WITHDRAWN

THE AUTOBIOGRAPHY
OF COLONEL
JOHN TRUMBULL

Library of American Art

THE AUTOBIOGRAPHY OF COLONEL JOHN TRUMBULL

Patriot-Artist, 1756-1843

Edited by Theodore Sizer

Kennedy Graphics, Inc. • *Da Capo Press*
New York • *1970*

This edition of
The Autobiography of Colonel John Trumbull
is an unabridged republication of the first edition
published in New Haven, Connecticut, in 1953. It is
reprinted by special arrangement with Yale University Press.

Library of Congress Catalog Card Number 79-116912

SBN 306-71242-3

Published by Da Capo Press
A Division of Plenum Publishing Corporation
227 West 17th Street, New York, N.Y. 10011

THE AUTOBIOGRAPHY OF COLONEL JOHN TRUMBULL

Published on the Foundation Established in Memory of

Henry Weldon Barnes of the Class of 1882, Yale College

1. Col. John Trumbull, painted by his fellow artist, Gilbert Stuart, at Boston in December 1818. (*Courtesy of Yale University Art Gallery*)

The Autobiography of Colonel

JOHN TRUMBULL

PATRIOT-ARTIST, 1756–1843

Edited by Theodore Sizer

CONTAINING A SUPPLEMENT TO

THE WORKS OF COLONEL JOHN TRUMBULL

NEW HAVEN: YALE UNIVERSITY PRESS, 1953

London: Geoffrey Cumberlege, Oxford University Press

This book is dedicated to the

FOUNDER

and to the Librarian and Staff, past and present,

of the

FRICK ART REFERENCE LIBRARY

the vast pictorial resources of which,

together with the learned assistance cheerfully rendered,

have turned drudgery into pleasure.

Contents

Illustrations

Preface

BY THE TIME John Trumbull, the "patriot-artist," came to live at New Haven in 1837 he had become a legend. One can well imagine a fond father pointing out to his son the tall, erect Colonel, who still retained his fine military bearing, and proudly saying: "There, my boy, goes Colonel Trumbull, General Washington's aide-de-camp!" This scene might have taken place on the elm-shaded streets of New Haven in 1840, nearly 2½ generations after the "glorious year" of 1775. Trumbull was a living embodiment of a heroic past. This, to the aged veteran, was soul satisfying.

But all was not well. For those who had helped to establish the nation there seemed to be a certain lack of understanding, a want of respect, on the part of the younger generation. It was becoming increasingly obvious to the proud old Colonel not only that his martial prowess stood in want of refurbishing but his intimacy with the Founding Fathers, his life among the great and near-great on both sides of the Atlantic, needed re-emphasizing. Although his 4 large historical compositions had been familiar to visitors to the new city of Washington for a dozen years or more, few realized that Trumbull had "assisted in saving the dome . . . and [the] central grandeur of the capitol" itself. Moreover he had been provoked; he had been made very angry. Although, according to the Holy Writ "anger resteth in the bosom of Fools" (Ecclesiastes 7:9), Martin Luther states: "when I am angry I can write, pray, and preach well, for then my whole temperament is quickened, my understanding sharpened, and all mundane vexations and temptations depart." (*Table-Talk*, Vol. *319.*) This was the case with the aged Colonel. His wits had been sharpened by real or supposed injuries. William Dunlap's *Arts of Design*, with its none too complimentary account of the patriot-artist's life, had appeared in 1834; the long, bitter battle over the New York academies had been fought and won by the younger men, resulting in the establishment (in 1826) of the National Academy of Design. This had been followed by the ignominious dissolution (in 1839) of the American Academy of the Fine Arts, of which Trumbull had been one of the original founders (in 1802) and president from 1817 to 1836. He was embittered. Clearly, things had to be set aright, the story of his rich and varied life told, and the new generation properly informed. These were the provocations which caused the octogenarian to write his autobiography.

The Colonel was an opportunist; he had always been; it was the key to his success. And now, once again, there was a favorable juncture of events. He found himself free of encumbrances. His beautiful but socially unacceptable wife had died some years before. His debts, incurred by his long, enforced stay in England during the War of 1812, had at last been settled. The troublesome administrative duties connected with the academy were over. His great work of visually recording the chief events of the Revolution, though short of his hopes and expectations, was completed. In a word, he was a free man. And he was very comfortable. His nephew-in-law, Benjamin Silliman, the eminent scientist, had persuaded him to give up his boarding house existence in New York and to make his home with the Silliman family at New Haven. The Colonel's old painting rooms at the American Academy had been partially destroyed by fire in March 1837 and were no longer available. The Sillimans lived in a prim, clapboard dwelling on Hillhouse Avenue, which, with its magnificent elms, was then one of the most beautiful streets in all America. Professor Silliman offered to remodel his house and to add an ample studio. The invitation proved to be irresistible; the promised space was provided. The old gentleman arrived with bag and an incredible amount of baggage in midsummer, 1837. Thus, in pleasant lodgings, amid sympathetic surroundings, encouraged and gently prodded by the kindly professor, Trumbull wrote the story of his life. He had not only a rich store of memories but an immense accumulation of letters, accounts, reports, and diaries to draw upon. The former army adjutant, meticulous by nature, had known how to preserve his papers. Like Horace Walpole, he was possessed with a passionate desire for posthumous fame.) Under such favorable circumstances, and with the documents at hand, the Life was produced. As chapter succeeded chapter, the old gentleman insisted upon reading them aloud to the tolerant, assembled Silliman family and a few select friends. At the end of each evening session he would serve the patient listeners with fruit and champagne.[1]

The *Autobiography, Reminiscences and Letters* was published (New Haven, New York, and London) in 1841, 2 years before the author's death. But alas, it was not a success. Professor Silliman observed:

. . . the book was a loss to the publishers and disappointed the distinguished author. Why? Was it not valuable and interesting? I thought it so and am still of the same opinion, and the colonel was liberal in its illustrations which were appropriate and in good taste . . . What is the cause? I apprehend it is to be found in the perverted taste of the age. The exciting tales which for an entire generation have formed the minds of the young and too often perverted those of the old, are not in harmony with the sober realities of life, and leave little relish for substantial and veritable history and biography. Had Col. Trumbull filled his book with gossip or even with those personalities—a fund of which were in his profession—I imagine it would have *taken* much better. Besides—a book that is got up in a dignified style and which would adorn a gentleman's library is now almost proscribed

[1] JT was, apparently, in the habit of using imported carbonated water with his brandy. His nephew-in-law, Prof. Benjamin Silliman of Yale, was "along with a number of other chemists of the time . . . interested in mineral waters since at the turn of the century it had become fashionable to serve drinks diluted with carbonated water." He wrote JT on 10 October 1806: "I have been informed that you have been in the habit of importing soda water from London. I presume that the empty bottles may not be of much use to you and I should be glad to purchase any you have, as I am constantly called upon to manufacture soda water, and I cannot procure any glass bottles which will not burst, nor any stone ones which are impervious to the fixed air . . ." From John F. Fulton and Elizabeth H. Thomson, *Benjamin Silliman, 1779–1864, Pathfinder in American Science* (New York, Henry Schuman, 1947), pp. 72–73, in which volume much information as to JT's later years is to be found.

and [as] it costs three dollars it finds few purchasers; while the dark crowded pages of the books of tales, cheap and enervating to the mind, go off at the first bid . . .[2]

Perhaps one cause of failure was the fact that many potential readers knew the author too well. In recent years he had become irritable, intolerant, and bellicose. He had not always been so. He had been a brilliant youth; success had come early. But he had reached the height of his creative powers before he was 40 and thereupon followed a long, steady, and unmistakable decline. Now he was 80 years old. The proud and punctilious old gentleman who grew up in an aristocratic 18th-century atmosphere had the great misfortune to live to the middle of the rough-and-tumble, democratic 19th century. The present had become intolerable. Consequently, his irritability and querulousness, if not forgivable, are understandable.

But the author's cantankerousness [3] was not the only cause of failure. Interest in America's recent past was then at a low point. Aristocratic Federalist ideals had been roughly swept aside by Jacksonian, shirtsleeve, democracy. The views, the account of the early achievements of an old-fashioned Federalist had but limited appeal. America was growing too fast to take lingering looks at her heritage. Tyler was president when the book appeared, and in England young Victoria sat upon the throne. The time was most inauspicious. The ebb of neglect in matters concerning the founding of the nation was reached in the post-Civil War period. The Centennial Exhibiton at Philadelphia in 1876 marked the first indication of the flow.[4] It was not until after World War I that early American pictorial art and craftsmanship were avidly studied, critically appraised, and eagerly collected. With our emer-

[2] Letter from Benjamin Silliman, New Haven, 25 July 1845, to Jabez Huntington of Norwich, Conn. (Yale Library.)

[3] A reputation that has been continuous. "John, the painter, a man who rarely erred by excess of meekness," was the way the Rev. Leonard Woolsey Bacon, Yale 1850, characterized him in an oration. See *The Lebanon War Office*, Jonathan Trumbull, ed. (Hartford, Connecticut Society of Sons of the American Revolution, 1891), p. 52.

[4] JT was represented by the large, full-length portrait of General Washington, painted in 1790 for the New York City Hall.

gence as a world power at the close of the second World War, interest has been redoubled. This is the time of neap tide.

Autobiographies are human documents and naturally reflect human frailties. Trumbull's, conceived in anger and written late in life, contains its full quota. As narrative it is uneven. Some of his papers and diaries he used unchanged; they alone contain the flavor and excitement of youth. The Rhine journey—an 18th-century adventure and a 19th-century commonplace—is charmingly recorded by the sensitive, well-educated colonial. Trumbull's fresh observations are of particular interest to the art historian. Those he met, what he saw, and what he thought, as he traveled about the Continent shortly before the French Revolution, are of concern to the historian of taste.

Were the *Autobiography* merely the record of an observant historical painter and ex-Revolutionary officer the tale would hardly be worth the retelling. But the cosmopolitan Colonel's acquaintanceship was wide. Nearly a quarter of his long life was spent in Europe; consequently, it assumes an international character. Through its pages walk the notables of his day—soldiers, statesmen, diplomats, merchants, bankers, architects, and fellow artists. Edmund Burke called on the imprisoned rebel officer and gave him advice on architecture. Goethe wrote his friend Schiller about the painter's "Battle of Bunker's Hill"; Walpole showed the Colonel through Strawberry Hill. William Beckford of "Fonthill Abbey" and Benjamin West, along with Trumbull, purchased some of the extensive Wadsworth landholdings in western New York state; Trumbull, as diplomat, conferred with the French Minister of Foreign Affairs, Talleyrand, and was invited to dine with him—Mme. de Staël and Lucien Bonaparte being present; the patriot-artist was the frequent bearer of messages from the Marquis de Lafayette to President Washington. Even in the American days the Colonel's life retained an interesting international flavor. Commission-seeking Italian sculptors came to his door for advice and introductions; the Colonel was instrumental in securing the services of a young English architect for the National Capitol—on which a Russian military engineer was (peaceably!) employed. Europe and America were culturally close during much of the artist's long life, and the Colonel knew the prominent people on both sides of the Atlantic.

Trumbull was considered by some to be pro-British; there is no doubt that he admired the well-ordered, cultivated English way of life. London was a pleasant place to live between 1780 and 1816, the years when he knew it. He was accused, with good reason, of celebrating British feats of valor in his painting. The youthful ex-rebel officer had gone to study art at London at the height of the Revolutionary War, and was imprisoned there as reprisal for the hanging of the popular Major André, whom he considered his "perfect pendant." It is rather touching that, years later, the Colonel designed the handsome casket in which André's remains were transferred from the site of the hanging to Westminster Abbey. Trumbull, a man of property and a staunch Federalist, was a political, not a social revolutionist.

The once rebellious New Englander was a versatile man. He was a historical and a religious painter, portrait painter, miniaturist, landscapist, amateur cartographer, designer of medals, and an architect of considerable ability. He was also an author, critic, and propagandist. We are apt to overlook the fact that, for a decade, the soldier-artist served as a diplomat. Scant attention has been paid to this phase of his many-sided career. (Documentation abounds; it is to be hoped that appropriate use will eventually be made of it.) Even the sources of his artistic development are diversified; colonial "primitivism," the long and powerful influence of his teacher, Benjamin West, that of Sir Joshua Reynolds and his school, of the charming and able Mme Vigée-LeBrun, the romantic Fragonard, and the two great champions of Classicism, the painter David and the sculptor Canova. He was a man of parts.

Trumbull holds a number of unique distinctions: he was (1) the earliest academically trained college graduate from the British-American colonies to become a professional painter (a fact which was too near to him to be noticed); (2) *par excellence,* the documentary recorder of the Revolutionary War; (3) the first American painter to be entrusted by the Federal Government with a large and important commission; [5] (4) the founder, as well as the architect, of the earliest art museum in America connected with an institution of higher learning, the Trumbull Gallery at Yale being among the earliest art museums in the Anglo-Saxon world; (5) the author of the earliest extended account of an individual American artist to be written and published in this country; [6] and (6) "the Oldest Surviving American officer of the Army of the Revolution." [7] If Trumbull was the architect of the 1793 First Presbyterian Church at Philadelphia, as he might have been, he has (7) the added honor of being among the first to introduce the neoclassic style in America. These are valid claims to a certain immortality. Any one of them merits the respectful consideration of the historian of American culture.

Professor Silliman inferred that, had the old Colonel not re-frained from gossip, the *Autobiography* would have sold better—even at $3.00 a copy. Trumbull, a gentleman of the old school, was aloof. He kept things to himself. There is no mention in the *Autobiography* of those matters which lay closest to his heart: his love for Harriet Wadsworth of Hartford; his sordid affair with a servant girl and their illegitimate son, John Trumbull Ray; his unaccountable marriage to a beautiful, obscure English girl (who comes off with but 6 lines at the time of her death) a dipsomaniac, who repeatedly mortified her abstemious husband; his long con-nection with the American Academy of none too happy memory;

[5] JT's contemporary, the painter and art historian William Dunlap, 1766–1839, wrote: "No American painter has ever received from government such patronage as Mr. Trumbull." *History of the Rise and Progress of the Arts of Design* (1918), 3, 76.

[6] There was a half-length edition of *The Life and Studies of Benjamin West, Esq. . . . Prior to His Arrival in England,* by the Scottish novelist, John Galt, published at Philadelphia in 1816, after the first London edition; 2d ed. London, 1817; Galt's full life (Pts. 1 and 2) appeared in London in 1820, the year of West's death. The encyclopedic, two-volume *Arts of Design* by William Dunlap was published at New York in 1834.

[7] So he described himself in a letter to the Hon. James Lanman of 6 January 1825. (New-York Historical Society.) On 26 September 1832 JT wrote: "Col. Trumbull, senior surviving Officer of the Revolutionary Army, has the Honor to request from the Secretary at War of the United States, an Audience of five minutes, on Business." (Yale Library.)

and his concern with his eyesight (of importance to the art historian). These are serious, though understandable, omissions. They complicated, conditioned, and saddened his life, and explain many of his otherwise unaccountable actions.

The *Autobiography* is a one-sided affair. About ten per cent of it is devoted to 2 years of military history and the figure the Colonel cut. Actually, he was Washington's second aide-de-camp for only 19 days—and he traded on that exalted position all his life. (He bore his military title, too, to the end of his days.) Sixty per cent of the life has to do with the 20 years spent in Europe. The author's 66 years lived in America are telescoped into 30 per cent of the 294 pages. In addition to this the old gentleman swept up and threw into a 142-page Appendix self-justifying documents of small interest to the present-day reader. All are referred to in this edition, but most are omitted. In their place other material of concern to us today—the hidden domestic matters which colored and conditioned his conduct—has been substituted.

Trumbull had a strong sense of his own dignity and of the dramatic. When he resigned his army commission he laid aside his "Cockade and Sword"; and it was the same in death as in life. The colonel's instructions for his burial were: "Place me at the feet of my great master"—beneath his portrait of General Washington. He lies buried, according to his wishes, in a vault in the Yale University Art Gallery. His tomb, in the gallery which he founded, bears the inscription: ". . . Patriot and Artist, Friend and Aid of Washington . . . To his Country he gave his SWORD and his PENCIL."

The *Autobiography* not only is a record rich in historical implications but contains, in spite of omissions, its share of human interest, of the bitter and the sweet of which life is made. As Trumbull the painter is chiefly significant as a *documentary* artist, so Trumbull the author is important as a *documentarian* of a heroic—and a critical—period in American history.

It was long my intention to write the life of the British-trained, French-inspired, American painter. My initial introduction to his work came in 1927 with my appointment to Yale, the direction of the Art Gallery, founded by Trumbull, being among my principal duties. Those who had, or believed they had, pictures by or manuscripts concerning Trumbull, wrote for information. It was my lot to answer such questions. Knowledge and insight were thus unwittingly and often reluctantly acquired.

Before proceeding with the life, it became increasingly evident that it would be necessary first to unscramble the cosmopolitan painter's vast and varied *oeuvre*, which had become entangled and obscured with that of his contempories and followers, worthy and worthless, and besmirched by the cunning output of the forger. This resulted in the publication, in October 1950, of *The Works of Colonel John Trumbull, Artist of the American Revolution* by the Yale University Press. About a thousand genuine items were listed; alleged works, left unrecorded, numbered nearly as many.

The life was eventually started and several chapters written. I found, however, that I was continuously and unavoidably quoting the *Autobiography* at great length or paraphrasing Trumbull's often brilliant accounts of events. In spite of its many and grave omissions, the author's inevitable bias, and (to us, to-day) misdirected emphasis, the book has the ring of authenticity. Trumbull was the witness of great events and he knew intimately the men who took leading parts in them. No biographer, no matter how sympathetic or understanding, could possibly make up for such contemporary genuineness. For this reason, as well as upon the advice of the editors of the Yale University Press, the partially written life was jettisoned in favor of editing the original *Autobiography*.

That long out-of-print volume is reprinted here, exactly as originally set forth, but for the quiet correction of a few minor typographical errors (probably due to the typesetter using a longhand MS). Trumbull's misspellings of proper names, however, have been retained, though corrected in the footnotes—and past confusion thus explained. The long topical listings at the head of each chapter and in the table of contents have been omitted and replaced with chapter titles and the far more convenient index. The editor has also taken the liberty of combining certain chapters. Instead of cutting the book into equal sections, as the author (or more probably the printer did), I have divided it into logical, chronological segments, which make some of the chapters short and others very long; but each is a complete unit. Otherwise the body of the *Autobiography* has been left quite undisturbed.

Much additional information of possible interest or use to readers to-day has been added in the footnotes and Appendix. Matters which the Colonel's contemporaries would have taken for granted receive the necessary explanation and elucidation. Full names, dates, and other lacking biographical data have been supplied. The present location of pictures referred to in the text is given wherever possible.

Since the publication of the check list in 1950, new pictures have come to light, "lost" pictures have been located, and others have moved. All of this was to be expected. In consequence a supplementary list, incorporating all such changes, has been added to this volume.

As the selected bibliography included in the *Works* (pp. 109–117) was comprehensive, it seems useless to duplicate it here. Note, however, has been made of the few publications which have appeared in the 3 intervening years. The 2 volumes are therefore mutually dependent.

The 6 June 1956 will mark the 200th anniversary of Colonel Trumbull's birth. This event, it is hoped, will give rise to further interest in the life and work of the visual historian of the American Revolution.

THEODORE SIZER

Davenport College
Yale University
July 1953

Acknowledgments

IN THE EDITING of a work such as this, it is the reference librarians on whom one most fully depends. Like the Royal Navy they are the "Silent Service"—efficient, willing, essential: it is they who are, basically, responsible for the achievements of others. I am vastly indebted to them. I wish to thank, especially, those at the Frick Art Reference Library, to whom this volume is gratefully dedicated; those of the university libraries of Yale, Princeton, Harvard, Columbia, and Michigan (the Clements Library); the Henry E. Huntington Library and Art Gallery (San Marino, Calif.), the United States Military Academy (West Point), the New-York Historical Society, the New York Public Library, the New Haven Colony Historical Society, the Connecticut State Library (Hartford), the Massachusetts Historical Society (Boston), the Boston Public Library, the Boston Athenaeum, the American Antiquarian Society (Worcester), the Historical Society of Pennsylvania (Philadelphia), the Chicago Historical Society, the Library of Congress, the National Archives (Washington), the Belgian Archives Centrales Iconographiques d'Art National (Brussels), and the City of Liverpool Public Libraries (England). To these unsung bibliographic heroes and heroines I make my bow.

It gives me great pleasure also to acknowledge the generous help afforded by the curatorial staffs of the Museum of Fine Arts (Boston), the Metropolitan Museum of Art, the Museum of the City of New York, the New-York Historical Society, the Art Institute of Chicago, the Detroit Institute of Arts, the Wadsworth Atheneum (Hartford), the Rijksmusem at Amsterdam, the National Portrait Gallery (London), and most of all, the Yale University Art Gallery.

In special matters I am indebted to Miss Maria Trumbull Dana, a Trumbull descendant, of New Haven (for material on Trumbull and Silliman); to Julian P. Boyd (Jefferson) and to Howard

C. Rice, Junior (Louis XVI's Paris), both of Princeton; Henry H. Reed, Junior, Assistant in City Planning at Yale (Versailles); Mme Henri Focillon (prerevolutionary Paris); the late James Wolcott Wadsworth, a descendant of Jeremiah and James Wadsworth, and his son, Reverdy Wadsworth (Trumbull's lands in western New York); Miss Katherine F. Adams and Faneuil Adams of Boston (Wadsworth matters); Talbot Hamlin and James G. Van Derpool of Columbia University, and Henry-Russell Hitchcock of Smith College (architecture); Helmut von Erffa of Rutgers (Benjamin West); Charles Coleman Sellers (the Peales); the late John Marshall Phillips, my successor at the Yale Gallery (for Trumbull's marriage record at St. Mary's, Parish of Hendon, London, besides much valuable help and advice); Josephine Setze (Yale collections); James Thomas Flexner of New York (painting); A. Hyatt Mayer of the Metropolitan Museum (prints); Charles Seymour of Yale (Houdon); Rev. Robert G. Armstrong, of Lebanon (the Meetinghouse); Samuel Flagg Bemis of Yale (diplomatic history); Carl F. Schreiber and Curt von Faber du Faur, both of Yale (matters German); Dr. John F. Fulton, Sterling professor of the history of medicine at Yale (medical matters; Benjamin Silliman); Albert Duveen and Henry Woodhouse, both of New York (Trumbull documents); the members of the Walpole Society (learned advice); and my colleagues Deane Keller, Lamont Moore, and Richard A. Rathbone (courage and forbearance). James Hatfield Daffer, Yale '50, and Norman Ernest Thomas, Yale '53, my last two "bursary boys," have done yeoman's service in searching old newspapers and periodicals, running down and identifying passages in forgotten books, reading and annotating endless reels of microfilm, and innumerable odd jobs. Both have unearthed much new material and have made "discoveries." Marjory Wilshire Nelson, once my secretary during some of my term as director of the Yale University Art Gallery, has been good enough to type, retype, and correct the copy. My son, Theodore Ryland Sizer, Yale '53, has read and corrected much of his father's faulty prose. My wife's patience in reading script and listening to the tales of old Colonel T. has been inexhaustible. Mary C. Withington, formerly of the library staff, recent compiler of the *Catalogue of Manuscripts in the Western Americana Collection, Yale University Library* (Yale University Press, 1952) has with great patience edited my manuscript. I am also deeply grateful to the staff of the Yale University Press.

Special thanks are due the New-York Historical Society, the Yale University Library, and the Walpole Society for their generous permission to reprint the articles which appear in the Appendix of this volume.

I am deeply grateful to the Associates in Fine Arts at Yale University—an organization which has done much to encourage the arts and strengthen the collections at Yale—for assistance in the publication of this volume.

Once again I wish to express my deep appreciation to the Trustees of the John Simon Guggenheim Memorial Foundation and the administrative officers of Yale University for their faith, encouragement, and assistance. These have made this volume possible.

I

Life at Lebanon and a Harvard Education 1756–75

THE families of Trumbull in New England have cause to believe themselves to be a branch of the Turnbulls of Scotland; of whose origin the Herald's office gives this history. In the —— year, —— king of Scotland, on a hunting party, was attacked by a bull, and his life was in imminent danger from the animal, when a young peasant threw himself before the king, and with equal strength, dexterity and good fortune, seized the bull by the horn, turned him aside, and thus saved the royal life. The king, grateful for the act, commanded the hitherto obscure youth to assume the name of Turnbull, gave him an estate near Peebles,[1] (which is still in the family,) and a coat of arms,—three bulls' heads, with the motto, *Fortuna favet audaci,*—still the bearings of the American branch.[1a]

The first person of the name known to be on record in the United States, is John Trumbull [2] of Rowley, in the county of Essex, Massachusetts, who was made a freeman in Boston, in 1640. He is understood to have emigrated from Cumberland or Lancashire in England, on the borders of Scotland. A son of this person, named also John,[3] removed to Suffield [4] in Connecticut; and one of his

1. 20 miles south of Edinburgh.

1a. The arms (argent, three bulls' heads razed, sable) have been adopted by Trumbull College, Yale University, and are described in *The Arms of Yale University and Its Colleges at New Haven* (New Haven, Yale University Press, 1948).

2. John Trumble (the present spelling of the name was not used until 1766) married Elinor Chandler, who died before he emigrated from Newcastle-on-Tyne, Northumberland, for Roxbury, Mass. Rowley is 30 miles north of Roxbury. His second wife was Anne, widow of Michael Hopkinson. After John Trumble's death in 1657 she married Richard Swann.

3. Not John, but Joseph Trumble, born at Rowley in 1647, removed to Suffield, Mass., in 1670, married Hannah Smith, died in 1685.

4. Suffield, 50 miles northeast of Lebanon, became a part of Connecticut in 1749.

sons, Joseph,[5] removed from Suffield to Lebanon.[6] This person was my grandfather, and was born at Suffield, 1679.

My father, Jonathan Trumbull,[7] was born at Lebanon in 1710. Joseph, his father, was a respectable, strong minded but uneducated farmer, who feeling the disadvantages of his own want of education, made it his first object to give to his children, this first blessing of social life; and at a very early age [8] my father was placed at Harvard College,[9] where he became a distinguished scholar, acquiring a sound knowledge of the Hebrew, as well as of the Greek and Latin languages, and of all the other studies of that day. He was graduated with honor in 1727. He died in 1785, having been governor of the state of Connecticut, by annual election, during the entire war of the Revolution; and was the only person who, being first magistrate of a colony in America, before the separation from Great Britain, retained the confidence of his countrymen through the Revolution, and was annually reëlected governor to the end of that eventful period.

My mother, Faith Robinson,[10] daughter of John Robinson,[11] minister of Duxbury in Massachusetts, was understood to be great granddaughter of John Robinson, the father of the pilgrims, who led our Puritan ancestors (his parishioners) out of England in the reign of James V, and resided with them some years at Leyden in Holland, until in 1620 they emigrated to Plymouth in Massachusetts, and there, among other acts of wisdom and piety, laid the

5. Capt. Joseph Trumble, 1679–1755, married Hannah Higley. He acquired a fine new home in Lebanon in 1740, in which the artist was later born. Though moved a little to the north in 1824 from its original site, it survives today practically unchanged. It is now owned by the Daughters of the American Revolution.

6. A name undoubtedly suggested by the presence of white swamp cedars.

7. See Clifford K. Shipton, *Sibley's Harvard Graduates* (Boston, Massachusetts Historical Society, 1951), 8 (1726–30), 267–300.

8. At thirteen.

9. The relatively obscure Jonathan Trumble was "ranked" 28th in his class of 37; his son Joseph was number 2 in the class of 1756 and his son Jonathan first in that of 1759. The artist had a deep sense of social superiority. William Dunlap observed (*Arts of Design, 2,* 13) that Trumbull "was emphatically well-born."

10. Married in 1735.

11. See Justin Winson, *A History of the Town of Duxbury, Massachusetts* (Boston, Crosby & Nichols, 1849), pp. 184–190.

foundations of that system of education in town schools, which has since been extended so widely over the northern and western parts of the United States, forming the glory and the defense, the *decus atque tutamen* of our country.

I was born at Lebanon on the 6th of June, 1756 [12]—the youngest child of these parents; and soon after my birth was attacked by convulsion fits, which recurred daily, and several times each day, increasing in violence and frequency until I was nearly nine months old,—the cause was hidden from the medical men of the vicinity,—when one of my father's early friends, Dr. Terry [13] of Suffield, who had become an eminent physician, called accidentally to make him a passing visit, and was requested to look at the unhappy child. He immediately pronounced the disease to be caused by compression of the brain, shewing my parents how the bones of the skull, instead of uniting in the several sutures, and forming a smooth surface, had slipped over each other, forming sensible ridges on the head, by which means the brain not having room to expand, convulsions followed. "Can the child be relieved?" was the anxious question.

"Nothing but the untiring care of the mother can effect a cure, and this can be done only by applying her hands to the head of the child daily, and many times a day, and gently and carefully drawing them apart. If the bones do not already adhere too strongly, it is possible that by this means they may be separated, and reduced to their proper junction in the sutures. If this had been attended to at the birth, it would have been easy; now, it is barely possible. Medicine is useless, and if relief cannot be obtained by this method, I know no other; and the poor

12. John was baptized at the First Congregational Church on 13 June 1756. There were 3 John Trumbulls, all contemporary and all residents of Connecticut: (1) the *artist* of Lebanon, 1756–1843; his second cousin, the *poet* and jurist of Hartford, 1750–1831; and the *printer* of Norwich, 1742–1802, no relation of the other two. There was a later fourth John Trumbull, 1784–1859, son of David Trumbull, the artist's brother, who used an "M" (standing for nothing) as a middle initial to distinguish him from his famous uncle, the artist.

13. Ebenezer Terry, 1696–1780, a man of wealth and prominence, settled in Enfield, Mass., in 1722.

child must either die early, or if he should live, become an idiot." [14]

My mother followed this prescription with unremitted care; by degrees favorable symptoms began to appear—the paroxysms of convulsion recurred less and less frequently, until at about three years old, the natural form of the head was restored, and they ceased entirely. Thus, by the kindness of Divine providence in making known the cause of the disease, and by the affectionate care of my mother, a life was snatched from early extinction, which has been prolonged to the unusual age of eighty five years;—through what strange vicissitudes, and for what purposes, the following pages will record.

My native place, Lebanon,[15] was long celebrated for having the best school in New England, (unless that of Master Moody [15a] in Newburyport, might, in the opinion of some, have the precedence.) It was kept by Nathan Tisdale,[16] a native of the place, from the time when he graduated at Harvard to the day of his death, a period of more than thirty years, with an assiduity and fidelity of the most exalted character, and became so widely known that he had scholars from the West India Islands, Georgia, North and South Carolina, as well as from the New England and northern colonies. With this exemplary man and excellent scholar, I soon became a favorite. My father was his particular friend; and my early sufferings, as well as my subsequent docility, endeared me to him. The school was distant from my father's house not more than three minutes' walk, across a beautiful green, so that I was

14. "Nutritional disturbances were common in Colonial days and the 'overlapping bones of the skull' represented nothing more than the late closure of the fontanelles, and convulsions were and are quite common childhood disturbances often without significance as far as later development is concerned." Dr. John F. Fulton, Yale University School of Medicine, letter, 24 December 1947.

15. There is a 1772 map of Lebanon as it was in JT's boyhood, with individual houses, bearing names of owners, in the Yale University Library. See Anthony N. B. Garvan, *Architecture and Town Planning in Colonial Connecticut* (New Haven, Yale University Press, 1951), Pl. 25, "Nathaniel Webb's survey of Lebanon 1772," opp. p. 57.

15a. Samuel Moody, preceptor of Dummer Academy from 1763 until his death in 1790.

16. 1731–87, Harvard 1749.

constant in my attendance; besides which, it was an excellent rule of the school to have no vacations, in the long idleness and dissipation of which the labors of preceding months might be half forgotten. Whether my mind, which had so long been repressed by disease, sprang forward with increased energy so soon as the pressure upon the brain was removed, I know not; but I soon displayed a singular facility in acquiring knowledge, particularly of languages, so that I could read Greek at six years old, at which age I remember to have had a contest with the late Rev. Joseph Lyman,[17] pastor of Hatfield in Massachusetts, a boy several years my senior. We read the five first verses of the Gospel of St. John; I missed not a word—he missed one, and I gained the victory. I do not mean to say that, at this time, I possessed much more knowledge of the Greek language, than might be taught to a parrot; but I knew the forms of the letters, the words, and their sounds, and could read them accurately, although my knowledge of their meaning was very imperfect.

My taste for drawing began to dawn early. It is common to talk of natural genius; but I am disposed to doubt the existence of such a principle in the human mind; at least, in my own case, I can clearly trace it to mere imitation. My two sisters, Faith [18] and Mary,[19] had completed their education at an excellent school in Boston, where they both had been taught embroidery; and the eldest, Faith, had acquired some knowledge of drawing, and had even painted in oil, two heads and a landscape. These wonders were hung in my mother's parlor, and were among the first objects that caught my infant eye. I endeavored to imitate them, and for several years the nicely sanded floors, (for carpets were then unknown in Lebanon,) were constantly scrawled with my rude attempts at drawing.

About the same time music first caught my attention. I heard a Jews-harp, delicious sound! which no time can drive from my en-

17. 1749–1828, a prominent theologian.

18. Faith Trumbull, 1743–75, married, in 1766, Jedediah Huntington, Harvard 1763, of Norwich, merchant and general in the Continental Army.

19. Mary Trumbull, 1745–1831, married, in 1771, William Williams, Harvard 1751, a signer of the Declaration of Independence, of Lebanon.

chanted memory! I have since been present at a commemoration of
Handel, in Westminster Abbey, and have often listened with rap-
ture to the celestial warblings of Catalani [20]—I have heard the
finest music of the age in London and in Paris—but nothing can
obliterate the magic charm of that Jews-harp, and even at this late
moment, its sweet vibrations seem to tingle on my ear.

At the age of four or five an accident befel me of a serious nature. After my recovery from my early sickness, I became the favorite plaything of my two sisters, who were more than ten years
my seniors. A door opened from their bed-room upon a flight of
stairs, leading direct to the ground floor, without a landing. I was
frolicking with them in this room with all the gaiety of young and
newly acquired health; the door was unfortunately open, and in
my race I plunged headlong down the stairs. I was taken up in-
sensible—my forehead, over the left eye, severely bruised; but I
soon recovered, and although for some time I squinted with the
left eye, no other evil was suspected, until several years after, when
happening to shut the right eye, I found I could not see. The optic
nerve must have been severely injured, for although the eye recovered entirely its external appearance, yet vision was so nearly
destroyed that, to this day, I have never been able to read a single
word with the left eye alone.[21]

20. Angelica Catalani, 1780–1849, famous Italian singer, spent seven years in
England. JT heard her in London sometime between 1808 and 1813.

21. This unfortunate accident affected and conditioned all his future work as
much as the "accident of birth." JT was troubled by his eyesight throughout his long
life. He wrote to Rufus King from London on 6 July 1809: "My pictures are arrived,
and I expect to have them home in a few days. We have taken a house for a year, No.
31, Argyle St. I am under the care of Mr. Phipps and hope that my Eyes will recover
their tone—the disorder is dryness and inflammation of the inner membrane of the
Eyelids, troublesome but he assures me not dangerous. I hope he is right." (New-
York Historical Society.) And on 30 April 1811 to Joseph Simonds: "The principal
motive for my present visit to this Country was to procure advice for a failure of my
Sight. I have had the Advice of the most eminent men to very little purpose, and
expect soon to return to America . . ." (New-York Historical Society.) In the Silliman family correspondence at the Yale Library there are many references to the subject: ". . . his eyes are still troublesome and deprive him intirely of the power of
employing or amusing himself." (22 February 1840.) Dr. Clement C. Clarke of
New Haven informs the editor that, in his opinion, this was conjunctivitis, "based on
a number of causes—chemical, physical, and bacterial . . . conceivably . . . a
vitamin deficiency as well." See "A note on Trumbull's Eyesight," App., pp. 325–327.

At the age of nine or ten a circumstance occurred which deserves to be written on adamant. In the wars of New England with the aborigines, the Mohegan tribe of Indians early became friends of the English. Their favorite ground was on the banks of the river (now the Thames) between New London and Norwich. A small remnant of the Mohegans still exists, and they are sacredly protected in the possession and enjoyment of their favorite domain on the banks of the Thames. The government of this tribe had become hereditary in the family of the celebrated chief Uncas. During the time of my father's mercantile prosperity, he had employed several Indians of this tribe in hunting animals, whose skins were valuable for their fur. Among these hunters was one named Zachary, of the royal race, an excellent hunter, but as drunken and worthless an Indian as ever lived. When he had somewhat passed the age of fifty, several members of the royal family who stood between Zachary and the throne of his tribe died, and he found himself with only one life between him and empire. In this moment his better genius resumed its sway, and he reflected seriously, "How can such a drunken wretch as I am, aspire to be the chief of this honorable race—what will my people say—and how will the shades of my noble ancestors look down indignant upon such a base successor? Can *I* succeed to the great Uncas? *I will drink no more!*" He solemnly resolved never again to taste any drink but water, and he kept his resolution.

I had heard this story, and did not entirely believe it; for young as I was, I already partook in the prevailing contempt for Indians. In the beginning of May, the annual election of the principal officers of the (then) colony was held at Hartford, the capital; my father attended officially, and it was customary for the chief of the Mohegans also to attend. Zachary had succeeded to the rule of his tribe. My father's house was situated about midway on the road between Mohegan and Hartford, and the old chief was in the habit of coming a few days before the election, and dining with his brother governor. One day the mischievous thought struck me, to try the sincerity of the old man's temperance. The family were seated at dinner, and there was excellent home-brewed beer on the table. I addressed the old chief—"Zachary, this beer is excellent;

will you taste it?" The old man dropped his knife and fork—leaned forward with a stern intensity of expression; his black eye sparkling with indignation, was fixed on me. "John," said he, "you do not know what you are doing. You are serving the devil, boy! Do you not know that I am an Indian? I tell you that I am, and that, if I should but taste your beer, I could never stop until I got to rum, and became again the drunken, contemptible wretch your father remembers me to have been. *John, while you live, never again tempt any man to break a good resolution.*" Socrates never uttered a more valuable precept—Demosthenes could not have given it in more solemn tones of eloquence. I was thunderstruck. My parents were deeply affected; they looked at each other, at me, and at the venerable old Indian, with deep feelings of awe and respect. They afterwards frequently reminded me of the scene, and charged me never to forget it. Zachary lived to pass the age of eighty, and sacredly kept his resolution. He lies buried in the royal burial-place of his tribe, near the beautiful falls of the Yantic, the western branch of the Thames, in Norwich, on land now owned by my friend, Calvin Goddard,[22] Esq. I visited the grave of the old chief lately, and there repeated to myself his inestimable lesson.

About this time, when I was nine or ten years old, my father's mercantile failure [23] took place. He had been for years a successful merchant, and looked forward to an old age of ease and affluence; but in one season, almost every vessel, and all the property which he had upon the ocean, was swept away, and he was a poor man at so late a period of life, as left no hope of retrieving his affairs. My eldest brother [24] was involved in the wreck as a partner, which rendered the condition of the family utterly hopeless. My mother and sisters were deeply afflicted, and although I was too young

22. A Massachusetts lawyer.
23. This was in 1766, when four ships belonging to Trumble, Fitch, and Trumble were lost with their cargoes—at a total loss of £10,000 to £12,000. The partnership had been formed in 1766 between Jonathan Trumbull, his son Joseph, and Col. Eleazer Fitch. The firm, operating chiefly from Norwich, Conn., built, bought, and chartered vessels, and traded with the West Indies and with Britain. About 60 vessels were thus engaged. See Isaac William Stuart, *Life of Jonathan Trumbull, Sen., Governor of Connecticut, 1769–1784* (Boston, Crocker & Brewster, 1859), pp. 114–124.
24. Joseph was then a bachelor of 29 living at Norwich.

clearly to comprehend the cause, yet sympathy led me too to droop. My bodily health was frail, for the sufferings of early youth had left their impress on my constitution, and although my mind was clear, and the body active, it was never strong. I therefore seldom joined my little schoolfellows in plays or exercises of an athletic kind, for there I was almost sure to be vanquished; and by degrees acquired new fondness for drawing, in which I stood unrivalled. Thus I gradually contracted a solitary habit, and after school hours frequently withdrew to my own room to a close study of my favorite pursuit. Such was my character at the time of my father's failure, and this added gloomy feelings to my love of solitude. I became silent, diffident, bashful, awkward in society, and took refuge in still closer application to my books and my drawing. The want of pocket money prevented me from joining my young companions in any of those little expensive frolicks which often lead to future dissipation, and thus became a blessing; and my good master Tisdale had the wisdom so to vary my studies, as to render them rather a pleasure than a task. Thus I went forward, without interruption, and at the age of twelve might have been admitted to enter college; for I had then read Eutropius, Cornelius Nepos, Virgil, Cicero, Horace and Juvenal, in Latin; the Greek Testament and Homer's Iliad in Greek, and was thoroughly versed in geography, ancient and modern, in studying which I had the advantage (then rare) of a twenty inch globe. I had also read with care Rollin's History of Ancient Nations, also his history of the Roman republic, Mr. Crevier's continuation of the History of the Emperors, and Rollin's Arts and Sciences of the Ancient Nations. In arithmetic alone I met an awful stumbling-block. I became puzzled by a sum in division, where the divisor consisted of three figures—I could not comprehend the rule for ascertaining how many times it was contained in the dividend; my mind seemed to come to a dead stand—my master would not assist me, and forbade the boys to do it, so that I well recollect the question stood on my slate unsolved nearly three months, to my extreme mortification. At length the solution seemed to flash upon my mind at once, and I went forward without further let or hindrance, through the ordinary course of fractions, vulgar and decimal, surveying, trigonometry, geometry, navigation, &c. &c., so that when I had reached the age of fifteen and a half years, it was stated by my good master that he could teach me little more, and that I was fully qualified to enter Harvard College [25] in the middle of the third or Junior year. This was approved by my father and proposed to me. In the mean time my fondness for painting had grown with my growth, and in reading of the arts of antiquity I had become familiar with the names of Phidias and Praxiteles, of Zeuxis and Apelles. These names had come down through a series of more than two thousand years, with a celebrity and applause which accompanied few of those who had been devoted to the more noisy and turbulent scenes of politics or war. The tranquillity of the arts seemed better suited to me than the more bustling scenes of life, and I ventured to remonstrate with my father, stating to him that the expense of a college education would be inconvenient to him, and after it was finished I should still have to study some profession by which to procure a living; whereas, if he would place me under the instruction of Mr. Copley,[26] (then living in Boston, and whose reputation as an artist was deservedly high,) the expense would probably not exceed that of a college education, and that at the end of my time I should possess a profession, and the means of supporting myself—perhaps of assisting the family, at least my sisters. This argument seemed to me not bad; but my father had not the same veneration for the fine arts that I had, and hoped to see me a distinguished member of one of the learned professions, divinity in preference. I was overruled, and in January, 1772, was sent to Cambridge, under the care of my brother,[27] who in passing through Boston indulged me by taking me to see the works of Mr. Copley. His house was on the Common, where Mr. Sears's elegant granite *palazzo* [27a] now stands.

25. Master Tisdale's prodigy was not an unusual case; his father entered Harvard at 13 and his cousin, John Trumbull the poet, was ready for Yale at 7½ and was honorably rusticated until 13. Benjamin Silliman also entered Yale at 13.

26. John Singleton Copley, 1738–1815, maintained a studio at Boston from about 1757 to 1775.

27. Probably Jonathan, who had graduated from Harvard in 1759 and in 1772, was a selectman of Lebanon.

27a. Designed by Alexander Parris for Col. David Sears in 1819, completed in 1821. A portion of this house is incorporated in the east side of the Somerset Club at 42 Beacon Street.

A mutual friend of Mr. Copley and my brother, Mr. James Lovell,[28] went with us to introduce us. We found Mr. Copley dressed to receive a party of friends at dinner. I remember his dress and appearance—an elegant looking man, dressed in a fine maroon cloth, with gilt buttons—this was dazzling to my unpracticed eye!—but his paintings, the first I had ever seen deserving the name, riveted, absorbed my attention, and renewed all my desire to enter upon such a pursuit.[29] But my destiny was fixed, and the next day I went to Cambridge, passed my examination in form, and was readily admitted to the Junior class,[30] who were then in the middle of the third year, so that I had only to remain one year and a half in college. My first anxiety was to know the actual studies and recitations of my class, and I soon found that I had no superior in Latin—that in Greek there were only two whom I had to fear as competitors, Mr. Pearson,[31] who afterwards became the professor of oriental languages, and Mr. Theodore Parsons,[32] brother of the late eminent judge, who died a few years after we graduated. This advanced state of my acquirements rendered unnecessary any exertion of study to maintain my footing with my class, and I was in no small danger of dropping into a course of idleness and vanity, and thence

28. Harvard 1756, a classmate of Joseph Trumbull; schoolmaster and politician.

29. The highly successful Copley was then making a good 300 gns. a year.

30. The class of 1773, consisting of 36 members, was the first to be listed alphabetically instead of according to social rank, in the *Quinquennial Catalogues* of Harvard University.

Being younger than most of his classmates, JT had few friends among them. Among lower classmen at Harvard then were Christopher Gore ('76), Rufus King and Thomas Dawes ('77).

The Yale class of 1773 also numbered 36, including Nathan Hale and James Hillhouse, treasurer of Yale from 1782 to 1832, who in 1793 gave JT some architectural employment.

JT lived, while at college, at the home of William Kneeland, Harvard 1751, tutor 1754–63. The house, built in 1635 by Gov. John Hayes, was approximately where numbers 100 and 102 Mt. Auburn Street now stand, between Eliot and Boylston Streets. Dr. Kneeland reported regularly to Governor Trumbull, stating that his versatile son was "modest and affable" and had "a natural genius and disposition for limning . . . an art I have frequently told him will be of no use to him." See *Autobiography* (1841), Appen., pp. 297–298.

31. Eliphalet Pearson, 1752–1826, who later became the first principal of Phillips Andover and Hancock professor of Hebrew and other oriental languages at Harvard.

32. Of Boston, 1751–79, to whom JT presented a drawing. See item 16 on p. 54.

perhaps into low company and base pursuits, when I fortunately learned that a French family, who had been removed with the other inhabitants of Acadie, by the political prudence of England, poor but respectable, were living in Cambridge, and had in some instances taught the French language. I went immediately to Père Robichaud,[33] as the worthy man was called, and was admitted as a scholar. This family, besides the parents, comprised several children of both sexes, some about my own age; in such society I made good progress, and there laid the foundation of a knowledge of the French language, which in after life was of eminent utility.[34]

In the mean time I searched the library of the college [35] for works relating to the arts, and among a few others of less importance, I found the "Jesuit's Prospective made easy, by Brooke Taylor." This I studied carefully, and still possess a book into which I copied most of the diagrams of the work. I found also, and read with attention, "Hogarth's Analysis of Beauty." [36] The library contained further a few fine engravings, and a set of Piranezi's prints [37] of Roman ruins; in the philosophical chamber were several of Mr. Copley's finest portraits,[38] and a view of an eruption of Mount

33. Probably: "Louis Robichaud, déporté à Salem, Massachusetts, qui se fit le consolateur et le père de ses co-exilés de la région de Boston." Antoine Bernard, *Le Drame acadien depuis 1604* (Montreal, Les clercs de Saint-Viateur, 1936), p. 340.

34. JT's ability to speak the language was the means of his later understanding and appreciating French art and thought.

35. James Winthrop, later wounded at Bunker's Hill, was librarian when Trumbull was an undergraduate. From the "Seniors' Library Charging Book," still in the College Library, it can be seen just what books he withdrew for protracted study. These were largely history, ancient and modern; and included an Italian grammar (did he have visions of Italy?), MacPherson's *Ossian* (he was to paint subjects from this 36 years later). The technical books were Roger de Piles, *Cours de peinture par principes,* Paris, 1708; *The Art of Painting,* translated by John Dryden (excerpts taken from Charles Alphonse du Fresnoy's *De arte graphica*) (London, 1716); Daniel Webb, *An Inquiry into the Beauties of Painting, and into the Merits of the Most Celebrated Painters Ancient and Modern* (London, 1740); John Joshua Kirby, *Dr. Brook Taylor's Method of Perspective Made Easy; both in Theory and Practice* (London, 1754), which JT refers to as "Jesuit's Prospective made easy."

36. Published in 1753, it became a veritable bible to the impressionable youth.

37. Giovanni Battista Piranesi, 1720–78. The 9 great volumes are still in the Harvard College Library.

38. Those of the Rev. Edward Holyoke, 10th president of Harvard, (Cat. No. H6), 1760; Thomas Hancock (H22), *ca.* 1764; Thomas Hollis (H25), 1766; Thomas

Vesuvius, painted in Italy, which, with the Piranezi, had been lately presented to the college by Thomas Palmer, Esq.[39] one of the alumni, who had travelled in Italy, and whom I had the pleasure to know afterwards in Berkeley square, London.

The principal college studies to which I paid much attention were moral and natural philosophy. Dr. Winthrop [40] was professor of the latter, and to his lectures I listened with great attention and pleasure. Electricity was of very recent discovery, and was a source of great admiration and delight. Chemistry as yet was in a manner unknown as a science, and formed no part of our studies.

At the same time I copied the painting of Vesuvius twice; [41] first with water colors on vellum, small; and afterwards in oil, the size of the original. One of these I presented to Professor Winthrop.

Among the engravings in the library, was one from a painting by Noel Coypel,—Rebecca at the well,[42] surrounded by a number of attendants. This I admired and copied in oil, the same size as the engraving; [43] the forms, expressions, characters, and light and shadow were before me; the colors I managed as well as I could from my own imagination. This received so much approbation

---

Hubbard (H79), *ca.* 1767; and the life-size replica of Nicholas Boyleston (H20), ordered by John Hancock, the treasurer of the College, in 1772, and paid for in 1773, the year young JT graduated. See *Harvard Portraits* (Cambridge, Harvard University Press, 1936). Copley's subsequent influence, especially through his portrait of Nicholas Boyleston, is strongly evident in such canvases of Trumbull's as the self-portrait, with the volume of Hogarth prominently displayed on the table, and the posthumous portrait of his brother Joseph. See Sizer, "John Trumbull, Colonial Limner," *Art in America*, 37 (1949), 190–201.

39. 1743–1820, who was only 14 when he entered Harvard; graduated in 1761.

40. John Winthrop, 1714–79, Hollis professor of mathematics and natural philosophy, father of Librarian James Winthrop.

41. Neither located; see items 17 and 18 on p. 54. The Italian original, "Last Eruption of Mount Vesuvius in 1767," which was the gift of Thomas Palmer in May 1772, has since disappeared. It was also copied by Washington Allston while an undergraduate at Harvard, 1796–1800. See Edgar Preston Richardson, *Washington Allston* (Chicago, University of Chicago Press, 1948), p. 183. In each instance it was the painter's first landscape in oil.

42. The engraving was made by Pierre Imbert Drevet after the painting of Antoine Coypel, 1661–1722.

43. This copy in oils, item 20 on p. 54, "Abraham's servant meeting Rebekah at the well, surrounded by her damsels," JT sold to his brother Jonathan for $10.00.

from the officers and students in college, that I ventured to show it
to Mr. Copley, and had the pleasure to hear it commended by him
also. The picture is still preserved in the family. In July, 1773, I
graduated without applause, *for I was not a speaker,* and returned
to Lebanon. Several circumstances prevented my forming intimate
connections while in college; I was the youngest boy in my class;
I had entered in an unusual way, (a sailor would say that I got in
at the cabin windows;) and I had too little pocket money to par-
take in any expensive gaieties, if my timidity and awkwardness had
not also prevented me from doing so. I formed therefore one, and
only one, intimate acquaintance. It was with Christopher Gore [44]
of Boston, an amiable boy, my junior in years, and in college rank.
This was the commencement of a friendship which lasted through
life. Gore became first a distinguished lawyer, then governor of
Massachusetts, and, in after life, it pleased Providence to bring us
frequently into near and intimate associations in important affairs.
—He is dead!

Not long after my return to Lebanon a letter came by the post,
and was first put into the hands of my father. He brought it to me,
and said, "John, here is a letter which I cannot read; I suppose it
must be for you; what language is it?" "Oh yes, sir, it is from my
friend Robichaud—it is French, sir." "What, do you understand
French? How did you learn it? I did not know that it was taught
in college." "It is not, sir, but I learned it in this gentleman's family."
"And how did you pay the expense? You never asked me for extra
allowance." "No, sir; I pinched my other expenses, and paid this
out of my pocket money." My father was very much pleased, and
soon after proposed to me to study Spanish. A ship from South
America, not long before, had been driven into New London by
stress of weather, and had there been condemned as unseaworthy.
The captain, of the name of Sistarri, a man of some education, was
residing in Hebron, a distance of five miles from Lebanon, and it
was from him my father proposed that I should learn. I very fool-
ishly declined it; I could never find in my own mind any other
cause for this absurdity, but that perverseness which seems in-
herent in our nature, and which leads us to undervalue the sugges-

44. 1758–1827, of "Gore Place," Waltham, Mass., Harvard 1776.

tions of others. I have frequently since repented of this folly, for the Spanish language has now become very important, and it has since cost me much laborious study to acquire a very imperfect knowledge of it.

At Lebanon I resumed the pencil, and painted the death of Paulus Emilius at the battle of Cannæ,[45] a passage of Roman history which I had always admired.

"Animæque magnæ,
Prodigum Paullum, superante Pœno."—*Horace.*

This was effected by selecting from various engravings such figures as suited my purpose, combining them into groups, and coloring them from my own imagination. One thing I attempted which I should now hardly venture upon—the clouds of dust by which the distant objects are obscured. This picture is in the Gallery at New Haven.[46]

In the autumn of this year, 1773, my excellent friend, Master Tisdale, had a stroke of paralysis, which disabled him entirely from performing his duties. He earnestly solicited me to take charge of his school until the event of his illness should be known; with the approbation of my father I did so, and during the winter had under my care seventy or eighty scholars, from children just lisping their A, B, C, to young men preparing for college, among whom were some my seniors. It was an arduous task, but a very useful one; my first entrance upon the realities, the sad realities of human life. In the spring, Mr. Tisdale recovered so far as to be able to resume his invaluable labors.

In the summer and autumn of 1774, the angry discussions between Great Britain and her colonies began to assume a very serious tone. As the low growling of distant thunder announces the approach of the natural tempest, so did these discussions give evident notice that a moral storm was at hand, and men began to

45. Item 21 on p. 54, now at Yale, Cat. No. 1832.100.

46. Shortly after JT returned home his father deflected his interest in "his pencil" to utilitarian map making. JT drew for him two maps (now in the Massachusetts Historical Society) of Connecticut's claims to western lands. See Theodore Sizer and Alexander O. Vietor, "John Trumbull, Cartographer," *Yale University Library Gazette,* 23 (1949), 137–139.

fear that the decision of these angry questions must ere long be referred to the *ultima ratio*.

I caught the growing enthusiasm; the characters of Brutus, of Paulus Emilius, of the Scipios, were fresh in my remembrance, and their devoted patriotism always before my eye; besides, my father was now governor of the colony, and a patriot,—of course surrounded by patriots, to whose ardent conversations I listened daily —it would have been strange if all this had failed to produce its natural effect. I sought for military information; acquired what knowledge I could, soon formed a small company from among the young men of the school and the village, taught them, or more properly we taught each other, to use the musket and to march, and military exercises and studies became the favorite occupation of the day.

Of these youthful companions, several became valuable officers in the war which soon followed. Two brothers, my very particular friends and companions, Judah and Roger Alden,[47] distinguished themselves. Judah commanded a company with which, in 1777, he covered the retreat of a reconnoitering column in West Chester country, and was killed in the defense of a bridge over the Bronx. Roger rose to the rank of major, and died lately, postmaster at West Point.

47. Both of Lebanon. Judah, captain of Webb's Additional Continental Regiment; Roger (Yale 1773), brigade major under General Huntington in 1777. JT painted Roger's portrait that year; see p. 55.

2

Soldier and Self-Taught Painter 1775–80

ON THE 19th of April, 1775, the tempest which had been long pre-paring, burst at Lexington in Massachusetts; the blood of our brethren cried from the earth, and the cry was heard throughout New England. In Connecticut, a provisional military organization already existed,[1] and the 1st regiment of Connecticut troops, com-manded by General Joseph Spencer,[2] started into view as by magic, and was on its march for Boston before the 1st of May. Of this regiment, I was adjutant. Gen. Spencer, a friend of my father, was somewhat advanced in life, brave but prudent, and it was arranged that I should be a member of his family—a sort of aid-du-camp.

When my mother was preparing and packing up my linen and clothes for this campaign, she said to me, "My son, when I recollect the sufferings of your infancy, with your present feebleness of con-stitution, and anticipate the hardships and dangers to which you are about to be exposed, I hardly dare to hope that we shall ever meet again; however, in all events, my dear son, I charge you so to conduct yourself, that if ever I do see you again, it may be with the pride and delight of a mother."

The regiment reached the vicinity of Boston early in May, and

1. Jedediah Huntington of Norwich wrote to Joseph Trumbull, the commissary general, at Cambridge, Mass., on 23 May 1775: "Bro. John is not determined whether to take under you or General Spencer." On 16 August 1775 he wrote from Roxbury Camp saying: "Am glad to be joined by Brother Jack—shall take him in with me and accomodate him as well as I can." (Connecticut State Library.)

2. 1714–89, chosen brigadier general of the Connecticut forces at the outbreak of the Revolution; left the forces when the Continental Congress raised Israel Put-nam of Connecticut to the rank of major general and commissioned Spencer, his superior, brigadier, two days later. He became major general in 1778 and resigned that year. The rank-conscious Spencer's conduct undoubtedly influenced JT's later behavior.

17

was stationed at Roxbury: the parade and alarm post was a field on the hill between the meeting-house and the then road, in full view of the enemy's lines at the entrance of Boston.

The entire army, if it deserved the name, was but an assemblage of brave, enthusiastic, undisciplined country lads; the officers in general quite as ignorant of military life as the troops, excepting a few elderly men, who had seen some irregular service among the provincials, under Lord Amherst.[2a]

Our first occupation was to secure our own positions, by constructing field-works for defense. The command of the Roxbury division, forming properly the right wing of the army, was entrusted to Gen. Thomas,[3] of Massachusetts, a brave and well educated man of fine talents, and who had seen some service; his head-quarters were on the hill, near the meeting-house.

Nothing of military importance occurred for some time; the enemy occasionally fired upon our working parties, whenever they approached too nigh to their works; and in order to familiarize our raw soldiers to this exposure, a small reward was offered in general orders, for every ball fired by the enemy, which should be picked up and brought to head-quarters. This soon produced the intended effect—a fearless emulation among the men; but it produced also a very unfortunate result; for when the soldiers saw a ball, after having struck and rebounded from the ground several times, (en ricochet,) roll sluggishly along, they would run and place a foot before it, to stop it, not aware that a heavy ball long retains sufficient impetus to overcome such an obstacle. The consequence was, that several brave lads lost their feet, which were crushed by the weight of the rolling shot. The order was of course withdrawn, and they were cautioned against touching a ball, until it was entirely at rest. One thing had been ascertained by this means, the caliber of the enemy's guns—eighteen pounds. Thirteen inch shells were also occasionally fired, some of which exploded, at first, to our no small annoyance and alarm; but some of these also being picked up, (having failed of igniting,) were carried to head-quarters, and by this means their dimensions were also ascertained.

2a. Jeffery Amherst, 1717–97.
3. John Thomas, 1724–76.

On the 17th of June, I was out at daybreak, visiting the piquet-guard of the regiment, which was posted in full view of Boston and the bay behind it, when I was startled by a gun, fired from a small sloop of war, lying at anchor between the town and Letchmere's point, about where the Cambridgeport bridge now is. It was the hour for the morning gun, but what, thought I, has this little thing to do with the morning gun, which is always fired by the admiral, on the other side of the town. It was very soon followed by another, apparently from the Somerset, sixty four,[3a] which lay between the north end of Boston and Charlestown. It soon became evident to us in Roxbury, that some movement was making in that quarter, but we knew not what. Although the distance between Roxbury and Charlestown, measured across the bay, on a direct line, might not exceed four miles, yet by the road, over the bridge, and through the town of Cambridge, it was not far from twelve. As the day advanced, the firing continued to increase, and our anxiety to know the cause was extreme; when at length, near noon, we learned that a detachment from Cambridge, had, during the preceding night, taken post on the hill behind Charlestown, and were engaged in throwing up a work. They had been discovered from the ships at daybreak, and fired upon. Charlestown and the hills behind it were in full view from the upper windows of headquarters, but the distance was too great for the naked eye to ascertain what was doing. It was about three o'clock when the firing suddenly increased, and became very heavy and continuous; and soon after, with the help of glasses, the smoke of fire-arms became visible along the ridge of the hill, and fire was seen to break out among the buildings of the town, which soon extended rapidly, and enveloped the whole in flames. We could ascertain by the receding of the smoke on the ridge of the hill, that our troops were losing ground, but we had no correct information of the result of the battle of Bunker's Hill,[4] until late at night.

3a. Guns.

4. Eleven years later JT painted his well-known, close-up scene of the battle— one of his most successful and spirited historical compositions. Of his six American and one British battle pictures this was the only action he actually witnessed, and even that was from afar.

In the mean time, when the firing became frequent and heavy, the troops in Roxbury were ordered under arms, and to their posts. Gen. Spencer's regiment was drawn up on their parade, in full view of the enemy's lines, and it was not long before we attracted their attention and their fire. Several of their heavy shot passed over us, and we were soon ordered to fall back to the hill above the meeting-house. It was my duty as adjutant to bring up the rear, and pick up stragglers. In crossing a stone fence, which the regiment in their retreat had nearly levelled, a soldier was on my right, not more than two feet distant, when I heard the rush of a heavy ball, and the poor fellow at my side fell, and cried out that he was killed. I looked at him—his limbs were all entire—I saw no blood, and naturally concluding that his fall was occasioned by extreme fear, I told him that he was not hurt, but only frightened, and bade him get up. He insisted that he could not rise, and I called some other soldiers to help him to the rear and to the surgeon. Some time after I enquired for him, and was told that he was dead. There was no external wound, but the body over the region of the heart was black from extravasated blood. It is said that the rush of a heavy ball, by its passage through the air, occasions a momentary vacuum; probably this ball passed close to the heart at the instant of a violent throb, (whether from fear or exertion,) and the blood-vessels, unsustained by the pressure of the atmosphere, gave way. In this manner I account for the effects produced by what is called "the wind of a ball." [5]

The regiment fell back to the summit of the hill, and we there passed the night on our arms. Charlestown, at that time, contained perhaps six hundred buildings of various sizes, almost all of wood, and lay full in our view, in one extended line of fire.

The British, victorious indeed so far as the possession of the field

5. ". . . the soldier killed by 'pressure of atmosphere' . . . was a figment of the Franco-Prussian War, which cropped up again in the first World War . . . There can be little doubt that airborne blast may produce unconsciousness and possibly death, but well authenticated instances of death from the proximity to the passing of a shell or to an explosion are very few. Generally the head is blown by the blast wave against a solid structure and the impact . . . is responsible for fatal issue." Dr. John F. Fulton. See also his "Blast and Concussion in the Present War," *New England Journal of Medicine*, 226 (1942), 1–8.

went, but fearfully cut up, were apparently not without apprehension that their obstinate enemy might rally and renew the action, and therefore kept up during the night a frequent fire of shot and shells in the direction of Cambridge. The roar of artillery—the bursting of shells, (whose track, like that of a comet, was marked on the dark sky, by a long train of light from the burning fuze)—and the blazing ruins of the town, formed altogether a sublime scene of military magnificence and ruin. That night was a fearful breaking in for young soldiers, who there, for the first time, were seeking repose on the summit of a bare rock, surrounded by such a scene.

About noon of that day, I had a momentary interview with my favorite sister,[6] the wife of Colonel, afterwards General Huntington, whose regiment was on its march to join the army. The novelty of military scenes excited great curiosity through the country, and my sister was one of a party of young friends who were attracted to visit the army before Boston. She was a woman of deep and affectionate sensibility, and the moment of her visit was most unfortunate. She found herself surrounded, not by the "pomp and circumstance of glorious war," but in the midst of all its horrible realities. She saw too clearly the life of danger and hardship upon which her husband and her favorite brother had entered, and it overcame her strong, but too sensitive mind. She became deranged, and died the following November, in Dedham.

Soon after that memorable day, General Washington arrived and assumed the command of the army.[7] A few days after his arrival, I was told by my eldest brother,[8] the commissary general, that the commander in chief was very desirous of obtaining a correct plan of the enemy's works, in front of our position on Boston neck; and he advised me (as I could draw) to attempt to execute a view and plan,[9] as a mean of introducing myself (prob-

6. Faith, wife of Jedediah Huntington.
7. 3 July 1775.
8. Joseph Trumbull.
9. This was the young, rankless adjutant's great opportunity. He drew nicely and clearly and had already had some practice in cartography with the maps of Connecticut's western claims, executed the year previous.

ably) to the favorable notice of the general. I took his advice and began the attempt, by creeping (under the concealment of high grass) so nigh that I could ascertain that the work consisted of a curtain crossing the entrance of the town, flanked by two bastions, one on the western and the other on the eastern side, and I had ascertained the number of guns mounted on the eastern, (their caliber was already known,) when my farther progress was rendered unnecessary by the desertion of one of the British artillerymen, who brought out with him a rude plan of the entire work. My drawing was also shown to the general, and their correspondence proved that as far as I had gone I was correct. This (probably) led to my future promotion; for, soon after, I was presented to the general, and appointed his second aid-du-camp; [10] the first was Thomas Mifflin [11] of Philadelphia, who was afterwards governor of the state of Pennsylvania, and president of Congress in 1783, when General Washington resigned his commission. Joseph Reed, [12] (also of Philadelphia,) was secretary, and Horatio Gates [13] adjutant general.

The scene at head-quarters was altogether new and strange to me, for the ruined state of my father's fortune, and the retirement in which he lived at Lebanon, had prevented my having seen much of elegant society. I now suddenly found myself in the family of one of the most distinguished and dignified men of the age; sur-

10. This was on 27 July 1775. In the General Orders for that day from "Head Quarters, Cambridge," it is recorded: "John Trumbull Esqr being appointed aid de Camp to his Excellency the Commander in Chief, he is to be obeyed as such," quoted by Trumbull in his pension file.

A rather complete military record is to be found in the Veterans' Administration papers in the National Archives, "Revolutionary War pension file of John Trumbull," No. S 14 718, with the soldier-artist's application for a pension dated 26 July 1832 (under the act passed by Congress on 7 June 1832). He was allowed $565.00 a year, payments commencing with 4 July 1831 and continuing until 3 September 1843 (he died 10 November 1843).

It is interesting to note that pay of a brigade major amounted to $33.00 and that of colonel to $50.00 a month. See *Journals of Continental Congress* (1775), 2, 220.

11. 1774–1800, aide from 4 July to 14 August 1775. Like JT he resigned from the army before the end of the war.

12. 1728/29–1806, was born in England of humble origin. He was commissioned a brigadier general on 17 June 1775 and major general on 16 May 1776.

13. 1741–85, lawyer and soldier.

rounded at his table, by the principal officers of the army, and in constant intercourse with them—it was further my duty to receive company and do the honors of the house to many of the first people of the country of both sexes. I soon felt myself unequal to the *elegant* duties of my situation, and was gratified when Mr. Edmund Randolph [14] (afterwards secretary of state) and Mr. Baylor [15] arrived from Virginia, and were named aids-du-camp, to succeed Mr. Mifflin and myself. Mifflin was made quarter-master general of the army,[16] and I a major of brigade at Roxbury.[17] In this situation I was at home, for it was but the duty of an adjutant upon an extended scale; the accuracy of my returns very soon attracted the notice of the adjutant general, (Gates,) and I became in some degree a favorite with him.

Nothing important occurred, until in March, the Roxbury division or right wing of the army, received orders to take possession of the heights of Dorchester. This was done in the evening of the 4th of March,[18] with perfect order, secrecy and success. Our movement was not discovered by the enemy until the following morning, and we had an uninterrupted day to strengthen the works which had been commenced the night preceding. During this day we saw distinctly the preparations which the enemy were making to dislodge us. The entire water front of Boston lay open to our observation, and we saw the embarkation of troops from the various wharves, on board of ships, which hauled off in succession, and anchored in a line in our front, a little before sunset, prepared to land the troops in the morning.

We were in high spirits, well prepared to receive the threatened attack. Our position, on the summits of two smooth, steep hills, were strong by nature, and well fortified. We had at least twenty pieces of artillery mounted on them, amply supplied with ammu-

14. Son of John Randolph of Virginia, appointed aide on 15 August 1775; Randolph succeeded Mifflin and Baylor took JT's place.

15. George Baylor, 1752–84, from the Shenandoah, was to carry the news of the victory of Trenton to Congress.

16. These two appointments were made on 15 August 1775.

17. JT now became brigade major for General Spencer as of 15 August 1775.

18. 1776, that is, after 11 months of comparative inactivity; the emotional JT was doubtlessly restive.

nition, and a very considerable force of well armed infantry. We waited with impatience for the attack, when we meant to emulate, and hoped to eclipse, the glories of Bunker's Hill. In the evening the commander in chief visited us, and examined all our points of preparation for defense. Soon after his visit, the rain, which had already commenced, increased to a violent storm, and heavy gale of wind, which deranged all the enemy's plan of debarkation, driving the ships foul of each other, and from their anchors, in utter confusion, and thus put a stop to the intended operation.

Within a few days the enemy abandoned Boston, and we entered it on St. Patrick's day, the 17th of March. It was a magnificent and beautiful sight—the numerous fleet of ships dropping down to the outer harbor and proceeding to sea. We viewed this triumphant and glorious scene with exultation, and at leisure, for it had been mutually stipulated that we would do nothing to interrupt the departure of the navy and army, on condition that they would commit no depredations on the town.

A strong detachment, commanded by General Thomas, was immediately ordered to reinforce the army in Canada, and the main body of the troops was marched towards New York, which was thought to be the probable scene of the future operations of the enemy; our troops moved to New London and there embarked for New York. Lebanon was nearly on the line of march, and I obtained an opportunity of seeing my parents and family, for a day or two, and proceeded to New York by land.

The brigade to which I was attached, was encamped on the (then) beautiful high ground, which surrounded Col. Rutgers's seat,[19] near Corlaer's Hook. In the levelling spirit of the age, all that part of the city is now flat as a table.

Nothing of military importance occurred during the months of April, May, and June. This time was passed in erecting works, to oppose the expected attack of the enemy, and in drilling the troops to a somewhat improved state of discipline.

Meantime, the affairs in Canada were in a deplorable state, and

19. Henry Rutgers, 1745–1830, Revolutionary officer, owned a large farm, the "Bouwery" (now known as the Bowery), on the lower East Side of Manhattan Island.

in addition to the reinforcement under command of General Thomas, which had been sent from Roxbury in March, another strong detachment, under the command of General Sullivan, was now ordered from New York to that quarter; and in June, General Gates, the late adjutant general, having been promoted to the rank of major general, was appointed to take the command of the northern department, (a term somewhat indefinite, as it afterwards proved,) but then understood to comprehend Canada and the northern frontier. He was expressly authorized to appoint his adjutant and quarter-master general. He offered me the first of these situations, the other to Morgan Lewis, Esq.;[20] both offices were accompanied with the rank of colonel.[21] I accepted with proud satisfaction the situation offered to me, resigned my place as major of brigade,[22] and on the 28th of June, 1776, embarked with General Gates and his suite for Albany.

The navigation of the North river by sloops, was at that time very different from the present mode by steam, and we were seven or eight days in reaching Albany, which may now be performed in almost as many hours. The general landed in the evening, and proceeded immediately to visit General Schuyler,[23] whom we found with his family, just seated at supper. I was very much

20. 1754–1844, Princeton 1773, deputy quartermaster general of the Northern Department from 12 September 1776 to the end of the war; chief of staff at Ticonderoga and Saratoga; later governor of New York. His portrait as governor by JT hangs in the New York City Hall.

21. General Gates was merely complying with his "Tables of Organization," or what the British would call his "War Estimate." The appointment was made on 12 September 1776; see Edmund C. Burnett, ed., Letters of Members of the Continental Congress (Washington, Carnegie Institution, 1923), Nos. 123 and 124, Elbridge Gerry and William Williams to Joseph Trumbull, of 12 and 13 September 1776, 2, 84–85. There are several other letters from Elbridge Gerry from Philadelphia, at this time, to Joseph Trumbull about JT's appointment and the dating of his commission. (Connecticut State Library.) John Hancock wrote to Joseph Trumbull from Philadelphia on 16 September 1776 announcing JT's appointment as deputy adjutant general of the army in the Northern Department. (Connecticut State Library.) JT clung tenaciously to the title of colonel throughout his long life.

22. After serving ten and a half months at that rank. Washington, too, was a major before he was 21.

23. Maj. Gen. Philip Schuyler, 1733–1804, later United States representative and senator from New York. JT painted him twice, in miniature, in 1792. (Yale and New-York Historical Society.)

struck with the elegant style of every thing I saw. We here learned
the news of fresh disasters in Canada, and the next morning, accompanied by General Schuyler, we departed on horseback for
Skeensborough, (now Whitehall.) The road as far as Saratoga was
good; thence to Fort Edward tolerable; but from that to the head
of Lake Champlain, bad as possible, and not a bridge over any of
the small streams and brooks which fall into Wood creek.

From Skeensborough we proceeded with all diligence by water
to Ticonderoga,[24] where we learned that the troops driven from
Canada were beginning to arrive at Crown Point. The two generals
went forward to that place without delay, leaving me, with orders
to examine (in company with Colonel Wynkoop,[25] who commanded at Ticonderoga) the ground on the east side of the lake,
since known by the name of Mount Independence, and the creek
which falls into the lake at the northern extremity of that peninsula.
We devoted the afternoon to a careful examination of the creek and
ground, and agreed in the opinion, that the spot was admirably
adapted for a military post. The next morning I went forward to
Crown Point, where I rejoined my general, and there saw, in all
their horrors, the calamities of unsuccessful war.[26]

Early in May, reinforcements from England had reached Quebec, and our troops were of course obliged to retire. They were
constantly harassed in their retreat, and in addition, the small pox,

24. The once-strategic Fort Ticonderoga, which has been restored as a museum
by the late Stephen H. P. Pell, preserves in its library the "Deputy Adjutant General's Orderly Book," Ticonderoga, 1776, kept by JT from July to November. Under
18 July it is noted that "Colonel John Trumbull is appointed Deputy Adjutant General to the Army, and is to be obeyed as such."

25. Cornelius D. Wynkoop, 1734–93, colonel of the 4th New York Regiment.

26. ". . . At this place [Crown Point] I found not an army but a mob, the scattered remains of twelve or fifteen very fine battalions, ruined by sickness, fatigue,
and desertion, and void of every idea of discipline or subordination. You will be surprised, sir, to know the real state of affairs in this department . . . Among the few
we have remaining, there is neither order, subordination, nor harmony; the officers
as well as men of one colony, insulting and quarreling with those of another . . .
Gen. Sullivan has set off for New York, indignant at being superseded by Gen. Gates
and Gen. Gates himself is superseded by Gen. Schuyler . . . In this manner we
now rest, and . . . my appointment is a little precarious . . ." JT to his father,
the governor of Connecticut, Ticonderoga, 12 July 1776, Autobiography (1841),
App., pp. 302–304.

in its most virulent and deadly form, had made its appearance among them. General Thomas died of this loathsome disease at Chambly, and the command devolved on General Sullivan,[27] who conducted this calamitous retreat in an admirable manner, but was driven, from post to post, until he reached St. John's, at the northern extremity of Lake Champlain. At that time no road existed on either side of the lake, and the only communication with Albany and the southern country was by its waters. General Sullivan having secured all the vessels and boats at St. John's, and destroyed all which were not necessary for the conveyance of his troops, by this means effectually prevented the immediate advance and pursuit of the enemy. Thus the wretched remnant of the army reached Crown Point in safety, but it is difficult to conceive a state of much deeper misery. The boats were leaky and without awnings; the sick being laid upon their bottoms without straw, were soon drenched in the filthy water of that peculiarly stagnant muddy lake, exposed to the burning sun of the month of July, with no sustenance but raw salt pork, which was often rancid, and hard biscuit or unbaked flour; no drink but the vile water of the lake, modified perhaps, not corrected, by bad rum, and scarcely any medicine.

My first duty, upon my arrival at Crown Point, was to procure a return of the number and condition of the troops.[28] I found them dispersed, some few in tents, some in sheds, and more under the shelter of miserable bush huts, so totally disorganized by the death or sickness of officers, that the distinction of regiments and corps was in a great degree lost; so that I was driven to the necessity of great personal examination, and I can truly say that I did not look into tent or hut in which I did not find either a dead or dying man. I can scarcely imagine any more disastrous scene, except the retreat of Buonaparte from Moscow—that probably was the very acme of human misery. I found the whole number of officers and men to be five thousand two hundred, and the sick who required the attentions of an hospital were two thousand eight hundred, so that when

27. Gen. John Sullivan, 1740–95, succeeded to the command of the Northern Army upon the death of Gen. John Thomas, 2 June 1776.

28. There is a "General Return of the Forces," dated Ticonderoga, 24 August 1776, signed by Gates, prepared and countersigned by JT in the Library of Congress.

they were sent off, with the number of men necessary to row them to the hospital, which had been established at the south end of Lake George, a distance of fifty miles, there would remain but the shadow of an army. Crown Point was not tenable by such a wreck, and we were ordered to fall back upon Ticonderoga immediately.

There my first duty was, in company with Colonel Wayne,[29] to make a second examination of Mount Independence. He joined in the opinion before expressed by Col. Wynkoop and myself, that the ground was finely adapted for a military post. At the northern point, it ran low into the lake, offering a good landing place; from thence the land rose to an almost level plateau, elevated from fifty to seventy-five feet above the lake, and surrounded, on three sides, by a natural wall of rock, every where steep, and sometimes an absolute precipice sinking to the lake. On the fourth and eastern side of the position ran a morass and deep creek at the foot of the rock, which strengthened that front, leaving room only, by an easy descent, for a road to the east, and to the landing from the southern end of the lake. We found plentiful springs of good water, at the foot of the rock. The whole was covered with primeval forest. . . .[30]

Part of the troops, as they arrived from Crown Point, being ordered to land and take post on this spot, proceeded to clear away the wood, and to encamp. The exhalations from the earth, which was now, for the first time, exposed to the rays of a midsummer sun, combined with the fog which rose from the pestilent lake, soon produced sickness in a new shape—a fever very nearly resembling the yellow fever of the present time—and it was not unusual to see the strongest men carried off by it in two or three days. The four Pennsylvania regiments, the *elite* of the army, were posted in the old French lines, which they were ordered to repair; and at all points the troops were actively employed in strengthening old works of defense, or in constructing new ones.

In the mean time, reinforcements were earnestly solicited from the New England states, and promptly sent on, so that the post soon assumed the aspect of military strength and activity. Ship carpenters were also requested from the eastern states, who were em-

29. The brave and impetuous Anthony Wayne, 1745–96, of Pennsylvania.
30. The country surrounding the fort has changed but little since JT's time.

ployed at Skeensborough in building the hulls of gallies and boats, with which to dispute the possession of the lake with the enemy, who were busy at St. John's in similar preparations; these gallies, as soon as launched, were sent down the lake to Ticonderoga, to be there equipped and armed. These naval preparations were made under the superintendence of Gen. Arnold,[31] and in this, as well as in every branch of the various duties, I had my full share.

The position of the army extended from Mount Independence on the right and east side of the lake, to the old French lines on the west forming our left, protected at various points by redoubts and batteries, on which were mounted more than a hundred pieces of heavy cannon. After some time, it was seen that the extreme left was weak and might easily be turned; a post was therefore established on an eminence, near half a mile in advance of the old French lines, which was called Mount Hope. Thus our entire position formed an extensive crescent, of which the center was a lofty eminence, called Mount Defiance, the termination of that mountain ridge which separates Lake George from Lake Champlain, and which rises precipitously from the waters of the latter to a height of six hundred feet. The outlet of Lake George enters Champlain at the foot of this eminence, and separates it from the old French fort and lines of Ticonderoga. This important position had hitherto been neglected by the engineers of all parties, French, English and American.

I had for some time, regarded this eminence as completely overruling our entire position. It was said, indeed, to be at too great a distance to be dangerous; but by repeated observation I had satisfied my mind that the distance was by no means so great as was generally supposed, and at length, at the table of Gen. Gates, where the principal officers of the army were present, I ventured to advance the new and heretical opinion, that our position was bad and untenable, as being overlooked in all its parts by this hill. I was ridiculed for advancing such an extravagant idea. I persisted however, and as the truth could not be ascertained by argument, by theory, or by ridicule, I requested and obtained the general's permission to ascertain it by experiment. General (then Major)

31. Benedict Arnold, 1741–1801, of Connecticut, patriot and traitor.

Stevens [32] was busy at the north point of Mount Independence in examining and proving cannon; I went over to him on the following morning, and selected a long double fortified French brass gun, (a twelve pounder,) which was loaded with the proof charge of best powder and double shotted. When I desired him to elevate this gun so that it should point at the summit of Mount Defiance, he looked surprised, and gave his opinion that the shot would not cross the lake. "That is what I wish to ascertain, Major," was my answer; "I believe they will, and you will direct your men to look sharp, and we too will keep a good look-out; if the shot drop in the lake their splash will easily be seen; if, as I expect, they reach the hill, we shall know it by the dust of the impression which they will make upon its rocky face." The gun was fired, and the shot were plainly seen to strike at more than half the height of the hill. I returned to head-quarters and made my triumphant report, and after dinner requested the general and officers who were with him to walk out upon the glacis of the old French fort, where I had ordered a common six pound field gun to be placed in readiness. This was, in their presence, loaded with the ordinary charge, pointed at the top of the hill, and when fired, it was seen that the shot struck near the summit. Thus the truth of the new doctrine was demonstrated; but still it was insisted upon, that this summit was inaccessible to an enemy. This also I denied, and again resorted to experiment. Gen. Arnold, Col. Wayne, and several other active officers, accompanied me in the general's barge, which landed us at the foot of the hill, where it was most precipitous and rocky, and we clambered to the summit in a short time. The ascent *was* difficult and laborious, but not impracticable, and when we looked down upon the outlet of Lake George, it was obvious to all, that there could be no difficulty in driving up a loaded carriage.

Our present position required at least ten thousand men, and an hundred pieces of artillery, for its doubtful security. I assumed that it would be found impossible for the government, in future campaigns, to devote so great a force to the maintenance of a single post; and as there was no road on either side of the lake by which

32. Ebenezer Stevens, 1751–1823, commanding officer of artillery in the Northern Department, commissioned major 7 November 1776.

an enemy could penetrate into the country south, he must necessarily make use of this route by water; and as the summit of Mount
Defiance looked down upon, and completely commanded the narrow parts of both the lakes, a small but strong post there, commanded by an officer who would maintain it to the last extremity,
would be a more effectual and essentially a less expensive defense
of this pass, than all our present extended lines.

On these principles I proceeded to draw up two memoirs, in
one of which was stated the number of men, *ten thousand*, with
the expense of their pay, subsistence, clothing, &c., and of artillery
at least *one hundred* pieces, with their attirail,[32a] ammunition, &c.,
necessary to the maintenance of the present system of defense; in
the other, an estimate of the expense of erecting a permanent work
on the summit in question, large enough to contain a garrison of five
hundred men, and mounting twenty five heavy guns, with the
ammunition, pay and provisions for that force for one year. The
relative expense of the two systems was as twenty to one nearly.
These memoirs I accompanied with plans of our present position.
I found time to draw up three copies,[33] both of the plans and
memoirs, one to be submitted to Gen. Gates, one to Gen. Schuyler,
and one to Congress. My other duties were so pressing that I could
proceed no farther; I have always lamented that I found it impossible to prepare one for my father, for among his papers it would
have been preserved. I have vainly sought a copy among the papers
of Gen. Schuyler and of Gen. Gates. Happily, however, I have lately
obtained, from among the papers of my father, a drawing of the
post made by me in the month of August and sent to him; an accurate copy of this is given in the annexed plate [in the 1841 edi-
tion], and sufficiently explains and confirms all that has been said
upon this subject.

The events of the succeeding campaign demonstrated the correctness of my views, for Gen. St. Clair [34] was left to defend Ticon-

32a. Gear, harnesses.

33. One now owned by Hall Park McCullough, New York; a sketch included in
a letter of 15 July 1776 to his brother Joseph, in the Connecticut State Library, may
be a second; the third is lost.

34. Brig. Gen. Arthur St. Clair, 1736 o.s.–1818, major general in 1777, of Pennsylvania.

deroga without any essential addition to the garrison which had been placed under his command by Gen. Gates in the preceding November, *because the Congress could not spare more men or means;* so that, when General Burgoyne[35] presented himself at Three Mile Point, no opposition could be hazarded to his movements, and instead of assaulting the works, (as had been formerly done by Gen. Abercrombie[36] in 1757,) he silently turned the left of the position, crossed the outlet of Lake George, and established a battery of heavy guns on the summit of Mount Defiance, the shot from which plunged into the old French fort and lines, and reached all points of Mount Independence, so that, as I had predicted, the whole position became untenable, and was immediately abandoned. General St. Clair became the object of furious denunciations, whereas he merited thanks, for having saved a part of the devoted garrison, who subsequently formed the nucleus of that force by which, in the course of the campaign, Gen. Burgoyne was ultimately baffled, and compelled to surrender his victorious army by the convention of Saratoga.

Early in October our naval preparations were completed, and our little fleet, composed of a brig, several gallies and gun-boats, mounting altogether more than one hundred guns, commanded by Generals Arnold and Waterbury,[37] proceeded down the lake to look for the enemy. His preparations were completed about the same time, and on the 11th of October the two fleets met, engaged, and we were defeated with total loss. Gen. Arnold ran the galley which he commanded on shore, and escaped with the crew; the other vessels were either taken or destroyed, and their crews, (with the exception of some who got on shore and straggled up to the army,) with Gen. Waterbury, remained prisoners of war.

On this occasion Sir Guy Carleton,[38] who commanded the hostile

35. John Burgoyne, 1722–92, soldier, statesman, dramatist, surrendered to General Gates at Saratoga on 17 October 1777, a subject which JT was to paint years later.

36. James Abercromby, 1707–81, supreme commander of all British forces in America in 1758.

37. David Waterbury, 1722–1801, colonel 5th Connecticut Regiment 1775, brigadier general Connecticut 1776, taken prisoner at Valcour's Island, 11 October 1776.

38. The first Lord Dorchester, 1724–1808, governor of Quebec in 1775.

fleet and army, behaved with a degree of humanity, as well as policy, which, if it had been generally employed by other royal commanders, might have exposed to great hazard the success of America. As soon as the action was over, Sir Guy gave orders to the surgeons of his own troops, to treat the *wounded prisoners* with the same care as they did his own men. He then ordered that all the other prisoners should be immediately brought on board his own ship, the Royal Charlotte, where he first treated them to a drink of grog, and then spoke kindly to them, praised the bravery of their conduct, regretted that it had not been displayed in the service of their lawful sovereign, and offered to send them home to their friends, on their giving their parole that they would not again bear arms against Great Britain until they should be exchanged. He then invited Gen. Waterbury to go below with him to his cabin, and requested to see his commission,—the moment he saw that it was signed by the governor of Connecticut, (my father,) he held out his hand, and aid, "General Waterbury, I am happy to take you by the hand, now that I see that you are not serving under a commission and orders of the rebel Congress, but of Governor Trumbull. You are acting under a legitimate and acknowledged authority. He is responsible for the abuse he has made of that authority. That which is a high crime in him, is but an error in you; it was your duty to obey him, your legitimate superior."

A few days after this defeat, a number of row-boats approached our advanced post, and there lay upon their oars with a flag of truce. I was ordered to go down and learn their object. I found Capt. Craig,[39] with Gen. Waterbury and the other prisoners who had been taken in the recent action; dismissed, as Sir Guy had promised, upon parole. The usual civilities passed between Sir James and me, and I received the prisoners; all were warm in their acknowledgment of the kindness with which they had been treated, and which appeared to me to have made a very dangerous impression. I therefore placed the boats containing the prisoners under the guns of a battery, and gave orders that no one should be per-

39. James Henry Craig, 1748–1812, of the 47th Regiment of Foot, who was severely wounded at Bunker's Hill, major general in 1794, afterward Sir James Craig, governor general of Canada, 1807–11.

mitted to land, and no intercourse take place with the troops on shore until orders should be received from Gen. Gates. I hurried to make my report to him, and suggested the danger of permitting these men to have any intercourse with our troops;—accordingly they were ordered to proceed immediately to Skeensborough, on their way home, and they went forward that night, without being permitted to land.

A few days after, the hostile army arrived at Crown Point, and a strong reconnoitering party was pushed forward to look at us. Upon the appearance of a number of boats at Three Mile Point, (so called from its distance from the old French fort,) our whole force was ordered under arms, and to occupy their several posts. Ticonderoga must have had a very imposing aspect that day, when viewed from the lake. The whole summit of cleared land, on both sides of the lake, was crowned with redoubts and batteries, all manned, with a splendid show of artillery and flags. The number of our troops under arms on that day (principally however militia) exceeded thirteen thousand. Our appearance was indeed so formidable, and the season so far advanced, (late in October,) that the enemy withdrew without making any attack, and we were enabled to dismiss great part of the militia, and prepare for winter quarters. The best of the troops were selected to remain in garrison during the winter, under the command of General St. Clair; the remainder moved off in succession for Albany, and on the 18th of November, Gen. Gates, with his staff, embarked on Lake George, on his way to that place.

My taste for the picturesque here received a splendid gratification. Some of the troops who had passed before us had landed on the west shore of the lake and lighted fires for cooking. The season was cold and dry—the leaves had fallen in masses—the fire had extended to them, and spread from ledge to ledge, from rock to rock, to the very summit, where it was from seven hundred to a thousand feet high. In parts the fire crept along the crevices of the rock; at times an ancient pine tree rose up a majestic pyramid of flame; and all this was reflected in the pellucid surface of the lake, which lay like a beautiful mirror in the stillness of the dark night, unruffled but by the oars of our solitary boat, and these were frequently suspended that we might enjoy the magnificent scene. No human habitation was exposed to danger, for none existed on that desolate and rocky shore. Snakes, bears and wolves were the only living things exposed to harm.

Late in the night we reached Fort George, at the head of the lake, and thence proceeded to Albany by land. There the general met an order from General Washington to hasten on with all the disposable troops, and join him behind the Delaware river. The best troops were selected, (the remainder being discharged into winter quarters,) and with these we proceeded by water as far as Esopus, (Kingston,) thence by land through the then uncultivated country of the Minisink, nearly on the route of the present Delaware and Hudson Canal—inclining to the left to Sussex court-house, in the hope of falling in with and joining the division of General Lee,[40] which we had learned was crossing Jersey. At Sussex, having learned Lee's unfortunate capture, we inclined to the right, crossed the Delaware at Easton, and marched through Bethlehem to Newtown, where we joined the commander in chief, a few days before his glorious success at Trenton.[41] News had just been received by him, that a detachment of the enemy had obtained possession of Newport and Rhode Island, and General Arnold and myself were ordered to hasten without delay to that quarter. When we arrived at Providence we found a body of militia already collected there, under the command of my first military friend, General Spencer. The enemy were quiet in Newport, and we in our quarters in and near Providence.

40. Maj. Gen. Charles Lee, 1731–82, of Virginia, son of the English Maj. Gen. John Lee. JT made a pencil sketch of him (now at Yale) for his projected historical picture, the "Attack on Charleston," S.C.

41. ". . . in November 1776, after the Enemy retired from the vicinity of Ticonderoga he accompanied Genl. Gates, with a Detachment of Troops to Newtown in pennsylvania, where they joined General Washington a few days before the glorious Event at Trenton" (on 26 December 1776). (JT's pension file, National Archives.) The artist began his small-scale "Battle of Trenton," which is now at Yale, at London in 1786, but it remained unfinished for 10 years. A large replica of this picture, now at the Wadsworth Atheneum, Hartford, Conn., was painted in 1832—56 years after the "glorious Event."

The 22d of February, 1777, terminated my regular military career.[42] The following letters [43] will explain the cause and manner.

To the Hon. John Hancock, Esq.,[44]
President of Congress.

> *Providence, R.I., Feb. 22, 1777.*

SIR—Lieut. Col. Meigs [45] has this day delivered to me a commission from the most honorable the continental Congress, appointing me deputy adjutant general in the northern department—an honor I had long despaired of.

I find the commission is dated the 12th of September, 1776, which, sir, is an insuperable bar to my accepting it.

I have served in that office since the 28th of June, by the appointment of the honorable Major General Gates, who was authorized to make the appointment, by particular instructions from Congress.

I expect, sir, to be commissioned from that date, if at all. A soldier's honor forbids the idea of giving up the least pretension to rank. I am, sir, &c. &c.

42. JT's army career lasted but 1½ years, from 3 May 1775 to 22 February 1777. That he had harbored some doubts about the retention of his rank may be inferred from a letter to his father dated simply "Ty: Sept. 1776": ". . . I find there is so much Ceremony in the Congress, that I am not to be appointed in this [session?], without a particular recommendation. As my Name has been mention'd by Genl Gates, I have informed my brother at York that I shall ask *no further recommendation*. I am very willing to return the Moment that my Country is desirous of it—or that Congress thinks they can better the Army, by appointing an officer in my place. You will not be surpris'd, Sir! if you should [hear?] me displaced—an Inferior Post I shall by no means accept—but either enter in the Fleet as a Volunteer—or return home." (William L. Clements Library, Ann Arbor, Mich.) JT's letters to his brother Joseph from Ticonderoga register his impatience in not receiving the commission for his colonelcy: "I shall wait a little longer at the price of my country—but not *much* longer by God!", 25 August 1776, and "My commission is not receiv'd yet—I look on myself *Insulted*," 4 November 1776. (Connecticut State Library.)

43. All of the following letters are given in the *Historical Magazine, 1*, (1857), 289–292, plus one from Lovell addressed simply to "J. Trumbull, Esq.," dated Philadelphia, 18 March 1777, to which Trumbull replied from Lebanon on the 26th, ". . . the omission of even the plain addition of Mr. to an officer who bore the Rank of Colonel, appears to me a *little* satirical . . ." Lovell's letter of 22 March 1777 is in *Letters of Members of the Continental Congress*, No. 415, 2, 308–309.

44. 1736/37–93, merchant and statesman of Massachusetts. JT was 21 when he wrote this letter and Hancock 40.

45. Return Jonathan Meigs, 1740–1823, then of Sherburne's Additional Continental Regiment, later colonel of the 6th Connecticut Regiment.

The commission in question was enclosed in the above, and by the same conveyance the following letter was sent to the Hon. James Lovell, Esq.,[46] member of Congress.

Providence, R. I., Feb. 22, 1777.

SIR—The occasion on which I write, will, I trust, justify my troubling you with this letter; I shall not, therefore, make any further apology for what might otherwise pass for presumption.

By this conveyance I have returned a commission which I lately received from Congress, accompanied by a short letter to the honorable president; and as my conduct may be blamed by those who are unacquainted with the treatment which I have received during the past campaign, I beg leave to give you the necessary information, and my reasons for this conduct, that you may have it in your power (as I trust you will feel the disposition) to justify me from any aspersions.

In August, 1775, I was honored with the commission of a major of brigade, in which office I served until the 28th of last June. In the beginning of that month, General Gates was promoted to the rank of major general, and was ordered to command in the Northern department. Among other powers contained in his instructions, he was particularly directed to appoint a deputy quarter-master general and a deputy adjutant general for the army on that station. On his return to New York, the general did me the honor to offer me the latter place, an offer which I accepted with gratitude and pleasure; and on the 28th of June, (having quitted my situation of major of brigade,) I sailed with the general for Albany. He immediately wrote to Congress that he had appointed Colonel Morgan Lewis and myself to the two offices mentioned, and desired that our commissions might be sent forward as soon as possible. No answer was received. On the last of July, or beginning of August, the major general sent Colonel Lewis to Congress, with a particular account of the state of affairs in that quarter—a detailed statement of wants—and again mentioned the affair of our commissions. After having waited five days in Philadelphia, and having been referred daily from this morning to to-morrow, Col. Lewis left the

46. 1737–1814, a delegate from Massachusetts to the Continental Congress.

city in disgust, and returned to Ticonderoga, without even a verbal answer to the dispatches which he had carried; nor was an answer received until two months from that time.

You may suppose our situation to have been uneasy, as any officer who chose to dispute our rank might do it with impunity. For this reason I determined to quit the army, the moment the dangers of the campaign should be past. I continued in service after the defeat of our fleet, and the retreat of the enemy into Canada, for no other reason but because my leaving the post before the danger was entirely past, might be imputed to improper motives. I attended my general to Albany in November, and thought that to be the long looked for opportunity, when the day before I meant to leave him, an express arrived from General Washington, requiring him to take down to his assistance the northern army, who were then going into winter quarters. I continued with the troops from the same cause as before. On my arrival at head-quarters I was ordered to attend General Arnold to this place, and have remained in this chaos, until this day, endeavoring to introduce some idea of regularity and discipline, and in the hope of an opportunity of attacking the enemy on Rhode Island. Our expectations are now destroyed by the impossibility of obtaining a number of troops sufficient for the proposed purpose, and another opportunity offers for my quitting with honor a service in which I have been able to acquire so little.

When length of service, an unimpeached character, and a forwardness to serve in a quarter where success was despaired of, is rewarded by *neglect,* we have reason to complain. But, sir, there was no occasion to add insult. I considered myself sufficiently affronted by being obliged to wait eight months for a commission. Congress needed not to wound my feelings further by sending me at length a commission, dated three months later than the time of my entering upon the service for which it was given.

I should have less reason to complain, did I not know that officers of the northern army, inferior in rank to myself, have been advanced and commissioned without the least difficulty. This prevents the hurry of business being alledged as an excuse for such treatment.

If I have committed any crime, or neglected any duty, since I engaged in the service of my country; if I have performed any action, or spoken a word in my public character, unworthy of my rank, let me be tried by my comrades and broke; but I must not be thought so destitute of feeling as to bear degradation tamely.

From this day, therefore, I lay aside my cockade and sword,[47] with the fixed determination never to resume them until I can do it with honor.

Thus, sir, I have given you the grounds of my conduct, and shall esteem it a favor if you will make use of this letter to justify me against any improper reflections which may be cast upon my character and conduct.

I have the honor to be, &c. &c.

To the above letter I received the following answer.

Philadelphia, March 22d, 1777.

Col. John Trumbull,

SIR—I wrote you a few lines by Mr. Bates,[48] in regard to your manner of returning your commission. I was not then aware of some circumstances attending your appointment, which have, upon this occasion, been since canvassed.

I shall not accurately enter upon a discussion of the propriety or impropriety of your resignation, but shall only, as an affectionate friend, give you this early intelligence of a number of facts, which will enable you to make a final determination of the matter.

The commissions of several, enclosed in letters of less apparent resentment than yours, had been readily admitted for resignation. Some cutting resolutions had been made upon the insolent passages of the late letters of ******, especially upon those parts which called for stigmas upon you or your brother. Immediately your letter is opened, and by your friends committed, instead of the resignation being instantly accepted, a favorable report was made,

47. "I lay aside my cockade and sword"—typical of JT's dramatic attitude. The version of the letter in the *Historical Magazine, 1,* 290, is "From this day, therefore, I lay aside my Cockade and Sword, with a Determination, *fixed as Fate,* never to resume them until I can do it with Honour." (The italics are JT's.)

48. "Mr. Bates," probably a Congressional employee; not mentioned in the Hancock papers.

but overruled by a motion to postpone the consideration. Upon this General Gates sent in a recommendatory letter, explaining the circumstances of your appointment. But this would not do. Congress is greatly piqued at the style and manner of your demand, in a case which will now appear to you in the line of favor, and not of strict right.

You are to know, that General Gates's power was in Canada, so that your appointment, before his entrance there, was not strictly proper. Whether your first commission was dated after any formal debate upon the point I cannot say, but that and your late one were of one date, founded on your nomination in Congress I suppose.

Every member is entirely willing to accord you a commission agreeable to the date you expect, but they are determined to lose even your acknowledged abilities, if they do not receive a different request from that now before them.

You were certainly unacquainted with the criticisms which may take place as to Gen. Gates's power of appointment out of Canada. You were also unacquainted with the provocations which have been given to Congress for attention to the style of their officers, prior to the receipt of yours. Gen. Gates is attached to you—the Congress admit your merit—and while they are disposed to give you a rank which shall save you from all appearance of demerit, they think that you yourself will judge the commission more valuable for proceeding from a body attentive to their own honor.

No time will be lost by this accident, if you determine to procure the commission by the method which I shall take the freedom to point out, because you may go on to act from certainty to receive it by the first opportunity after your letter shall arrive here.[49]

49. Elbridge Gerry wrote to Joseph Trumbull on 26 March 1777: ". . . I am informed that upon a report of the Board of War upon your Brother's Letter, Congress discovered a Resentment at the disrespectful Freedom expressed therein, and would not consent to give him a Comm. of an earlier Date. I think he had a Right to his Claim, but cannot altogether approve of the Stile in which he addressed the Legislative authority of the Continent. It is the fixed Determination of Congress to preserve the civil above the military . . ." *Letters of the Members of the Continental Congress*, No. 419, 2, 311. The President of Congress wrote to General Gates on 29 April 1777: ". . . it is not the intention of Congress that Mr. Trumbull should be reappointed." *Ibid.*, No. 466, 2, 347. William Williams, Trumbull's brother-in-law, wrote to Joseph Trumbull from Yorktown 28 November 1777: "If Jack had really an

To the Hon. John Hancock, Esq., &c. &c.

SIR—Since I addressed a letter to your honor from Providence, enclosing my commission, I have been led to find that I was mistaken in the apprehension that my appointment to the office of deputy adjutant general on the 28th of June, (from which time I have acted,) was so much in the usual manner, as to render the commission bearing an after date a decisive degradation, when compared with the usual practice. But the same desire of serving my country in the most effectual manner, which has governed my actions in the whole course of my adjutancy, since the day of my first appointment, leads me to be anxious that I may not be under any appearance of disgrace from any circumstance in the date of my commission, as this would lessen my most vigorous exertions; therefore, I entreat that your honor would move the honorable Congress to favor me with a commission consonant in date to my appointment by Gen. Gates. Assuring them of my zeal for the service of the United States, and of my highest respect for their body, I am, &c. &c.

I do not affect to point out a verbal model for you; it is the tenor only; with something similar you may be sure of an instant compliance here. The delay therefore depends on yourself; I hope you will make none,

And am, &c. &c.   J. LOVELL.

To this I returned the following answer.

Lebanon, March 30th, 1777.

To the Hon. James Lovell, Esq., &c. &c.

SIR—I was yesterday honored by the receipt of your letter of the 22d inst. and have considered its contents.

I acknowledge the kind intentions of my friends in having my former letter committed, and shall remember the service they meant to do me with gratitude; but I designed to have my resig-

---

Inclination to have continued in the Army, I have no doubt he might have obtained Justice in the matter he complained of, and wo'd have done real Service, and been also a Brigr. Genl . . ." *Ibid.,* No. 759, 2, 573. One wonders if he did want to continue in the army.

nation accepted, nor can I consent to the method which they propose of regaining the post which I have quitted.

It is perhaps true that my appointment by Gen. Gates was not *strictly* proper; but, he could not be the less a judge of military merit, from being by mere accident deprived of the command which he expected; and as the office in question in the northern army was vacant, and no rival to my pretensions offered, had I not good ground to expect that his recommendation would still be attended to? and was it not a compliment justly due to him, when Gen. Schuyler, our proper commanding officer, not only made no objection to my appointment, but even wrote in my favor?

It had ever been the custom of the army, to date commissions from the day on which the offices were entered upon by the appointment or recommendation of the general; and I had no reason to expect that I should be the person in whom the innovation was to commence.

Though my appointment may not have been *strictly* valid, yet from former practice in similar cases, my authority and rank had been admitted; and to sink under the command of men whose superior in rank I had been acknowledged, though perhaps not established, tasted indeed too loathsome of degradation.

I can see nothing in my former letters at which the honorable Congress can, with propriety, take umbrage. There is not in either of them, a sentiment or a word of disrespect to them; there is not a sentiment or word which I wish altered. They are written with freedom—a freedom which it would illy become the representatives of a free state to discourage. Neither can I suppose that any preceding insolence of other men, can influence so wise a body as the Congress in forming their judgment of me, or (when it is seen that there is no expression of designed insult or disrespect in what I wrote) that I shall be condemned for the sins of others.

I have never asked any office in the public service, nor will I ever; the very request would acknowledge and prove my unworthiness. If my services have not rendered me deserving of the notice of my country; if the manner in which I discharged the duties of the office which I have resigned, did not entitle me to the commission with which I expected to have been gratified,—

surely my request cannot, and it is well that I have ceased to serve.

I forbear to say any thing further upon a subject now of perfect indifference to me, and will only add my sincere thanks to you and my other honorable friends in Congress, for having interested themselves in my behalf on this occasion. At the same time I regret that by this means the appointment of a necessary officer has been delayed; *since I cannot ask,* and therefore do not expect, the return of my commission. I am, &c. &c.

The "line by Mr. Bates" referred to in the foregoing letter from Mr. Lovell, did not come to my hands until that had been received and answered. The difference of style deserves to be remarked, and it would puzzle a wise man to account for it, except by a whimsical sickliness of pride, which we would not willingly have supposed, could have influenced so respectable and wise a body as Congress were believed to be at that early day.

A copy of that letter follows.

Philadelphia, March 16th, 1777.

Col. John Trumbull,

My dear sir—I have received your letter of the 22d of February, and though aware of the manly sensibility which governed you on the late occasion, yet I am sorry that any accident should have given you this particular occasion of showing yourself a man of spirited honor.

Your character is unblemished in the opinion of those who should have forwarded your commission; therefore I have attributed past omissions on their part to accident—I cannot think of design—in what has happened.

I showed your letter to Gen. Gates, who had before made the most honorable mention of you to me. He will not do without you; therefore, if the proper alteration of date is made, I will not think you can obstinately disappoint *his* hopes, to say nothing of mine.

Perhaps before I put a wafer to this, I may have a word or two more to say on this subject. I took up my pen to prevent missing an opportunity, through the haste of the bearer, of assuring you of the esteem of, &c. &c.

J. Lovell.

In explanation of this singular correspondence, it is proper that I should add the following anecdote.

While I was in General Washington's family, in 1775, Mr. Hancock made a passing visit to the general, and observing me, he enquired of Mr. Mifflin who I was, and when told that I was his fellow aid-du-camp, and son of Gov. Trumbull, he made the unworthy observation, that *"that family was well provided for."* Mr. Mifflin did not tell me this until after he (Mr. Hancock) had left headquarters, but then observed that he deserved to be called to an account for it. I answered, "No, he is right; my father and his three sons are doubtless well provided for; we are secure of four halters, if we do not succeed." Gen. Gates was intimate with Mifflin and knew this anecdote at the time, and probably had mentioned it to Mr. Lovell, as indicative of a spirit of ill will to my father and his family which might have caused the delay and neglect in forwarding my commission, and hence probably the apologetic paragraph in the letter "by Mr. Bates."

Thus ended my regular military service,[50] to my deep regret, for my mind was at this time full of lofty military aspirations.

I returned to Lebanon, resumed my pencil, and after some time went to Boston, where I thought I could pursue my studies to more advantage. There I hired the room which had been built by Mr. Smibert,[51] the patriarch of painting in America, and found in it several copies by him from celebrated pictures in Europe, which were very useful to me, especially a copy from Vandyck's celebrated head of Cardinal Bentivoglio,[52]—one from the continence

50. "The final Settlement & close of his Accounts was made at Albany in the month of May 1777—by John Carter, the accounting officer of the Northern Department;—which Settlement may perhaps be found among the papers of that day, in the Treasury." (JT's pension file, National Archives.)

51. John Smibert, 1688–1751, accompanied Dean (afterward Bishop) George Berkeley to America, as professor of drawing in the proposed college in the Bermudas. He settled at Boston in 1730. His house was in Queen Street, between the Town House (the old State House) and the Orange Tree, now Nos. 5, 7, and 9 Scollay Square. For the Smibert painting room Trumbull paid, to 16 November 1779, £61.6 "in old emission currency." See Henry Wilder Foote, *John Smibert* (Cambridge, Harvard University Press, 1950), for Smibert's posthumous influence on JT.

52. Smibert's copy, after Sir Anthony Van Dyck, 1599–1641, is now lost. JT gave his to Harvard College in 1791 (now hanging in Eliot House). See item 37, p. 55.

of Scipio, by Nicolo Poussin,[53] and one which I afterwards learned to be from the Madonna della Sedia by Raphael.[54] Mr. Copley was gone to Europe, and there remained in Boston no artist from whom I could gain oral instruction; but these copies supplied the place, and I made some progress.

At this period, 1777–8, a club was formed in Boston of young men fresh from college, among whose members were Rufus King,[55] Christopher Gore,[56] William Eustis,[57] Royal Tyler,[58] Thomas Dawes,[59] Aaron Dexter,[60] &c. &c.,—men who in after life became distinguished. The club generally met in my room, regaled themselves with a cup of tea instead of wine, and discussed subjects of literature, politics and war. About this time arrived in Boston from South America a singular person, who announced himself as Dr. Korant; his complexion was unusually dark, countenance serious, manners monastic, but evidently a man of extensive learning, speaking several modern languages fluently—English tolerably, Spanish in perfection. The society of the Jesuits had been recently suppressed, and the general impression was, that Dr. Korant was an ex-Jesuit. The club thought that the society of such a man was worth courting, and he was invited to our meetings. After we had become acquainted, one of our members asked the doctor what he thought of our political state. "Gentlemen, you are all lately from college, and of course you remember the Latin adage—*Procul a Jove, procul a fulmine.* I have always admired that proverb; for if

53. Smibert's copy after Nicolas Poussin, 1594–1665, is at the Walker Art Gallery, Bowdoin College, Brunswick, Maine; JT's copy is now lost. See item 45 on p. 55.

54. Now in the Uffizi, Florence; Raphael Sanzio, 1483–1520, of Urbino.

55. 1755–1827, Harvard 1777, later United States senator from Massachusetts and minister to Great Britain.

56. Governor and United States senator from Massachusetts, and commissioner to Great Britain, who, with Rufus King, remained a close, life-long friend of the artist.

57. 1750–1825, Harvard 1772, later served as surgeon in the Revolutionary army, member of Congress, secretary of war, minister to Holland, governor of Massachusetts.

58. 1757–1826, Harvard 1776, of Massachusetts, playwright and jurist. See item 67 on p. 56.

59. 1757–1825, Harvard 1777, jurist. See item 66 on p. 56.

60. 1749–1829, Harvard 1776, later Erving Professor of Chemistry and Materia Medica at Harvard College.

at any time the thunderbolt of Jove seemed to menace me, I would
retire to a great distance and be safe; but you seem to have in every
town and village, a number of little Joves, each armed with a little
thunderbolt, (committee of safety,) which though less terrible
than the bolt of imperial Jove, are each of them sufficient to destroy
the peace and happiness of an individual, and so numerous, and
planted over all the country, that there is no possibility of escape.
I do not like that."

The war was a period little favorable to regular study and deliberate pursuits; mine were often desultory. A deep and settled
regret of the military career from which I had been driven, and to
which there appeared to be no possibility of an honorable return,
preyed upon my spirits; and the sound of a drum frequently called
an involuntary tear to my eye.

In the year 1778, a plan was formed for the recovery of Rhode
Island [61] from the hands of the British, by the coöperation of a
French fleet of twelve sail of the line, commanded by the Count
D'Estaing,[62] and a body of American troops, commanded by Gen-
eral Sullivan. The fleet arrived off New York early in July, and in
August sailed for Rhode Island. I seized this occasion to gratify
my slumbering love of military life, and offered my services to
General Sullivan, as a volunteer aid-du-camp. My offer was ac-
cepted, and I attended him during the enterprise.

The French fleet, which had passed Newport, and lay at anchor
above the town, were drawn off from their well selected station by
a clever manœuvre of Lord Howe,[62a] the very day after the American army had landed on the island. The two fleets came to a partial
action off the capes of the Chesapeake, in which they were separated by a severe gale of wind; the French, more damaged by the
tempest than by the enemy, put into Boston to refit, and General
Sullivan was left to pursue the enterprise with the army alone. The
enemy shut themselves up in Newport, while he advanced to the

61. Drafts of several of JT's letters from Rhode Island to his father are to be
found in the former's letter book in the Library of Congress.

62. Charles Hector, comte d'Estaing, 1729, guillotined 1794, vice-admiral 1778,
admiral 1792.

62a. Richard Howe, commander of the British fleet, elder brother of General Sir
William Howe.

town in admirable order, and the place was invested in form.

It soon became evident that the attempt was vain, so long as the enemy could receive supplies and reinforcements by water, unmolested; so soon as it was ascertained that the French fleet would not resume its station, the enterprise was abandoned—on the night between the 28th and 29th of August, the army was withdrawn, and reoccupied their former position on Butts' Hill, near Howland's ferry, at the north end of the island.

Soon after daybreak the next morning, the rear-guard, commanded by that excellent officer, Col. Wigglesworth,[63] was attacked on Quaker, otherwise called Windmill Hill; and Gen. Sullivan, wishing to avoid a serious action on that ground, sent me with orders to the commanding officer to withdraw the guard. In performing this duty, I had to mount the hill by a broad smooth road, more than a mile in length from the foot to the summit, where was the scene of the conflict, which, though an easy ascent, was yet too steep for a trot or a gallop. It was necessarily to ride at a leisurely pace, for I saw before me a hard day's work for my horse, and was unwilling to fatigue him.

Nothing can be more trying to the nerves, than to advance thus deliberately and alone into danger. At first, I saw a round shot or two drop near me and pass bounding on. Presently I met poor Col. Tousard,[64] who had just lost one arm, blown off by the discharge of a field piece, for the possession of which there was an ardent struggle. He was led off by a small party. Soon after, I saw Capt. Walker,[65] of H. Jackson's regiment, who had received a musket ball through his body, mounted behind a person on horseback. He bid me a melancholy farewell, and died before night. Next, grape shot began to sprinkle around me, and soon after musket balls fell in my path like hailstones. This was not to be borne,—I spurred on my horse to the summit of the hill, and found myself in the midst of the melée. "Don't say a word, Trumbull," cried the gallant commander, "I know your errand, but don't speak; we will beat them

63. Edward Wigglesworth, 1742–1826, colonel of the 13th Massachusetts Militia.
64. Lieut. Col. Louis de Tousard, d. 1821, a French volunteer in the Continental Army in 1777.
65. Lieut. Richard Walker of Massachusetts, of Col. Henry Jackson's Additional Continental Regiment, killed at Quaker Hill 29 August 1778.

in a moment." "Col. Wigglesworth, do you see those troops crossing obliquely from the west road towards your rear?" "Yes, they are Americans, coming to our support." "No, sir, those are Germans; mark, their dress is blue and *yellow*, not buff; they are moving to fall into your rear, and intercept your retreat. Retire instantly— don't lose a moment, or you will be cut off." The gallant man obeyed reluctantly, and withdrew the guard in fine style, slowly but safely. . . .

As I rode back to the main body on Butts' Hill, I fell in with a party of soldiers bearing a wounded officer on a litter, whom I found to be my friend, H. Sherburne,[66] brother of Mrs. John Langdon [67] of Portsmouth, New Hampshire, a fellow volunteer. They were carrying him to the surgeons in the rear, to have his leg amputated. He had just been wounded by a random ball while sitting at breakfast. This was a source of lasting mortification, as he told me afterwards,—"If this had happened to me in the field, in active duty, the loss of a leg might be borne, but to be condemned through all future life to say I lost my leg under the breakfast table, is too bad." Mr. Rufus King was acting that day as a volunteer aid-du-camp to General Glover,[68] whose quarters were in a house at the foot and east of Quaker Hill, distant from the contested position of the rear-guard a long mile. The general and the officers who composed his family were seated at breakfast, their horses standing saddled at the door. The firing on the height of the hill became heavy and incessant, when the general directed Mr. King to mount and see what and where the firing was. He quitted the table, poor Sherburne took his chair, and was hardly seated, when a spent cannon ball from the scene of action bounded in at the open window, fell upon the floor, rolled to its destination, the ancle of Sherburne, and crushed all the bones of his foot. Surely there is a

66. Henry Sherburne, 1755–76, killed in the Montgomery-Arnold expedition to Quebec, second son of John and Catherine Cutt (Moffatt) Sherburne.

67. Elizabeth Sherburne, 1761–1813, daughter of John and Mary (Moffat) Sherburne, married John Langdon, 1741–1819, United States senator from New Hampshire and five times governor of the state, in 1777. His stately mansion, built in 1784, is now owned by the Society for the Preservation of New England Antiquities.

68. Brig. Gen. John Glover, 1732–97, of Massachusetts. In 1779 he succeeded General Sullivan in command of the Providence department.

providence which controls the events of human life, and which withdrew Mr. King from this misfortune.

Soon after this, as I was carrying an important order, the wind, which had risen with the sun, blew off my hat. It was not a time to dismount for a hat. I therefore tied a white handkerchief round my head, and as I did not recover my hat until evening, I formed, the rest of the day, the most conspicuous mark that ever was seen on the field—mounted on a superb bay horse, in a summer dress of nankeen—with this head-dress, duty led me to every point where danger was to be found, and I escaped without the slightest injury. It becomes me to say with the Psalmist, "I thank thee, Oh thou Most High, for thou hast covered my head in the day of battle!" [69] For never was aid-du-camp exposed to more danger than I was during that entire day, from daylight to dusk.

The day was passed in skirmishing, and towards evening a body of the enemy (Germans) had pushed our right wing, and advanced so far as to endanger themselves. I was ordered to take Gen. Lovell's [70] brigade of Massachusetts militia, and aid in repulsing them; this brigade was very much weakened by the withdrawal of many officers and men, in consequence of the army having been left by the French fleet. For this reason I drew up the brigade in line, and disregarding their original distinctions of regiments and companies, told them off into ten divisions; assigned their officers among them, wheeled them off into column, and advanced toward the scene of action, intending to pass beyond the enemy's flank, and to attack his rear. As we advanced, the noise of the conflict seemed to retire, until we approached a small wood skirting the open fields, which lay in the direction of our march. This wood was occupied by a party of the enemy, whom it concealed from our view, while the fire which they opened upon us as we advanced, marked their position. As was common they fired too high, and their shot passed over our heads, doing no harm. In front of the wood, at a distance of thirty or forty yards, ran a strong stone fence, such as are common in Rhode Island. Generally, on such an occasion, this

69. Not the exact wording either of the Book of Common Prayer or of the King James Version of the Bible for Psalm 140:7.

70. Brig. Gen. Solomon Lovell, 1731/32–1801.

fence would have been made use of as a breastwork to protect us
from the enemy's fire; but as my men had hitherto kept their order
perfectly, and seemed to be in no degree disconcerted by the
sound of the balls, which whistled over their heads, (perhaps they
did not understand it,) I became elated with the hope of doing
something uncommon, and therefore determined not to make use
of this wall for defense, but to attack. For this purpose it was necessary to remove such an obstacle, for in attempting to climb over it
all order would infallibly be lost. I therefore moved on until the
front division of the column was within ten yards of the wall, and
then gave the word of command as if on parade, "Column, halt—
leading division, ground your arms—step forward, comrades, and
level this fence, it stands in our way—quick, quick!" The order was
obeyed with precision; the fence was leveled in an instant, and we
resumed our forward march without having a man hurt. From that
moment the firing from the wood ceased, and we could find no
enemy; they had been already engaged with, and overmatched by
other troops, before we approached, and when they saw our cool
manœuvre, they probably mistook us for veterans coming to the
rescue, and prudently withdrew.

Still I hoped to be able to strike an important blow, and requested General Lovell to incline his march to the right, (by which
means his movement would be screened from the view of the enemy
by the form of the ground,) to move slowly and carefully, and to
keep the men together in their actual order. I rode forward to re-
connoitre and ascertain the position of the enemy. As I rose the
crest of the hill, I saw the German troops, who had just been re-
pulsed, in evident disorder, endeavoring to re-form their line, but
fatigued, disconcerted and vacillating. I thought it a glorious moment, and hurried back to my brave column with the intention of
leading it (under cover of the ground) into the rear of the enemy's
flank. Judge of my vexation, when I found my men, not in slow
motion and good order, as I had directed, but halted behind another
strong fence, dispersed, without the shadow of order, their arms
grounded, or leaning against the fence, exulting in their good conduct and success in having made the enemy run. I was cruelly disappointed; but as the success of the blow which I had meditated
depended entirely upon rapidity of movement, and much time must

be wasted before we could recover our original order and be prepared to move, I gave up my projected attack, and returned to make my report to my general.

The next day the army kept their ground on Butts' Hill, collected our wounded, buried the dead, and while we made a show of intending to maintain our position, were really busied in preparing for a retreat, which was effected during the following night, by transporting the whole in boats, across Howland's ferry to Tiverton, without the loss of a man, or of the smallest article of stores.

The entire conduct of this expedition, and of this retreat, (as well as of that from Canada,) was in the highest degree honorable to General Sullivan.

As soon as we had left the island, I took leave of my general, sent my servant back to Lebanon, with a descriptive letter to my father, a drawing of the field, and the sword which I had taken from its owner, a German sub-officer, my trophy of the action; and then took my own course to Boston, where I arrived on the second day, with strong symptoms of severe indisposition. Excitement of mind and fatigue of body had quite overpowered and prostrated my strength; I immediately took some cooling medicine and went to bed. Before I rose next morning, a visit from Governor Hancock [71] was announced. He followed the servant to my bedside, and with great kindness insisted that I should be removed to his house immediately, where, if my illness should become serious, I could be more carefully attended than was possible in a boarding-house. I made light of my illness, and with many thanks declined his pressing invitation. But it was a proud and consoling reflection, that he who had been president of Congress at the time of my resignation, and who had both signed and forwarded the misdated commission which had driven me from the service, had now witnessed my military conduct, and seen that I was not a man *to ask*, but *to earn* distinction.[72]

71. John Hancock did not become governor until September 1780; JT was then in London.

72. Washington wrote to his former aide from his headquarters at Morristown, N.J., 26 March 1780: "In answer to your letter of the 10th of this month, I have enclosed you a certificate expressing in general terms my sense of your services. For want of a knowledge of the ranks which you may have held at different times, and

I soon recovered, and resumed the pencil, pursuing the study of painting with great assiduity during the following year. My friends, however, were not satisfied with my pursuit, and at length succeeded in persuading me to undertake the management of a considerable speculation, which required a voyage to Europe, and promised (upon paper) great results. They were to furnish funds, I to execute the plan, and share with them the expected profits. Accordingly, in the autumn of 1779, I gave up my studies in Boston, and returned to my father's house in Lebanon, to prepare for the voyage.

During this residence in Boston, I became acquainted with Mr. Temple,[73] afterwards Sir John, and consul general of Great Britain in New York. He was married in Boston to a daughter of Gov. Bowdoin,[74] and had also high connexions in England. He seemed to be regarded by both parties as a neutral person, and was occasionally permitted to pass from one to the other. He was acquainted with Mr. West[75] in London, and strongly urged me to go there and study with him. Connected as I was, and personally hostile as my conduct had been, I did not believe that this could be done with safety, during the war; but Mr. Temple was confident, that through the influence of his friends in London, he could obtain permission for me from the British government. He soon after went to London, and before I was ready to embark on my commercial pursuit, I received information from him, that he had seen Lord George Germaine,[76] the British secretary of state—had represented to him my wish to study painting under Mr. West—had explained my connexions, my past military pursuits, &c., concealing nothing—and

the periods of your service I could not make it more particular, but if you are desirous of one comprehending these matters and will send me the proper dates etc. I shall make a certificate agreeably." (Library of Congress, Manuscript Division, Vol. 131–75.)

73. Sir John Temple, 1732–98, 8th baronet; Trumbull painted his portrait in 1784.

74. James Bowdoin, 1726–90, merchant, Revolutionary statesman, governor of Massachusetts 1785–87.

75. Benjamin West, 1738–1820, of Pennsylvania, was most helpful to visiting American students.

76. George Sackville Germain, 1716–85, commissioner of trade and plantations, 1775–79, and secretary of state for the colonies to 1782.

had received for answer, "that if I chose to visit London for the purpose of studying the fine arts, no notice would be taken by the government of my past life; but that I must remember that the eye of precaution would be constantly upon me, and I must therefore avoid the smallest indiscretion,—but that so long as I avoided all political intervention, and pursued the study of the arts with assiduity, I might rely upon being unmolested."

Thus, in the event of failure of my mercantile project,[77] the road was open for pursuing my study of the arts, with increased advantages.

The following is a list [78] of drawings and pictures executed before my first voyage to Europe, and before I had received any instruction [79] other than was obtained from books.[80]

1. A head of General Wolfe, from an engraving in the Gentleman's Magazine.

2. Fire-works in London, on the occasion of the peace of Aix la Chapelle, in 1748; copied in Indian ink, from an engraving, A. D. 1770, ætat. 14.

3. View of part of the city of Rome.

4. The Virginia water, in Windsor Park.

5. The Crucifixion of our Savior.

77. The artist sprang from a race of merchants; throughout his long life he continuously vacillated between art and trade; a good commercial speculation ever held an irresistible attraction. He wrote his father on 3 February 1780 from Boston about "the price of indigo in foreign markets." He suggested that "it might be proposed to the council [of Connecticut] . . . if they see fit . . . [to] entrust me with the agency . . . to supply them . . . with military clothing, woolens and linen . . ." *Autobiography* (1841), App., pp. 308–309.

78. This list is based on an earlier one (now in the Yale University Library) recording the work executed prior to 1789, which in turn was "copied from an early book which was ruined by the damp." See Sizer, "An Early Check List of the Paintings of John Trumbull," *Yale University Library Gazette*, 22 (April 1948), 116–123.

79. Not quite correct: the works of Copley exercised a profound and lasting impression; imported European paintings and copies after them, especially those by Smibert, and those owned by John Hancock, and European paintings had their influence on the work of young JT.

80. Among the books the artist may have consulted was Charles LeBrun's *Traité des passions* (Paris, 1698), of which there are many later editions, as a sheet of sketches at Yale, dated 1778, seems to indicate. JT was later to admire greatly the work of this painter.

6. The family arms—first attempt in oil colors—age 15.

7. Ruins of the Temple of the Sun, &c., Palmyra, from an engraving in the Gentleman's Magazine; given to Master Tisdale.— *The preceding were done at Lebanon, before going to college.*

8. The Crucifixion, in water colors, from a print by Rubens.

9. Portrait of Dr. and President Holyoke, from one of Mr. Copley's pictures; given to Mrs. Kneeland, his daughter.

10 to 15. Six small portraits of eminent men, Newton, Locke, &c. &c.; given to Mr. Isaiah Doane.

16. Britannia, in Indian ink; given to Theo. Parsons.

17. Eruption of Mount Vesuvius, small, water colors, on vellum; copied from the Italian picture in the philosophical lecture room, and given to Professor Winthrop.

18. The same in oil, size of the original.

19. Miniature of Rubens; given to Mr. F. Borland.

20. Abraham's servant meeting Rebekah at the well, surrounded by her damsels; copied in oil from an engraving after the picture by Noel Coypel, in the library of Harvard College, same size as the engraving; in possession of Daniel Wadsworth, Esq., of Hartford.— *These at Cambridge.*

21. Death of Paulus Emilius at the battle of Cannæ, my first attempt at composition, many figures; done at Lebanon in oil, 1774, age 18; now in the Gallery at New Haven.

22. Portraits of my father and mother, heads in oval spaces, surrounded by ornamental work, from Houbraken's heads—Justice and Piety, &c.; in possession of Professor Silliman.

23. Brutus condemning his Sons—original design, at Lebanon, 1777; given to my eldest brother—perhaps at Windham, in the possession of the relatives of his wife, Miss Dyer.

24. Portrait of my brother David, a small whole length, standing in a landscape, 1777; in possession of his widow at Lebanon.

25. Crucifixion, a small single figure.

26. Head of myself, half size; given to my sister, the late Mrs. Williams.

27. Portrait of Maj. Gen. Jabez Huntington of the militia, whole length, half size of life, 1777; possession of his family.

28. Portraits of my brother Jonathan, his wife and daughter—group, heads size of life, 1777; in possession of Professor Silliman.

29. Portrait of myself, head size of life.

30. Brutus and his friends, at the death of Lucretia—half length, reversed; copied in part from a print after Gavin Hamilton, partly original, 1777; in possession of Peter Lanman, Esq., Norwich.

31. Elisha restoring the Shunamite's son, on a half length cloth; in possession of Joseph Trumbull, Esq., of Hartford.

32. Portrait of Elisha Williams, head the size of life.

33. Portraits of my parents—group, size of life, on a half length cloth reversed; my father dressed in a blue damask night gown; in possession of Joseph Trumbull, Esq., Hartford.

34. Portrait of Major Roger Alden, small head—not bad.

35. Portrait of my sister-in-law, Mrs. Amelia Trumbull, widow of my eldest and favorite brother.

36. Portrait of Jabez Huntington, Jr.—*These at Lebanon.*

37. Head of Cardinal Bentivoglio; copied from Smibert's copy of Vandyck's celebrated portrait in the Florence Gallery.

38. Heads of two boys, (Charles and James 2d,) copied from Smibert's copy of Vandyck's beautiful picture.

39. Head of Dr. Franklin—a fur cap—from a French print.

40. Head of James Wilkinson, small.

41. Head of Mr. Edward Gray, size of life.

42. Head of Mrs. Edward Gray, size of life.

43. Head of Mr. Cutler, small.

44. A Nun by candlelight; copy.

45. The Continence of Scipio; copied, with essential variations, from Mr. Smibert's copy of N. Poussin; at Mr. Wadsworth's, Hartford, in perfect preservation.

46. St. Paul preaching at Athens; a drawing in Indian ink.

47. Half length portrait of Washington; copy from Peale.

48. Landscape, from a print after Salvator Rosa; in possession of Joseph Trumbull, at Hartford.

49. Head of Rubens, ⎱ copied from pictures in possession of
50. Head of Vandyck, ⎰   Gov. Hancock.

51. Portrait of Mr. Ben. Call,—head size of life.

52. Portrait of my eldest brother Joseph, *from memory,* after his death; half length, size of life.—*These at Boston.*

53. Col. Wm. Williams, ⎱ heads.
54. Mrs. Williams, my sister, ⎰
55. A Monk at his Devotion, by lamplight; copy.
56. Copy of 52, for his widow, my sister-in-law.
57. Gen. Washington, half length, from memory.
58. A Madonna; copy.—*These at Lebanon, 1778.*

59. Miss P. Sheaffe, ⎫ small heads, from life, on oval plates of
60. Miss A. Sheaffe, ⎬ copper; given to Mrs. Sheaffe.
61. Miss S. Apthorp, ⎭
62. Myself.
63. Belisarius, *date obolem,* the principal figure copied from Strange's engraving, after Salvator Rosa; several figures of Roman soldiers, ruins, &c. added,—on a half length cloth; in possession of Joseph Trumbull, Esq. at Hartford—good.

64. Landscape, sunset; composition, as companion for 48; possession of Joseph Trumbull, Esq. Hartford—not bad.

65. Portrait of Benj. Hitchburn, half length—not bad.

66. Portrait of Thomas Dawes, head—very respectable.

67. Head of Royal Tyler, with both hands—a respectable portrait.

68. The Dying Mother and Infant, an abortive attempt at the celebrated Greek story,—the mother, mortally wounded, repelling the child from her bosom, lest he should drink her blood.—*These at Boston, 1779.*[81]

81. Of these, located and lost pictures are as follows (all are in oil unless otherwise noted):

1–2. Unlocated.   3. Rome, water color, based on a print, the earliest surviving work of the artist in any medium; Yale, No. 1928.26.   4–19. Unlocated.   20. Rebecca at the Well, based on a print; Mrs. John DeForest Haskell, Wakefield, Nebr. 21. Paulus Emilius, probably based on several prints; Yale, No. 1832.100.   22. The artist's parents; estate of William Brownell Goodwin, Hartford, Conn.   23–25. Unlocated.   26. Self-portrait, his earliest; Dr. George E. McClellan, Woodstock, Conn. 27. Gen. Jabez Huntington, pose derived from a print, probably after Salvator Rosa; Connecticut State Library, Hartford.   28. Jonathan Trumbull, Junior, his wife Eunice Backus, and their daughter Faith (later Mrs. Daniel Wadsworth), in the early Copley manner; Yale, No. 1920.2.   29. Self-portrait, with a volume labeled

"Hogarth" (*The Analysis of Beauty* [London, 1753]) and a palette (the colors on which are laid out in seven "classes" in the manner described by Hogarth) on the table. Close in style to Copley's "Nicholas Boylston"; Museum of Fine Arts, Boston, Mass., No. 29.791. 30. Brutus, partly after a print; Yale, No. 1942.111. 31. Elisha, based on prints; Mrs. John T. Roberts, Hartford, Conn. 32. Unlocated. 33. The artist's parents, again inspired by Copley's "Nicholas Boylston" of 1772 at Harvard College; Connecticut Historical Society, Hartford, No. 72. 34–35. Unlocated. 36. Jabez Huntington, the general's grandson; Yale, No. 1938.272. 37. Cardinal Bentivoglio; Harvard University, No. H24. 38–45. Unlocated. 46. St. Paul, ink drawing; Fordham University, New York. 47. Washington, after the 1776 portrait by Peale (now at the Brooklyn Museum); see C. C. Sellers, *Portraits and Miniatures by Charles Willson Peale* [Philadelphia, American Philosophical Society, 1952], pp. 220–221), copied at John Hancock's home at Boston; Yale, No. 1870.2. 48. Landscape, based on a print (unlike Salvator Rosa); Daughters of the American Revolution, Jonathan Trumbull House, Lebanon, Conn. 49–51. Unlocated. 52. Joseph Trumbull in the Copley manner; Mrs. John T. Roberts, Hartford, Conn. 53. William Williams; Dr. George E. McClellan, Woodstock, Conn. 54. Mary Trumbull Williams; same as above. 55. Unlocated. 56. Joseph Trumbull, replica; Pilgrim Hall, Plymouth, Mass. 57. Washington. (JT took this portrait to London with him and presumably gave it to his master, Benjamin West. It was No. 123 in the sale of the "pictures of the late Benjamin West, Esq., P.R.A.," by George Robins, 22 June 1829.) 58–62. Unlocated. 63. Belisarius; Henry Austin Stickney, New York. 64. Landscape, in the manner of Gaspar Dughet and Claude Lorraine, based on a print; Jonathan Trumbull Lanman, Junior, Cross River, N.Y. 65–68. Unlocated.

The following work, unrecorded by the artist, may be assigned to him on stylistic or internal evidence: Brutus, earliest surviving work in oils, 1771 at Lebanon; Wadsworth Atheneum, Hartford, Conn., No. 1844.9. Jonathan Trumbull, Senior, 1774 at Lebanon; unlocated. Jonathan Trumbull, Senior, in a Houbracken frame, similar to No. 22, 1774 or 1775 at Lebanon; Yale, No. 1797.1. The artist's parents, replica of No. 22, 1775 at Lebanon; Connecticut Historical Society, No. 103. Maps, the Colony of Connecticut, 1774 and 1775 at Lebanon; Massachusetts Historical Society, Boston, Mass. Military maps of Boston, 1775 at Boston; unlocated. Military maps of Ticonderoga, 1776 at Ticonderoga; two unlocated, one, Hall Park McCullough, New York. Rev. Abel Stiles, about 1777 at Woodstock, Conn.; unlocated. Mrs. Abel (Alethea Robinson) Stiles, the artist's aunt; same as above. Jonathan Trumbull, Junior, his wife and child, preliminary drawing for No. 55; unlocated. Architectural drawing of an Anglo-Palladian Villa, 1777 at Boston; New-York Historical Society, New York. St. Paul preaching, probably similar to No. 46, 1778 at Boston; unlocated. Rev. Joseph Buckminster, D.D., probably 1779 at Boston, in manner close to Copley's "John Hancock" of 1765 (then in John Hancock's house, now at the Museum of Fine Arts, Boston); Yale, No. 1864.1.

See Sizer, "John Trumbull, Colonial Limner," *Art in America* (October 1949), pp. 191–201.

3

The Rebel at London and His Enforced Return
to America 1780–83

I EMBARKED at New London about the middle of May, 1780, on board a French ship (La Negresse) of twenty-eight guns, bound to Nantes.[1] She was an armed merchant ship from Hispaniola, which had been driven into New London by stress of weather, and having repaired her damages, now sailed for her original destination, having on board a valuable cargo of sugar and coffee. The Trumbull frigate [2] got under weigh with her, and kept company for three days, until she was clear of the coast, and out of the usual track of the English cruisers. I had one fellow passenger, Major Tyler [3] of Boston, who like myself had been an officer in the American army, and took this voyage for the purpose of settling some mercantile concern of his father, who was lately dead.

Our passage was pleasant; we met neither enemy nor accident, and in about five weeks saw the coast of Europe. As we approached, a lofty wall of rock rose before us, and the officers of the ship (who did not know the coast) were extremely anxious until we got a pilot on board. He steered directly for the reef, which was tremendous, and appeared to have no opening; an opening there was, however, for which the pilot directed our course, and which we at

1. "Col. John sailed . . . for France the 7th of May last." Jonathan Trumbull to Horatio Gates, dated Lebanon, 25 July 1780, "Trumbull Papers," *Collections of the Massachusetts Historical Society*, Ser. 7 (Boston, 1902), *3*, 85. His mother, Faith Robinson Trumbull, died 29 May 1780, five days after her son sailed for Europe.

2. The artist's father maintained a considerable fleet of merchantmen operating chiefly from the ports of Norwich and New London.

3. John Steel Tyler was a major in Jackson's Continental Regiment prior to March 1779; in 1779 he was a lieutenant colonel of the Massachusetts Militia.

length saw, in appearance not wider than the ship. The officers, crew and passengers were breathless as we approached the reef, the rocks composing which were, in parts, as high as the ship's masts, and on which the waves of the Atlantic beat with fury. With the swiftness of an arrow, the ship shot through the opening, which as we passed, did not appear to be much wider than her main studding-sail booms; and in an instant we found ourselves in an extensive basin, calm as a mill-pond; it was a part of Quiberon bay. The old pilot turned proudly to the captain, and said, "*Mon capitaine, vous voila en sureté; les Anglois ne vous trouveront jamais içi.*" (Captain, here you are safe; the English will never find you here.)

As we stood across the bay towards the entrance of the beautiful Loire, and approached the land, I was very much struck with the total dissimilitude to the shores of America; there all is new, here all things bore marks of age; the coast was lofty, the very rocks looked old; and the first distinct object, was an extensive convent, whose heavy walls of stone seemed gray with age, and were surrounded by a noble grove of chestnut trees, apparently coeval with the building. We soon entered the river, and the next day we landed at Nantes. Here all was indeed new—a city built with white stone—some imposing remains of ancient Roman architecture—a seaport of great bustle and activity—and a people whose appearance, manners and language, were entirely strange. I had flattered myself that I knew something of the French language, but I here found that the language of books and of educated people was not that of the market, or the port, especially at Nantes,[4] where all partook largely of the *patois* of Brettany. Mr. Tyler and myself remained here two or three days only, and then set off in company for Paris *en poste*. He knew not a word of the language, and I had the sole management of the journey, which lay upon the beautiful banks of the Loire, and led us through Angers, Tours, Blois and Orleans, to Paris. Here bad news met us. Charleston in South Caro-

4. JT wrote his father from Nantes on 15 June 1780: "I shall go on to Paris in two days; this is, when I am become a Frenchman, and dressed *à-la-mode*." *Autobiography* (1841), App., p. 310. His accounts (in the Yale University Library) show bills for "a Suit of clothes at Nantes . . . buckles, Hatter and Hosier." Dress was always an important factor in the artist's long life.

lina was taken,[5] and the British were overrunning the southern states, almost without opposition.

This news was a *coup de grâce* to my commercial project,[6] for my funds consisted in public securities of Congress, the value of which was annihilated by adversity. The study of the arts remained as a last resort, and I resolved to go to London, and there wait a possible change. I therefore remained but a short time in Paris, where I knew few except Dr. Franklin,[7] and his grandson, Temple Franklin; [8] John Adams,[9] and his son, John Q.,[10] then a boy at school, of fourteen; and Mr. Strange,[11] the eminent engraver, and his lady. As I was sitting one morning with Mrs. Strange, a fashionable old French lady came in to make her a visit. She was splendidly dressed, but her face was very brown and wrinkled, with a spot of bright red paint, about the size of a dollar, on the centre of each cheek, then the indispensable mark of a married lady. With difficulty I suppressed the desire to laugh, which convulsed me; Mrs. S. observed it, and when her visitor was gone, gravely asked me what so much amused me. "My dear madam, to see how very strangely extremes meet. In my own country, I have often seen a squaw, dressed in finery—old, dusky, wrinkled—with a dab of pure vermillion on each cheek, and little thought that the poor old savage was dressed in the height of Parisian fashion."

5. Charleston was taken on 12 May 1780, after a vigorous siege of 6 weeks. Trumbull had it in mind to paint the "Attack on Charleston" as one of the historical series. Of the 15 projected subjects 8 only were painted.

6. The painter was a curious combination of a Yankee trader and a romanticist. He wrote his father upon arrival, from Nantes, 15 June 1780: ". . . 'Tis the sword only that can give us such a peace as our past glorious struggles have merited. The sword must finish what it has so well begun . . ." *Autobiography* (1841), App., pp. 310–311.

7. Benjamin Franklin, 1706–90, then sole plenipotentiary to France. His appearance at this precise time may be learned from his portrait painted by Joseph Silfrede Duplessis, exhibited at the Paris Salon in 1779, a replica of which, belonging to the Boston Athenaeum, hangs in the Museum of Fine Arts, Boston.

8. William Temple Franklin, *ca.* 1760–1823, was secretary to his grandfather at Paris.

9. 1735–1826, then commissioner to France, minister to United Provinces in 1780, later 2d president of the United States.

10. 1767–1848, later 6th president of the United States.

11. Robert Strange, 1721–92, married Isabella, the daughter of William Lumisden of Edinburgh. Strange was knighted in 1787.

Having obtained from Dr. Franklin a line of introduction to Mr. West, I set off for London, travelling through Péronne, Cambray, Lisle, &c. to Ostend, and there embarked for Deal, (which was then the regular packet communication between England and the continent.) Arrived in London,[12] I took lodgings near the Adelphi, and sent immediate notice of my arrival to my friend Mr. Temple, whose address I knew; by him the secretary of state was informed of my residence. The next morning information to the same effect was lodged at the secretary's office, by a committee of American loyalists, who thought they were doing the state some service; but they received the incomprehensible rebuke, "You are late, gentlemen; Mr. Trumbull arrived yesterday at three o'clock, and I knew it at four. My eye is upon him, but I must observe to you, that so long as he shall attend closely to the object of his pursuit, it is not the intention of government that he shall be interrupted."

I presented the letter of Dr. Franklin to Mr. West, and of course was most kindly received. His first question was, whether I had brought with me any specimen of my work, by which he could judge of my talent, and the progress I had made; and when I answered that I had not, he said, "Then look around the room, and see if there is any thing which you would like to copy." I did so, and from the many which adorned his painting-room, I selected a beautiful small round picture of a mother and two children. Mr. West looked keenly at me, and asked, "Do you know what you have chosen?" "No, sir." "That, Mr. Trumbull, is called the Madonna della Sedia, the Madonna of the chair, one of the most admired works of Raphael; the selection of such a work is a good omen; in an adjoining room I will introduce you to a young countryman of ours who is studying with me—he will shew you where to find the necessary colors, tools, &c., and you will make your copy in the same room." Here began my acquaintance with Mr. Stuart,[13] who was afterwards so celebrated for his admirable portraits. With his assistance I prepared my materials, and proceeded to my work.

12. July 1780.

13. Gilbert Stuart, 1755–1828, of Rhode Island, arrived at London in November 1775.

When Mr. West afterwards came into the room, to see how I went on, he found me commencing my outline without the usual aid of squares. "Do you expect to get a correct outline by your eye only?" "Yes, sir; at least I mean to try." "I wish you success." His curiosity was excited, and he made a visit daily, to mark my progress, but forbore to offer me any advice or instruction. When the copy [14] was finished, and he had carefully examined and compared it, he said, "Mr. Trumbull, I have now no hesitation to say that nature intended you for a painter. You possess the essential qualities; nothing more is necessary, but careful and assiduous cultivation." With this stimulant, I devoted myself assiduously to the study of the art, allowing little time to make myself acquainted with the curiosities and amusements of the city.

At the close of Mr. West's residence in Italy, in 1762, he stopped at Parma long enough to make a small copy of the celebrated picture by Correggio,[15] called the St. Jerome of Parma,[16] which is universally regarded as one of the three most perfect works of art in existence. I have since seen several copies, by eminent men; one by Annibal Caracci,[17] in the collection of the marquis of Stafford; [18] another by Mengs,[19] in the possession of the widow of the well known Mr. Webb,[20] at Bath; and in 1797, I saw the original in the Louvre at Paris, and have no hesitation to give it as my opinion, that Mr. West's copy approaches much nearer to the exquisite delicacy of expression and harmony of clair-obscure of the original, than any other I have seen. I cannot compare the color, for when I saw the original it was in a room adjoining the gallery of the

14. JT's copy of West's copy of the "Madonna della Sedia" was stolen from the Yale Gallery about 1880.

15. Antonio Allegri da Correggio, 1494–1534, Italian painter of the Lombard school, whose work was exceedingly popular in the 18th century.

16. Still hanging in the Museum at Parma.

17. Annibale Carracci, 1560–1609, Italian painter of the Bolognese school, whose work was much admired at the time.

18. Granville Leveson-Gower, first marquis of Stafford, 1721–1803, former president of the Privy Council and later Lord Privy Seal, a man of great wealth and much political influence.

19. Anton Raphael Mengs, 1728–79, German historical painter, long a resident of Rome.

20. Daniel Webb, 1719?–98, author of several theoretical works on art.

Louvre, under the hands of some mender of pictures, who deserves to be flayed alive for the butchery which he was inflicting upon this exquisite work. He had cleaned the body of the infant, and whole centre of the picture, till all the original surface color was taken away, and nothing was left but the dead coloring of blue-black and white; so that whatever may be its present appearance, it certainly is no longer the hand of Correggio, but of the cleaner. This picture early attracted my attention, but the number of figures and complexity of the composition deterred me from attempting to copy it; after having finished my Madonna, I resolved to attempt it, and with the approbation of my master, I commenced,—again without squares, and trusting to my eye alone. I had not advanced far, when an event occurred, which had well nigh put an end to my pursuit of the arts forever.[21]

On the 15th of November, 1780, news arrived in London of the treason of Gen. Arnold,[22] and the death of Major André.[23] The loyalists, who had carefully watched my conduct from the day of my arrival, now thought themselves certain of putting an end to my unintelligible security and protection. Mr. André had been the deputy adjutant general of the British army, and I a deputy adjutant general in the American, and it seemed to them that I should make a perfect *pendant*. They however took their measures with great adroitness and prudence, and without mentioning my name, information was by them lodged at the office of the secretary of state, that there was actually in London (doubtless in the character of a spy) an officer of rank of the rebel army, a very plausible and

21. Not long after the artist's arrival at London he painted, from memory, a small full-length portrait of General Washington (now at the Metropolitan Museum of Art, New York). This portrait was engraved in mezzotint by Valentine Green, London, 1781; head used on the United States postage stamp, Washington Bicentennial issue, No. 712, 7¢, black, 1932. Six of JT's portraits and two of his historical scenes have been used on United States stamps. See Sizer, "Trumbull's Paintings on Postage Stamps," *The American Philatelist*, 62 (June 1949), 704–706.

22. The plot of Benedict Arnold to surrender West Point was discovered on 23 September 1780 by the capture of Major André.

23. John André, hanged at Tappan, N.Y., 2 October 1780. See Winthrop Sargent, *The Life and Career of Major John André* (Boston, Ticknor & Fields, 1861). In 1821 Major André's remains were translated from Tappan, to Westminster Abbey, London. JT designed the sarcophagus. See App., pp. 365–368.

dangerous man, Major Tyler. In the very natural irritation of the moment, a warrant was instantly issued for his arrest. This warrant was placed in the hands of Mr. Bond [24] of the police, and the additional instruction was given to him by the *under* secretary, Sir Benjamin Thompson, afterwards Count Rumford,[25] (himself an American loyalist,) that "in the same house with the person who is named in this warrant, lodges another American, who there are strong reasons for believing to be the most dangerous man of the two,—although his name is not inserted in the warrant, you will not however fail, Mr. Bond, to secure Mr. Trumbull's person and papers for examination, as well as Major Tyler." This took place on Saturday. On Sunday, Winslow Warren [26] of Plymouth, who was a somewhat amphibious character, and withal young, handsome and giddy, dined at Kensington with a party of loyalist gentlemen from Boston, when the arrest of Mr. Tyler for high treason, and his probable fate, became a subject of conversation at dinner. Tyler and Warren, from similarity of character, had become companions in the gaieties of London, and the moment Warren learned the danger of his friend, he excused himself from sitting after dinner to wine, by pretending an engagement to take tea with some ladies at the east end of the city; and knowing where Tyler was engaged to dine, he drove with all haste, found him, and warned him of his danger. Of course he did not return to his lodgings, but prudently and safely made his escape to the continent. In the mean time, a few minutes after Tyler went out on Sunday morning, a party of the police were stationed in an opposite ale-house, to watch for him. I knew nothing of what was thus passing around me, and went out and returned several times during the day. In the evening I drank

24. Unidentifiable; possibly Nathaniel Bond, 1754–1823, admitted to the Inner Temple in 1773, who later had a distinguished legal and political career; or John Bond, Inner Temple same year; or George Bond, 1750–96, sergeant-at-law 1786 and member of the Middle Temple.

25. 1753–1814, of Massachusetts, British-American scientist and adventurer.

26. 1759–91, son of Gen. James Warren and Mercy Otis (sister of James Otis), left Boston June 1780, ship captured by British, passengers taken to Newfoundland, proceeded to England, returned to the United States in 1785, commissioned lieutenant, killed at St. Clair's defeat at the Forks of the Miami River, Ohio, in a memorable encounter with the Indians, died unmarried.

tea with Mr. and Mrs. Channing [27] of Georgia, and did not return home until past eleven o'clock; I found the mistress of the house sitting up, waiting for us; I asked for Tyler, and was answered that he was not yet come in. Soon after, we were startled by a loud knock at the door, and the servant came in to say, that it was a well dressed gentleman, who enquired for Mr. Tyler. "Aye," said I, "some of his merry companions, for another frolic." Some time after, the knock was repeated, and the servant announced that the same gentleman had enquired again for Mr. Tyler, and on being told that he was not yet come in, desired to see me. On entering the passage, I saw a very respectable looking, middle aged man, and requested him to walk into the parlor. He began with saying, "I am very sorry that Mr. Tyler is not at home, as I have business of importance with him; in short, sir, I have a warrant to arrest him." I replied, "that I had for some time been apprehensive that he was spending more money than he could afford." "You misunderstand me; I have a warrant to arrest the Major, not for debt, but for high treason; and, my orders are, at the same time, to secure your person and papers, Mr. Trumbull, for examination." A thunderbolt falling at my feet,[28] would not have been more astounding, for conscious of having done nothing politically wrong, I had become as confident of safety in London, as I should have been in Lebanon. For a few

27. Probably John Channing, owner of a plantation on the Savannah River, near Savannah, and his wife. See *Georgia Gazette* for 7 March 1793: "John Channing, late of London, deceased . . ."

28. There is a contemporary account, with the page heading, "Rebel Spy taken up and committed," and the title, "Examination and Committment of JOHN TRUMBULL, Esq; for High Treason," in *The Political Magazine and Parliamentary, Naval, Military, and Literary Journal* (November 1780), *1*, 738–740. The article contains 3 letters, described as "extraordinary correspondence," found in JT's possession; one to his father, the governor, dated 8 September 1780 (found on the prisoner's person), one from W. T. Franklin, written from Passy on 3 October, and one from William White of Lyme in Dorset, dated 12 November (these two found "in his bureau, at his residence in George street Yorkbuildings, at a Mr. Bushel's"). The account states "that the prisoner behaved much like a gentleman, making no attempt to escape . . . he is a genteel looking man, about thirty-five years of age, and rather of a sallow complexion." It was JT's traveling companion, Tyler, who got him in trouble.

There is no mention of JT's arrest as a reprisal for the hanging of Major André.

moments I was perfectly disconcerted, and must have looked very like a guilty man. I saw, in all its force, the folly and the audacity of having placed myself at ease in the lion's den; but by degrees, I recovered my self-possession, and conversed with Mr. Bond, who waited for the return of Mr. Tyler until past one o'clock. He then asked for my papers, put them carefully under cover, which he sealed, and desired me also to seal; having done this, he conducted me to a *lock-up house,* the Brown Bear [29] in Drury Lane, opposite to the (then) police office. Here I was locked into a room, in which was a bed, and a strong well armed officer, for the companion of my night's meditations or rest. The windows, as well as door, were strongly secured by iron bars and bolts, and seeing no possible means of making my retreat, I yielded to my fate, threw myself upon the bed, and endeavored to rest.

At eleven o'clock next morning, I was guarded across the street, through a crowd of curious idlers, to the office, and placed in the presence of the three police magistrates, Sir Sampson Wright,[30] Mr. Addington,[31] and another. The situation was new, painful, embarrassing. The examination began, and was at first conducted in a style so offensive to my feelings, that it soon roused me from my momentary weakness, and I suddenly exclaimed, "You appear to have been much more habituated to the society of highwaymen and pickpockets, than to that of gentlemen. I will put an end to all this insolent folly, by telling you frankly who and what I am. I am an American—my name is Trumbull; I am a son of him whom you call the rebel governor of Connecticut; I have served in the rebel American army; I have had the honor of being an aid-du-camp to him whom you call the rebel General Washington. These two have always in their power a greater number of your friends, prisoners, than you have of theirs. Lord George Germaine knows under what circumstances I came to London, and what has been my con-

29. The Brown Bear is described that year in *The Complete Modern London Spy* ("written by a Gentleman of Fortune" and revised by Richard King, Esq., London, 1780) as "a house equally frequented by bloods, bullies, pimps, chairmen, and those persons who are unfortunate enough to be shut out of their lodgings . . ." (p. 77).

30. Magistrate for the County of Middlesex, served in the Bow Street office.

31. William Addington also magistrate for the County of Middlesex, serving at Bow Street.

duct here. I am entirely in your power; and, after the hint which I have given you, treat me as you please, always remembering, that as I may be treated, so will your friends in America be treated by mine." The moment of enthusiasm passed, and I half feared that I had said too much; but I soon found that the impulse of the moment was right, for I was immediately, and ever after, treated with marked civility, and even respect.

Other business of the office pressed, so after a few words more, I was ordered in custody of an officer to Tothill-fields Bridewell,[32] for safe keeping during the night, to be ready for a further examination the next day. I had not entirely recovered from the shock of this most unexpected event, so I drifted with the stream, without further struggle against my fate, *and I slept that night in the same bed with a highwayman.*

The next day, I was brought up to a second examination before the same magistrates. I had avowed the crime of which I stood accused—bearing arms against the king—and little else remained to do, but to remand me to prison. The clerk was ordered to make out my mittimus; I took the liberty to look over him, and found he was directing it to the keeper of Clerkenwell prison.[33] The mob of the preceding summer, called Lord George Gordon's mob,[34] had in their madness destroyed all the prisons in London except this,

32. Bridewell, now Westminster House of Correction, built in 1622, enlarged in 1778, replaced by a new prison in 1834. Some indication of the appearance of the interior of the prison (about 1730) may be derived from Plate IV of William Hogarth's "Harlot's Progress." The *Oxford Dictionary* defines the noun "bridewell" as a "house of correction, gaol," derived from "St. Bride's Well, near London."

Writ of commitment for high treason dated 20 November 1780 and writ of discharge from Tothill Field Prison, 12 June 1781, make the period of the artist's incarceration less than 8 months. Among JT's prison papers is a filled-out form, dated 4 December 1780: "To the Governor of Tothill-Fields, Bridewell, or his Deputy. DETAIN in your Custody the Body of John Trumbull he being further charged . . . upon Oath and upon his Confession of having been guilty of the Crime of High Treason committed within His Majesty's Colonies and Plantations in America . . ." The admission slip to the Bridewell is dated 20 November 1780 (drafts of JT's accounts, correspondence, arrest, imprisonment, and discharge at the Connecticut State Library).

33. The House of Detention, Clerkenwell, established in 1774 and rebuilt in 1818 and 1845.

34. 1751–93, a younger son of Cosmo George, 3d duke of Gordon. He was responsible for the tragic anti-Catholic riots of June 1780.

and of course it was filled to overflowing with every class of male-factors. This I knew, and therefore remonstrated against being placed in such detestable companionship. Sir Sampson answered with great civility, and apparent kindness, "We must necessarily place you in confinement, Mr. Trumbull, and unfortunately this is the only prison within our jurisdiction which remains unburnt; but if you will write a note to Lord George Germaine, I will myself take it to his lordship, and I have no doubt but you will receive a favorable answer." I wrote a few words, and Sir Sampson soon returned with a very civil verbal answer from Lord George, "expressive of regret for what had happened, as being entirely unknown to him, until it was too late to interfere; that he was disposed to grant any alleviation which was in his power; that therefore, I might make choice of any prison in the kingdom, from the Tower down, as the safety of my person, not the infliction of inconvenience or vexation, was the only object of the government."

A little enquiry satisfied me that it would be folly to select the Tower for my place of residence, as I should have to pay dearly for the honor, in the exorbitance of fees; and as I had been pleased with the quiet of Tothillfields, and the civility of the people, I chose that, and was remanded to the care of Mr. Smith, the keeper of that place, who having been butler to the duke of Northumberland, had the manners of a gentleman, and always treated me with civility and kindness.

The building which bears the name of Tothill-fields Bridewell, was a quadrangle of perhaps two hundred feet—an old and irregular building—the house of the keeper occupying one angle and part of a side; the entrance, turnkey's room, tap-room, and some space for prisoners, and a small yard, another side; the female apartments and yard occupy the third; and the fourth was little more than a high brick wall. Besides the yards, a pretty little garden was enclosed within the walls; all windows looked upon the interior of the square. Its situation was behind Buckingham house, towards Pimlico.

After the first shock, during which I cared not where I slept, or what I ate, I hired from Mr. Smith, the keeper, one of the rooms of his house, for which I paid a guinea a week. It was a parlor on the ground floor, about twenty feet square; the door opened upon the hall of the house, at the foot of the stairs, and was secured by a strong lock and bolts. Two windows looked upon the yard, and were also firmly secured by strong iron bars. The room was neatly furnished, and had a handsome bureau bed. I received my breakfast and dinner,—whatever I chose to order and pay for, from the little public house, called the *tap*. The prison allowance of the government was a penny-worth of bread, and a penny a day; this I gave to the turnkey for brushing my hat, clothes and shoes. Besides these comforts, I had the privilege of walking in the garden. Every evening when Mr. Smith went to his bed, he knocked at my door, looked in, saw that I was safe, wished me a good night, locked the door, drew the bolts, put the key in his pocket, and withdrew. In the morning, when he quitted his own apartment, he unlocked my door, looked in to see that all was safe, wished me a good morning, and went his way.

The moment when Mr. West heard of my arrest, was one of extreme anxiety to him. His love for the land of his nativity was no secret, and he knew that the American loyalists (at the head of whom was Joseph Galloway,[35] once a member of Congress from Pennsylvania) were outrageous at the kindness which the king had long shewn to him, and still continued; he dreaded also the use which might be made to his disadvantage of the arrest for treason, of a young American who had been in a manner domesticated under his roof, and of whom he had spoken publicly and with approbation. He therefore hurried to Buckingham house, asked an audience of the king, and was admitted.

Mr. West began with stating what had induced him to take the liberty of this intrusion,—his anxiety lest the affair of my arrest might involve his own character, and diminish his majesty's kindness,—spoke of my conduct during the time he had known me, as having been so entirely devoted to the study of my profession as to have left no time for political intrigue, &c. &c. The king listened with attention, and then said, "West, I have known you long, and have conversed with you frequently. I can recollect no occasion on which you have ever attempted to mislead or misinform me, and

35. 1731–1803, prominent American Loyalist.

for that reason you have acquired my entire confidence. I fully believe all that you have now said, and assure you that my confidence in you is not at all diminished by this unpleasant occurrence. I am sorry for the young man, but he is in the hands of the law, and must abide the result—I cannot interpose. Do you know whether his parents are living?"

"I think I have heard him say that he has very lately received news of the death of his mother; I believe his father is living."

"I pity him from my soul!" He mused a few moments and then added, "But, West, go to Mr. Trumbull immediately, and pledge to him my royal promise, that, in the worst possible event of the law, his life shall be safe." [36]

This message was immediately delivered, and received, as it deserved to be, with profound gratitude. I had now nothing more to apprehend than a tedious confinement, and that might be softened by books and my pencil. I therefore begged Mr. West to permit me to have his beautiful little Correggio, and my tools;—I proceeded with the copy, which was finished in prison during the winter of 1780–81, and is now deposited in the Gallery at New Haven.[37]

But, with every alleviation, confinement within four walls soon became irksome, and with the advice of some friends, (for my friends [38] were permitted freely to visit me,) I resolved to endeavor to force myself to a legal trial; for the tide of military affairs, as well as of public opinion, began to run in favor of America, and it was believed that no jury could be found, who would enforce the penalty of the law. I therefore consulted an eminent lawyer—the Hon.

36. "The favor which was thus done to me by the king, in promising me pardon, if I should be brought to trial for treason, and condemned, merits my grateful remembrance . . ." *Autobiography* (1841), App., p. 312. Seventeen pages, 312–329, are devoted to the artist's arrest and confinement—letters to his father, to Lord George Germaine, to Edward Chamberlayne, solicitor of the Treasury, Counselor John Lee of Lincoln's Inn, and to Edmund Burke.

37. The St. Jerome (of Parma), Yale University Art Gallery, No. 1832.94. Not only was JT furnished pictures to copy but he was privileged to employ a model. Some of his studies of the male nude, dated "Tothill fields, 1780," are now at Fordham University, New York.

38. Among these friends was his fellow student, Gilbert Stuart, who painted his portrait (head only); the remainder of the seated figure, and the prison-barred window, were done by JT (now at the Pilgrim Society, Plymouth, Mass.).

John Lee [39]—and received for answer, that the suspension of the act of habeas corpus, rendered such a measure impossible, and that my only hope was, by impressing the minds of ministers with a sense of the uselessness of severe measures, in the actual state of the dispute, and thus inducing them to release me, as a step towards conciliation.

In the course of the winter, I received kind visits from many distinguished men, among whom were John Lee, lately attorney general, Charles J. Fox,[40] and others. Mr. Fox was very kind; he recommended a direct application to ministers, on the ground of impolicy, and added, "I would undertake it myself, if I thought I could have any influence with them; but such is the hostility between us, that we are not even on speaking terms. Mr. Burke [41] has not lost all influence—has not thrown away the scabbard, as I have; I will converse with him, and desire him to visit you." A few days after, Mr. Burke came to see me, and readily and kindly undertook the negotiation, which after some unavoidable delay, ended in an order of the king in council to admit me to bail, with the condition

39. 1733–93, king's counsel, later solicitor general and attorney general. "Mr. John Lee, a councellor of eminence, member of parliament, and a friend of our country, . . . immediately honored me with a visit in prison," the artist to his father, letter dated Amsterdam, 13 July 1781. *Autobiography* (1841), App., p. 334.

40. Charles James Fox, 1749–1806, leader of the opposition to Lord North.

41. Edmund Burke, 1729–97, friend of America, whose study in the aesthetics of romanticism, *A Philosophical Enquiry into the Origin of Our Ideas of the Sublime and Beautiful* (London, 1756), young JT must have known. The latter addressed a long letter to the British statesman on 10 May 1781, after having "suffered six months' imprisonment." *Autobiography* (1841), App., pp. 321–324. "Mr. Burke," JT explained, "called on me immediately after he had received this letter, and assured me of his hearty efforts in my favor; that he had already seen Lord George Germaine, and, from what passed in their conversation, he had hopes of effecting my discharge. However, after having attempted all rational methods, if they should not succeed, he would then, if agreeable to me, and as a dernier resort, bring it before Parliament, as an act of injustice which their honor was interested to redress. Mr. Fox called on me the next day, and assured me of his entire concurrance with Mr. Burke; and, after a few days' delay with forms of law and want of precedent, a discharge was sent me from the privy council . . ." *Ibid.*, p. 323. JT's original letter to Burke of 10 May 1781, enclosing copies of those to Lord George Germaine of 20 January 1781 (*ibid.*, pp. 317–318) and to Mr. Chamberlayne of 20 February 1781 (pp. 318–319), are in the possession of Lord Fitzwilliam of Milton Hall, Peterborough, England, as is JT's letter to Burke of 25 June 1781, written in gratitude shortly after his release.

that I should leave the kingdom in thirty days, and not return until after peace should be restored. Mr. West and Mr. Copley became my sureties,[42] and I was liberated in the beginning of June,[43] after a close confinement of seven months.

During this time, and amid the variety of crime with which I was surrounded, I necessarily saw much of the dark side of human character, and met with some traits of deep interest; but their narration can do no good—the world is already too deeply read in evil. I remained in London a few days,[44] and then determined to return to America by the shortest route, Amsterdam. Again I crossed from Deal to Ostend, and there was joined by my friend, Mr. Temple, who had the same intention of returning to America. We travelled together, and at Antwerp met with a little adventure sufficiently ridiculous, as well as annoying, to merit notice.

The morning after our arrival at Antwerp, we rose early, that we might have time to view some of the curiosities of the city, especially the cathedral. We took a guide, but reached the cathedral too early; morning mass was being celebrated, during which the finest paintings, &c., could not be seen. Not to lose time, our guide offered to conduct us to the house of a gentleman in the vicinity, who possessed (he said) one of the finest collections of paintings in the city. We went, were admitted,—shown into a neat parlor, and desired to wait; we expected to see some upper servant to guide us. A young gentleman soon came in, dressed very well, but somewhat negligently, who we soon discovered could neither speak English nor French, but as far as signs could go, he was very attentive and civil. He left the room for a moment, and I seized the

42. At £100 each, plus £200 furnished by the artist, a total of £400.

43. 12 June 1781. "I was discharged with an injunction to quit the kingdom within thirty days." *Autobiography* (1841), App., p. 324.

44. Horace Walpole, *Anecdotes of Painting in England* (London, 1760–95), 5, 112, wrote on 31 August 1781: "Mr. Trumbull, who obtained his discharge from prison on condition that he would quit the kingdom, set off last week for Boston in New England. This gentleman, during his confinement, amused himself with painting, in which he had been regularly educated. Some beautiful strokes of the above gentleman's pencil were admired in the royal academy, without an idea that they came from the gloom of a prison. Ingenuity and a fine taste, combined with judgment and accuracy procured him no inconsiderable share of credit in his profession."

opportunity to ask Mr. Temple, as being better acquainted with European manners than I was, "whether this could be the master of the house, or only his valet, or *maitre d'hotel*." "Certainly not the master," said he; "we cannot suppose that he would be so attentive to strangers at so early an hour." The gentleman returned, showed us from one apartment to another, pointing out, with great assiduity and precision, the finest pictures, and this with a manner so entirely polished, that my heart misgave me as we approached the last of the suite of rooms; there, however, I did what was customary—offered him silver for his attention. He smiled, *like a gentleman,* and succeeded in making us understand that the *servant* was at the door. Never was I more mortified. It was a direct insult to offer money to the master of the house, and argued gross ignorance in us to mistake the master for a servant. Every way it was a most mortifying blunder, and I felt the dread of being recognized so severely, that I carefully avoided going again to that house, when afterward I passed some days in Antwerp.

We passed through Bergen-op-Zoom,[45] and visited the fortifications, then the finest in Europe; thence passed through Williamstadt to Rotterdam; slept there, saw the statue of Erasmus, and other curiosities of the city, and passed on through Gorcum, &c., by the canal, to Amsterdam.[46]

The next day I called at the counting-house of Messrs. John De Neufville & Son,[47] and there found important letters from my father. This house was then in high mercantile repute, and favor-

45. Situated on the right bank of the Scheldt. The town was fortified in the mid-16th century; the fortifications were greatly strengthened at the end of the 17th and extended in the 18th.

46. JT wrote his father from Amsterdam, 8 July 1781, about his call upon the banking house of Lane, Son & Frazer, London: "on the subject of their Debt" (William L. Clements Library, Ann Arbor, Mich.), and on 10 July 1781, "I have the happiness . . . [of] informing you that I obtain'd an order of the Privy Council for my discharge on the 12th ult°, thro' the intervention of liberal men, & arriv'd in this place on the 6th inst in perfect health. My confinemant was not rigorous and I had the happiness to enjoy my health & spirits thro' the whole, & the few friends I had were permitted to visit me." ("Trumbull Papers," 3, 238.)

47. The De Neufvilles had kept Jonathan Trumbull informed about his son's apprehension and release. The young painter was well received and hospitably entertained by the bankers, from whom he borrowed funds for his return journey.

able to the cause of America; the other great houses of Amsterdam, the Hopes,[48] Willinks,[49] &c. were in the English interest. I had seen the junior partner of this house in London, (the son,) and requested that any letters which might come to their hands, to my address, might be retained. Mr. De Neufville invited me to accept an apartment in his house, which I did. I found that one of the packets from my father contained authority and instructions to negotiate a loan in Holland, for the state of Connecticut.[50]

On consulting with Mr. John Adams,[51] whom I again met here, endeavoring in vain to accomplish a similar purpose for the United States, I learned that the moment was entirely unfavorable, that he was unable to succeed for the nation, and of course I could not hope to do better on the credit of a small state, which was comparatively unknown in Europe. My friends, the De Neufvilles and the Van Staphorsts,[52] the only considerable capitalists from whom I had reason to entertain any expectations, expressed the same opinion, and therefore I gave up the attempt. Thus was I baffled at every point—my original mercantile speculation—my flattering pursuit of the arts—and now this honorable gleam of hope, all seemed to fade and elude my grasp;—nothing therefore remained but to yield to circumstances, and find my way back to America, and the quiet of home, as soon as possible.

Two opportunities offered for America; one was a small fast sailing merchant vessel, unarmed, and relying entirely upon her speed

48. The well-known banking house of Hope & Co. See J. E. Elias, *De Vroedschap van Amsterdam, 1578–1795* (2 vols., Haarlem, 1903–05), p. 933, and *Burke's Landed Gentry* (1939), p. 1150.

49. The Willinks, a distinguished merchant family; Wilhem Willink, 1750–1841, alderman of Amsterdam, honorary member of the State Council of the Netherlands, was then head of the firm. See *Deutsches Geschlechterbuch, 23* (1913), 426; E. B. F. F. Wittert van Hoogland, *Bijdragen tot de geschiedenis der Utrechtsche ridderhofsteden en heerlijkeden* (The Hague, 1912), 2, 193; and *Nederland's patriciaat* (1950).

50. Again business, see letter dated Amsterdam, 20 July 1781, to his father, *Autobiography* (1841), App., pp. 335–337.

51. Then in the Netherlands attempting to negotiate a loan; envoy to the court of St. James 1785–88.

52. It is impossible to tell which members of the family JT might have seen. See W. C. Mees, "Brieven van een bezorgde moeder," *Jaarboek van het Genootschap Amstelodamum* (Amsterdam, 1947), pp. 120–121.

to avoid the British cruisers which she must expect to meet; the
other was the South Carolina, commanded by Commodore Gillon,[53] a frigate of the first class, too strong to fear any thing less
than a ship of the line. My friend, Mr. Temple, wisely chose to
go in the small ship, and arrived at Boston in three weeks. Several
other gentlemen were going on board the South Carolina; [54] they,
as well as Mr. Gillon, urged me to go with them, and unfortunately
I separated from my friend.

The story of this ship has been the subject of much discussion
since, as well as of several publications. The want of funds or credit,
and the dread of those who had advanced money for her outfit,
occasioned her officers (after she had been permitted to drop down
to the Texel) to run her out of the roads, and to anchor on the outside, beyond the jurisdiction of the port, at the distance of more
than a league from land. Here several of us passengers went on
board, and on the 12th of August, soon after sunrise, the wind began to blow from the northwest, directly on shore, with every appearance of a heavy gale. The proper thing to have done, was to
have run back into the Texel roads, but that we dared not do, lest
the ship should be seized. We dared not run for the English channel lest we should fall in with British cruisers of superior force.
The gale soon increased to such a degree, that it would have been
madness to remain at anchor on such a lee shore. The only thing
which could be done, therefore, was to lay the ship's head to the

53. Alexander Gillon, 1741–94, of South Carolina, merchant and naval officer.
The artist wrote his father from Bilboa on 11 October 1781: "I mention the name
of Mr. Gillon, with a promise of giving you his history, an odious task, which I should
not have impos'd upon myself were his character only interesting in private life . . ."
The long letter is published in full in the "Trumbull Papers," op. cit., pp. 285–289.
In another letter to his father, dated 23 October 1781, he speaks of "the villainy of
Mr. Gillon." Autobiography (1841), App., p. 316.

". . . with the highest pleasure I can inform your Excell. that Coll. John Trumbull is on board the Charleston frigate . . . the frigate mounted 28–36 pounders on
one deck and 12–12 pounders on her quarter deck, 55Q men equipage . . ." J. G.
Diriks to Gov. Jonathan Trumbull, 24 September 1781, "Trumbull Papers," op. cit.,
pp. 278–279.

54. The South Carolina "mounted 28 long 42-pounders on her main deck, and
16 long twelves on her forecastle and quarter-deck, and she had a compliment of
550 men," Hulbert Footner, Sailor of Fortune, The Life and Adventures of Commodore Barney, U.S.N. (New York and London, Harper, 1940), p. 93.

northeast, and carry sail. A fog soon came on, so thick that we could hardly see from stem to stern; the gale increased to a very hurricane, and soon brought us to close-reefed topsails; the coast of Holland was under our lee, and we knew that we were running upon the very edge of the sands, which extend so far from the shore, that if the ship should touch, she must go to pieces before we could even see the land, and all hands must perish. We passed the morning in the deepest anxiety; in the afternoon we discovered that we had started several of the bolts of the weather main-chain plates. This forced us to take in our close-reefed topsails, as the masts would no longer bear the strain of any sail aloft, and we were obliged to rely upon a reefed foresail. By this time, we knew that we must be not far from Heligoland, at the mouth of the Elbe, where the coast begins to trend to the northward, which increased the danger. At ten o'clock at night, a squall struck us heavier still than the gale, and threw our only sail aback; the ship became unmanageable, the officers lost their self-possession, and the crew all confidence in them, while for a few minutes all was confusion and dismay. Happily for us, Commodore Barney [55] was among the passengers, (he had just escaped from Mill prison in England,)—hearing the increased tumult aloft, and feeling the ungoverned motion of the ship, he flew upon deck, saw the danger, assumed the command, the men obeyed, and he soon had her again under control. It was found, that with the squall the wind had shifted several points, so that on the other tack we could lay a safe course to the westward, and thus relieve our mainmast. That our danger was imminent no one will doubt, when informed that on the following morning, the shore of the Texel Island was covered with the wrecks of ships, which were afterwards ascertained to have been Swedish; among them was a ship of seventy-four guns, convoying twelve merchantmen—all were wrecked, and every soul on board perished. The figure-head of the ship-of-war, a yellow lion, the same as ours, was found upon the shore, and gave sad cause to our friends for believing, for some time, that the South Carolina had perished.

When the gale subsided, we stood to the northward, made the

55. Joshua Barney, 1759–1818, of Maryland, ardent Federalist, naval officer, sailed privateers for the Cabots of Beverly, Mass. See Footner, *op. cit.*

Orkneys,[56] then Shetland, and when off Faro encountered another gale, more furious, if possible, than that of the 12th, but we had now sea-room and deep water. In the night, however, the ship labored so heavily as to roll the shot out of her lockers; several of us passengers had our cots slung in the great cabin, over the guns, which were forty-two pounders, and it was by no means a pleasant sight to see several dozens of these enormous shot rolling from side to side of the ship, with the roar of thunder, and crushing all that stood in their way, whether furniture, trunks or chests, while we hung over them swinging in our canvass bags. This difficulty was overcome, and the rolling of the shot stopped, by throwing the people's hammocks among them.

Another danger was also apprehended—that some of the immense heavy guns might break loose. They were secured by running one of the cables outside, fore and aft, in front of the open port-holes, and passing strong lashings around that; by this addition to the usual ringbolts, all was held safe until the gale was over.

We had now cleared the land of the British islands, and were off the west coast of Ireland, when it was thought to be necessary to examine into the state of our provisions and water. The enormous heavy metal of the ship rendered necessary a very strong crew, and so injudicious was the construction of the ship, that when the men, &c. were accommodated, too little room remained for provisions, water and stores. This examination showed that we were short; consequently, instead of continuing our course for America, it was determined to bear away for Corunna in Spain, the nearest friendly port. We arrived in safety, in a few days. There we found the Cicero,[57] a fine letter of marque ship, of twenty guns and one hundred and twenty men, belonging to the house of Cabot [58] in Bev-

56. The artist made a number of drawings, in ink and wash, of the Shetlands and of Bilboa and environs, all from shipboard, most of which are now at the Yale University Art Gallery. See Sizer, *Works of . . . Trumbull*, pp. 85–87, and Jean Lambert Brockway, "Early Landscape Drawings by John Trumbull," *American Magazine of Art*, 5 (January 1933), 35–38.

57. A privateer of 200 tons, commissioned January 1781. See L. Vernon Briggs, *History and Genealogy of a Cabot Family* (2 vols., Boston, Goodspeed, 1927), *1*, 94–97.

58. The house of John & Andrew Cabot carried on a large trade with Spain. Their correspondents at Bilboa were Gardoqui & Sons. See Briggs, *op. cit.*, *1*, 87, and

erly. She was to sail immediately for Bilboa, there to take on board
a cargo, which was lying ready for her, and to sail for America.
Several of us, (among whom were Major Jackson,[59] who had been
secretary to Col. John Laurens,[60] in his late mission to France,
Capt. Barney, Mr. Bromfield,[61] and Charles Adams,[62]) tired of the
management of the South Carolina, endeavored to get a passage
to Bilboa, on board of this ship, and were permitted to go on board
their prize, a fine British Lisbon packet. The usual time required
to run from Corunna to Bilboa was two to three days. We were
again unfortunate; the wind being east, dead a-head, we were
twenty one days in making the passage, and, as if Jonas himself
had been among us, at the end of eighteen days, we fell in with a
little fleet of Spanish coasters and fishermen, running to the westward before the wind, who told us that when off the bar of Bilboa,
they had seen a ship and two brigs, which they believed to be
British cruisers, and cautioned us to keep a good look-out. Capt.
Hill [63] of the Cicero, immediately hailed his prize, a ship of sixteen
guns, and a fine brig of sixteen guns, which was also in company,
and directed them to keep close to him, and prepare to meet an
enemy. At sunset we saw what appeared to be the force described,
and about midnight found we were within hail. The Cicero ran
close alongside of the ship, and hailed her in English—no answer;
in French—no answer. The men, who were at their guns, impatient
of delay, did not wait for orders, but poured in her broadside; the
hostile squadron (as we supposed them) separated, and made all
sail in different directions, when a boat from the large ship came
alongside with her captain, a Spaniard, who informed us that they

---

Octavius T. Howe, "Beverly Privateers in the American Revolution," *Transactions
of the Colonial Society of Massachusetts,* 24 (1922), 318–435.

59. William Jackson, 1759–1828, aide to Major General Lincoln, later assistant
secretary of war.

60. Lieut. Col. John Laurens, 1754–82, of South Carolina. JT painted Laurens
posthumously in the "Surrender at Yorktown" (No. 32 in the key). See "Continental
Light Infantry Officer," *Journal of Military Collectors & Historians,* 5, June 1953,
50–51.

61. Probably Henry Bloomfield, 1751–1837, merchant.

62. Charles Adams, 1770–1880, son of John and Abigail Adams.

63. Capt. Hugh Hill, born in Ireland in 1741, cousin of Andrew Jackson.

were Spanish vessels from St. Sebastians, bound to the West Indies
—that his ship was very much cut in her rigging, but happily, no
lives lost. He had mistaken us for British vessels, and was delighted
to find his mistake. We apologized for ours, offered assistance, &c.
and we parted most amicably. Soon after, we entered the river of
Bilboa, and ran up to Porto Galette. The disabled ship with her
comrades put into Corunna, where it was found that one of our
nine pound shot had wounded the mainmast of our antagonist so
severely, that it was necessary to take it (the mast) out, and put in
a new one. This was not the work of a day, and her consorts were
detained until their flag ship was ready. In the mean time, we had
almost completed taking in our cargo at Bilboa, when a messenger
from Madrid arrived, with orders to unhang the rudders of all
American ships in the port, until the bill for repairs of the wounded
ship, demurrage of her consorts, &c. &c., was paid. We were thus
detained in Bilboa [64] until the 10th of December, and even then
had to encounter one more vexation and delay.[65]

At the entrance of the river of Bilboa is a bar, on which the water
is so shallow, that a ship of the Cicero's size can pass over, only at
spring tides. When we dropped down from Porto Galette, we found
the wind at the mouth of the river, blowing fresh from the northward, which caused such a heavy surf upon the bar, that it was impossible to take the ship over. We were obliged to wait until the
wind lulled, and then the pilot insisted that he could not take her
over safely, until the next spring tide. Several of the passengers
thought it was folly to remain on board, consuming the ship's stores,
and proposed to the captain that we would go back to Bilboa for a
few days. He acceded, promising to send up a boat for us, when-

64. JT spent 15 ducats on the voyage to Bilboa. He gave £1 to "Seamen for
saving a Boy who had fallen overboard." While in Spain he purchased taffeta, silk,
velvet, chambray, and nankeen, obviously for his father's firm. See accounts in the
Yale Library.

65. Benjamin Franklin wrote to JT informing him, that his father had placed a
bill of exchange on Paris for 1350 Livres Tournois at his disposal. This letter (now
in the Huntington Library), dated Passy, 26 November 1781, was answered on 8
December 1781 from Bilboa. JT notified Franklin that he had drawn the draft, adding: "I beg leave to congratulate your Excellency upon the capture of Lord Cornwallis, & the very flattering situation of our Affairs in America." (Trumbull's draft
of this letter is in the Yale University Library.)

ever he might have a prospect of getting to sea. We went, and amused ourselves among the friends we had made; on the third or fourth day, we were walking with some ladies in the Alameda, a public walk which ran upon the bank of the river, when we espied a boat coming up with sails and oars, which we recognized as being from below. One of her men sprang on shore, and ran to us, with the information that the Cicero, and other vessels, had got over the bar that morning at eight o'clock, and were standing out to sea, with a fair wind—that Capt. Hill desired us to make all possible haste to get on board—that he would stand off and on for a few hours, but not long, as he could not justify it to his owners. We, of course, made all possible haste, but the distance from town was eight or nine miles, and when we got down, it was near three o'clock, and the ship was out of sight. We obtained a spy-glass, ran to the top of the house, and could thence discern a ship in the offing, apparently standing in. We persuaded ourselves that it must be the Cicero, and bid for a boat and crew to put us on board. The pilots made great difficulty—the sea was very rough—the ship was too far out—perhaps it was not the Cicero—they thought it was not; all this was said to work up the price. On the other hand, we were desperate; among us we could not muster twenty guineas to carry us through the winter, and the bargain was at last made, at a price which nearly emptied all our pockets, and before sunset we got on board the Cicero, in the Bay of Biscay, two or three leagues from land. The mountains of Asturia were already covered with snow, but the wind was fair, and we went on our way rejoicing.

No accident befel, until the last day of our passage. We saw the land of America, (the Blue Hills of Milton, near Boston,) in the afternoon of a beautiful day in January; [66] at six o'clock, P. M., we laid the ship's head to the eastward, and stood off under easy sail until midnight, when we hove about, and stood in to the westward, under the same sail, expecting to find ourselves at sunrise, at about the same distance from the land, and all was joy and merriment

66. Gardner Weld Allen, "Massachusetts Privateers of the Revolution," *Collections of the Massachusetts Historical Society*, 77 (1927), 99, quotes the *Boston Gazette*, 28 January 1782: "Capt. Hill, in the letter of marque ship *Cicero*, arrived at Beverley on Monday last, in six weeks from Bilboa . . . Passengers, Col. John Trumbull, Son of his Excellency the Governor of Connecticut . . ."

on board, at the near approach of home. One honest old tar was happily on the lookout, and at three o'clock sung out from the fore-castle, "breakers! breakers! close under our bow, and right ahead!" He was just in time; the crew, though merry, were obedient, and flew upon deck in time to escape the danger. We found we were close upon the rocks of Cape Ann. We must have been drifted by a very strong current, for our course had been judicious, and could never have brought the ship there. Before noon, we were safe in the port of Beverly, where we found eleven other ships, all larger and finer vessels than the Cicero—all belonging to the same owners, the brothers Cabot—laid up for the winter. Yet such are the vicissitudes of war and the elements, that before the close of the year they were all lost by capture or wreck, and the house of Cabot had not a single ship afloat upon the ocean.[67] In the evening, after we got into port, a snow storm came on, with a heavy gale from the eastward. The roads were so completely blocked up with snow, that they were impassable, and we did not get up to Boston until the third day; but, *per tot discrimina rerum,* I was at last safe on American land, and most truly thankful.

I returned to Lebanon, as soon as possible, and occupied myself with closing all accounts respecting my unfortunate mercantile experiment. My reflections were painful—I had thrown away two of the most precious years of life—had encountered many dangers, and suffered many inconveniences, to no purpose. I was seized with a serious illness, which confined me to my bed, and endangered my life; and it was autumn before I had recovered strength sufficient to attempt any occupation.

My brother [67a] was engaged in a contract for the supply of the army. It was necessary to have a perfectly confidential agent residing with the army, to superintend the faithful execution of the contract there. He offered me this situation, and as soon as I had

67. "This statement of Mr. Trumbull ('We found we were close upon the rocks . . . not a single ship afloat upon the ocean') demands considerable credulity, for it is extremely doubtful whether eleven vessels larger than the *Cicero* entered Beverly harbor during the war, and while Mr. Cabot, in common with all owners of armed vessels, suffered severe losses in 1782, yet the *Cicero, Revolution* and *Buccanier* were all profitably cruising at the end of the year . . ." L. Vernon Briggs, *op. cit.,* pp. 96–97.   67a. David Trumbull, 1751–1822.

recovered sufficient strength, I commenced my duty at the quarters of the army, on the North river—presented myself to my early master and friend, General Washington, and was very kindly received. I remained at New Windsor [68] during the winter of 1782 and 1783. Here we received the news of the signing of the preliminary articles of peace, and an end was thus put to all further desultory pursuits. It was now necessary to determine upon a future occupation for life. The gentlemen with whom I was connected in the military contract proposed a commercial establishment, in which they would furnish funds, information and advice, while I should execute the business, and divide with them the profits. The proposal was fascinating, but I reflected that if I entered upon regular commerce,[69] I must come in competition with men who had been educated in the counting-house, and my ignorance might often leave me at their mercy, and therefore I declined this offer. My father again urged the law, as the profession which in a republic leads to all emolument and distinction, and for which my early education had well prepared me. My reply was, that so far as I understood the question, law was rendered necessary by the vices of mankind—that I had already seen too much of them, willingly to devote my life to a profession which would keep me perpetually involved, either in the defense of innocence against fraud and injustice, or (what was much more revolting to an ingenuous mind) to the protection of guilt against just and merited punishment. In short, I pined for the arts, again entered into an elaborate defense of my predilection, and again dwelt upon the honors paid to artists in the glorious days of Greece and Athens. My father listened patiently, and when I had finished, he complimented me upon the able manner in which I had defended what to him still appeared to be a bad cause. "I had confirmed his opinion," he said, "that with proper study I should make a respectable lawyer; but," added he, "you must give me leave to say, that you appear to have overlooked, or forgotten, one very important point in your case." "Pray, sir," I rejoined, "what was that?" "You appear to forget sir, that

68. New York; site of the last of the Revolutionary camp grounds.
69. Again JT's vacillation between the life of an artist and that of a merchant.

Connecticut is not Athens;" [70] and with this pithy remark, he bowed and withdrew, and never more opened his lips upon the subject. How often have those few impressive words recurred to my memory—"Connecticut is not Athens!" The decision was made in favor of the arts. I closed all other business, and in December, 1783, embarked at Portsmouth, New Hampshire, for London.[71]

70. Italics JT's; one of the most frequently quoted passages in the *Autobiography*.
71. Thus, these two years spent in America are passed over in a page or two. He busied himself in making a few landscape sketches and painting portraits.

4

Europe and Great Expectations 1784–89

I ARRIVED in London in January, 1784, went immediately to Mr. West,[1] and was received most cordially.

My father had written a letter to Mr. Edmund Burke,[2] expressive of his gratitude for the kindness shown to his son when in prison, and commending me to his future protection. This letter I early presented, and was most kindly received. "Your father speaks of painting as being the great object of your pursuit; do you not intend to study architecture also," asked Mr. Burke.[3] I replied, "that I thought I knew enough already, for my purpose in backgrounds, &c." "I do not mean that, Mr. Trumbull; you are aware that architecture is the eldest sister, that painting and sculpture are the youngest, and subservient to her; you must also be aware that you belong to a young nation, which will soon want public buildings; these must be erected before the decorations of painting and sculpture will be required. I would therefore strongly advise you to study architecture thoroughly and scientifically, in order to qualify yourself to superintend the erection of these national buildings— decorate them also, if you will."

1. The return to West's studio marks the beginning of a period, lasting but a decade, of JT's most spirited and aesthetically satisfactory work, a period which came to an abrupt close in 1794, when the painter deserted art for diplomacy; he never "came back."

2. This letter, dated Lebanon, 8 October 1783, is preserved in the Sheffield Central Library, Sheffield, England. It says, in part: "I . . . recommend him to your future protection during his residence in England, whither he returns to pursue his favorite Study of the Pencil." The painter himself wrote to Burke on 20 April 1783. This and an earlier letter from the Bridewell of 19 May 1781 are also in the Sheffield Library. I am endebted to my former student, Robert A. Smith, for bringing these letters to my attention.

3. Cf. with Professor Silliman's story, p. 375.

This was wise and kind advice, and I had afterwards sufficient evidence of my own want of wisdom in neglecting to follow it; a few of the hours of evenings, which, with all my fancied industry, were trifled away, would have sufficed for the acquisition of thorough architectural knowledge.

Mr. Burke was the personal friend of Sir Joshua Reynolds,[4] and when I mentioned my predilection for history, and spoke of my intention to study especially under Mr. West, he did not appear to regard this preference with cordiality. I went on, however, painting by day at Mr. West's house, and in the evening, drawing at the academy.[5] Here I frequently sat by the side of Lawrence, (afterwards Sir Thomas,) [6] so celebrated for his exquisite portraits; his manner there, was, to finish elaborately, such parts of the model before him as struck his taste;—of course he rarely had time to work up the other parts of his figure with equal care, *and the whole was not unfrequently, out of drawing.* The consequence of this bad habit of study may often be traced in his paintings.

In the early part of my studies, in 1784, my friend, Col. Wads-

4. 1723–92, first president of the Royal Academy (in 1768), at this time the dominant figure in British painting.

5. JT painted by day at West's and attended classes at the Royal Academy School at Somerset House evenings; for the results see *Works*, pp. 90–91. (Fortunately he did not go in for his master's dirty browns; his realistic color was, in part, due to his admiration of Rubens.)

The literary sources of JT's work are of interest. Hogarth's *Analysis of Beauty* was the greatest. He undoubtedly was familiar with *The Art of Painting* by Charles Alphonse du Fresnoy (2d ed., London, 1716). Among that author's precepts are: "XII Let . . . the Figures dispos'd in Grouppes: And let those Grouppes be separated by a void space . . . XIII The Figures in the Grouppes, ought not to have the same Inflections of the Body, nor the same Motions; nor should they lean all one way, but break the symmetry, by proper Opposition and Contrastes . . ." JT's best historical pictures follow this system of grouping. He had known the work of the French art historian, Roger de Piles, *The Principles of Painting* (London, 1743), since his undergraduate days at Harvard (he read a French edition of 1708). From JT's sketch books it is evident that he became familiar with the work of John Caspar Lavater of Zurich, *Essays on Physiognomy* (4 vols., London, 1789), or the later, smaller edition, London, 1797. From an examination of the young painter's work it may also be assumed that he was familiar with *The Artist's Repository and Drawing Magazine, Exhibiting the Principles of the Polite Arts in Their Various Branches* (London, C. Taylor, 1785), 1.

6. Thomas Lawrence, R.A., 1769–1830, succeeded Reynolds as painter in ordinary to George III in 1792, knighted in 1815.

worth, and his son, were in London, and I was desired to paint their portraits. I attempted it—the father dressed in gray cloth, sitting, the son leaning on his shoulder—small, whole length figures.[7] This picture still exists, in possession of Mrs. Terry [8] of Hartford, the daughter of the former and sister of the latter of these two gentlemen, and is, in truth, bad enough. I had the vanity, however, to take it to show to Sir Joshua Reynolds; the moment he saw it, he said, in a quick sharp tone, "that coat is bad, sir, very bad; it is not cloth—it is tin, bent tin." The criticism was but too true, but its severity wounded my pride, and I answered, (taking up the picture,) "I did not bring this thing to you, Sir Joshua, merely to be

7. Representing Jeremiah Wadsworth, 1743–1804, of Hartford, Conn., merchant and banker, former commissary general of the Continental forces, and his son, Daniel Wadsworth, 1771–1849, future banker, art patron, and founder of the Wadsworth Atheneum at Hartford. The little picture (now the property of Faneuil Adams of Cambridge, Mass.) is in the artist's "hard-as-nails," early Copley manner. Sir Joshua's biting remark so mortified the young JT that he abandoned his New England manner of painting and adopted the softer, more fluid style then current in England. The little double portrait marks the great turning point of the artist's career.

The abrupt change in style is well illustrated in the little group portrait of "Mr. afterwards Sir John Temple & family—four small whole lengths, on a Kitkat cloth: given to Sir John, and still preserved in the family," now in the possession of George Temple Bowdoin of Oyster Bay, Long Island, N.Y., and in a "Small whole length of Mrs. Church, child & Servant on a Kit Kat cloth—recd. 20 Guineas" (Mrs. John Barker—Angelica Schuyler—Church, young Philip Church, and servant), belonging to Peter Butler Olney of New York and Old Saybrook, Conn. See Sizer, "An Early Check List of the Paintings of John Trumbull," *Yale University Library Gazette*, 22 (April 1948), 116–123.

The Trumbull and Wadsworth families had long been intimate, Hartford being but 30 miles from Lebanon. Jeremiah followed JT's oldest brother, Joseph Trumbull (d. 1778), as commissary general. He also acted as supply officer for Rochambeau's troops. After the close of the war he had hastened to France to present his accounts and stopped at London, probably to further private mercantile ventures on his return. While there he might have fired West, JT, and others with accounts of the immense tract of land in the Genesee River district of northwestern New York, which he had recently acquired from the original Phelps-Gordon purchase. A few years later, in 1790, a large slice of wilderness was taken up by young, adventuresome relatives of his, James Wadsworth of Durham, Conn., Yale 1787, and his brother William. JT, West, and their eccentric English friend, William Beckford, were to become involved in the Genesee Tract. See Sizer, "John Trumbull, 'Patriot-Painter,' in Northern New York," *New York History*, 31 (July 1950), 283–293.

8. Mrs. Nathaniel Terry (Catherine Wadsworth), 1774–1841, a miniature of whom JT painted in 1792 (now at Yale).

told that it is bad; I was conscious of that, and how could it be otherwise, considering the short time I have studied; I had a hope, sir, that you would kindly have pointed out to me, how to correct my errors." I bowed and withdrew, and was cautious not again to expose my imperfect works to the criticism of Sir Joshua.[9]

In the summer of 1785, I finished, for Mr. West, a copy of his glorious picture of the battle of La Hogue,[10] on cloth, a few inches larger on every side than the original. This work was of inestimable importance to me, and soon after, I composed and painted the picture of "Priam returning to his family with the dead body of Hector," [11] which is now in the Atheneum at Boston.

In the autumn of the same year, I was invited by the Rev. Mr. Preston [12] of Chevening, in Kent, to pass a week at his house, in company with Mr. West's eldest son. The library of Mr. Preston

9. JT exhibited "The Deputation from the Senate Presenting to Cincinnatus the Command of the Roman Armies," "four small figures on a half-length cloth," which he painted in 1784, to the Royal Academy (No. 153) that year. It was sold with the effects of Benjamin West by George Robins "in the splendid gallery, Newman Street, London," 22 June 1829 (No. 179), the second day of the three-day auction. Both the painting and the preparatory sketch (1st Silliman Sale, Philadelphia, No. 121) are unlocated. West also owned an unidentifiable "Portrait of a Lady" by JT, No. 170 in the same London sale, and the engraving of JT's "Bunker's Hill."

10. West's original picture, 60 by 83 inches, celebrating the English and Dutch victory over the French fleet in 1692, is the property of the Duke of Westminster and hangs at Eaton Hall, Eccleston, Chester, England; JT's copy of it is unlocated.

11. In 1786 JT exhibited but one picture, painted in 1785, at the Royal Academy. Contemporary comment is to be found under "Miscellanies" in The Artist's Repository and Drawing Magazine, 4 (1786), 25: "No. 132, Priam returning with the Body of Hector, by Mr. TRUMBULL, is a considerable advance on his picture of last year [there were actually 3 pictures, Nos. 72, 94, and 432]; the colouring is more brilliant, and we think we foresee much improvement of this young artist in character, which will greatly assist his pencil." This picture is now deposited by the Boston Athenaeum at the Museum of Fine Arts, Boston. Although it was painted the same year as David's celebrated neoclassical composition, the "Oath of the Horatii," now in the Louvre, it is in the manner of West's "Agrippina Landing at Brundisium with the Ashes of Germanicus," painted 18 years earlier for the Archbishop of York and now at Yale. Benjamin Robert Haydon, 1786–1846, referring to West's work, stated: "His Venuses looked as if they never had been naked before, and were too cold to be impassioned; his Adonises dolts; his Cupids blocks—unamorous." Autobiography and Memoirs (new ed., New York, Harcourt, Brace, n.d.), 2, 465. JT, the Connecticut Calvinist, painted few nudes.

12. Samuel Preston, 1774–1803, rector of St. Botolph's Church at Chevening, son of William Preston of Oxford.

(which at his death he bequeathed to the library of Philadelphia, where it now is) was rich in works relating to the arts, and among others were the Trajan, Antonine and other columns, the triumphal arches, bas-reliefs, &c. &c., of Rome; these I studied attentively. Here also, I made my first attempt at the composition of a military scene, taken from the war of the Revolution; it was a small sketch in Indian ink, on paper, of the death of General Frazer,[13] at Behmus's heights; and here I was introduced to the learned and excellent Earl and Countess of Stanhope.[14]

Upon my return to town, I resumed my studies with Mr. West, and at the academy, with ardor; and now began to mediate seriously the subjects of national history, of events of the Revolution, which have since been the great objects of my professional life. The death of General Warren at the battle of Bunker's Hill,[15] and of Gen. Montgomery in the attack on Quebec,[16] were first decided

13. Simon Fraser, British brigadier; the action at Bemis' Heights, near Saratoga, took place on 7 October 1777; the sketch is unlocated. It is interesting to note that the first of the projected series of historical paintings, though never executed, was in celebration of British valor.

14. Philip Stanhope, 1717–86, 2d earl, family seat at Chevening, married Grisel Hamilton, daughter of Charles, Viscount Binning.

15. Maj. Gen. Joseph Warren of the Massachusetts Militia. Trumbull witnessed the battle from across Boston Harbor on 17 June 1775. See p. 19. Abigail Adams in a letter to her sister, Mrs. Shaw, from London, 4 March 1786, wrote of this painting: "To speak of its merit I can only say that in looking at it my whole frame contracted, my blood shivered, and I felt a faintness at my heart. He [Trumbull] is the first painter who has undertaken to immortalize by his pencil those great actions, that gave birth to our nation. By this means he will not only secure his own fame, but transmit to posterity characters and actions which will command the admiration of future ages, and prevent the period which gave birth to them from ever passing away into the dark abyss of time." Charles Francis Adams, ed., *Letters of Mrs. Adams, the Wife of John Adams* (Boston, Wilkins, Carter, 1948), p. 277.

16. Maj. Gen. Richard Montgomery of the Continental Army; the action took place on 31 December 1775. These two spirited paintings, the earliest of the "national history," are the most successful of the 8 completed. Trumbull made replicas of most of his historical paintings; he did not finish with the business until 1834 or 49 years after he had begun the series. See Sizer, *Works of Trumbull*, pp. 71–78.

The dramatic representation of the death of a historic personage was a popular subject at the time, particularly among the American painters then working at London. Benjamin West painted his celebrated "Death of Gen. Wolfe," at Quebec, now at the National Gallery of Canada, Ottawa, in 1771. It was engraved by William Woolett of London. John Singleton Copley's "Death of Major Pierson" of 1783, now at the Tate Gallery, London, was engraved by James Heath. Other than these death

upon. These were the earliest important events in point of time, and I not only regarded them as highly interesting passages of history, but felt, that in painting them, I should be paying a just tribute of gratitude to the memory of eminent men, who had given their lives for their country. These pictures (which are now in the Gallery at New Haven) were both painted in the room of Mr. West, and when the Bunker's Hill was pretty far advanced, he said to me one day, "Trumbull, will you dine with me to-morrow? I have invited some of our brother artists, and wish you to be of the party." He received his friends in his painting-room, where by his direction, my picture was standing in an advantageous light. Among the guests was Sir Joshua Reynolds, and when he entered the room, he immediately ran up to my picture,—"Why, West, what have you got here?—"this is better colored than your works are generally." "Sir Joshua," (was the reply,) "you mistake—that is not mine—it is the work of this young gentleman, Mr. Trumbull; permit me to introduce him to you." Sir Joshua was at least as much disconcerted as I had been by the *bent tin;* the account between us was fairly balanced.

Mr. West witnessed the progress of these two pictures with great

---

scenes on the field of battle was Copley's famed "Death of Chatham" of 1781, also at the Tate, engraved by Francesco Bartolozzi of London. "Twenty-five hundred prints from the large engraving made from this canvas were sold in a very short time." John Hill Morgan, "John Singleton Copley," The Walpole Society *Note Book* (1938), p. 41. Trumbull, obviously, had in mind such successes.

The time lag between event and pictorial recording should be noted. For instance, JT's West-inspired "Bunker's Hill" was painted after the lapse of 11 years, West's celebrated "Death of Gen. Wolfe" was 12, and Copley's "Death of Chatham" of 1783, 5.

One wonders whether West might not have thought of the painting of scenes of the American Revolution. As historical painter to the king he was, of course, precluded from such a course. His unfinished "American Peace Commissioners," owned by Henry Francis du Pont at Winterthur, Del., might be taken as an indication.

In connection with these battle pieces and heroic death scenes it should be noted that "the legend that Benjamin West's 'Death of Wolfe' was the first battle piece [the event taking place in a region unknown to the Greeks and Romans] ever painted in contemporary costume, has been four times refuted within recent memory." See Edgar Wind, "Penny, West, and the 'Death of Wolf," *Journal of the Warburg and Courtauld Institute,* 10 (1948), 162–65, and the same author's "The Revolution of History Painting," *Journal of the Warburg Institute,* 2 (1938), 116–127.

interest, and strongly encouraged me to persevere in the work of
the history of the American revolution, which I had thus commenced, and recommended to me, that I should have the series
engraved,[17] by which means, not only would the knowledge of
them, and of my talent, be more widely diffused, but also, in small
sums from many purchasers, I should probably receive a more
adequate compensation for my labor, than I could hope from the
mere sale of the paintings, even at munificent prices. He proceeded to detail to me a history of his own method, and of his success in the publication of the engravings from his history of Eng-

17. JT's historical pictures were all painted for the engraver; he expected to make
a fortune from the sale of the engravings. He wrote his brother Jonathan from London on 14 December 1785: "My Prospects are exceedingly changed since I last
wrote you—the rapidity of my advances in the Art has exceeded my most sanguine
expectations—and even hopes. I have begun upon the plan which has always been
my object: the American War. I am now painting the Death of Warren at Bunker
Hill: Mr. West and other artists of Eminence encourage & even praise my success.
M[r] W[est] has suggested to me a plan . . . to go on with a series of these pictures & to publish prints from them . . . [John Barker] Church has offer'd to lend
me whatever money I may have occasion for & another Gentleman will advance all
the money on condition of a Share in the prints—but the more I can keep the Business in my own hands & the less I am oblig'd to the assistance of strangers, the more
I shall be pleas'd." On 4 March 1786: ". . . my first picture of Bunker's Hill . . .
almost finished & met much approbation; the second, of Montgomery's death before
Quebec, is now far Advanc'd, & has rec'd from the few Judges who have seen it,
still warmer praise: Mr. West & Mr. Copley particularly encourage me to go on &
assure me that I have no reason to doubt the entire success of my prints: I cannot
believe they wish to deceive me, nor can I see a reason why they should. I shall
proceed therefore, tho the Expence must be very considerable." And on 24 May
1786: "My plan is far more compleat than I had flattered myself to expect: the two
first pictures are finish'd, & meet with increased approbation. I am highly fortunate
too in the friendship of Mr. Church who continues to supply me with Cash . . .
Mr. West, whose friendship is unexhaustible, has propos'd to me a subject of the
History of this Country [Gibraltar], at once popular, sublime, & in every respect perfect to the pencil . . ." (Yale Library.)
    ". . . he approached his subject from the patriot's rather than the painter's point
of view. He was filled with the seriousness of his time, with the sense of responsibility
to the grave issues through which the young nation was progressing . . ." Charles
Henry Caffin, *The Story of American Painting* (New York, Stokes, 1907), pp. 50 and
53. The observation is correct; JT was a stickler for accuracy of such things as military accoutrements, wherein lies his importance as a documentarian; the two
Baroque-like compositions, "Bunker's Hill" and "Quebec," the earliest and, inci-
dentally, the finest of the series of his "national history," have considerable aesthetic
interest quite apart from the subject matter.

land, and explained to me, with the kindness of a father, all the intricacies of such an enterprise—the choice of engravers, printers, publisher, &c. &c.

My only objection to this was, that the necessary superintendence would require more time and attention than I was willing to spare, from the direct pursuit of my studies. I was conscious of having entered upon the profession at too late an hour, and feared to divert my mind from the unremitted course of study which I had so successfully pursued during the last two or three years. This objection was removed; Mr. West was well acquainted with an Italian artist, by the name of Antonio di Poggi,[18] of very superior talents as a draughtsman, and who had recently commenced the business of publishing. He suggested that Mr. Poggi might be advantageously taken into connection, as the publisher, for which his great precision and elegance of drawing peculiarly qualified him. After some reflection, I determined to pursue the course thus pointed out to me; [19]—I entered into an agreement with Mr. Poggi for the publication of the two paintings now in hand; and while he sought for engravers, I continued to work upon the pictures. He soon found that there was not, at the time, a single engraver in England, disengaged, of sufficient talent to be safely employed in a work of the first class, as we meant this to be; [20] he therefore soon went to the continent, in pursuit of this, in connection with his other affairs; when the two pictures were finished, I took them with

18. He is listed as an exhibitor (in 1776 and 1781) at the Royal Academy as "Anthony Poggi, Painter, Rome."

19. JT lost no time in making known his intentions of painting a series for the purpose of engraving. The subject matter, obviously, was more popular in France than in England. The following announcement was printed this year:
"*Précis Historique* sur la Bataille de BUNKERS-HILL, donnée près de Boston dans le Massachuset le 17 Juin 1775, pour servir d'explication au prémier des XIV Tableaux représentants les evenemens les plus mémorables qui ont contribués à établir l'independance DES XIII PROVINCES-UNIES DE L'AMÉRIQUE SEPTEN-TRIONALE. Peints par le Colonel TRUMBULL, Américain & qui vont être gravés en taille-douce par les plus habiles Artistes de l'Europe, London, 1786 . . ." and "Précis Historique sur l'Expédition CONTRE LE CANADA . . ." (John Carter Brown Library, Providence, R.I.)

20. Obviously, English engravers were not anxious to participate in the making of prints depicting the military triumphs of the rebellious colonists.

me, and joined him at Paris,—with the great object of finding proper engravers.

On this occasion, Mr. Adams,[21] (minister of the United States in London,) and other friends, gave me letters of introduction to a number of important persons in Paris; from which I entertained hopes of a pleasant reception; and Mr. Vander Gucht,[22] a dealer in pictures in London, requested me to deliver a letter to Mr. Le Brun,[23] his correspondent in Paris; from this I expected nothing, as I had little acquaintance with Mr. Vander Gucht, and supposed it merely a letter of business. It happened, however, that when I reached Paris, every person to whom the letters of Mr. Adams and other friends were addressed, was in the country, and the letters of course useless, while that to Mr. Le Brun, aided by the sight of my pictures, made me known to all the principal artists and connoisseurs in Paris.

In the summer of 1785,[24] political duties had called Mr. Jefferson,[25] then minister of the United States in Paris, to London, and there I became acquainted with him. He had a taste for the fine arts, and highly approved my intention of preparing myself for the accomplishment of a national work. He encouraged me to persevere

21. John Adams, envoy to the Court of St. James from May 1785 to February 1788.

22. Benjamin Van der Gucht, d. 1794, portrait painter, picture restorer, and art dealer, patronized by the best society.

23. Jean-Baptiste Pierre LeBrun, 1748–1813, grandnephew of the painter, Charles LeBrun. His place of business was at 67, rue de Cléry. His beautiful and talented wife, Mme Vigée-LeBrun, 1755–1842, the celebrated portrait painter, had much influence on JT's current and later work.

24. JT's brother, Jonathan, wrote him 4 December 1784, of their father, the old governor: "His mind dwells much on his absent Son; and the longing Wish of his Heart is, that he may live to see him once more returned to his fond embraces . . ." and on 27 August 1785 he informed him of his death ten days previously: ". . . our Dear & respected parent . . . expired amidst the groans and Tears of his friends like one gently falling asleep, without a sigh or a pang he closed his Eyes upon the Scenes of Mortality . . ." (Jonathan Trumbull, Junior, Collection, Connecticut State Library, Hartford.)

25. The recent accounts of Thomas Jefferson by Marie Kimball, *Jefferson, the Scene of Europe, 1784 to 1789* (New York, Coward-McCann, 1950), and Dumas Malone, *Jefferson and the Rights of Man* (Boston, Little, Brown, 1951), illustrated by JT's pictures, contain illuminating accounts of the intimate friendship, at the time, between diplomat and painter.

in this pursuit, and kindly invited me to come to Paris, to see and study the fine works there, and to make his house my home, during my stay.

I now availed myself of this invitation, and went to his house, at the Grille de Chaillot,[26] where I was most kindly received by him. My two paintings, the first fruits of my national enterprise, met his warm approbation, and during my visit, I began the composition of the Declaration of Independence, with the assistance of his information and advice.

Through the acquaintance which I formed with the principal artists, David [27] in particular, who became and continued my warm and efficient friend, I had the best opportunity of seeing all that related to the arts, in Paris and its vicinity. At the same time, Mr. and Mrs. Cosway,[28] of London, were in Paris; he (then the admired miniature painter of the day) had been invited by the Duke of Orleans,[28a] to paint the duchess and her children. I became acquainted and intimate with them, and availing myself of all these advantages, I employed myself, with untiring industry, in examining and studying whatever had relation to the arts. I kept a journal of each day's occupation, which has narrowly escaped perishing by dampness, but by considerable labor has been saved in part, and will form the two following chapters.

In May, 1777, immediately after my resignation, my military

26. For a well-illustrated description of Jefferson's Paris residence see Howard C. Rice, *L'Hôtel de Langeac, . . . 1785–1789* (Monticello, Va., Thomas Jefferson Memorial Foundation, 1947).

27. Jacques Louis David, 1748–1825, leader of the classical movement in painting, exerted a strong influence on JT, whose charming miniature of Catherine Wadsworth, painted in 1792 (Yale), is quite similar in feeling to David's Mme Serizat of 1795 (Louvre).

28. Richard Cosway, 1740?–1821, the best English miniaturist at this time and principal painter to the Prince of Wales, also influenced JT. His beautiful wife, Maria Louisa Catherine Cecilia (Hadfield) Cosway, 1759–1838, born in Florence of English or Irish parents, was a close friend of Jefferson's. See Malone, *Jefferson*, pp. 160–183, Helen Duprey Bullock, *My Head and My Heart, A Little History of Thomas Jefferson and Maria Cosway* (New York, Putnam, 1945), in which there are many references to Trumbull, and Elizabeth Cometti, "Maria Cosway's Rediscovered Miniature of Jefferson," *The William and Mary Quarterly*, 9 (April 1952), 152–155, for an account of the replica of Jefferson's miniature JT made for Maria Cosway.

28a. See note 56 below.

accounts were audited and settled at Albany, by the proper accounting officer, John Carter. This gentleman who, soon after, married Angelica,[29] the eldest daughter of General Schuyler, resided in 1778 and 1779, in Boston, where I was studying, and the acquaintance which commenced at Albany was continued. On my return from Europe in 1782, he was one of the contractors for the supply of the American and French armies, in company with my friend Col. Wadsworth of Hartford. After the preliminaries of peace were signed, these gentlemen proposed the commercial connection which I declined; and when I resolved to return to London for the purpose of studying the arts, I purchased from Mr. Carter, a bill of exchange upon a banking house in London, with the full amount of all my disposable means, which were small enough to begin such a course with.

In London, 1784, my acquaintance with this gentleman was renewed, under the name of John Barker Church,[30] (Carter had been but a *nom de guerre,*) where he lived in great elegance, a member of Parliament, &c. &c.; and although I was now but a poor student of painting, and he rich, honored, and associated with the great, Mr. Church continued to treat me on the footing of equality, and I frequently dined at his table with distinguished men, such as Sheridan,[31] &c.

In 1786, Mr. Church called upon me, one morning very early, and said, with a little hesitation, "I am glad to find you at home and alone, Trumbull; I wish to ask you a question, at which I hope you will not take offense." "Certainly, my friend, you can say nothing at which I can be offended." "I wish to know then, how your money holds out." "Almost exhausted." "I should think so; I cannot comprehend how you have made it last so long; now do not regard this as an enquiry of silly curiosity; I hear very favorable accounts of your industry and probable success, and was afraid that the want of money might oblige you either to relax your studies, or to ask pecuniary favors from strangers. My real business, therefore, is to

29. Angelica Schuyler, daughter of Maj. Gen. Philip Schuyler, was married in 1777. JT painted her portrait, with her son Philip and servant, at London in 1784. See note 7 above.
30. 1748–1808.
31. Richard Brinsley Sheridan, 1751–1816, British dramatist and politician.

ask, that you will consider me as your banker, and that whenever you may have occasion for fifty, one hundred, or five hundred pounds, you will go to no one else, but apply to me, and you shall always have it, on your personal security. I shall ask no guarantee or endorser—your simple receipt only, and five per cent. interest."

Instances of patronage like this, to young men studying the fine arts, I presume are uncommon, and deserve to be gratefully remembered. By reference to my accounts at that time, I find that I availed myself of my friend's singular kindness to a considerable amount, and for several years; and when the account was closed by my final payment of the balance due on the 5th of March, 1797, I made an entry, of which the following is a copy: "The kindness of Mr. Church, in advancing me, at times when my prospects were not the most promising, and on my personal security merely, the sums which form the above account, will forever deserve my most sincere acknowledgments; without such aid, my subsequent success would have been checked by pecuniary embarrassments.— J. T."

The façade of the cathedral of Abbeville [32] is very good Gothic, but the interior is entirely destitute of any ornament in sculpture or painting worthy to be remembered. At Moulines, is nothing worth naming. At Amiens, the cathedral is a noble Gothic building; the chapels have been mostly repaired and modernized within a few years; the ornaments principally sculpture, and some parts tolerably well, but nothing of a high class; the pulpit in the body of the church, is worthy of notice for the elegance of the design. It is supported by the four cardinal virtues, large as life, and on the canopy, an angel holding the sacred volume, *"sic age, ut vivas,"*— the angel is finely conceived. A statue of St. Charles Borromeo,[33] on the right side of the church, as you enter, and near the choir, is one of the best things here; the devotion with which he contemplates the cross is well conceived and executed. A monument behind the great altar is also good. Several figures of the Virgin, with the infant Jesus, are well in the disposition of the upper parts, but

32. St. Vulfran, a late Gothic church; there is no cathedral at Abbeville.
33. Executed in 1755 by the Amiens sculptor, Jean-Baptiste Michel Dupuis, 1698–1780.

generally the lines of the lower part of the figure are too parallel, straight, and tasteless. Here are also some alto-relievos of Gothic sculpture in wood, lives of saints, &c., worthy to be attended to; the compositions have great simplicity and nature. Some others in gold, &c., on the sides of the great altar, are shown as fine, but are only tolerable. In painting, there is nothing worthy to be remembered; an offering of the three kings, by Parrocel,[34] is most striking, but has little real merit.

The stables of the Prince of Condé,[35] at Chantilly, are said to be the grandest in the world; the architecture simple, and well adapted to the purpose of the building, the circus particularly. The fountain in the centre of the stables is a good design; the horses and figures which hold them, very well executed; the other ornaments of stags' heads, &c., are well conceived and executed. The chateau has nothing particularly fine, in architecture, sculpture or painting.

PARIS.

The façade of the old Louvre is fine, *very fine* indeed; the very best thing which I have as yet seen. The Tuilleries is the vilest possible jumble of antique and Gothic, perfectly, utterly bad. The Palais Royal[36] is magnificent, and in good taste; Place de Louis quinze,[37] so far as regards the architecture of the Garde Meubles

34. "Côté sud . . . Chapelle Saint-Pierre et Saint-Paul . . . le tableau du retable (l'Adoration des Mages) d'un des Parrocel (peut-être Ignace)," 1668–1722, Amédée Boinet, *La Cathédrale d'Amiens* (Paris, Henri Laurens, 1922), pp. 117–118.

35. The Grandes-Ecuries, built in 1719–35 by John Aubert, were capable of stabling 240 horses.

36. Contemporary description is to be found in such guide books as the *Almanach du voyageur à Paris . . . Ouvrage utile aux citoyens, & indispensable pour l'étranger, Par M. T.* [Luc Vincent Thiéry], (Paris, Hardouin, 1783), and the *Guide des amateurs et des étrangers voyageurs . . . aux environs de Paris* (Paris, Hardouin & Gattey, 1788). These volumes were combined and expanded, in 1787–88, in the *Guide des amateurs et des étrangers voyageurs à Paris et aux environs de Paris par Thiéry.* This edition of the guide was indexed by Marc Furcy-Raynaud in 1928 in the *Publication de la Société Française de Bibliographie* (Paris, Auguste Picard, 1928), which makes it especially useful in locating works of art. See also Charles Kunstler, *La Vie quotidienne sous Louis XVI* (Paris, Hachette, 1950). The Palais Royal was built in 1629–34 for Richelieu, known as the Palais Cardinal, bequeathed to Louis XIII and called Palais Royal.

37. First laid out by Louis XV after whom it was named; became the Place de

du Roi,[38] is good, but the effect of the square is destroyed, by being cut into numberless small parts, divided by heavy balustrades of stone and deep trenches; the little abominable buildings, like watchhouses, are vile, and the statue itself,[39] with its accompaniments, bad; the horse is the best part; the caryatides at the angles of the pedestal are vile, and the bas-reliefs little better.

Count de Vaudreuil [40]—house and furniture elegant and magnificent in a high degree—few pictures, and mostly of the modern French school; some fine drawings and sketches by Rubens; [41] Madame Le Brun's portrait of herself,[42] Venus binding Cupid,[43] from which the print is done, and some others, possess great merit; architecture and figures, by Mr. Robert,[44] is a fine picture, in which the aerial perspective is beautiful; a village feast, small, by Le Prince,[45] is better drawn, with more elegance of character than

la Révolution; at the end of the Reign of Terror name changed to Place de la Concorde. A view of the Place Louis XV and views of many of the buildings to which the author refers are to be found in Marcel Poëte, *Une vie de cité Paris de sa naissance à nos jours* (Paris, Auguste Picard, 1925), in the chapter on "Le Dix-huitième siècle." Le Sage, *Le Géographe parisien, ou le conducteur chronologique et historique des rues de Paris* (2 vols., Paris, 1769), and Albert Babeau, *Paris en 1789* (Paris, Firmin-Didot, 1892), are also helpful.

38. Garde-Meuble de la Couronne, "L'Hôtel du Garde-Meuble occupe toute la colonnade de la place de Louis XV, du côté des Tuileries; la porte d'entrée est rue S. Florentin . . ." Thiéry, *Almanach*, p. 206.

39. The bronze equestrian statue of Louis XV by the academic sculptor, Edme Bouchardon, 1698–1762, erected in 1763, replaced in 1792; a small-scale model is in the Salle de Houdon at the Louvre.

40. Joseph François de Paul, comte de Vaudreuil, 1740–1817, lieutenant general, "grand-fauconnier de France." The count sold part of his great collection in November 1784, the catalogue being composed by "the artist, J. B. P. LeBrun," dealer in "old masters." A second sale took place in November 1787; M. LeBrun was again responsible for the catalogue.

41. JT was an admirer of the work of the great Flemish master, Peter Paul Rubens, 1577–1640, especially his small sketches of battle scenes. The "Battle of Bunker's Hill" and the "Attack on Quebec," both recently executed, are distinctly baroque in feeling. Evidently he was already well acquainted with Rubens' work through engravings and such of his pictures as he had seen at London.

42. There are two self-portraits in the Louvre.

43. A pastel, executed for comte de Vaudreuil by Vigée-LeBrun; J. B. P. LeBrun Sale of 1814.

44. Hubert Robert, 1733–1808, French painter of romantic architectural subjects.

45. Jean Baptiste Le Prince, 1734–81, French painter and etcher of romantic genre scenes.

Teniers,[46] with great beauty of execution; Bacchanals, by Poussin,[47] very good.

Sunday, August 5th. Went with Mr. Jefferson [48] and others to see the ceremony of crowning the *rosière* of Sarennes, a village near St. Cloud, four miles from Chaillot. Every year, the most amiable, industrious and virtuous poor girl of the parish is elected, who is received by all the village, and a crowd of strangers, in the church with great solemnity; the service is performed, a sermon preached, and the ceremony of crowning with roses is performed, with the benediction of a bishop. The *rosière* of the year, with the preceding candidates, is arranged on the right of the bishop—their parents and friends with them; the crown of flowers is placed by a little girl, daughter of the seigneur of the parish, with the *benedicite*

46. Either David Teniers, the Elder, 1582–1649, or his son, David, the Younger, 1610–90, Flemish genre and landscape painters.

47. Nicolas Poussin, chief exponent of the French classical tradition, painted four bacchanals for Cardinal Richelieu in 1641, two of which are in the National Gallery, London. A third, "Une fête en l'honneur de le Dieu Pan," was item 28 in the LeBrun Sale of 1787.

48. Jefferson wrote to his friend, Antoine Jean Marie Thevenard, 1733–1815, later minister of Marine (1791), vice-admiral (1791) and count (1810), from Paris, 5 May 1786: "In England I met with Mr. Trumbul a young painter of great & increasing reputation who proposes to employ himself solely in painting the events of the American war . . . He will come to Paris next month to take the pictures of Count Rochambeau, the M. de la Fayette & other characters of this country who bore principal parts in the war . . ." (Huntington Library, San Marino, Calif.) He also wrote to Francis Hopkinson from Paris, 14 August 1786: ". . . our countryman Trumbul is here, a young painter of the most promising talents. He brought with him his Battle of Bunker's Hill & Death of Montgomery to have them engraved here, & we may add, to have them sold; for like Dr. Ramsey's history, they are too true to suit the English palate . . ." President Stiles (1727–95) of Yale College noted in his diary for 16–22 August 1787: "Jefferson . . . says Col. Trumbull bro't to Paris 2 Pictures or Paintings admired by the Connaiseurs, & that he is excellent in this Art." Franklin Bowditch Dexter, *The Literary Diary of Ezra Stiles* (New York, Scribner, 1901), 3, 276. Lafayette wrote to Jefferson from Luneville, 30 August 1786: "I am Sorry, My dear Sir, not to have been in Paris to welcome Mr. Trumbul, and to offer him what little services may lay in my power . . . it will be a sincere satisfaction for me to see a Gentleman who does honour to America, whose family and person I have a great regard for, and whose talents are employed the very way I wanted. Be pleased to present my compliments to him, and tell him I hope, and wish to see him before he goes . . ." Gilbert Chinard, *The Letters of Lafayette and Jefferson* (Baltimore, Johns Hopkins Press, 1929), pp. 106–107.

of the bishop, and accompanied by music; the *rosière* is then conducted home, attended by the clergy, music and company, when she receives three hundred livres—the annual legacy of a clergyman, whose institution this is. Returned to Paris on foot, over the Pont de Neuilly, a very beautiful stone bridge over the Seine; the floor of this bridge is horizontal; it consists of seven arches, which have a beautiful degree of lightness; these arches, which in fact and intrinsically are hemispherical, are sloped from one fourth of the piers on each side to the outer face, so that the arch externally appears to be a very flat ellipse, but within and under the centre of the bridge, they are hemispheres.

Monday, 6th. Went with M. and Madame Houdon,[49] to the *salon* on the Boulevards, to see his little Diana in marble, a very beautiful figure—an honor not only to the artist, but to the country and age in which he lives. She is represented as in the chase, the bow in one hand, an arrow in the other, running; the countenance animated with a noble severity, a dignity worthy the chastity and virtues of the goddess.

From the *salon*, went to Mr. Girardon's, where is a beautiful bronze of the same figure,[50] large as life, and some clever pictures; several by Vernet [51] were standing in the *salle a manger*, but could

49. JT's friend, Jean Antoine Houdon, 1741–1828, the celebrated French sculptor, had recently returned from the United States, where he had visited Washington at Mount Vernon for the purpose of making studies for the marble statue now directly under the dome of the Capitol at Richmond, Va. Years later, in 1805, Houdon was elected an honorary member of the American Academy of the Fine Arts.

In the mémoire of his work communicated to his friend Bachelier on "20 vendémiaire An III" (1794), Houdon mentions four versions of his "Diana," including "le marbre de petite proportion," which he notes as having belonged to "feu d'Ormesson." The List is published in Georges Giacometti, *La Vie et l'oeuvre de Houdon* (2 vols., Paris, A. Camoin, 1929), *1*, 65–67.) The whereabouts of the reduced marble version is unknown today. Giacometti (*op. cit.*, 2, 246) cites some evidence that it might have been in Sir Richard Wallace's possession in London in 1874.

50. The "Diana" is clearly the bronze version made in 1782 for Girardot (not Girardon) de Marigny. (Exhibited at the Salon of 1783; acquired in 1870 by Lord Hertford; then Yerkes Collection, New York; and now in the Huntington Library, San Marino, Calif.) Another, later bronze example is in the Louvre and a third cast, made in 1839, is now at Tours.

51. A family of French painters, JT probably refers to Carle Vernet, 1758–1835, historical and animal painter.

not be seen. We then went to Mr. Pinceau's,[52] a gentleman singularly curious for his anatomical preparations in wax. The human body is here seen modelled in wax, shewing not only the external muscles, and the vessels of the heart and viscera, but likewise the internal distribution of the arteries, &c. You here may see, also, the anatomy of various animals, both skeletons and injected blood-vessels; the various states of an egg, until it becomes a chicken, &c. &c.

The Bibliothèque du Roi.[53] Here are a great number of curious works; busts of Voltaire, Franklin, de Suffrein,[54] &c. The library is open every Tuesday and Friday, to all who choose to read; the books, a vast collection, are generally old and worn. The Parnassus

52. This fascinating gentleman, "Monsieur Pinceau," is unidentified; the name, "Mr. Pencil," might possibly be a *nom de guerre* for some sculptor-anatomist. Thiéry, however, in his *Almanach du voyageur à Paris* for 1783 mentions a "cabinet d'Anatomie": "Le Cabinet de M. Sue, Professeur d'Anatomie au College Royal de Chirurgie, réunit une collection précieuse de tout ce qui peut piquer la curiosité d'un connoisseur en ce genre. L'ordre qu'y a mis M. Sue son fils, en rend le coup-d'oeil agréable, & facilite beaucoup l'étude de L'Anatomie (p. 162 and, in the 1787 ed., *1*, 404). There were a number of celebrated surgeons of that name in 18th-century Paris, among them Jean Sue, 1699–1762, and his son Pierre Sue, 1739–1816, a scholar and author who became librarian of the École de Santé. Jean's brother, Jean-Joseph Sue, 1710–92, *dit de la Charité*, was professor of anatomy at the Royal Academy of Surgery. He and his surgeon son, another Jean-Joseph Sue, 1760–1830, built a remarkable anatomical collection, which is evidently that mentioned by Thiéry. This last Sue gave the collection to the École des Beaux-Arts, of which he was professor of anatomy, in 1829. Although JT spoke fluent French he probably did so with a New England accent. It is not inconceivable, too, that the collection formed by the Jean-Joseph Sues became confused in his mind with the name of the well-known Pierre Sue; "Pierre Sue," might, in Yankee-French, come to be "Pinceau"—at least, the editor chooses to believe that this is the case. For JT's often fantastic spellings of French proper names see p. 118, n. 160. (La Bibliothécaire en chef at the Muséum National d'Histoire Naturelle, Paris, confirms this: ". . . nous avions cherché à la Faculté de Médecine et à l'Académie de Médecine . . . Nos recherches ont été négatives. Nous croyons que vous avez trouvé la solution et qu'il s'agit de *Pierre SUE*.")

53. Now the Bibliothèque Nationale.

54. Houdon did François Marie Arouet de Voltaire, 1694–1778, in 1778 (and another version, without the wig, in 1779) and Benjamin Franklin in 1778. That of Pierre André de Suffren de Saint Tropez, 1726–88, naval hero, was executed in 1786 and shown in the Salon of 1787. JT might have seen plasters of these overwhelmingly strong busts.

of France [55] is here seen, in sculpture,—a rock, steep, rugged, and difficult of ascent; Pegasus at the top; and at various points of the ascent, little statues of the elegant and favorite French poets, prettily enough conceived, and some parts beautifully executed. The great globes, twenty or twenty five feet in diameter, are very fine. Here also are many models of machines belonging to the Duke of Orleans,[56] which are placed here while the Palais Royal is repairing; they represent various manufactures, as mills, furnaces, glass-houses, China works, &c. &c.

From the Bibliothèque du Roi, we went to the Salle des Antiques, in the old Louvre, where are the statues, casts, bas-reliefs, &c. of the Academy. The casts from some of the antique statues which are deposited here, are very fine, and there are some statues in marble of modern men, of great merit, particularly that of Tourville,[57] by Houdon; this has a grandeur and simplicity about it worthy of any age; the air and dress of the head in particular are charming. In fact, here is a collection worthy of a great nation, but kept in a state of dirt and disorder that would disgrace a plaster-shop; many of the fine things are broken and mutilated, and the whole has the appearance of having never been cleaned, since they were deposited there.

Hence to the apartments of the Academy in the Louvre, through the Hall of the Farnese Hercules, so named from an admirable cast of the statue, which adorns this room;—to the Salle du Conseil,

55. A contemporary description of this complicated, symbolic bronze monument, "À la gloire de la France et de Louis le Grand, et à la mémoire immortelle des illustres Poëtes et des illustres Musiciens François . . ." by Évrard Titon du Tillet, 1677–1762, dedicated 1717, is to be found in [N. H. Le Prince] Essai historique sur la Bibliothèque du Roi (Paris and Berlin, 1782), pp. 124–133.

56. Louis Philippe Joseph, duc d'Orléans, 1747, guillotined 1793, liberal, reformer, revolutionist, known as Philippe-Égalité, son of Louis Philippe d'Orléans, and father of Louis Philippe, king of France.

57. Anne Hilarion de Costentin, comte de Tourville, 1642–1701, illustrious naval officer under Louis XIV. The full-length, marble, life-size statue, now at Versailles, of the 17th-century admiral was ordered by Angiviller for the series of "grands hommes" for a gallery in the Louvre. Shown in the Salon of 1781, it could well have been lying about in 1786 (waiting for a permanent place) in the Académie store-rooms.

which, with the antichamber through which you pass, is adorned with the *morceaux de reception* and portraits of the academicians of the institution; among them are many fine things, but not in that careful preservation which could be wished.

We then went to the Gallery of the Academy, in which are the battles of Alexander, by Le Brun; [58] in point of composition, these are among the finest things which have ever been produced— *perhaps the finest.* The drawing is good, though the style of the figures is heavy, and the coloring unpleasant in a high degree. It is impossible to see these superb things to any advantage, as the *morceaux de réception* of several living artists are standing on easels before them; among these, Madame Le Brun's Peace and Plenty [59] holds a conspicuous rank; the coloring is very brilliant and pleasing. Chiron teaching Achilles the use of the bow, is a very good picture, by M. Reynaud; [60] the body of Achilles beautiful, both in drawing and color; the head not quite so well, something in the outline of the right cheek and eye seems incorrect, but the action and expression of both figures are well understood. Andromache lamenting the death of Hector,[61] by David, is a picture of much merit, with some defects; the style of the drapery is too little, too much cut up; the expression well, and the drawing pretty good. These are the best of the present artists. The rooms in which the

58. The "History of Alexander the Great" series of Charles LeBrun, 1619–90, painter to Louis XIV. JT was naturally interested in battle scenes.

59. "Peace Bringing Back Plenty," Vigée-LeBrun's reception piece for the French Academy, painted in 1783, a Rubensesque picture; now in the Louvre. Interesting comparisons can be made between such similar works as Vigée's portrait of the painter, Hubert Robert, of 1788 (Louvre) and JT's miniature of the Italian sculptor, Giuseppe Ceracchi, 1792 (both Yale and Metropolitan Museum of Art); Vigée's Mme Molé Raymond, 1786 (Louvre), and JT's miniature of Harriet Chew, 1793 (Yale); and Vigée's charming and vivacious portrait of her daughter of about 1793 (Museum of Fine Arts, Boston) and the miniature of Capt. Thomas Youngs Seymour, 1793 (Yale). JT admired the lady and her work extravagantly. See Sizer, "The John Trumbulls and Mme Vigée-LeBrun," *The Art Quarterly* (Detroit Institute of Arts), *15* (Summer 1952), 170–178.

60. JT made a pen sketch, now at Yale, of this newly finished picture, "The Education of Achilles by the Centaur Chiron," by Jean Baptiste Regnault, painted in 1782; now in the Louvre.

61. David's "La Douleur d'Andromaque sur le corps d'Hector," painted in 1783; now at the École des Beaux-Arts, Paris.

students draw from the life, of which there are two, are much smaller, and less convenient than that in London. The specimens of sculpture which we see here, are much superior to the painting. The apartments of the Academy are extensive and princely, but kept in very bad order. In one of the model rooms, is a small picture by a young man, just gone to study at Rome, which has much simplicity and nature; it gives fair promise of future excellence. It is a style of which one may venture to say, that assiduous study will improve into the dignity of Poussin.

From the Academy, went to the Palais Royal, where we found workmen employed in taking down the old gallery,[62] in order to rebuild the whole, in a modern style; the pictures taken down, and placed in the middle of each room, on great easels, and obliquely to the light, resting partly upon each other, and with such small intervals that it was impossible to view the large pictures with any advantage or satisfaction. The collection [63] is most princely; the best works of the first masters are to be found here—the Sacraments, by Poussin [64]—Murder of the Innocents, by Le Brun [65]— the Cupid making his Bow, by Correggio [66]—the dead Christ, by Annibal Caracci [67]—sketches and pictures, by Rubens,[68] in pro-

62. Undertaken by Philippe-Egalité, duc d'Orléans, in 1781–86.

63. See Pierre d'Espezel, Le Palais-Royal (Paris, Calmann-Lévy, 1936), pp. 98–99. The pictures which JT saw and describes have been dispersed. They are now to be found in Buckingham Palace, the National Gallery, the Dulwich Gallery, and Wallace Collection, all of London; the Fitzwilliam Museum at Cambridge, England; in the Louvre; Borghese Palace, Rome; and in the museums of Berlin and Antwerp. The proper identification of the picture JT admired is difficult if not impossible. There is a two-volume MS at the Frick Art Reference Library, New York, entitled "Recueil de catalogues des principales collections de tableaux" (1774), in which 85 pictures in the Palais Royal are described, 2, 98–103.

64. Probably the "Jesus Christ Instituting the Sacrament of the Eucharist" now in the Louvre, Nicolas Poussin, collection of Louis XIII.

65. Charles LeBrun's "terribly fine" "Massacre of the Innocents," painted in 1657. See Jean Paul Richter and John C. L. Sparkes, Catalogue of the Pictures in the Dulwich College Gallery (London, Spottiswoode & Co., 1880), p. 91, No. 252; now at Dulwich College.

66. Possibly the "Education of Cupid," painted in 1521, in the National Gallery, London, "Venus and Cupid," after Correggio, at the Dulwich College Gallery, or some other picture with a changed attribution.

67. Possibly the "Pietà," school of Lodovico Carracci "formerly attributed to

fusion—the best things of Teniers—in short, the best works of
every great man. Few however of these fine works can be advantageously seen, while the apartments remain in their present state
of disorder. Here is also a duplicate or copy of the head of Christ
crowned with thorns, which Mr. West possesses, but if *by* Guido,[69]
certainly very much inferior to that, in color, execution and expression. The Annibal Caracci is superb, but I think not quite
equal in color, execution or preservation to that of M. Au Frere; [70]
but in composition, it will scarcely be thought inferior. Le Brun's
Murder of the Innocents is *terribly* fine; maternal horror and distress are too wonderfully represented.

From the Palais Royal we went to the new church of St. Genevieve; [71] it is unfinished, but the entrance at the grand portico is
really in a fine style of architecture, and to judge from that part of
the interior from which the scaffolding is removed, and which is
nearly finished, the whole will be one of the most elegant works in
Europe. The general plan appears to resemble St. Stephen's,[72] Wal-
brook, but on a much larger scale; all the ornaments are intended to
be of sculpture only, in white stone; no paintings are to be admitted
in the church. The exterior has much novelty and elegance.

To the church of the Carmelites; [73] rich without taste; several
large pictures by Champagne; [74] one said to be by Guido, the

Annibale Carracci," at the Dulwich College Gallery, "The Dead Christ on the Knees
of the Virgin" at the Louvre, or a lost picture.

68. There is a "Judgment of Paris" from the Orléans Collection in the National
Gallery, London. Rubens' sketches were always of interest to JT.

69. Guido Reni, 1575–1642, of Bologna; not the "Ecce Homo" in the Louvre, from
the collection of Louis XIV; undoubtedly a reattributed picture.

70. Possibly Louis-Stanislas Fréron, a literary figure, son of Élie-Catherine Fréron,
1719–76, a famous critic of the 18th century.

71. The church of St. Geneviève (patron saint of Paris) was begun during the
reign of Louis XV by the architect Jacques Germain Soufflot. It became the Panthéon
in 1791. This imposing building in the form of a Greek cross, with its magnificent
dome, was justly admired by the architectural-minded JT.

72. A noble church built 1672–79 by Sir Christopher Wren.

73. The Église des Carmélites on the rue St. Jacques in the faubourg St. Jacques.
The pictures in the church are listed in the MS "Recueil de catalogues," 2, 103.

74. Philippe de Champagne, 1602–74, first painter to Marie de Médicis, employed to decorate the Luxembourg Palace and this church. JT might be referring
to his "Announciation" in grisaille or to the "Announciation . . . and a Glory of

Visitation of the Virgin, very unworthy of so great a name, except the head of the Virgin, and two little angels over her. The Magdalen of Le Brun, Madame de la Valiere,[75] is a charming picture; the coloring much superior to that of his works in general. Here are also one or two large pictures, said to be by his hand, but very inferior.

Tuesday, August 7th. Went to the house of the Count D'Orsay,[76] said to be one of the most superb in Paris; it is in truth overloaded with elegance; the furniture is expensive and rich, to a fault; the eye can find no rest; the windows, in one of the apartments looking upon the garden, are of plate glass, only two pieces in each. The picture room contains the most beautiful collection of perfect little things that I have ever seen together; the Visitation of the Virgin, by Rubens [77]—the taking down from the Cross, by Rembrandt [78] —an Infant Saviour, by Vandyck [79]—are superb. Teniers, Paul Potter, Wouvermans, Mieris, Metzu, Netscher, Van Oort,[80] &c. &c., have precious specimens here. Small bronze copies of the finest antique statues, the choicest porcelain, &c. &c. literally crowd every apartment. The dining room is magnificent, ornamented with marble copies of some of the best antiques; the columns which separate the windows are of green and white marble; the windows are of plate glass, of prodigious size; but in my opinion, this room has one

---

Angels" by Guido Reni in the Louvre. The positive identification of church pictures, with their often faulty 18th-century attributions, is difficult if not impossible. The well-illustrated catalogue, *Peintures méconnues des églises de Paris, retour d'évacuation,* Y. Bizardel (Preface) and Jean Verrier (Introduction) (Paris, Musée Galliera, 1946), is helpful.

75. Charles LeBrun's "The repentant Saint Magdalen renouncing the vanities of this life" is in the Louvre. The features of the saint are supposed to be those of the beautiful Louise Françoise de la Baume–Le Blanc de la Vallière, 1644–1710.

76. Pierre Gaspard Marie Grimod, comte d'Orsay, b. 1748; the Hôtel d'Orsay is on the rue de Varenne.

77. Possibly the picture now at the Musée des Beaux-Arts, Strasbourg.

78. Possibly the "Descent from the Cross" now in the Widener Collection in the National Gallery of Art, Washington, D.C. (the history of which can only be traced to 1834), or more likely that in the Hermitage at Leningrad, which was acquired in 1815; both justly famous pictures.

79. Unidentified.

80. David Teniers, Paul Potter, Jan Wouwerman, Frans van Mieris, Gabriel Metzu, Caspar or Constantine Netscher, Lambert or Adam van Moort, Dutch and Flemish genre and landscape painters of the late 16th and 17th centuries.

inexcusable fault,—it looks upon the court yard, where is all the dirty business of the stables, &c., objects far from pleasing to contemplate, in convivial hours.

From the Maison D'Orsay, to the Hotel des Invalides.[81] This is a noble institution; the buildings are extensive and well planned, equal to the accommodation of six thousand men; at present, there are only four thousand seven hundred. The church in which the service is performed is plain; through it you pass to the dome, which is truly one of the most beautiful pieces of architecture in this kind that has hitherto been executed. It is light and airy in its proportions—the sculpture well wrought—the paintings barely tolerable —the whole clean and well kept—the four chapels, in the angles of the dome, are very elegant and rich; but among all the paintings, whether of the chapels or the dome, there is nothing worthy of much attention. The centre of the dome is the best, and in one apartment adjoining the Salle du Conseil there is a small picture, said to be the original design from which this centre was painted, which is very well, much better in truth than the great work. The Salle du Conseil contains a number of portraits of great men, but in general intolerably bad.

Passy. The view of Paris from the house formerly occupied by Dr. Franklin [82] is very beautiful. La Muette,[83] a small house of the king, is pretty; Madrid,[84] an old Chateau near the Bois de Boulogne, built by Francis the 1st, in great Gothic grandeur, to elude a parole which he had given to remain a prisoner at Madrid; the Pont de Neuilly [85] is still more beautiful at a second view than at the first.

Wednesday, August 8th. Went with the Marquis Trotti [86] to M.

81. Founded by Louis XIV as a home for disabled soldiers; the dome, one of the most impressive in France, by Jules Hardouin Mansard, was justly admired by JT. It appears in the background of his portrait of Louis Guillaume Otto, comte de Mosloy, painted some years later, as well as in Hyacinthe Rigaud's portrait of the architect now in the Louvre.

82. From 1777 to 1785. The Hôtel de Valentinois is on the corner of rue Raynouard and rue Singer.

83. Château de la Muette or La Meute, a hunting lodge rebuilt by Louis XV.

84. Château Madrid, demolished 1793 and 1847.

85. Constructed in 1768–74 by Jean Rodolphe Perronet, spanning the Seine.

86. Probably Marchese Ludovico Trotto, 1729–1808, or possibly his son Lorenzo Galeazzo, born 1759 (whose title of marquis, however, was not confirmed until 1817). The Trotti were an ancient Milanese family.

Houdon's, and afterwards to MM. Martinis [87] and Güttenberg's.[88] Proposal made to Güttenberg to come to England, to engrave one of my pictures,—a plain, honest German, industrious, and ambitious of fame, and one of the best engravers at present in France. Thence to the church of Notre Dame [89]—Gothic, but not the grand style; ornamented with many paintings of the French school, of which no one made sufficient impression upon me to be particularly remembered; they appeared to be not above mediocrity. To the church of St. Sulpice [90]—Grecian architecture, but heavy, clumsy, and unpleasing; some pictures, but none of a high class; St. Jerome,[91] in the first chapel on your right, as you enter the church, is a finely colored picture, but incorrect in the drawing, and there is a Nativity [92] in a chapel near the choir, still on the right hand, which I could not approach near enough to see well, but it appeared to be a sweet thing, and over it was another small picture of three half figures; the Creator and two Angels adoring, which, at the distance from which I saw it, had a very good effect, and beautiful color.

Thursday, August 9th. Went to the Luxembourg palace [93] with Mr. and Mrs. Cosway, Mons. Belesaire,[94] *architecte du Roi,* the Marquis Trotti, &c. &c. Saw the Gallery of Mary de Medici, painted by Rubens [95]—the Empire of Color, Allegory, and Composition.

87. Pietro Antonio Martini, 1739–97, engraver from Palma, worked both at Paris and London.

88. Heinrich Guttenberg, 1745–1818, engraver from Nuremberg, worked at Rome and Paris.

89. Archaeologically if not aesthetically the most interesting of the great Gothic cathedrals of France.

90. This dull building (1650), was designed by Louis Levau, in the classical or what JT chose to call the "Grecian" style. JT's observations have a contemporary ring.

91. According to the present curé (1952) of the church "the St. Jerome disappeared during the Revolution and all the furniture; the altar was destroyed except the Chapel of the Virgin."

92. The "Nativity" by Carle van Loo, 1705–65, painted in 1746, is still *in situ.*

93. The present Senate of the French Republic, built in 1615–27 for Marie de Médicis, widow of Henry IV, by Saloman de Brosse.

94. Claude Billard de Bélisart, became architect to Louis XVI in 1781.

95. The Salle Rubens in the Louvre contains 18 of the 21 large allegorical paintings depicting the life of Marie de Médicis, designed in 1621–25 by Rubens for the Luxembourg Palace.

The gallery is in so decayed a state as to be supported by props, to prevent its falling; the pictures want cleaning, the varnish being so chilled as to destroy, in a great degree, their effect, but still enough is visible to charm every spectator. The Death of Henry is in the best state, and is indeed a model of grandeur in composition, and of splendor of coloring; the richness, the glow, and at the same time the truth of color and effect, is wonderful, and the drawing generally more correct than I had been taught to expect. The picture at the end of the gallery—France—is the most perfect of all, and appears to have been painted entirely by the hand of Rubens; splendor and harmony are here wonderfully united—the truth of nature, and the glow of a nature superior to ours. From the condition in which the building is at present, there is great difficulty in obtaining permission to see the paintings; Mr. Cosway obtained it through Madame de Polignac,[96] and I owe this almost greatest pleasure I ever received from the arts, to his politeness. In the other parts of the palace there is nothing of art worth seeing. The gardens are pleasant, but as well as the building, very much out of repair.

Went thence to the apartments of the Sieur David, in the old Louvre; took the liberty to introduce myself; found him a pleasant, plain, sensible man of perhaps thirty five or forty years of age. Found a picture finished of the three Horatii receiving their swords from their father, and swearing to use them bravely in the service of their country, before their famous battle with the three Samnites; figures large as life, the story well told, drawing pretty good, coloring cold;—Belisarius receiving alms, likewise large as life—as well composed and drawn as the other, and better colored.[97]

Again went to the apartments of the Academy—magnificence,

96. Yolande Martine Gabrielle de Polastron, *ca.* 1749–93, wife of Armand Jules François Polignac, 1745–1817, an intimate of Marie Antoinette.

97. As court painter to Louis XVI, David received living quarters in the former royal residence. The "Oath of the Horatii" was begun at Rome in 1784 and exhibited at Paris in 1785. This picture, 130 by 168 inches, is now in the Louvre. A smaller version, 50 by 65 inches, originally owned by JT's friend Count Vaudreuil, is now in the Toledo Museum of Art. His "Bélisaire demandant L'Aumone," painted in 1784, was exhibited at the Salon in 1785, is now in the Louvre. JT had painted the same subject in 1778 at his home at Lebanon, Conn.

neglected and decaying. The pictures of Le Brun [98] are by no means so pleasing as the prints; the coloring is all that is bad, and after seeing such works of Rubens, quite insufferable; the flesh is a dirty, brick dust red—shadows more heated than the light—violent red near the extremities of the pictures, and even in the distances; in short, while they have infinite merit as compositions, and great in point of drawing, they are, as colored pictures, bad as possible.

Thence, to the *Jardin du Roi.*[99] The collection of plants is very great, beautifully disposed, and kept in perfect order; the cabinet of natural history perfectly arranged, but, if what I saw be the whole, by no means so extensive or various as that of Sir Ashton Lever.[100]

Friday, August 10th. Went to the Sorbonne.[101] The church [102] is very good architecture; no paintings worthy of much notice. The monument of Cardinal Richelieu is finely conceived and executed; the figure of Science weeping at his feet, is, of all the marble I ever saw, the most expressive; it is the only thing of this kind which ever forced an involuntary tear from my eye—such dignity of sorrow, yet so simple and unaffected, so directly addressed to all the tender feelings, that the heart which does not melt before it, must be still harder and more cold than the marble. In one of the halls for disputation is a whole length portrait of the Cardinal, very finely painted, and worthy of Vandyck; this hall contains many other pictures, unworthy to be remembered. Here, two learned young men were carrying on a most edifying theological dispute in Latin, upon the merits of Judas and the degree of his sins, before two grave doctors, who sat wisely nodding over their theses, and a most attentive audience, consisting of one young man.

Went again to the church of St. Genevieve, and through every

98. Charles LeBrun; JT's observation is good.
99. The present Jardin des Plants, founded in 1636.
100. 1729–88, English naturalist and collector.
101. Founded in 1253 by Robert de Sorbon, chaplain to St. Louis.
102. The Church of the Sorbonne was rebuilt in the mid-17th century by Jacques Lemercier for Cardinal Richelieu, minister of Louis XIII. The cardinal's tomb was designed by Charles LeBrun and sculptured by François Girardon during Louis XIV's reign.

part of it, to the highest scaffolding of the dome, the inner columns of which seemed just carried up to their height, and the workmen laying up the arches of the intercolumniations, which are to form the windows; the external colonnade was carried to about half its height—the diameter of its columns here is about four feet; to the summit of the dome, above what is now finished, will be near one hundred feet. The view of Paris from this highest scaffolding is magnificent and vast; it was a very fine day, so that the eye, without interruption, wandered over the immense extent of buildings, which lay beneath it. The Tuilleries,[103] the Louvre,[104] with the church of Notre Dame, St. Sulpice, the dome of the Invalides, the Bastille, the Salpetriere,[105] Val de Grâce,[106] and a vast number of inferior buildings, towering above the dwelling houses. The extent of the city; the vast and opulent country, terminating partly in rough and broken hills, partly in a fine champaign, ornamented with the palaces of Meudon [107] and St. Cloud; [108] the aqueduct of Marly,[109] the convent of Mount Calvaire,[110] and a number of other splendid buildings, form altogether a *coup d'œil* entirely superior to any thing I have heretofore seen.

Dined to-day (the 10th) at Mons. Le Brun's, the Count Vaudreuil, M. Menagiot,[111] Le Brun *l'aîné*,[112] &c. &c. Madame Le Brun is one of the most charming women I ever saw; her pictures have great merit, particularly a portrait of herself and her daughter, which is not yet finished; in the composition of this picture there is a simplicity and sweetness worthy of any artist, and a brilliancy

103. The Palais des Tuileries, once the center of Paris, was destroyed by the mob in 1871.

104. Then the deserted royal residence; not used as a museum until 1793.

105. The Salpêtrière or saltpeter factory, then used as a hospital.

106. Designed by François Mansard, in the style of St. Peter's at Rome.

107. The two royal châteaux at Meudon were destroyed in 1803 and 1871.

108. Nothing remains of the château, burned during the occupation of the Germans in 1870.

109. The aqueduct was constructed by Louis XIV to convey water from the Seine to Versailles.

110. The convent Dames du Calvaire, founded by Marie de Médicis, was located on the rue de Vaugirard near the Luxembourg Palace.

111. François Guillaume Ménageot, 1744–1816, who was appointed director of the French Academy at Rome in 1787.

112. Presumably J. B. P. LeBrun's father.

of coloring quite charming. Among female names, Angelica [113] alone can come in any competition with Madame Le Brun. After dinner, the Sieur David, with one of his friends, did me the honor to visit my pictures; his commendation, I fear, was too much dictated by politeness.

Saturday, August 11. Breakfasted with Mr. and Mrs. Cosway, M. D'Hancharville,[114] M. Belesaire, Marquis Trotti, &c. Went to Madame Guyard's [115]—a plain, diverting woman; thence to M. Vincent [116] in the Louvre, a very elegant gentleman and good artist; saw his picture of Pœtus and Arria,[117]—full of expression and energy;—also his Henry IV, of France, meeting Sully wounded,[118] —the characters good, drawing fine, coloring a little weak, effect too broken and *éparpillé* [scattered], but close attention to the costume of the time, and great propriety and simplicity of action and expression. From M. Vincent's, I went to see M. Pajou,[119] sculptor, in the Louvre; his works (*à mon avis*) by no means equal to those of Houdon;—thence to M. Boileau,[120] and M. Paillet.[121]

August 12th. Went to Versailles,[122] with Mr. and Mrs. Cosway,

113. The beautiful and admired Angelica Kauffmann, 1741–1807, Swiss-born historical and portrait painter, royal academician in 1769, the year of its founding.

114. Pierre François Hugues, *dit* d'Hancharville, 1719–1805, author, classical archaeologist, and antiquarian.

115. Laurent Guyard, 1723–88, sculptor, pupil of Bouchardon.

116. François André Vincent, 1746–1816, historical painter, honorary member of the American Academy of the Fine Arts in 1805.

117. Subject from Tacitus (*Annals*, XVI, 34); picture not in the Louvre; present location unknown.

118. "Henri IV recontre Sully blessé," painted in 1786; in the Louvre.

119. Augustin Pajou, 1730–1809. JT's opinion of his work would be sustained today.

120. Jacques Boileau, 1752–93, future Girondist, member of the Convention, voted for the death of Louis XVI.

121. Probably the Paillet described in Thiéry, *Guide* (1787), *1*, 424; a painter and picture dealer who remodeled the Hôtel de Bullion on the rue Coquillière and made a public auction room there. He also executed orders for foreigners.

122. Principal pictures listed in the MS "Recueil de catalogues," *2*, 107–111. Jefferson wrote to Col. David Humphreys from Paris on 14 August 1786: "Your friend, Mr. Trumbull, is here at present. He brought his Bunker's Hill and Death of Montgomery to have them engraved here. He was yesterday to see the King's collection of paintings at Versailles, and confessed it surpasses everything of which he even had an idea. I persuaded him to stay and study here, and then proceed to

MM. D'Hancharville, Poggi, Bulfinch,[123] Coffin,[124] &c.—quite undress,—the chapel, antichamber, gallery, &c., magnificent in the
highest degree. Saw here the whole length portrait of King Charles
I,[125] engraved by Strange—the most perfect and loveliest of Vandyck's portraits that has come to my view. In the same apartment
are three Labors of Hercules, by Guido,[126] very fine; that with the
hydra almost the same as Raph West's [127] etching, the upper part
of the figure perfectly the same. Adoration of the Kings, by Rubens,[128] an admirable composition; the expression and color of
the old man's head in the centre is particularly fine, and a black
face of vast dignity. A Holy Family, by Vandyck,[129] is very fine.
In other apartments, we saw the works of Paul Veronese,[130] of the

---

Rome . . ." *The Writings of Thomas Jefferson*, Andrew A. Lipscomb, ed. (Washington, Thomas Jefferson Memorial Assn., 1904), pp. 400–401.

123. Charles Bulfinch, 1763–1844, architect, Harvard 1781, then traveling in
Europe, returned 1787; JT was to see much of him in later years.

124. Possibly Sir Isaac Coffin, 1759–1839, captain (later admiral) in the Royal
Navy, then in France prior to his appointment to the command of the "Thisbe" in
1786.

125. Sir Anthony Van Dyck's celebrated portrait of Charles I, still in the Louvre,
engraved by Sir Robert Strange. One can readily understand JT's enthusiasm for this
portrait.

126. The "Labors of Hercules" by Guido Reni, from the collection of Louis XIV,
much admired in JT's day, now in the Louvre. It is interesting to note that Samuel
F. B. Morse, 1791–1872, Yale 1810, pupil of Benjamin West in 1811, painted a large
"Dying Hercules," the same subject as one of the three Guido Reni's JT admired. It
was evidently inspired by an engraving after Guido Reni by William Cooke, dated
1807, which he might have seen at West's studio in the newly published *Historic
Gallery of Portraits and Paintings . . . Ancient and Modern* (7 vols., London,
Vernor, Hood & Sharpe, 1807–19), illustrated. (It is the engraving which often
offers the key to painting in prephotographic days.) The painting was exhibited in
1813 at the Royal Academy (No. 359) and brought the young artist considerable
acclaim. The 8 by 6½ foot painting is now at Yale. See Dunlap, *Arts of Design*
(1918), 3, 90–91.

JT and Morse, 35 years his junior, were to become rival portrait painters and
antagonists in the controversies over the academies in the 1820's at New York.

127. Raphael Lamar West, 1769–1850, Benjamin's older son, painter, etcher, and
lithographer.

128. A large picture, 110 by 85 inches, painted 1627–28; now in the Louvre.

129. Collection of Louis XIV; now in the Louvre.

130. 1528–88; Louis XIV had a half dozen works by this "Painter of Pageants,"
Venetian school, at Versailles; all are now in the Louvre.

Caracci,[131] Le Brun; particularly the Tent of Darius,[132] so much admired by the French. The composition is undoubtedly very fine, but the drawing in some parts not correct, especially the right arm of Alexander; it is too small for the character, or even for the other parts of the figure; the coloring, as in the other pictures of this series, utterly bad; the characters and expression are all good —some of them admirable. I cannot like Paul Veronese; his outline is so universally and equally hard, that his figures have the appearance of being cut out in pasteboard, and stuck upon the canvass; his local colors are certainly fine. In this apartment one of his famous works hangs, as the companion of the Tent of Darius; but I cannot like it—his characters are often vulgar.

The gallery looking over the gardens, is most splendid; the material, solid variegated marble; the ornaments are bronze gilt, the statues marble, and very fine; the view from the windows, magnificently beautiful. The apartments of Madame Adelaide [133] are simple and elegant; her workshop, in which she is alternately joiner, carver, turner, engraver, &c., is curious and complete. The apartments of the royal children, neat and simple; the dauphin is a beautiful boy; Madame, no beauty, but pleasing; Monsieur,[134] very young and pretty. The theatre is very elegant, after designs by Le Brun, the ornaments are principally figures in bas-relief, gilt, and very fine.

131. There were four Carracci—Ludovico, 1555–1619, Agostino, 1557–1602, Annibale, 1560–1609, and Antonio, son of Agostino. It is interesting to note JT's interest in the work of the eclectic painters of the Bolognese school at this date.

132. Charles LeBrun's picture, from the collection of Louis XIV; now in the Louvre.

133. Marie-Adélaide, 1732–1800, the 8th child and favorite daughter of Louis XV and aunt of Louis XVI, one of the "filles de France," known as mesdames. For a description of Le Grand Cabinet de Mesdames (rooms 52 to 56 on the Galerie basse), see Charles Mauricheau-Beaupré, Versailles, l'histoire et l'art, guide officiel (Paris, 1949), p. 82.

134. Louis XVI and Marie Antoinette had but 3 children: the Dauphin, Louis Joseph, their first-born son and second child; Madame, Marie Thérèse Charlotte, the eldest child and only daughter, who later married her cousin Louis, duke of Angoulême, son of Charles X, and was known as Madame Royale; and Monsieur, Louis Charles, 1785–95, the 2d son, duke of Normandy, who, upon the death of his brother in 1789, became the Dauphin, and, after the execution of his father in 1793, was referred to by his émigré adherents as Louis XVII.

In the apartments of the Count D'Angervilliers,[135] *intendant des ponts et chaussées,* (of roads and bridges,) is a collection of the most precious things I have yet seen; a Holy Family with Angels, by Correggio,[136] in fresco, covered with plate glass, in point of taste and elegance is a most lovely composition; the Marriage of St. Catherine in oil, half figures, large as life, an enchanting picture —nothing can exceed the gracefulness of the three hands of the Virgin, St. Catharine and the Infant [137]—the coloring exquisite. Titian, Raphael, Julio Romano, the three Caracci, &c. &c.[138] have their place here; but, for color, composition and expression, nothing can excel a Rubens. Lot and his family leaving Sodom [139]—the tender regret, the pity, the reluctance, with which the good old man quits the place where he had so long lived, his eyes cast up to heaven, as if praying that even yet his countrymen might be spared, is wonderfully expressed. The amiable, the heavenly manner of the angel who hastily leads him forward, pointing to happier and more virtuous scenes; the trembling hesitation of the wife, who is even urged forward, by another heavenly comforter; the beauty and resignation of one of the daughters, and the meretricious carelessness of the other; the heavens filled with ministers of the divine vengeance, urging on the tempest of lightning and fire upon the devoted city, forms altogether a scene, the most sublime in imagination, the most perfect in expression, and most splendid in coloring, that I have ever seen from this great man! Vandyck, Teniers, &c., complete this precious little cabinet, with their most choice specimens.

The Royal Collection—*Maison de surintendance*—I had no im-

135. Charles Claude Labillarderie, comte d'Angiviller, died 1810, "directeur général des bâtiments du roi de France, jardins, manufactures et academies," *Biographie universelle, Supplément,* 1834, 56, 319–320.

136. Possibly Correggio's tiny "Sainte Famille," on *copper,* from the collection of Louis XIV; now in the Louvre.

137. Now in the Louvre, collection of Louis XIV. The disposition of the hands in this composition might have suggested a somewhat similar treatment in JT's "Sortie Made by the Garrison of Gibraltar," the first version of which he finished the following year, 1787, at London and gave to his master, Benjamin West.

138. Titian and Raphael, giants of the High Renaissance; Giulio Romano, 1499–1546, painter and architect, pupil and heir of Raphael; Ludovico, Annibale, and Agostino Carracci, founders of the Eclectic school of painting at Bologna.

139. "Lot departing from Sodom," dated 1625; now in the Louvre.

agination of ever seeing such works in existence. Here is Michael Angelo, a marble painted on both sides with the story of David and Goliah,[140] figures large as life, and in perfect preservation; for grandeur and correctness of drawing, admirable,—action, expression and composition, very fine, but the color not to be mentioned. Of Leonardo da Vinci, here are several heads and in perfect preservation; [141] and the picture,[142] of which the sketch is at Somerset House, a charming composition. Here too is the famous Holy Family by Raphael,[143] engraved by Edelinck. This exquisite work was painted on wood, which was perishing by worms and decay; it has been transferred to canvass lately, as well as many others, and is perfectly and successfully cleaned, and in fine preservation. Another large picture, and several small ones by him, are also here. Titian [144] has several fine heads. The Caracci, Guido, Julio Romano, Paul Veronese, Tintoret, Rubens, Vandyck, Teniers, Berghem, &c. &c.,[145] have here fine things. The collection is in fact composed of the finest works of the first masters, many of which are in perfect condition; and much care seems to have been and to be taken, to restore and preserve those which were in a decaying state. Some of the finest pictures, particularly of Raphael,[146] which had been done on wood, (thick plank,) were in a very bad state, and the

140. By Daniele Ricciarelli, called Daniele da Volterra, on *slate*, presented to Louis XIV in 1715 as the work of Michelangelo; now in the Louvre.

141. The heads by Leonardo da Vinci, 1452–1519, could have been "La Belle Féronnière" and the "Mona Lisa," from the collection of Francis I; now in the Louvre.

142. "The Virgin, the Infant Jesus and St. Anne," painted ca. 1506–10, from the collection of Louis XIV; now in the Louvre. The full-size cartoon on brown paper, ca. 1499, then in the Royal Academy's Somerset House, is now in Burlington House.

143. Known as the "Grande Sainte Famille de François Ier"; now in the Louvre. Gerard Edelinck, 1640–1707, engraver of Antwerp and Paris; see Charles LeBlanc, *Manuel de l'amateur d'estampes* (Paris, É. Bouillon, 1854?–90?), 2, 183.10.

144. Titian, 1477–1576; the "Portrait of Francis I" was in that monarch's collection. Louis XIV had 3 portraits in his, including the celebrated "Man with the Glove"; all now in the Louvre.

145. Guido Reni, painter of the Eclectic school; Jacopo Robusti, Il Tintoretto, 1518–94, Venetian; Nicolaes Berchem, 1620–83, Dutch genre and landscape painter and etcher.

146. Painting on a wooden panel covered with plaster (gesso) was the usual Italian Renaissance practice. There are a half dozen Raphaels on panels from the Royal Collections at Versailles now in the Louvre, "La Belle Jardinière," acquired by Francis I, being the most notable.

world owes much to the man, whose ingenuity has discovered a method of transferring them to canvass. By this means many are perfectly restored, and in a state to endure to future ages, for them to admire and imitate.

The gardens of Versailles must be seen; they cannot be described. I had expected to see immense monuments of labor and bad taste, where nature was overwhelmed in art; but I was disappointed. There is much more of nature than I expected; and the art, though perhaps too lavish, yet so vast, so magnificent, as to bear down all criticism. The *orangerie* is a noble work, worthy of those days when the baths of Rome were erected; the approach to the Egyptian statue, (which is fine,) has the gloomy solemnity and grandeur of an ancient temple. The bath of Apollo is very fine, both in idea and execution; the *petit bosquet* in which it is enclosed is charming.[147] The Fountain of the Giants [148] has grandeur of imagination, and the beautiful fairy-like scene, where the court sometimes dance, surrounded with trees and flowers—the colonnade with its numerous fountains—the grand cascade, are all delightful. The evening was advancing, and the growing obscurity of twilight left the imagination at liberty to vary and veil the forms of objects to suit its own taste. We left the gardens at half past eight, and were in Paris a little after ten, most heartily fatigued. I had indeed seen too much. It was an effort of no little difficulty to recall even the imperfect traces of memory, which I endeavor here to preserve.

Monday, August 13th. Again at the Louvre; saw the part of the Royal Collection which is there; among them are numberless inestimable things. Rubens, his wife and two children,[149] a beautiful small sketch which was sometime since in England, and for which

147. Designed by André LeNôtre, 1613–1708, for Louis XIV. The Bosquet des Bains d'Apollon are in marked contrast to the axial rigidity of the gardens. The little grove with its sculptured nymphs disporting themselves beneath a great artificial rock, is a contemporary work—to which JT always responded—of the romantic painter Hubert Robert.

148. Probably the "Fountain of Enceladus," 1675–76, in spite of the fact that there is but one giant. See Mauricheau-Beaupré, *op. cit.*, p. 140.

149. Rubens' second wife, "Helena Fourment and Her Two Children," 44½ by 32¼ inches, painted about 1636, purchased by Louis XIV in 1685.

the king paid one thousand pounds, is here; a very fine portrait by Vandyck,[150] some sweet things by Teniers,[151] seven specimens of the Chevalier Vanderwer,[152] from the collection of Sir Gregory Page.[153] Wouvermans, Berghem, Vandervelde, Ostade, Rembrandt,[154] &c. &c., are here in such numbers as to fatigue the eye, and all of the very first class. In another apartment, among many fine things, is the martyrdom of a saint, (I think Hubert,) by Rubens; [155] figures larger than life, grand and terrible in the highest degree. They have cut out the tongue of the sainted bishop, and one of the executioners gives it to a dog; the head of the saint, and that of the villain who has the bloody knife in his mouth, are wonderfully fine. Another apartment contains Poussin's [156] pictures of the elements, of which water or the Deluge, is generally considered a very fine work; a very beautiful landscape by Rubens [157] —an assumption of the Virgin by a multitude of little angels,[158] exquisitely colored, and his famous boors merry making, in the

150. There were a dozen or more portraits by Sir Anthony Van Dyck in the collections of Louis XIV, XV, and XVI.

151. David Teniers, the Younger; there are 15 in the Louvre, 6 of which belonged to Louis XVI.

152. The Chevalier Adriaen van der Werff, 1659–1722, painter and architect of Rotterdam; the "seven specimens" are in the Louvre, 6 of them from the collection of Louis XVI.

153. Sir Gregory Page, ca. 1695–1775, baronet (1714) of Greenwich. See G. E. Cokayne, Complete Baronetage (1906), 5, 24; and Frits Lugt, Répertoire des catalogues de ventes publiques (La Haye, Martinus Nijhoff, 1938), for the sales of 1775 and 1783. There is reference to the "Cabinet de M. Le Baron Gregoire Page . . . à sa Maison à Blackhead près de Greenwich" in the MS "Recueil de catalogues," 1, 5–8, with the note: "Cette collection n'existe plus, ayant été disparée par vente publique—Depuis quelques Années [1786]."

154. Van der Velde, a family of Dutch painters of the 17th century; Adriaen van Ostade, 1610–85, Dutch genre painter and etcher; JT did not admire the work of Rembrandt as he did that of Rubens.

155. Not a Christian martyrdom but the bloody story of "Thomyris and Cyrus" from Herodotus; a large picture, 110 by 78 inches, painted 1630–32, collection of Louis XIV; still in the Louvre.

156. Nicolas Poussin; his 4 paintings of the seasons, now in the Louvre, were in the collection of Louis XIV.

157. Possibly Rubens' fine "Tournament by the Castle Moat," painted 1636–39, from an "ancienne collection"; in the Louvre.

158. "La Vierge aux anges" or "Madonna with the Holy Innocents," 54 by 39 inches, painted about 1615, collection of Louis XIV; now in the Louvre.

manner of Teniers. This is one of the finest things imaginable, for color, composition, character, humor and landscape—painted on pannel, and in perfect preservation. The seaports of France, by Vernet,[159] and many fine things of the Italian and Flemish schools, are here.

Dined, in company with Mr. Jefferson, at the Abbés Chassí and Arnout in Passy; [160] a *jour maigre,* or fast day, but the luxury of the table in soups, fish and fruits, truly characteristic of the opulent clergy of the times. After dinner, visited Madame De Corny.[161]

Tuesday, August 14th. Morning, visited Mons. David, and Mons. Julien,[162] sculptor; afternoon, the Count Vaudreuil, Madame Le Brun, MM. Menageot, D'Hancharville, Mr. and Mrs. Cosway, &c.; saw the pictures, and had the politeness to commend them.

Wednesday, August 15th. At mass at the Eglise St. Roch,[163] with M. Boileau, to hear M. Balbastre; [164] introduced to him. Dined with the Count de Vaudreuil, in company with Madame Le Brun, the Abbé St. Nom,[165] Count Parois,[166] M. Menageot, M. Robert, and others.

159. Joseph Vernet, 1714–89, the ports of Marseilles, Toulon, Cette, Bordeaux, Bayonne, Dieppe, La Rochelle, Rochefort, etc., painted between 1754 and 1765; now in the Louvre; again JT's interest in contemporary art.

160. JT's spelling is quite incorrect for the Abbés Chalut and Arnoux. They lived on the heights of Passy, not far from Franklin's house, friends of Franklin, John and Abigail Adams, and Jefferson. JT's spelling of foreign proper names is notoriously bad. His mistakes are not only phonetic but typographical, arising from the transcribing of old diaries and papers and lack of careful proofreading. The monocular JT often complained of his eyesight; when he wrote the *Autobiography,* at the age of 84 or 85, it must have been getting much worse.

161. Wife of Louis Dominique, Éthis de Corny, "a liberal minded friend of Lafayette and the American Republic . . . , who had a pretty house on the rue Chausée d'Antin." See Malone, *Jefferson,* p. 70.

162. Pierre Julien, 1731–1804, a classical sculptor.

163. A florid baroque church built during the reigns of Louis XIV and XV by the architects Jacques Lemercier, Robert de Cotte, and his son Jules de Cotte.

164. Claude Louis Balbastre, 1729–99, celebrated organist, of St. Roch and later of Nôtre Dame.

165. Jean Claude Richard, abbé de Saint-Non, 1727–91, distinguished amateur etcher, writer, and philosopher, in charge of the Abbaye de Poultières, in the diocese of Langres.

166. JT probably refers to Jean Philippe Guy LeGentil, marquis de Paroy, 1750–1822, painter, engraver, and inventor, son of Guy LeGentil, chevalier de Saint-Louis, gentilhomme ordinaire de la Chambre de Roi, marquis de Paroy (in 1754).

Thursday, August 16th. Saw at M. Massard's,[167] the Murder of the Innocents, a copy from Rubens,[168] and touched by himself—a wonderful composition. Went again to the Palais Royal; saw an admirable landscape by Rubens; Hampton Court; King Charles I, in the character of St. George,[169] protecting his queen from the dragon, spectators, &c.,—beautiful works of Correggio, Raphael, Titian, Guido, &c.

Friday, August 17th. The Count de Moustier,[170] Marquis Cubiere,[171] M. D'Hancharville, M. Boileau, called to see my pictures [172]—expressions of great civility. Went to see the collection of the Duke de Praslin; [173] some exquisite pictures by Murillo,[174] &c.; the most extraordinary Rembrandt I have met with; Gerard Dow,[175] Teniers, Count ——, M. Robert, &c. saw my pictures. * * * *

Saturday, August 18th. Visited Sir John Lambert's [176] collection—a fine portrait by Vandyck; [177] a very fine Teniers, himself, wife and family, near his house; [178] a Holy Family, by Rubens; [179] a Visitation, by M. Fragonard,[180] a most striking picture, small;

167. Jean Massard, 1740–1822, engraver.

168. The original Rubens, *ca.* 1635, is now at the Alte Pinakothek at Munich.

169. JT's punctuation is confusing. He probably refers to the "Landscape with St. George," painted by Rubens in 1629–30 for Charles I. Horace Walpole of Strawberry Hill, Twickenham, is responsible for identifying the landscape as the banks of the Thames at nearby Richmond but a few miles down river from Hampton Court. The picture now hangs in Buckingham Palace.

170. Éléonore, François Élie, count, then marquis de Moustier, 1751–1817, general and diplomat, minister to the United States 1787–89.

171. Simon Louis Pierre, marquis de Cubières, 1747–1821, scientist, friend of artists and men of letters.

172. "Bunker's Hill" and "Quebec."

173. Renault César Louis de Choiseuil, duc de Praslin, 1735–91, general, or, more probably, Antoine César, duc de Choiseuil-Praslin, 1756–1808, his son.

174. Bartolomé Esteban Murillo, 1617–82, of Seville.

175. Gerard Dou, 1613–75, Dutch genre painter.

176. Sir John Lambert, 1728–99, grandson of Sir John Lambert (d. 1722), a wealthy merchant of London and director of the South Seas Company.

177. Unidentified.

178. "Teniers' Château at Perck" by David Teniers, Junior; now in the National Gallery, London.

179. Possibly the "Holy Family with St. George and Other Saints" by Rubens, from the Angerstein collection; now in the National Gallery, London.

180. Jean Honoré Fragonard, 1732–1806, painter and etcher, see Baron Roger

the effect aërial, mystical, &c.—cost three hundred pounds.

August 19*th*. Here my manuscript fails me; I presume that one if not two sheets, have perished entirely. Of the next fragment, one half of four pages are consumed vertically; that is, half of each line only remains. This begins with the 10th of September, commencing my journey to Frankfort. I very much regret the loss of these twenty days; for, after fifty years, memory unaided, can do little to restore the chasm. I distinctly recollect, however, that this time was occupied with the same industry in examining and reviewing whatever relates to the arts, and that Mr. Jefferson joined our party almost daily; and here commenced his acquaintance with Mrs. Cosway, of whom very respectful mention is made in his published correspondence. In the course of this interval, I became acquainted with the Count de Moustier, afterwards minister to the United States, and his sister, the Marquise de Brethon.[181] She was a most interesting little woman, who had been married to an abandoned brute, with whom it was impossible for any woman of delicacy, or of any sense of virtue, to live. She was therefore separated from him, and went with the Count, her brother, soon after to the United States, where she became unpopular in consequence of her dispirited, retired, melancholy manners, which, if her domestic history had been known, would, I trust, have endeared her to my fair countrywomen.

By M. de Moustier, I was presented to the Count de Vergennes,[182] the Baron Breteuil,[183] and other great men of the day. I became known also to the Marquis de Biceore,[184] and de Cu-

---

Portalis, *Honoré Fragonard* (Paris, J. Rothschild, 1889), 2, 291, "La Visitation de la Vierge. Tableau d'un mérite éminent tant par la pureté du dessin que par la finesse de la touche et l'intelligence de la lumière qui est portée à la plus haute perfection . . . vente Lambert et du Porail (1787) 6000 livres . . ."

181. Madame de Bréhan, not his sister but sister-in-law (which "aroused considerable comment"), an artist, friend of Maria Cosway. See Malone, *Jefferson*, pp. 197–198.

182. Charles Gravier, comte de Vergennes, 1717–87, minister of foreign affairs under Louis XVI, 1774–87.

183. Louis Auguste de Tonnelier, baron de Breteuil, 1733–1807, diplomat.

184. Unidentified; JT's spelling is most certainly incorrect.

biere,[185] who married a beautiful young woman, daughter of the Countess de Bonouil,[186] herself one of the most splendid women I ever met, and moving at this time in the first and highest orders of society. In 1795, being in Paris soon after the death of the miscreant Robespierre,[187] I found the beautiful Madame de Bonouil in an obscure garret, with barely the means of existence. In 1799, I met her in London, living in a pretty house near Hyde Park, apparently at her ease. Soon after she was sent to St. Petersburg by Buonaparte, who knew well how to choose his agents. She was there at the coronation of the Emperor Alexander,[188] and wrote to her court the following account of the ceremony: *"L'Empereur y marchoit en grand procession. Les assassins de son père le precedoient. Ceux de son grand père le suivoient. Et les siens l'entourent de tout part."* [189] (The Emperor walked in grand procession. The assassins of his father walked before him. Those of his grandfather followed him. And his own surrounded him on all sides.) This letter was intercepted, and the beautiful diplomatist was conducted in safety to the frontiers, and there dismissed, with the injunction never to enter the Russian dominions again, under penalty of losing her exquisite head.

September 9th. Left Paris in the diligence for Metz, on my route to Frankfort sur Maine,[190] where (at the great fair) I had appointed

185. Michel de Cubières, 1752–1820, poet, writer, and dramatist, associated with, but not the husband of, Fanny de Beauharnais, joined her salon and became its leading figure in 1781; went with her to Italy in 1789; upon his return aided the revolutionists.

186. Possibly JT refers to Marie Françoise (Mouchard) Beauharnais, called Fanny de Beauharnais, 1737–1813, authoress, wife of Claude Beauharnais, from whom she was separated; her salon, at her father's house in the Montmartre, was famous. She had 2 daughters, Marie Françoise, born in 1757, and Anne Amédée, born in 1760.

187. Maximilien François Marie Isidore Robespierre, born 1758, beheaded 28 July (10 Thermidor) 1794.

188. Emperor of Russia, 1801–25.

189. More correctly: "L'Empereur y marchoit en grande procession. Les assassins de son père le precedoient. Ceux de son grand père le suivoient. Et les siens l'entouroient de toute part."

190. Frankfurt-am-Main or Frankfort-on-the-Main, manufacturing and commercial city in Hessen-Nassau.

to meet M. Poggi.[191] The environs of Paris on this route are uninteresting. Dined at Meaux, a small dirty city. The country through
which we travelled in the afternoon was fine; slept at La Ferté en
bois.

Sept. 11th. Country uninteresting. Dined at Epernay, in Champagne, where lived M. Lochet Duchumet,[192] one of our fellow
passengers, a considerable wine merchant. He insisted upon my
visiting his wine cellar, and tasting his champagne wine. The cellar
is cut two stories deep, in that solid white rock of which Paris is
built, and which underlies a considerable part of France. At the
depth of this lower cellar the temperature is always equal, and the
wine is kept in perfection; it was the finest I have ever tasted; the
price in the cellar is six francs per bottle. Supped and slept at
Chalons. The canal which is here commencing, to connect the
Maine with the Loire, with the bridge across the Marne, are elegant, useful, and noble works. The country from Epernay is mountainous, much resembling the county of Litchfield. In this part of
Champagne, on the southern side of the hills, grows the fine blue
grape: the meadows on the banks of the Marne are principally rich
pasture and meadow; the country behind rising, and covered very
much with cornfields, but a poor soil. From Chalons to Clermont in
Auvergne,[193] the country is rough but beautiful; covered with
corn, orchards of apples and pears, vineyards and wood, delightfully interspersed: it reminded me of the North River near Fishkill.
Clermont is a fortified town, small, but strong,—a fine hospital
here, . . . a part of the . . . who was with the legion de Lauzun.

191. Anthony Poggi, JT's publisher, though hardly mentioned in this account,
went ahead to arrange about the engraving of the "Battle of Bunker's Hill" with the
Stuttgart engraver, Johann Gotthard von Müller, 1747–1830. This was the main
purpose of the trip. "I will beg you to inform Mr. Trumbull that I have already had
two conferences with Mr. Muller and that he will undertake the engraving of Bunker's Hill at the price of 1000 pounds and which I have agreed to give him rather than
lose so great an artist. . . ." Copy of a letter (evidently sent to JT), dated Stutgard
31 July 1788, from Poggi to his wife at London. (Yale Library.) The high prices
demanded—and received—by reproductive engravers of the 18th century are
worthy of note.

192. Lochet du Chenet, given in B. C. Gournay, *Tableau général du commerce,
des marchands, négocians, armateurs . . . Années 1789 et 1790* (Paris, 1790), as
one of the 8 "négocians en vins" at Epernay.

193. Clermont-en-Argonne.

The road leads through a beautiful, variegated rough country to Metz. I had taken cold, and the jolting of a wretched carriage had given me such a severe pain in my back, that on our arrival, I was hardly able to get out of the diligence. My suffering caught the attention of an old invalid soldier, who served the hotel as a sort of *valet de place:* he assisted me, and offered to cure me—which he did, by administering when I got into bed, a basin of hot tea, apparently of peppermint, which brought on a profuse perspiration, and effected a cure.

Metz being a frontier town, is very strongly fortified, and garrisoned with several thousand men. The Moselle, on which it is situated, is not navigable, and therefore it has little commerce; the principal part of the town is occupied by public and military buildings, the Hotel du Government, new, &c. In the morning I learned, that being so near the frontier, no public carriage was established to any farther point, and therefore my journey to Frankfort was interrupted. Spent the day in strolling about the town. Went to mass in the cathedral; found the building old Gothic; service uninteresting as usual; music pretty good. Viewed the fortifications, barracks, and found every thing connected with the military in excellent condition.

Sept. 14th. Left Metz for Frankfort, in a small neat chariot with a pair of horses, which I engaged to carry me in three days for six Louis d'ors, being a Louis a day for six days, to go and return. To lighten the expense, I admitted as a companion a German musician, returning from Paris to Erfuth—a heavy, silent man, speaking French no better than myself, and for German, a most wretched provincial *patois:* neither of us had any knowledge of the part of the country through which lay our road, and we formed a strange association. For a few miles, the road was good and the country pleasant; afterwards poor and sandy. Breakfasted at —— four leagues from Metz, in a house which poverty and filth seemed to have chosen for their residence: very bad food, scarcely two cups to be found in the house, and apparently not a decent utensil or article of furniture,—great quantities of wild pears, of which we made good use. Stopped at ——, where are some decent houses and a convent of Benedictines; a regiment of cavalry stationed here, are the principal support of the town. Stopped at a miserable village entirely German; supped *maigre*, being Friday: the house almost destitute of furniture or comfort of any kind. All this day the country poor and road bad. Eleven leagues from Metz.

Sept. 16th. In the morning passed through Saarbruck, the residence of ——, a pretty little town; houses neat and good, some of them really elegant and of good architecture. There are several very pretty seats in the neighborhood. The small river Saar, on which the town stands, is navigable for boats, and has a handsome bridge. In the neighboring hills are iron mines, several fine forges for iron and steel, and of course, considerable commerce. The road is sandy and bad; the country clear, with tolerable crops of Indian corn, pumpkins, &c. At four o'clock supped at St. Embright, on very good coffee, bread and butter, &c.; the china handsome; the inhabitants appear to live comfortably;—the country woody and sandy—principal food of the poor appears to be potatoes, and bread of Indian corn, but bad; the soil is poor until very near Erbach. In this vicinity is the palace [194] of the Duke de Deux-pont,[195] prince of this country, and cousin of Count Maximilian Deuxpont,[196] colonel of the regiment royal Allemand, one of the four superb infantry regiments who served in America under the

194. Residence of the counts of Erbach.

195. French Deux-Ponts, German Zweibrücken, Roman Bipontium. Charles Theodore, the elector palatine, from 1777 to 1799, succeeded to the dukedom and electorate of Bavaria at the death, in 1777, of Maximilian III Joseph, the last of the Bavarian line of the Wittelsbachs.

196. Maximilian Joseph, 1756–1825, head of the Zweibrücken branch of the Wittelsbach family, inherited Bavaria and the palatinate; elector from 1799 to 1805; king of Bavaria, as Maximilian I Joseph, from 1806 to 1825. JT is confused; Count Maximilian Deux-Ponts, born 1756, king of Bavaria, was not a colonel in Rochambeau's forces (See *My Campaigns in America: A Journal Kept by Count William de Deux-Ponts, 1780–81*, Boston, J. K. Wiggin & Wm. Parsons Lunt, 1868, pp. xii–xiii.) The two who fought in the American war were Christian, comte de Forbach, marquis de Deux-Ponts, 1752–1817, morganatic son of Christian IV de Deux-Ponts, served in America from 1775 with the rank of colonel, promoted to brigadier general of infantry for his conduct at Yorktown 1781; and Guillaume, comte de Deux-Ponts, 1754–1807, colonel Royal-Deux-Ponts from 1777 to 1782. See Baron Ludovic de Contenson, *La Société des Cincinnati de France et la guerre d'Amerique, 1778–1783* (Paris, Auguste Picard, 1934), p. 169. The portrait of one of the Colonel Deux-Ponts (it is impossible to determine which) was included by JT in his "Surrender of Lord Cornwallis at Yorktown," No. 1 in the Key.

Count Rochambeau; [197] this residence appears to be fine and finely situated. The Count Maximilian [198] was made king of Bavaria by Napoleon; the present king is his son, the king of Greece his grandson. Supped at Erbach on milk soup, that is, boiled bread and milk, fresh pea soup, broiled chicken, and a sallad of potatoes half boiled, sliced; raw onions, do. dressed with oil and vinegar, very good.

Sept. 17th. Rose at five o'clock; dined at ——. The country more mountainous, wooded and sandy. Afternoon, passed over a very rough country resembling the highlands of New York; the road bad, running between two mountains rising high upon the sides of a small stream. Stopped and slept at a solitary post-house, in the wildest and most picturesque situation. Rose at four o'clock, the 18th, and set off for Turckheim: a few miserable houses are scattered along the roadside, which runs through an almost desert, among the wildest mountains, as far as Frankenstein: here we left the mountains and entered upon the valley of the Rhine. The country is now rich with vines and various cultivation;—several villages in sight. Manheim visible in the distance, backed by a range of very high mountains, (Heidelberg and part of the Black Forest, the eastern boundary of the valley.) The prospect is rich and luxuriant; but the crops which we pass are lean and bad, the weather having been unfavorable, produce and vegetation is backward. The vintage of Champagne and all this country, is made towards the end of September.

Sept. 18th. Four leagues from Worms. The country here is rich, and abundantly cultivated in vines, corn, potatoes, turnips, radishes, &c. The manner of planting vines is different from what is usual in Champagne, and generally throughout France; they are here planted like Indian corn, in rows, but not quite so distant. Each vine is trained to about three feet high, beyond which height the plant is seldom permitted to rise; the field has thus the appearance of a cornfield. In some places, the field in ploughing is divided into lands; on the edge of each land is one row of vines, the space between is devoted to corn, potatoes, turnips, &c., and

197. Jean Baptiste Donatien de Vimeur, comte de Rochambeau, 1725–1807, commander of the French forces in the Revolutionary War.
198. Prince Otho, son of Louis I of Bavaria, became king in 1832.

here the row of vines is permitted to rise higher, and to spread themselves upon slips of board extended from prop to prop, a kind of espalier. At four o'clock passed through the city of Worms, the first impression of which was favorable. At almost every window we passed, was a beautiful and well dressed young lady;—whether our eyes were prejudiced by the long tract of desolate frontier country, through which we had passed, we could not decide; but we thought the women here were in general remarkably pretty. The town is old, the houses neglected, ill built, and apparently in decay. The cathedral [199] is a very clumsy, heavy, Gothic building; we stopped a few minutes to see the interior, but found we could not have admittance unless we waited longer than was convenient, and we concluded from the style of the exterior, that we did not lose much. The fortifications,[200] which were Gothic, were miserable and in ruins. It would give great pleasure to see rising upon the ruins of war, the habitations of peace and industry; but such pleasure is not to be expected in a country like this, where the inhabitants hold even their lives at the will of an arbitrary and despotic prince. "Sic nos non nobis," is a reflection which is painfully forced upon the mind at every step. The soil is abundantly luxuriant in various productions; but in the midst of plenty, the inhabitants, although numerous, appear to be wretched: to support the pride and pomp of one family, the happiness of the people is sacrificed.

September 19*th.* At six o'clock reached Openheim, a wretched old Gothic town, once walled, now in decay. We here crossed the river Rhine, which is at this place twice the width of Hartford ferry, very deep and rapid. The boat was of a singular construction: a platform of twenty five or thirty feet square is laid upon two boats placed parallel to each other; over this platform is erected a sort of gallows of strong timber, twenty feet high, over which passes a strong hawser, at one end connected with a windlass, at the other, and at a considerable distance, to a boat, and this boat is made fast

199. The cathedral of Saints Peter and Paul is one of the finest examples of Romanesque architecture in the Rhineland.

200. Again JT's military eye for fortifications, though ancient.

again by an iron chain to another, and so on for six or eight; the last boat is firmly anchored or moored in the middle of the stream, there is no tide in the river, and the force of the current acting upon these boats and their rudders, which are presented obliquely to it, maintains a constant effort to carry the whole down the river—counteracted by the connected boats; this communicates a swinging motion to the ferry-boat, which sets it across the river in a very short time. On each side of the river is a short wharf, one end of which is secured to the shore, the other supported by a large boat, of the same height above the water as the platform of the ferry-boat, which rising or falling as the surface of the river, carriages may be driven in and out with perfect ease and safety.

The country from this landing to Gohrah, two and a half leagues, is like the other side of the river, a perfect garden, and the road fine. At Gohrah, for the first time in all this ride, I met children coming from school. Education and liberty would convert this country into an earthly paradise; but, an ox saddled and harnessed in a cart like a horse, formed a sad contrast of ignorance.

From Gohrah at twelve o'clock, for Frankfort, six leagues. After the first two miles, the road was very deep sand; soil poor, covered with a growth of white birch and small stunted pines. Walked a great part of the distance, and amused myself with trying to talk German with a corporal and his party of soldiers, of Hesse Darmstadt. At the distance of a mile and a half came in view of Frankfort, most delightfully situated in a beautiful fertile valley on the banks of the Maine, the distance formed by high mountains; the whole scene recalling most forcibly the beauties of my native country. As we approach, the town appears large and handsome, and on entering the gate of the small town opposite, we find it strongly fortified; the river passing through the town, is crossed by a bridge, very high, and built of stone. Passed through a considerable part of the town, to arrive at the lodgings which had been secured for me by M. Poggi, where I found myself very well accommodated; the town very full of strangers, come to attend the fair.

The 21st was passed in running about the town, and seeing the

engravings in aqua-tinta of two clever artists; those of Madame
Prestor [201] have very great merit. Saw also the collection of pictures
of Mons. Stadle,[202] the only one in the town; it contains some
tolerable pictures, and good architectural drawings; the proprietor
a very amiable, gentleman-like man. The environs of the town are
extremely beautiful; the land divided into small portions of one
half to two acres, cultivated in the highest perfection and most
charming variety, and on most of these little spots, a tastefully
ornamented summer-house. The Jews' quarter is a very narrow
street, or rather lane, impassable for carriages, with the houses
very lofty, old-fashioned and filthy, not more than a quarter of a
mile long,—no cross avenue or alley, and a strong gate at each end,
carefully closed and secured at tattoo-beat, after which no one is
allowed to go out or enter, and whoever is found out of the quarter
after this time, is secured by the city guard and confined. This
quarter is said to contain ten thousand of this miserable people;
how such a number can exist in such a narrow space is almost incredible, yet here (at one of the entrance gates) I saw them
crowded together in filth and wretchedness, calculated to generate
disease. And how were they to escape from a fire, after the two
only avenues were closed for the night?—Men, women and children must be in imminent danger of perishing. The sight of such
misery was most painful, and the reflection of the possible, nay,
probable, consequences appalling.

In the evening I went to the theatre, (strange transition!) which
is a very neat small building; the actors tolerable; music excellent;
company numerous and genteel—some elegant women—many
very well dressed and beautiful young creatures; the whole *coup
d'œil* striking.

Sept. 22d. Went to see the cathedral; old, Gothic, overloaded
with bad ornaments.[203] In this building is performed the corona-

201. Maria Catherina Prestel, 1747–94, wife of Johann Gottlieb Prestel (separated in 1786), both etchers in aquatint.
202. Johann Friedrich Städel, 1728–1816, Frankfurt banker, founder of the Städel
Art Institute, containing a notable collection of Old Masters.
203. A many pinnacled building of the 13th to 15th centuries.

tion of the king of the Romans; the choir of the cathedral, the council-room, &c. are remarkable for their great antiquity, and the council-room is decorated, or rather filled and crowded, with vile portraits of all the emperors. Here is also kept sacredly, the Golden Bull, or Magna Charta of Germany, dated 1230, and containing the constitution of the empire.

Frankfort contains forty thousand inhabitants, free, and carrying on an extensive commerce with the interior of Germany. The fairs are held spring and fall, continuing three weeks; that of the fall is the most important, during which it is calculated that at least ten thousand persons are attracted to this temple of commerce, from all parts of Europe, besides a great number of nobility and gentry, who resort to the place for amusement. The city is generally well built, with some broad handsome streets, and magnificent public buildings and hotels, of which the Maison Rouge is the finest. I dined once at this house, at the *table d'hôte*, with at least two hundred persons of all descriptions, from princesses and princes of the empire, who were there from curiosity, down to Jews and Gentiles of all descriptions, from the merchant to the pedlar, all seeking whom they might devour, at least plunder. The river Maine, on which the town is built, is about as wide as the Connecticut at Hartford, and from eight to ten feet deep at ordinary times —smooth, but somewhat rapid.

I embarked at 10 o'clock for Mayence on the Rhine, on board a boat filled with two or three hundred people of all classes and nations, without one acquaintance, and speaking hardly a word of German. Fortunately, there were among the number some very genteel and intelligent people speaking French, and in their society I passed the day very agreeably. Down the river to Mayence, the country is fertile and beautiful, with several picturesque small towns.

Arrived at Mayence at four o'clock; was conducted by M. C. Haberle [204] of Erfuth, a gentleman of the university here, and a

---

204. Carl Constantine Haberle, born at Erfurt in 1764, was then a student at the University of Mainz (founded in 1477 and closed in 1796, revived in 1946), became a professor at the University of Budapest in 1814.

fellow passenger in the boat, to see the cathedral,[205] of rich but heavy Gothic architecture; no paintings of value; the choir of new Gothic Grecian.[206] There are, in some of the chapels, pictures in fresco [207] of some merit; and a —— not yet finished, by the principal canon of the cathedral, is a beautiful little work, of real Greek taste. The citadel stands upon the height of ground above the town, and is a fine specimen of modern fortification. Within the citadel is preserved what remains of an ancient tower, said to be the monument of Drusus; [208] in the neighboring country are many remains of ancient Roman works and buildings.

Mayence is the Maguntium [209] of Cæsar, and when the water of the river is low, the remains of a Roman bridge [210] may still be seen, at the lower part of the town, supposed to be of his time, and indeed to have been constructed by him across the Rhine. The view from the citadel is fine, overlooking the city, the river, and opposite country. The principal street of the town is handsome; upon it are placed the electoral stables, and in the lower part, on the bank of the Rhine, stands the electoral palace,[211] externally an old, irregular Gothic building; the interior said to be decent, not magnificent; I did not enter it, but made a slight drawing [212] of the river front. The city contains thirty thousand inhabitants, a nunnery with its

205. Cathedral of St. Martin, a Romanesque building of the 11th century. Trumbull seems to have had little understanding of the Romanesque style.

206. "Gothic Grecian" is a contradiction of terms. He undoubtedly refers to the Brendelsches Chorgestühl, a curious combination of rococo with fluted Ionic pilasters. The principal choir stalls, by Ludwig Hermann, 1767, are consistently rococo. A mixture of late rococo with the neoclassical is to be found in the work of Adam Friedrich Oeser, 1717–99, of Leipzig.

207. JT probably meant wall painting (in oil) and not *buon fresco* (water color on wet plaster).

208. The Citadel built about 1660; the Drususstein is said to have been erected by the Roman legions in honor of the stepson and general of the Emperor Augustus, Drusus Senior, 39–38 B.C., who fortified the Rhine.

209. The Roman Castrum Mogontiacum or Magontiacum.

210. Built by the Emperor Domitian in A.D. 83–89.

211. There is some confusion here. The Electoral Palace is a rigid Renaissance building begun in 1627 and finished in 1678, enlarged in 1750–52, see illustration. *Enciclopedia italiana* (1934), *21*, 940.

212. Sketch not located.

dependencies, an university, &c.—mechanics, shopkeepers, &c., and has considerable commerce.

Sept. 23d. Embarked for Cologne, in a boat, i. e. a batteau with oars and an awning. Again very fortunate in my companions; the person whom I first met was M. Herry [213] of Antwerp, at whose house my friend, Major Brice [214] of Maryland, formerly lived when studying painting in that city—I found M. Herry a very agreeable young man, speaking both French and English tolerably, and possessing great love for the arts, and considerable skill in painting. Our other companions, Mons. and Madame Payen [215] of Maestricht, a very pleasant couple, who spoke French well, returning from a visit to his parents in Switzerland; and with them, under their protection, was a beautiful and amiable young lady, very like Mrs. Langdon [216] of Portsmouth; she had been for two years at Lausanne with an aunt, and was the daughter of General Gresnier,[217] in the service of Holland, residing at Breda, and commandant of Gertruydenbergh. Several others were on board the boat, to our great vexation, for we had understood it to have been engaged for our party exclusively; however, as they were all decent people, we reconciled ourselves to our fate, soon became acquainted, and at ten o'clock left Mayence. The morning was fine, the sky and the river clear and undisturbed, the country surrounding us rich, various, and bright, in the distance lofty mountains terminating the scene; the banks of the river covered with villages, and boats and barges crossing and recrossing, some coming up the river, others following us down.

At twelve o'clock we spread our little repast, consisting of a pair of roasted chickens and some veal, with good bread and some bottles of fine wine; the want of plates and dishes was supplied by bits of clean paper, the knives out of our pockets, and two tumblers

213. Probably Antoon Herry, historical painter.

214. Jacob Brice of Baltimore, who served in various Maryland regiments from 1776 to 1783, an original member of the Society of the Cincinnati of Maryland.

215. Unidentified, possibly a member of the large family of architects from Tournai. JT made a pencil sketch of Mrs. Payen; now lost.

216. Elizabeth Sherburne, wife of John Langdon of Portsmouth, N.H.

217. David Grenier, 1721–90, a Swiss (family from Vaud).

we had to divide between the ladies and gentlemen. The singularity of our meeting, the oddity of our table, the whimsical mixture and confusion of languages, with the delightful beauty of the weather and the scene, all conspired to make our dinner the most charming party possible, and no travellers ever were happier than we. At two o'clock we went on shore a few minutes at Bingen, a small town on the west bank of the river, seven leagues from Mayence, at the entrance of the highlands, which are picturesque in the highest degree, far superior in grandeur to the highlands of the North River. The stream is contracted to a very narrow space, restrained between high mountains, rocky, wild, precipitous, and every summit ornamented with the ruins of some ancient Gothic castle, overhanging the river and subject country, like the eyrie of an eagle. The river just below Bingen runs rapidly; the channel is interrupted by rocks, but not dangerous; on one of these (not larger than Pollipell's island) [218] is a formidable structure in stone, intended probably for a prison in ancient days.[219] Soon after entering the channel between the mountains, the weather became obscure, then squally, and at four o'clock the wind blew violently in gusts, and we were very happy, when with some difficulty we reached a little landing-place on the west side, where we got safely on shore; the ladies were excessively frightened, and in truth with good reason. There was no house near to shelter or defend us from the storm; a few osiers, which had been cut and made into bundles by basket-makers, were all we could find to protect us from the rain. We reassured the ladies, drank a tumbler of wine, and walked on in a little foot-path until the wind abated, the lovely little girl leaning on my arm for support; we resembled a scene of ancient story, knights and damsels, and difficulties and dangers. We soon recovered spirits to amuse ourselves with our adventure, and recollecting passages of poetry and romance, we returned cheerfully to our boat. The weather cleared, and we went on pleasantly to

218. Pollepel (Polopels, now Bannerman's) Island is just above West Point, near the east bank of the Hudson River, Putnam County, N.Y.

219. The Mouse Tower or Mäuse-Turm, early 13th century, built for the purpose of collecting river toll. According to legend Archbishop Hatto of Mainz was devoured alive by mice in the 10th century.

Bacherach, a village on the west shore, four leagues below Bingen, where we landed at seven o'clock. The ladies, after their fatigue and alarms, went immediately to rest; we supped pleasantly, and slept soundly.

At six o'clock next morning breakfasted together, and pursued our voyage. The morning was squally, but the mountainous scene through which we were passing was picturesque in the highest degree; every moment presented some new change of form or effect, some ruined castle in a new point of view—scenes sometimes pleasant, sometimes terrible, always grand. The gleams of sunshine and alternate squalls, which at times concealed, and then again unveiled the mountains, enriched the beauty of the day, but destroyed its pleasures and even comforts, for the frequent rain rendered our boat damp and cold, and the sudden violence of the wind was at times dangerous.

At twelve we repeated our little dinner, but not with the same pleasure as before. The sky was gloomy, the water rough, the wind frequently violent, with heavy rain, so that we were glad to shrink and cower under the canvass shelter of our awning, which was often in danger of being blown away. In the afternoon the weather became still more unpleasant. We landed for a few minutes, at Coblentz; the town large and well fortified, the citadel strong, and the castle of Ehrenbrietzen [219a] on the opposite shore, placed on the lofty summit of an almost inaccessible rock, frowning on all below, river, town and country, with a stern and solemn grandeur. Coblentz is eleven leagues from Biberach, and twenty-two from Mayence. We resumed our seats in the boat, and went on to Neuwidt, a beautiful little village on the eastern shore, like Esopus.[219b] Here we landed at seven o'clock; the evening dark, rainy, tempestuous; found our way to an inn, and inquired for Madame, the mother of Mademoiselle Gresnier, who had arranged to meet her daughter here, and conduct her to Breda. Having established the ladies in a comfortable room, I ran with M. Payen to the *pension*, (boarding-house,) where we found the mother, an elegant elderly

219a. The ancient Fortress of Ehrenbreitstein.
219b. On the Hudson River, 8 miles south of Kingston, New York (see p. 35), which reminded JT of Neuwied on the Rhine.

woman, a sister somewhat older than Mademoiselle, and two fine chubby little boys, brothers, who were here at school. The people of the house were agreeable, and all, as well as Madame Gresnier, received the news of the young lady's arrival with the transports of real and undisguised affection. A carriage was immediately sent for the ladies, and M. Payen and myself were *commanded* to stay to supper and accept beds. The ladies soon arrived, and the meeting was the most tender and interesting I ever witnessed; the transports of filial and maternal affection were seen in their most lovely forms, and we passed an evening of such amiable, virtuous joy, as I shall never forget. An elegant little English supper closed the scene, and I took leave of this most estimable family and society, not without deep regret; all the parties gave me their address, and received mine in exchange. We parted, I believe with a mutual, sincere hope, that we might meet again.

Sept. 24th. At seven o'clock, M. Herry and myself embarked at Neuwidt; the weather still rainy and cold, with heavy wind. We found it advisable to land at nine o'clock at Andernach, a small town one league below Neuwidt, on the opposite shore. Service was performing in the church; we attended for an hour, and at ten returned to our boat; found that the wind had rather increased, and the water was very rough, but once more we attempted to descend the river. Soon, however, we found our situation very disagreeable and hazardous; the wind increased to a very heavy gale, the water was violently agitated, and we were glad to reach the shore again, at a little village opposite, at the distance of a mile. The gale increased to such a degree, (blowing directly up the river,) that we gave up all hope of being able to proceed by water, and inquired if it were possible to obtain post-horses; and to our great mortification learned that Andernach, which we had just quitted with no small risk, was a post-town, and that there was no practicable road down the east side of the river where we are, nor any horses. It remained, therefore, only to recross the river, and this was not only unpleasant, but dangerous. The desire to get on our way, and our reluctance to spend one, perhaps two or three days, in a miserable dirty little village, at length determined us to hazard the attempt. M. Herry having on board the boat a chaise, (cabriolet,) in which he had travelled from Dresden to Mayence, was so kind as to offer me a seat in it, and the river was all that obstructed our going forward. We therefore hired a larger boat, with fresh and skilful hands, shifted our baggage on board her, embarked, and in a few minutes found ourselves safe on shore, a short distance below Andernach, where we landed the chaise and our baggage. Meantime the tempest increased, with violent rain; I had not even a great-coat, and was thoroughly wet before we could finish our labor and secure our effects above the bank of the river, and out of its reach. There were no houses near, but at length we observed at some distance a little chapel, by the roadside, which might afford some shelter from the rain; we ran thither, carrying with us our little basket of eatables, and a couple of bottles of wine, and there made our dinner, waiting for horses, which we had sent for to the town. The little chapel proved to us the most delightful refuge; some poor Italian travellers on foot, were driven to the same shelter by the storm; we shared our provisions and wine with them, and enjoyed more satisfaction in this wretched little hovel, than is perhaps commonly seen in palaces. After waiting two hours, until one o'clock, we at last got horses, mounted the chaise, and proceeded on our journey, leaving our bottles, basket, glass, the fragments of our dinner, a small box, &c., in the entrance of the chapel, as a memorial of gratitude for the shelter which we had received, and for the benefit of any poor creature who might be our successor. The wind, still furious, blew directly in our faces, and the front of the cabriolet was open, but we were safe on land, and that reflection, when we looked towards the river, which the continuance of the gale had by this time rendered terrible, comforted us for the cold and rain to which we were still exposed. We went on in this weather six hours, to Remagh, eighteen miles, or six leagues. Here for want of horses, we were again detained nearly two hours; having resolved to travel all night, we at length obtained horses, and went to Bonne, the residence of the Elector of Cologne. Arrived there at twelve o'clock; the storm still continued, and we were most excessively cold; the gates of the town were shut, but after some delay we gained admission, and were directed to an inn, where we found a fire and something to eat, which was the summit of our wishes; we warmed ourselves, devoured a leg of mutton, drank a couple of bottles of excellent *vin du Rhine*, and at two o'clock proceeded to Cologne, arrived at sunrise, procured fresh horses and went on to Dormagh, breakfasted, changed horses and went on to Dusseldorf, where we arrived at two o'clock, having travelled twenty five leagues in as many hours. The last twelve hours had been free from rain and violent wind, but very cold. Passing in this rapid way, and in the night, there was very little opportunity to form a just opinion of the country; I can only say, judging from the time we were passing through it, that Bonne is not large, and upon the same principle, that Cologne is; the latter is old and very ill built, but well paved. The road which we have passed, is in general good, frequently close on the bank of the Rhine; the river under you and a precipice of rock hanging over you, and frequently hardly width to admit two carriages to pass. From Cologne to Dusseldorf, the country is flat, highly cultivated and beautiful; the mountains continue as far as Bonne, from thence to Cologne the country is somewhat rough. We no longer see any vines.

Sept. 25th. At Dusseldorf, a small pleasant town, pretty well built, paved and fortified; the only thing to be seen in it is the electoral palace, and of that, there is nothing worth notice, except the gallery of paintings,[220] which is extensive and truly fine. The gallery is divided into five apartments, of which the first contains a number of choice works of eminent masters, Italian and Flemish, among which several hunting pieces, the animals by Snyders,[221] and one with figures, by Rubens; portraits, by Vandyck; [222] a large historical composition, by G. Crayer; [223] the Wise and Foolish

220. The arrangement of the pictures on the walls of this once famous gallery may be seen from the beautifully engraved plates in Nicolas de Pigage, *Estampes du catalogue raisonné et figuré des tableaux de la Galerie Electorale de Dusseldorff*, 1778. The pictures were removed to Munich in 1805 and now hang in the Alte Pinakothek.

221. Frans Snyders, 1576–1657, Dutch painter of animals, friend and coworker of Rubens.

222. There are 29 pictures, including 18 portraits, by Van Dyck at Munich.

223. Possibly a mistake on JT's part; the only picture at Düsseldorf by Caspar de Crayer (ca. 1584–1669), of Antwerp, at the time of his visit, was the "Virgin and the Infant Jesus, Enthroned, Surrounded by Several Saints," *Estampes du catalogue raisonné*, No. 12, Pl. III; picture now reattributed; present location unknown.

Virgins, by Schalken;[224] one very fine Teniers,[225] &c., are the finest of this division. In the second are several fine works by Vandyck, as the dead Christ and attending angels, a superb picture; Susannah and the Elders, St. Sebastian, the Virgin and Child, &c. Here is also the celebrated master-piece of Gerard Dow,[226] admirably painted, but the subject detestably low. In the third is a beautiful Christ and Magdalene, by Barroccio,[227] sweetly colored; the Murder of the Innocents by Annibal Caracci,[228] grand expression and coloring; St. John in the Desert, by Raphael,[229] beautiful drawing, character and expression, and tolerable color; single figure, young, and large as life; Ascension of the Virgin, by Guido,[230] not one of his choice works; and a multitude of other fine things, which it would require a volume to characterize, and a year to view. The fourth is devoted to the Vanderwerfs, which, of all the celebrated pictures I have ever seen, appear to me to be the very worst—mere monuments of labor, patience, and want of genius. Two Rembrandts,[231] one a Crucifixion, the other a Descent from the Cross, small figures, are very fine. A Jordaens,[232] the Satyr and the Pedlar, is charming, equally for color, expression and design; the figures are large as life; the subject perfectly suited to the painter. The fifth apartment may properly be called the monument of Rubens,[233] and magnificently worthy of him; it contains near fifty of his most extraordinary works, and nothing by any other hand. They are of such variety in subject and style, as

224. Godfried Schalcken, 1643–1706, Dutch painter and etcher, *ibid.*, No. 12, Pl. XXIV. Again, with reattribution; location unknown.
225. There are 14 pictures by David Teniers the Younger at Munich.
226. Gerard Dou; of the 4 pictures at Munich, 2 hung at Düsseldorf, the "Herring Woman" and the "Mountebank," either of which fits the description.
227. "Noli me tangere" by Federico Barocci, 1526–1612, of Milan.
228. No longer attributed to Annibale Carracci, but to Daniele Crespi, *ca.* 1590–1630, of Milan; *ibid.*, No. 114, Pl. XII; now in the State Picture Gallery, Schleissheim.
229. No longer attributed to Raphael; *ibid.*, No. 165, Pl. XIV; not in the Alte Pinakothek, Munich, probably in some provincial museum under another name.
230. Attribution to Reni no longer valid; *ibid.*, No. 201, Pl. XVI; not listed in the Munich catalogues of 1911 or 1936; present location unknown.
231. Rembrandt Harmensz van Rijn, 1606–69, of Amsterdam.
232. Jacob Jordaens, 1593–1678, of Antwerp.
233. There are 75 paintings by Rubens at the Munich gallery.

would almost inspire a doubt of their being the fruits of one mind, but that we see the hand and the color which are so peculiarly and exclusively his. The subjects vary, from the very lowest ribaldry and profligacy of human nature, to the most sublime conceptions of religion and poetry. The first on the right hand of the entrance is a small picture, figures not more than a foot high—a marauding party of soldiers pillaging the house of a peasant; the commander, a vulgar profligate, is seated in a pompous attitude, in the assumed character of a gentleman, and directing a scoundrel of the lowest class in his attempt to search the person of the unhappy dame of the cottage, who struggles stoutly, but in vain, against the brutal strength of the ruffian; all the accompaniment of birds and animals of a rustic yard, are intermingled with the plunderers, and the whole has such a hurry of vulgar distress, the expressions and characters so appropriate, that one would suppose the painter to have passed a life in studying similar scenes. But what a transition do we see in a neighboring picture, the Resurrection of the Just,[234] which is painted on a pannel not more than twenty by thirty inches —upright, the ground white—an unfinished sketch or study. In parts of some of the figures the outline is visible on the white ground, untouched—no correction, no repetition of line—correct and elegant, and graceful as Raphael. This most exquisite work consists of young women and children, aided by intermingled angels, mounting from earth to heaven; the forms are all correct as Raphael, all elegant as Correggio; the drawing of the most refined purity and grace; the color pure, delicate, and rich, but not gaudy—in some parts very thin, in others the ground visible; and all this accompanied with such expressions of joy, of gratitude, of humility, as are rarely seen. The entire group seem to be in motion, and you gaze lest they should escape and soar out of human sight; the whole effect is aërial, the color delicately bright and luminous. This appears to have been the study for a companion of the neighboring picture of the Fall of the Damned, which is

234. Or "The Assumption of the Righteous," a panel 46½ by 36¼ inches. The "Fall of the Damned," 112½ by 88¼ inches. JT had good reason for his enthusiastic admiration for these masterpieces. See *Katalog der Älteren Pinakothek zu München* (Munich, 1925).

larger, and more finished—a scene as tremendous as the other is lovely. The drawing in this is less correct, but the color, the characters, the expressions, the attitudes, tremendously fine. In the upper part is a figure in the attitude of the fighting gladiator, reversed, struggling against a demon, who endeavors to drag him to the immeasurable gulf; in others, the various vices of mankind are characterized, going reluctantly to their reward; near the bottom are laughing devils, dragging by their hair their wretched victims up a stream of liquid and burning brimstone; while the lowest part of the surface is filled with lions, tigers, and other savage beasts, tearing and devouring promiscuously each other and the miserable dregs of human nature. As a whole, this picture presents to the eye and mind, a scene of horror never before imagined. In other parts of this room are various other works—history, portrait and landscape—all fine, but those which I have attempted to describe, transcendently so. If I possessed the Resurrection of the Just, small and unfinished as it is, I would not give it in exchange for the entire Luxembourg gallery, for the Family of Lot [235] at Versailles, nor indeed for any or almost all the specimens of the art which I have seen. This little picture establishes the claim of Rubens to a place among the highest, most chaste, and most correct of the profession; no hand but his has touched, no mind but his could have conceived, these two wonderful compositions.[236]

The reflection here occurs to me, that there is in nature, in the laws of optics, an insurmountable difficulty in rendering a large work equal to a small; in small, the eye is near its object, and without change of place can compare the parts with the whole; not so in large,—while at work, the eye must be almost equally near the surface, but can form no judgment of the relation of the parts to the whole, without removing to a distance. I am not certain that I am right, but at present I believe the theory.

The garden of the Elector, near the town, is the only other place worth notice. Living is here very cheap, and the wine of the country

235. "Lot departing from Sodom," 4 figures and 2 angels, 29½ by 47 inches, dated 1625, is a comparatively dull picture; now in the Louvre. See Edward Dillon, *Rubens* (London, Methuen, 1909), Pl. 284.
236. This observation concurs with contemporary opinion.

not only cheap but excellent; access of artists to the gallery perfectly easy, forming great attractions for the residence of young
students. I lodged at the great fair of Heidelberg, and remained
in Dusseldorf three days, most beneficially employed.

Sept. 29th. At four o'clock, A. M., M. Herry having sold his
cabriolet, we mounted (for the first time to me) a German post-
waggon, for Aix la Chapelle; the most detestable carriage, I believe,
that is now used in any civilized country. It was indeed a mere
waggon, and a very bad one, without springs of any kind, covered
with painted canvass instead of windows, and the apertures closed
with sides of leather. We were eight passengers inside, and five
out—crowded, jolted, and bruised most unmercifully; the weather,
violent wind, with rain and cold. Quitted the banks of the Rhine
near Dusseldorf, dined at Juliers, a small fortified town, eleven
leagues from that place, and in the evening reached Aix la Chapelle,
now famous for little else than its baths, which are convenient and
medicinal, and its gambling houses, which are as systematic, extensive, elegant and infamous, as almost any in Europe. The country through which we have travelled to-day, is finely cultivated and
flat, until we approach Aix, when it begins to be undulating and
broken; the town is not fortified, but large, ill built, and dirty.

Sept. 30th. At half past six, we mounted the diligence for Liege
—(that for Maestricht, which we wished to have taken, being full)
—the day windy and wet; the company of Brabant, and all speaking
French. The country through which we pass, is the territory of
Liege, beautiful and finely cultivated, but the road bad. Entered
Liege at seven o'clock, by a long and good bridge over the Meuse,
which runs through the town.

October 1st. Could get no carriage to go on towards Antwerp,
every body being gone to Aix la Chapelle, to see an ascension of
Blanchard's balloon.[237] Amused ourselves with going first to see
the citadel, from whence is a fine view of the town, and of a most
delightful, variegated, and well cultivated country; the Meuse,

237. Jean Pierre Blanchard, 1753–1809. The military-minded JT was interested
in such instances. In 1784 he started but never finished a composition, "Lunardi's
Balloon," from an ascent made at London by the Italian balloonist, Vincenzo Lunardi,
1756–1806.

larger than the Thames at Richmond, and navigable, wanders through a most fertile valley, and divides the town into two large and several small parts, crossed by one long bridge of six arches and several small ones. The citadel stands on the highest ground near the town, and is a pretty good fortification, but very much out of repair. It contains a well, which is very curious, being cut (principally through rock) to a depth level with the river, which cannot be less than five hundred feet, I believe much more, as a bundle of straw, ignited for the purpose of shewing us the depth, was forty seconds in falling to the water. The palace of the prince bishop [238] is an old Gothic building, forming a square, larger than the Exchange of London; the style very bad, the apartments unadorned. The cathedral [239] and some other churches which we ran through are very bad Gothic; not one tolerable painting could we find, nor any thing grand and noble, except the gates of some chapels in the cathedral, which are of brass and fine; a grand balustrade of brass and marble likewise surrounds and encloses the choir of the cathedral. The town is old, large, ill built and dirty, containing more beggars and fewer pretty women than any other of equal size I ever saw. The manufactures are principally of iron; coal is found in abundance, but, before they burn it, it is broken into a coarse powder, mixed with clay, and formed into cakes, like brickbats; thus is formed a fuel incomparably more filthy than the coal alone, and which renders both inhabitants and streets, and atmosphere, dirty in the extreme. Here is also a manufacture of calimanco.[239a] In the evening we went to the theatre; very little company, but the actors and music tolerable; the piece, Richard Cœur de Lion.

On the 2d of October, we took the diligence for Brussels. The country, soon after quitting Liege, from hilly becomes flat, and so continues, beautifully cultivated. At about nine leagues from Liege, we entered the Emperor's dominions, where the custom-

238. Palais des Princes Évêques, a flamboyant Gothic building, now the Palais de Justice.

239. Cathedral of St. Paul, 13th century, finished in the flamboyant style of the 16th.

239a. Calamanco, a glossy woolen stuff, much used in the 18th century.

house officers were particularly careful in their visit; the wiseacres pretended to mistake me for some foreign dealer in small wares or jewelry, returning from the fair at Frankfort, and searched my little trunk and baggage with great care; they found a trifling piece of cambric, on which they demanded the duty, amounting to five pence and a half, and by their useless severity lost a *douceur* of much more value, which I should have given them, had they behaved with civility. Came on to Louvain, famous at present for its university,[240] general stupidity and strong beer. The town is in a very ruinous state, the buildings old and Gothic; the Maison de Ville, however, is a very fine specimen of ancient Gothic.

Oct. 3d. We left Louvain, and travelling through a rich and beautiful country, we arrived at Brussels at eleven o'clock. This town is large, clean, well paved, and the streets tolerably broad; the old part of the town ill built—the quarter adjoining the park very elegant. The park [241] itself is a beautiful little square, elegantly variegated with three grand walks, which unite in front of the Maison de Conseil,[242] (an elegant building,) and a number of smaller irregular ones. At the end of the park is the Vauxhall,[243] an imitation of that in England. The buildings which surround the park are new and of good architecture; the situation elevated and superb. The cathedral [244] church is an ancient Gothic building, richly but heavily decorated within; many paintings, but none very good, except one by Rubens, (Christ's charge to Peter,) [245] and in this the drawing is inferior to his works in general, and the color not in his best style, but the characters and expression are

240. The celebrated university founded in 1426.

241. Laid out a dozen years earlier, in 1774.

242. The Palais de la Nation, the present meeting place of the Belgian parliament, erected in 1779–83, and therefore very new. JT admired the neoclassical architecture of his own day.

243. Le Vaux Hall, situated in the Parc Royal, was built in 1780 after the design of the architects Vanderstraeten père and Montoyer and transformed into a theater in 1782; it still exists and is used for art exhibitions.

244. The Church of SS. Michael and Gudula, "Ste. Gudule," often misnamed "cathedral," a 13th- to 17th-century building.

245. The Rubens' "Christ's Charge to Peter" or "Feed My Sheep" is now in the Wallace Collection, Hertford House, London.

fine. Here is also a small head of a lady by Vandyck,[246] very good; some landscapes, with sacred stories, by Artois; [247] a picture by Otho Venius; [248] and others by J. Van Cleve,[249] and several of the early masters.

October 4th. We saw the court or palace; [250] it is near the park, contains some very elegant apartments, with very fine tapestry of Brussels and of the Gobelins,[251] and two pieces of inlaid wood, very uncommon; they are historical compositions, executed at Neuweid by David Routgen,[252] in 1779, after the design of Jan Zeck,[253] of the same place. These compositions are very good, the

246. Portrait of Anne-Marie Schotte (or Schotti), painted in 1627–28, believed to have been destroyed in 1794, possibly survives; see Henri Velge, *La Collégiale des Sts. Michelet et Gudule à Bruxelles* (Brussels, A. Dewit, 1925), p. 299, and Max Rooses, *Van Dyck* (Brussels, 1902), p. 85.

247. A series of 9 landscapes (said to represent the environs of Brussels) by Jacques Arthois, 1613–84?, of Brussels, 7 of which still survive in the Church of Ste. Gudule.

248. "The Carrying of the Cross" by the Flemish painter, Otho van Veen, 1556–1629, is now in the Musée des Beaux-Arts at Brussels, having been taken from the church in 1794.

249. There are 4 pictures by Joos Van Cleve (Jan Van Cleef), 1646–1716, dated 1698, still in the Chapel of the Magdalene, see Velge, *op. cit.*, p. 300, and J. B. Descamps, *Voyage Pittoresque de la Flandre et du Brabant, avec des réflexions relativement aux arts et quelques gravures* (Rouen and Paris, Desaint, 1769), p. 57.

250. The Palais du Roi dating from 1740.

251. The making of tapestries gave great distinction to Brussels in the 16th and 17th centuries. The Manufacture des Gobelins, the most renowned of the French tapestry factories, was established by Louis XIV.

252. David Roentgen, 1743–1807, a German-born "ébeniste" of great originality, succeeded his father, Abraham Roentgen, in 1774, as head of the cabinet works founded by the latter at Neuwied-sur-Rhin. The greatest vogue for this type of intarsia (true inlay) and especially marquetry (a later development, a veneer process) was between 1780 and 1790. It is possible that the two "pieces of inlaid wood . . . historical compositions" which JT saw are those now in the Vienna Museum für Kunst und Industrie, representing the "Continence of Scipio" (a subject which JT once painted) and the "Rape of the Sabines"; they have the inscriptions: "Jan Zick delineavit et David Roentgen fecit in Neuwied Ao 1779"; they were ordered by Prince Charles of Lorraine for the wall decoration of the Audience Hall in his palace at Brussels; inherited by the Archduke Albert of Saxe-Teschen; reproduced by Hans Huth, *Abraham und David Roentgen* (Berlin, Deutscher Verein für Kunstwissenschaft, 1928), Pls. 92, 93.

253. The painter and architect Januarius Zick, 1730–97, worked with David Roentgen after 1773 supplying designs for the cabinetmaker.

drawing correct and spirited, heads and characters fine, the extremities well finished, the figures half the size of life; they are executed in various colored wood, upon a ground of pale straw-colored satin wood, and so well as to produce a very pleasing effect of clair-obscure. Saw very few pictures; one by Verague [254] of Louvain, a bad thing, though in this country he has reputation.

The Maison de Ville [255] is Gothic; the Tower fine; the Chambre des Etats [256] is a very handsome apartment. Here is a portrait of the present emperor,[257] by Herreyns [258] of Mechlin, who is the most esteemed painter of the present day in this country; the picture approaches nearly to the style of Dance,[259] but not so good. The theatre is handsome, larger than any I have seen except those of Paris and London, the actors and music good, the company genteel, and very well dressed. The general language of all genteel people is French, and almost all speak some English. The little theatre on the park, where the actors are children, is pretty, and the performances amusing. In the church of Petits Carmes [260] is another fine picture by Rubens, (Christ appearing to his disciples,) [261] beautifully composed and colored, but not well drawn; the altar-piece, the Assumption of the Virgin,[262] is called Rubens' also, and his composition it certainly is, and very fine, but I believe the execution to be principally by some scholar; the parts are doubtless by his own hand. Here also are copies of several other works of this master, one especially representing the triumph of the church over

254. Either Jean Joseph Verhaghen, 1726–95, or his brother, Pierre Joseph Verhaghen, 1728–1811, both popular painters from Louvain. Pierre became the official painter to Prince Charles of Lorraine.

255. The Hôtel de Ville, a remarkable and noble monument; the lofty tower was completed in 1454. Although appreciative JT had no great enthusiasm for the Gothic.

256. Salle du Conseil Communal, the old Salle des États de Brabant.

257. Joseph II, 1765–90, son of Maria Theresa, emperor 1780–90.

258. Guillaume Jacques Herreyns, 1743–1827.

259. Sir Nathaniel Dance-Holland, bart., 1734–1811, son of the elder George Dance and brother of George Dance, architects.

260. Église des Carmes, rue des Petits Carmes, demolished in 1811.

261. "Christ Appearing to His Disciples" by Rubens has disappeared.

262. The "Assumption of the Virgin," partially painted by Rubens, from the Carmelite Church, now hangs in the Musée des Beaux Arts, Brussels. There were 10 copies after Rubens hanging in the church before the pillage of 1794.

infidelity, bad in truth, but valuable because the original has been destroyed by fire; painted by a monk of this order.

Oct. 5th. Visited several other churches, old, Gothic, bad as are the paintings which load and encumber them. Saw also the collection of Mons. Lavocat,[263] in which are several pretty little specimens of the Flemish school, and among others is one by Jan Schooreel,[264] who was born in 1495, spent some time in Italy, and died in 1562. The subject is a Descent from the Cross; the composition exactly the same as that of Rubens' celebrated picture in the cathedral of Antwerp. M. Lavocat read to me a history of the picture, by which it appeared that it was in the cabinet of Rubens at the time of his death; the probability is, therefore, that he took this as his model for the great picture; differences there certainly are, and all in favor of Rubens; but still, not only the composition of the whole, but of every figure, is essentially the same in both, the variations being in the arrangement of the hair, the folds of the drapery, the character not the airs of the heads, and the tint of the background, which in the small picture is universally very dark; the heads of the Savior and Mother are also surrounded by a glory in gold. There are two or three other private collections in this town, but very difficult of access.

The new palace of the archduke at Laaken,[265] three miles from the city, near the canal at Antwerp, is an elegant building; the park and gardens are in the English style, very simple, finely varied, spacious and noble; the building and its decorations are not indeed yet finished, but enough is done to convey a fine idea of simple grandeur and good taste. Unfortunately for the gratification of our curiosity, the court dined there, so that we could not see the apartments. The Chinese tower,[266] or pagoda, on the high ground behind

263. Unidentified; probably JT's error, "Monsieur l'avocat ——?," and the lawyer's name left blank.

264. Jan van Scorel; the picture is now in the Museum Kunstliefde at Utrecht, Holland.

265. The royal château at Laeken, built by the architects Montoyer and Payen, in 1782–84, for Duke Albert of Saxe-Teschen.

266. An early example of chinoiserie, possibly designed by the architects of the château, erected in 1784 (it had 11 stories), taken down before 1794 when the

the palace, has a fine effect, and commands a most extensive view; in fine weather, Antwerp may be seen distinctly.

In the evening we went to the theatre, where an opera was very well presented; the music and actors fine. I became acquainted with Madame Ploetinks,[267] Rue de la Madeleine, one of the handsomest and loveliest women I ever saw—the precise style of beauty which Vandyck so loved to paint.

The most obvious remark which a stranger makes in this elegant place, is its wonderful cheapness; for very decent lodgings three nights, three suppers, and one breakfast, I paid only five shillings sterling, and for a dinner, which I was curious to see, only ninepence; the dinner consisted of soup, boiled mutton and turnips, *bouilli* with greens, roast mutton, veal and fowls, all very good, with a dessert of excellent bread, butter and cheese, nuts, pears, &c., and we drank as much very good strong beer as we pleased. How such a dinner could be given for such a price is to me inconceivable. The best houses around the park, and some of them are very elegant, let for £150 per annum. A single man, who does not keep a horse, may live here very genteelly for £100 per year.

October 6th. Took the barge for Antwerp on the beautiful canal, the banks adorned with country seats; quitted the boat at two o'clock; at —— crossed a small branch of the Scheldt, and took the diligence for Antwerp; the road fine, bounded by rows of trees so closely planted as to shut out the view of the country almost entirely. At five o'clock arrived at L'Hotel de l'Empereur, Place de Mer.

In November, 1786, I returned to London; my brain half turned by the attention which had been paid to my paintings in Paris, and by the multitude of fine things which I had seen.

I resumed my labors, however, and went on with my studies of other subjects of the history of the Revolution, arranged carefully the composition for the Declaration of Independence, and prepared it for receiving the portraits,[268] as I might meet with the

château was sold; the present 5-storied pavilion was erected for Leopold II in the 1860's.

267. Unidentified; Pletinckx?

268. This is an important statement as to the artist's mode of procedure. JT's

distinguished men, who were present at that illustrious scene. In the course of the summer of 1787, Mr. Adams [269] took leave of the court of St. James, and preparatory to the voyage to America, had the powder combed out of his hair. Its color and natural curl were beautiful, and I took that opportunity to paint his portrait in the small Declaration of Independence. I also made various studies for the Surrender of Lord Cornwallis,[270] and in this found great difficulty; the scene was altogether one of utter formality—the ground was level—military etiquette was to be scrupulously observed, and yet the portraits of the principal officers of three proud nations must be preserved, without interrupting the general regularity of the scene. I drew it over and over again, and at last, having resolved upon the present arrangement, I prepared the small picture to receive the portraits. Some progress was also made in the composition of some of the other subjects, especially of the battles of Trenton [271] and Princeton,[272] for which I made many studies upon paper.

---

earliest sketch, on the same paper as a floor plan of Independence Hall by Jefferson, dated Paris, September 1786, is at Yale. Other sketches of the interior of Independence Hall, all of 1790, are in the Historical Society of Pennsylvania, Philadelphia. The original painting, finished before 1797, is at Yale; replicas are in the Rotunda of the Capitol at Washington (with figures the size of life), painted in 1818, and at the Wadsworth Atheneum, Hartford (figures half the size of life), painted in 1832.

269. John Adams, 2d president of the United States.

270. 19 October 1781. The original, finished in 1797, is at Yale and the large replica, finished in 1820, at Washington. Two interesting studies, both of 1787, are in the Detroit Institute of Arts. Jefferson owned a study (10 by 20 inches) of this date, exhibited at the Boston Athenaeum in 1828 (No. 310), now lost. The small oil (20 x 30 inches) for the engraving is at Yale. For other studies see Sizer, *Works . . . of Trumbull*, pp. 75–76.

271. Original at Yale, replica, 1830, at the Wadsworth Atheneum. One preliminary sketch is at Yale; 3 others known to exist are unlocated.

272. In 1786–87 JT executed a preliminary study of the "Battle of Princeton," which, being too large for the engravers, he left unfinished. The final picture was painted in the decade 1787–97; both are at Yale. An enlarged replica, painted 1830–31, is at the Wadsworth Atheneum. The Princeton University Library possesses 6 preliminary sketches, Col. Ralph H. Isham and Hall Park McCullough, both of New York, one each. These "studies on paper," with sketches in ink and in pencil at Yale, form the most complete record which survives of the artist's method of picture making. See Sizer, "Trumbull's 'The Battle of Princeton,'" *Princeton University Library Chronicle*, 12 (1950), 1–5.

In May of this year, (1787,) M. Poggi told me the story of the
sortie from Gibraltar,[273] which had taken place in 1781; we were
walking in Oxford street, in early twilight—I went to my lodgings,
and before I slept, put upon paper a small sketch of the scene, now
in possession of the Atheneum, Boston.[274] I was pleased with the
subject, as offering, in the gallant conduct and death of the Spanish
commander, a scene of deep interest to the feelings, and in the
contrast of the darkness of night, with the illumination of an extensive conflagration, great splendor of effect and color. I therefore
proceeded to paint a small picture in colors, on cloth, fourteen by
twenty one inches; [275] this was carefully finished, and afterwards
presented to Mr. West, as an acknowledgment of gratitude for his
liberal and parental instruction and kindness. I soon discovered,
however, that I had committed a great error, in dressing my principal figure in *white* and scarlet, supposing that to have been the
uniform of the Spanish artillery. I therefore, in conformity with the
advice which Mr. West had always given me, instead of attempting alterations, determined upon painting a second study,[276] on a

273. The sortie made by the British garrison took place on 27 November 1781.
JT explained to his brother Jonathan: "Give the Devil his due . . . upon this principle I shall paint a passage or two of British History—the Sortie of the Garrison of
Gibraltar . . . I shall do first" (London, 27 February 1787), and "I am now busy
in a picture of the Sortie made by the Garrison of Gibraltar in '81—addressed to the
Vanity and Nationality of John Bull; this is agreed to be engrav'd here by the best
of the English Artists . . ." (London, 3 September 1788—both letters Yale Library.)
    The high point, aesthetically speaking, in the long career of JT was reached in
his 30th year, in 1786, with the painting of "Bunker's Hill," "Quebec," and "Gibraltar." Washington Allston, painter, author, and pupil of Benjamin West, wrote from
London on 25 August 1801 to Charles Fraser, the miniature painter, at Charleston,
S.C.: "By the by, how long do you suppose Trumbull was about his 'Gibraltar'? It
is truly a charming picture; but he was a whole year about it, therefore it ought to
have been better. I have no idea of a painter's laboring up to fame. When he ceases
to obtain reputation without it, he becomes a mechanic. Trumbull is no portrait
painter. By this picture alone he has gained credit. But it is indeed credit purchased
at a most exorbitant interest." Jared B. Flagg, *The Life and Letters of Washington
Allston* (New York, Scribner, 1892), pp. 45–46. Allston, like JT, was a Harvard
graduate (in 1800, 27 years after JT). His comments upon JT's work (excepting the
latter's portraits in miniature of the 1790's) are, on the whole, just.
    274. And is still there in a bound volume containing many sketches of this action.
    275. Now lost.
    276. Now at the Cincinnati Art Museum. JT wrote his brother on 27 February
1789: ". . . I have labour'd for a long time past, & have now almost compleated a

cloth twenty by thirty inches, the size of my American works; and as I knew that by painting them, I had given offense to some extra-patriotic people in England, I now resolved to exert my utmost talent upon the Gibraltar, to show that noble and generous actions, by whomsoever performed, were the objects to whose celebration I meant to devote myself. I therefore studied this with great care, and obtained successful portraits of the officers who were engaged. This picture pleased, but I was not satisfied with all its parts; my Spanish hero seemed to express something approaching to ferocity, and several other parts appeared to me not well balanced; it was sold to Sir T. Baring [277] for five hundred guineas. I resolved upon painting a third, on a surface six feet by nine,[278] which would give

Picture which [in] spite of prejudice, begins to be look'd upon with pleasure & to be rank'd as one of the best modern productions of the Pencil. I have been offer'd a very princely price for it: but it is my next business to avail myself to the full extent of the public partiality, & I have therefore declined selling it with the Hope of finding a better reward from the curiosity of the Town. The annual exhibition of the Royal Academy has become a regular public amusement, & in a great City like this, being frequented by a vast number of people, is productive of a considerable sum, usually about £3,000 pr An.—this first gave M. Copley, our countryman, the Idea of exhibiting his famous picture of the death of Lord Chatham, & it prov'd a very profitable speculation . . . I confess I tremble for the consequences of the experiment . . . every tongue of Envy will be busy in recalling all my past sins of Rebellion in America . . ." (Yale Library.) Writing at London 36 years later, in 1825, James Elmes noted in "Character of Trumbull, the American Historical and Portrait Painter," *The Art and Artists*, 3, 199–200: "Mr. Trumbull, although an American, studied and pursued his profession for a long time in this country . . . [he] was a man of considerable power. His well-known 'Sortie of Gibraltar,' the original sketch of which has lately been exhibited at the Suffolk Street exhibition, was a very fine picture, but worth, it is true, everything else that he has ever done." Copley's "Gibraltar" represented the repulse of the Spanish floating batteries on 13 September 1782; JT's was of an incident occurring on 27 November 1781; Sir Joshua Reynolds' celebrated portrait of Lord Heathfield, holding a symbolic key of Gibraltar in his hands, painted in 1787, is in the National Gallery, London.

277. Sir Thomas Baring, 1772–1848, baronet (1793), of Stratton Park, was in the East India Company's service, 1790–1801, and partner of Baring Brothers, London. He was known for his fine taste and magnificent collection of pictures.

278. Deposited by the Boston Athenaeum with the Museum of Fine Arts, Boston. A spirited, well-composed and executed painting, the most successful of the artist's large-scale historical groups. The intertwining hands in the center of the composition are reminiscent of those in Tintoretto's "Bacchus and Ariadne" in the ducal palace at Venice, a picture which JT must have known through an engraving. Benjamin West had a large collection of engravings after the Italian masters.

to my principal figures, half the size of life; in this, my Spanish hero was thrown in an attitude like the dying gladiator, (the head studied from my friend Lawrence.) [279] Being finished in the spring of 1789, it was exhibited at the great room, Spring Garden,[280] entrance of St. James' park; and notwithstanding that I was a foreigner, not only without family connections or friends to support me, but with the remembrance of my adventure in 1780 still rankling in some minds, it attracted the public attention in a satisfactory degree. The military were partial to it, and I seldom looked into the room without being cheered by the sight of groups of officers of the Guards, in their splendid uniforms.

At this time, the king had a severe attack of that distressing illness, which some years after proved fatal; a regency was talked of; and even the ministry of the regent were arranged in common conversation. Lord Moira,[281] afterwards the Marquis of Hastings, who had served in the American revolution, was expected to be minister at war; and at this time, gave a splendid dinner to a number of military officers of rank. My picture became a subject of conversation at table, and caught his lordship's ear. "What painting is that of which you speak so highly, gentlemen?" He was told the subject. "And who is the artist?" Upon being told my name, he said with feeling, "Gentlemen, nothing done by that man, ought ever to be patronized by officers of the British army." I was told this anecdote

279. JT noted in a sketch book, now at the Boston Athenaeum, where the study of Lawrence is to be found: "The above Head was sketched in 1789 from Sir Thomas Lawrence with whom I was then intimate; and who did me the Favor to act as model for my dying Spaniard; in the last picture. I have lately been told by Mr. Robert Gilmor that Sr Thomas informed him that he had never set for his portrait, except on this occasion to me:—this therefore may be regarded as an unique resemblance of that very eminent and estimable man." Robert Gilmor, Junior, 1774–1848, Baltimore merchant, partner in the shipping house of Robert Gilmor & Sons, a liberal patron of art and collector of note, a friend and patron of JT; see Anna Wells Rutledge, "Robert Gilmor, Jr., Baltimore Collector," *The Journal of the Walters Art Gallery*, 12 (1949), 19–40.

280. The hall was hired from Thomas Hammersley from 11 April to 4 July 1789 for £150 4s.

281. Francis Rawdon-Hastings, 1st marquis of Hastings and 2d earl of Moira, 1754–1826, fought in the American Revolution. Trumbull painted him in his "Bunker's Hill," No. 17 in the key.

the next day, by my friend, Lieut. Col. Smith [282] of the Guards, who was present at the dinner, and at the same time lieutenant governor of the Tower.

After such an interdict, I of course saw few gentlemen in military uniform at my exhibition; it succeeded, however, better than I had reason to expect. A very fine engraving was afterwards made from the picture by Sharpe,[283] and the picture itself is now placed in the gallery of the Atheneum at Boston, by which institution it was purchased.

Among those who saw this picture at Mr. West's, before its public exhibition, was the celebrated connoisseur, Horace Walpole,[284] afterwards Lord Orford, who, on being asked his opinion, declared, "that he regarded it as the finest picture he had ever seen, painted on the northern side of the Alps."

Before the picture was exhibited, I was offered twelve hundred guineas, (six thousand dollars,) for it, which I refused, under the persuasion that the exhibition, the print, and the ultimate sale of the picture,[285] would produce more; the event has proved, that I made a mistake.

282. Mathew Smith, major of the Tower of London, 1793–1812; see Thomas Preston, *The Yeomen of the Guard: Their History from 1485–1885* (London, Harrison & Sons, 1885), p. 158. His name does not appear in the War Office records.

283. William Sharp, 1749–1824, of London, "on the purely technical side . . . one of the most accomplished of all the reproductive line-engravers of the eighteenth century . . ." Arthur M. Hind, *A History of Engraving & Etching* (Boston & New York, Houghton Mifflin, 1923), p. 205.

284. Horace Walpole, 1717–97, author, critic, and collector, of "Strawberry Hill," Twickenham, 3d son of the statesman and great collector of pictures, Robert Walpole. The younger Walpole exerted a tremendous influence on the arts. JT owned and read his *Anecdotes of Painting.* Walpole's high opinion of JT's "Sortie from Gibraltar," certainly one of his finest historical compositions, must have been pleasing to him. JT's name, along with that of his painter friend, James Northcote, 1746–1831, appears in the "Book of Visitors at Strawberry Hill, 1784–1796," under the date of 31 August 1787. The entry is marked "and myself," which indicates that Walpole acted as guide, as he did only for intimate friends or highly distinguished visitors. See Horace Walpole, *Correspondence with Mary and Agnes Berry,* W. S. Lewis and A. Dayle Wallace, eds., 2, 229, Yale Edition of Horace Walpole's Correspondence, 12 (New Haven, Yale University Press, 1944).

285. Purchased in 1828 by the Boston Athenaeum for $2,000. See Mabel Munson Swan, *The Athenaeum Gallery, 1827–1873* (Boston, Athenaeum, 1940), pp. 111–

In the autumn of 1787, I again visited Paris,[286] where I painted the portrait of Mr. Jefferson [287] in the original small Declaration of Independence,[288] Major General Ross [289] in the small Sortie from Gibraltar, and the French officers in the Surrender of Lord Cornwallis, at Yorktown in Virginia. I regard these as the best of my small portraits; they were painted from the life, in Mr. Jefferson's house.[290]

I was again in Paris in the early autumn of 1789, and witnessed the commencement of the French revolution—the destruction of the Bastile,[291] &c.—and on one occasion attended the Marquis de

---

112. In later years Trumbull made 3 or 4 replicas of this picture. One of the poorest, painted about 1840, probably after the William Sharp engraving as the original was unavailable, is at Yale. See Sizer, *Works . . . of Trumbull*, pp. 76–77.

286. He might have seen the "Death of Socrates," executed that year (now at the Metropolitan Museum in New York) in the studio of his friend David. JT's "I Was in Prison and Ye Came unto Me" (now at Yale), painted at New York in his old age, seems to indicate this.

287. JT's most successful portrait of the statesman.

288. 21⅛ by 31⅛ inches, at Yale. Note that JT calls it simply the "Declaration of Independence," never the "*Signing of* the Declaration of Independence."

289. Charles Ross (d. 1797), major general 1781; lieutenant general 1793. On the night of 26/27 November 1781 he commanded a force of some 2,000 men in a sortie from the garrison. See Francis Nevile Reid, *The Earls of Ross and Their Descendants* (Edinburgh, T. & A. Constable, 1894), p. 74.

290. The Hôtel de Langeac, adjoining the Grille de Chaillot, at the corner of the Champs Élysées and the rue de Berri. JT wrote his brother Jonathan from Paris on 6 February 1788: "I have been in this capital of dissipation and nonsense near six weeks for the purpose of getting the portraits of the French Officers who were at York Town, and have happily been so successfull as to find all those whom I wished in town. I have almost finished them, and shall return to London in a few days:— they are Rochambeau, DeGrasse, De Barras, Viomenil, Chastellux, St. Simon, the young Viomenil, Choizy, Lauzun, de Custine, de Laval, Deuxponts, Pherson, & Damas, besides the Marquis La Fayette . . ." (Yale Library.)

291. 14 July 1789. The rioting and attack began several days earlier. In July 1789 Lafayette was appointed commanding general of the National Guard. "From the 14th to the 22nd of July, Lafayette, at the risk of his life, saves with his own hand seventeen persons in different quarters." Taine, *1*, 46. "In Paris the number of paupers has been trebled; there are thirty thousand in the Faubourg Saint-Antoine alone." Taine, *1*, 3. See Hippolyte Adolphe Taine, *The French Revolution*, John Durand, trans. (New York, Henry Holt, 1878), and Brand Whitlock, *LaFayette* (New York and London, D. Appleton, 1919), *1*, 342. Both the marquis and his son George Washington Lafayette were elected honorary members of the American Academy of the Fine Arts with much pomp and ceremony at New York in 1824.

La Fayette in a successful attempt to calm a mob, (principally *ouvriers*,) in the Fauxbourg St. Antoine. Soon after, the Marquis invited me to breakfast with him at an early hour, and alone. I went; he immediately entered upon a long conversation, of which the following is an outline.

He began by saying, "I am very desirous, Mr. Trumbull, that the President of the United States, (Washington,) should be accurately informed of the state and prospects of the affairs of France. I have not leisure to write so much at large, as would be necessary to make myself well understood, and knowing that you are about to return immediately to America, and knowing also upon what terms you are with him, I have asked this interview, that I may without interruption, explain myself fully to you, and I confidently hope, that immediately upon your arrival, you will communicate the same to him.

"You have witnessed the surface of things; it is for me to explain the interior. The object which is aimed at by the Duke de la Rochefaucault,[292] M. Condorcet,[293] myself, and some others, who consider ourselves leaders, is to obtain for France a constitution nearly resembling that of England, which we regard as the most perfect model of government which is hitherto known. To accomplish this, it is necessary to diminish, very essentially, the power of the king; but our object is to retain the throne, in great majesty, as the first branch of the legislative power, but retrenching its executive power in one point, which, though very important in the British crown, we think is needless here. The peerage of France is already so numerous, that we would take from our king the right of creating new peers, except in cases where old families may become extinct. To all this, the king (who is one of the best of men, and sincerely desirous of the happiness of his people,) most freely and cordially consents.

"We wish a house of peers with powers of legislation similar to

292. François Alexandre Frédéric, duc de La Rochefoucault-Liancourt, 1747–1827, philanthropist, grand master of the wardrobe to Louis XV and Louis XVI, member of the Assembly in 1789.

293. Marie Jean Antoine Nicolas Caritat Condorcet, 1743–94, mathematician and philosopher, member of the Assembly in 1791, noted as much for his political violence as for his scientific eminence.

that of England, restricted in number to one hundred members, to be elected by the whole body from among themselves, in the same manner as the Scotch peers are in the British parliament. This part of our plan meets no opposition, for, in the first place, it is an acquisition of immense importance to the body at large, to possess a share in the power of giving laws to the nation; and in the second, it offers to every individual a chance of being one of the distinguished hundred.

"We wish as the third branch of the legislative body, a house of representatives, chosen by the great body of the people from among themselves, by such a ratio as shall not make the house too numerous; and this branch of our project meets unanimous applause.

"From this representation, it might fairly be believed that our purpose was already attained, and that there remained nothing to be done but to put the machine in motion. But unhappily there is one powerful and wicked man, who, I fear, will destroy this beautiful fabric of human happiness—the Duke of Orleans. He does not indeed possess talent to carry into execution a great project, but he possesses immense wealth, and France abounds in marketable talents. Every city and town has young men eminent for abilities, particularly in the law—ardent in character, eloquent, ambitious of distinction, but poor. These are the instruments which the Duke may command by money, and they will do his bidding. His hatred of the royal family can be satiated only by their ruin; his ambition probably leads him to aspire to the throne.

"You saw the other day in the mob, men who were called *les Marseillois, les patriotes par excellence.* You saw them particularly active and audacious in stimulating the discontented artisans and laborers who composed the great mass of the mob; to acts of violence and ferocity; those men are in truth desperadoes, assassins, from the south of France, familiar with murder, robbery, and every atrocious crime, who have been brought up to Paris by the money of the Duke, for the very purpose in which you saw them employed, of mingling in all mobs, and exciting the passions of the people to frenzy.

"This is the first act of the drama. The second will be to influence the elections, and to fill the approaching Assembly with ardent, inexperienced, desperate, ambitious young men, who, instead of proceeding to discuss calmly the details of the plan of which I have given you the general outline, and to carry it quietly into operation, will, under disguise of zeal for the people, and abhorrence of the aristocrats, drive every measure to extremity, for the purpose of throwing the affairs of the nation into utter confusion, when the master spirit may accomplish his ultimate purpose."

This conversation was prophetic, for soon after, Mr. Pethion,[294] the lawyer of Chartres, which gave his second title to the Duke of Orleans and Chartres, became mayor of Paris, and the next Assembly was filled with unprincipled young men, who pushed every thing to excess, and brought upon France and all Europe such a series of crime, disaster and blood, as the world never before saw, and all this under the abused names of liberty, equality, and the rights of man.

Soon after this conversation I returned to London, and Mr. Jefferson having obtained leave of absence for a short time, to return to America, and finding no ship in any port of France convenient for his family and himself, desired me to engage one in London, to receive him on board at Cowes.[295] I did so, and we sailed on the same day, in different ships, for the United States; he for Norfolk in Virginia, I for New York.[296]

In the course of this summer, Mr. Short,[297] who had been the

294. Jérôme Péthion de Villeneuve (also spelled Petion), ca. 1753–92, was one of the outstanding figures in the first years of the French Revolution, mayor of Paris, November 1790, voted for the death of Louis XVI.

295. Drafts of JT's letters addressed to the Rt. Hon. William Pitt, the prime minister, requesting facilities concerning Jefferson's return to the United States, dated London, 24 September and 10 October 1789, copies of which he sent to President Washington on 29 November 1789, are in the Library of Congress. Jefferson sailed in October 1789 and arrived at Monticello two days before Christmas. He did not return again to France.

296. Before JT left London he made a careful "account of paintings . . . copied from an early book which was ruined by damp" in which he lists [33] works. See Sizer, "An Early Check List of the Paintings of John Trumbull," *The Yale University Library Gazette*, 22 (April 1948), 116–123.

297. William Short, 1759–1849, graduated in 1779 from William and Mary College where he was one of the founders of the Phi Beta Kappa Society, private secretary to Jefferson, secretary of the legation and chargé d'affaires at Paris after Jefferson's departure, 1789–92, then minister to Holland.

secretary of Mr. Jefferson during his entire mission, having expressed a disposition to leave the situation, for the purpose of returning to the United States, and entering upon the studies necessary for a profession in future life, the following letters were written.

Paris, May 21, 1789

To John Trumbull, London.

DEAR SIR—I have not yet received my leave of absence, but I expect it hourly, and shall go off within an hour after I receive it. Mr. Short will stay till I come back, and then I think he has it in contemplation to return to America; of this however I am not sure, having avoided asking him, lest he should mistake mere curiosity for inclination. If he does not go, all which I am going to say may be considered as *non avenu;* if he goes, would you like his office of private secretary? Its duties consist almost entirely in copying papers, and were you to do this yourself, it would only occupy now and then one of your evenings; and if you did not choose to do it yourself, you can hire it done, for so many sous a sheet, as it is rare that there is any thing secret to be copied. Sometimes, indeed, there is a squall of work, but it can be hired, and comes very rarely. The salary is three hundred pounds a year, which is paid by the public. I have given Mr. Short his lodging and board, and shall do the same to you with great pleasure.

I think it will not take a moment of your time from your present pursuit; perhaps it might advantage that, by transferring it for a while to Paris, and perhaps it may even give you an opportunity of going to Italy,[298] as your duties, performed by another during your absence, would cost a very little part of your salary. Think of this proposition, my dear sir, and give me your answer as soon

298. JT's stylistic development would have been quite different, in all probabilities, if he had accepted this thoughtful offer. It is to be regretted that the 33-year-old painter rejected the opportunity. See Otto Wittmann, Junior, "The Italian Experience (American Artists in Italy 1830–1875)," *American Quarterly, 4* (Spring 1952), 4.

JT in sending to Jefferson, on 10 July 1789, a draft of a bill then before Congress, added, in postscript: "An Inflammation in my Eyes has occasioned me to make use of another hand in copying the above" (Library of Congress), a serious matter for an artist, especially for one who possessed but one good eye.

as you can decide to your satisfaction, sending it after me to America, if I should be gone there. I should wish to know while there, because if you do not accept, I must bring from thence some other proper person.

But, whether you accept or not, be so good as to keep it secret till the moment of its execution, unless you choose to mention it to Mr. West, for the purpose of consulting him, (under the same injunction.) Observe, this need neither hasten nor retard your trip to America.

I am, with sincere esteem,
Dear sir, your friend and servant,
Thos. Jefferson.

Paris, June 1st, 1789.

John Trumbull,

Dear Sir—Your favor of the 26th of May came to hand yesterday. As you express yourself doubtfully on the proposition in my last, and it may be because I did not sufficiently explain the event which may give place for that arrangement, I will observe to you, that Mr. Short and myself came here with an idea of staying but two years, because my commission was limited to that. Dr. Franklin's departure [299] produced another commission to me, to remain here indefinitely. Though I do not propose to be very long in any office, yet as long as I remain in any, I believe I shall prefer the present one. This will be for some years, if it depend upon myself; but I am going out of life—Mr. Short is coming in. He has never viewed his present situation but as temporary; his views are justly directed to something permanent, independent, in his own country, and which may admit him to marry; his talent, his virtues, and his connections, ensure him any thing he may desire. Perhaps he has already let pass the most favorable opportunity of putting himself in the way of preferment; but these opportunities will recur. His letters to me during his absence, showed to me that he thought it time to return to his own country, and some expressions in conversation make me suppose that he means to do it on my return. I have not asked his decision, lest he might mistake my wishes. He

299. He left France, never again to return, on 12 July 1785 from Passy.

put himself under my guidance at nineteen or twenty years of age; he is to me therefore as an adopted son, and nothing is more interesting to me, than that he should do what is best for himself. It is on this principle alone that I shall acquiesce in his leaving me, because I am persuaded that he will obtain better positions. Your great pursuit, on the contrary, renders a continuance in Europe more eligible to you, and it was the expectation that a residence here might be thought advantageous, which permitted me to indulge the wish that you would accept of Mr. Short's place, if he should decide to quit it. I hope from your letter, that you are not indisposed to it, and be assured that I shall do every thing in my power, to make the office further your improvement, and not obstruct it. I shall be happy to meet you in America, and to know there your decision, though it would be more convenient to me, to know it before, because I might be on the lookout for a person, if your decision is contrary to my wish. In all cases, I am, with sincere esteem and attachment, dear sir,

Your affectionate friend and servant,

THOS. JEFFERSON.

London, June 11th, 1789.

To Thos. Jefferson, Esq., &c. &c., at Paris.

DEAR SIR—I have received yours of the 1st, by the last post, and am happy that you find the account correct; since writing that, you will have received by Mr. Broome,[300] the bill of exchange. You will receive by the diligence to-morrow, Sterne's Sermons, Tristram Shandy, and the Sentimental Journey, unbound; [301] being all of his works which have been published by Wenman,[302] in his very small size; they cost eight shillings, sixpence.

If my affairs were in other respects as I could wish them, I should have given at once a positive answer to your proposition. It would have been an answer of thankfulness and acceptance, for nothing

300. Probably Samuel Broome, *ca.* 1735–1810, of Broome and Platt, leading mercantile house in New Haven, Conn., of the period; brother of John Broome, a well-known New York merchant.

301. Laurence Sterne, 1713–68, *The Sermons* (1760–69), *Tristram Shandy* (1760–67), and the *Sentimental Journey* (1768).

302. J. Wenman, publisher, 144 Fleet Street, London.

could be proposed to me more flattering to my pride, or more consonant, at least for a time, to my favorite pursuit. The greatest motive I had or have for engaging in, or for continuing my pursuit of painting, has been the wish of commemorating the great events of our country's revolution. I am fully sensible that the profession, as it is generally practiced, is frivolous,[303] little useful to society, and unworthy of a man who has talents for more serious pursuits. But, to preserve and diffuse the memory of the noblest series of actions which have ever presented themselves in the history of man; to give to the present and the future sons of oppression and misfortune, such glorious lessons of their rights, and of the spirit with which they should assert and support them, and even to transmit to their descendants, the personal resemblance of those who have been the great actors in those illustrious scenes, were objects which gave a dignity to the profession, peculiar to my situation. And some superiority also arose from my having borne personally a humble part in the great events which I was to describe. No one lives with me possessing this advantage, and no one can come after me to divide the honor of truth and authenticity, however easily I may hereafter be exceeded in elegance. Vanity was thus on the side of duty, and I flattered myself that by devoting a few years of life to this object, I did not make an absolute waste of time, or squander uselessly, talents from which my country might justly demand more valuable services; and I feel some honest pride in the prospect of accomplishing a work, such as had never been done before, and in which it was not easy that I should have a rival.

With how much assiduity, and with what degree of success, I have pursued the studies necessarily preparatory to this purpose, the world will decide in the judgment it shall pass on the picture (of Gibraltar) [304] which I now exhibit to them; and I need not fear that this judgment will deceive me, for it will be biased here, to a favorable decision, by no partiality for me, or for my country.

But, while I have done whatever depended upon my personal exertions, I have been under the necessity of employing, and rely-

303. A New England, Calvinistic point of view, ill-suited for a creative artist.
304. Probably the version now owned by the Boston Athenaeum and deposited at the Museum of Fine Arts, Boston, finished in April 1789 at London.

ing upon the exertions of another. The two paintings which you saw in Paris three years ago, (Bunker's Hill and Quebec,) [305] I placed in the hands of a print-seller and publisher, to cause to be engraved, and as the prospect of profit to him was considerable, I relied upon his using the utmost energy and dispatch; instead of which, three years have been suffered to elapse, without almost the smallest progress having been made in the work. Instead therefore of having a work already far advanced to submit to the world and to my countrymen, I am but where I was three years since, with the deduction from my ways and means of three years' expenses, with prospects blighted, and the hope of the future damped by the experience of past mismanagement. And the most serious reflection is, that the memory and enthusiasm for actions however great, fade daily from the human mind; that the warm attention which the nations of Europe once paid to us, begins to be diverted to objects more nearly and immediately interesting to themselves; and that France, in particular, from which country I entertained peculiar hopes of patronage, is beginning to be too much occupied by her own approaching revolution, to think so much of us as perhaps she did formerly.

Thus circumstanced, I foresee the utter impossibility of proceeding in my work, without the warm patronage of my countrymen. Three or four years more must pass before I can reap any considerable advantage from what I am doing in this country, and as I am far from being rich, those years must not be employed in prosecuting a plan, which, without the real patronage of my country, will only involve me in new certainties of great and immediate expense, with little probability of even distant recompense. I do not aim at opulence, but I must not knowingly rush into embarrassment and ruin.

I am ashamed to trouble you with such details, but without them, I could not so well have explained my reason for not giving you at once a decided answer. You see, sir, that my future movements depend entirely upon my reception in America, and as that

305. "The Death of Gen. Warren at the Battle of Bunker's Hill" (now at Yale) was finished in March 1786 at London and "The Death of Gen. Montgomery in the Attack on Quebec" (also at Yale) in June 1786.

shall be cordial or cold, I am to decide whether to abandon my country or my profession. I think I shall determine without much hesitation; for although I am secure of a kind reception in any quarter of the globe, if I will follow the general example of my profession by flattering the pride or apologizing for the vices of men, yet the ease, perhaps even elegance, which would be the fruit of such conduct, would compensate but poorly for the contempt which I should feel for myself, and for the necessity which it would impose upon me of submitting to a voluntary sentence of perpetual exile. I hope for better things. Monuments have been in repeated instances voted to her heroes; why then should I doubt a readiness in our country to encourage me in producing monuments, not of heroes only, but of those events on which their title to the gratitude of the nation is founded, and which by being multiplied and little expensive, may be diffused over the world, instead of being bounded to one narrow spot?

Immediately therefore upon my arrival in America, I shall offer a subscription for prints to be published from such a series of pictures as I intend, with the condition of returning their money to subscribers, if the sum received shall not prove to be sufficient to justify me in proceeding with the work; and I shall first solicit the public protection of Congress.

I am told that it is a custom in France, for the king to be considered as a subscriber for one hundred copies of all elegant works engraved by his subjects; that these are deposited in the Bibliothèque du Roi, and distributed as presents to foreigners of distinction and taste, as specimens of the state of the fine arts in France. Would this be a mode of diffusing a knowledge of their origin, and at the same time a lesson on the rights of humanity, improper to be adopted by the United States? And if the example of past greatness be a powerful incentive to emulation, would such prints be improper presents to their servants? The expense would be small, and the purpose of monuments and medals as rewards of merit, and confirmations of history, would receive a valuable support, since perhaps it may be the fate of prints, sometimes to outlast either marble or bronze.

If a subscription of this sort should fill in such a manner as to justify me, I shall proceed with all possible diligence, and must of course pass some years in Europe; and as I have acquired that knowledge in this country which was my only object for residing here, and shall have many reasons for preferring Paris hereafter, I shall in that case be happy and proud to accept your flattering proposal. But if, on the contrary, my countrymen should not give me such encouragement as I wish and hope, I must give up the pursuit, and of course I shall have little desire to return for any stay in Europe. In the mean time, viewing the absolute uncertainty of my situation, I must beg you not to pass by any more favorable subject which may offer, before I have the happiness to meet you in America, which I hope will be ere long.

I have the honor to be, very gratefully,

Dear sir, your most faithful servant,

JOHN TRUMBULL.

5

Active Years in the New Republic 1789–94

I ARRIVED in New York on the 26th of November, 1789,[1] where I found the government of the United States organized under the new constitution, General Washington president.[2] I lost no time in communicating to him the state of political affairs, and the prospects of France, as explained to me by M. La Fayette,[3] and having done this, proceeded immediately to visit my family and friends in Connecticut. My excellent father had died in 1785, at the age of seventy-five.[4] My brother,[5] and my friend, Col. Wadsworth[6] of Hartford, were members of the house of representatives in Con--

1. JT wrote to Jefferson, with whom he was still on good terms, from New York on 26 November 1789, congratulating him on his return and informing him that he had "landed on Monday, the 23rd," the winds having been favorable. (Huntington Library, San Marino, Calif.) The observant Ezra Stiles, president of Yale College, noted in his diary for 1 December 1789: "This Eveng. Col. Jno. Trumbull the Painter & Mr. Bill Hillhouse arrived from London." Dexter, *Literary Diary of Ezra Stiles*.

2. Inaugurated at New York on 30 April 1789.

3. The Marquis de Lafayette, 1757–1834. His portrait is included in JT's "Surrender at Yorktown," No. 19 in the Key.

4. Jonathan Trumbull, Senior, 1710–85, the legendary "Brother Jonathan." JT painted his distinguished father a half dozen times.

5. Jonathan Trumbull, Junior, 1740–1809, 2d son of the above, member of the 1st, 2d, and 3d Congresses, speaker of the House in 1791, like his brother John a staunch Federalist. JT painted a miniature (now at Yale) of Jonathan at Philadelphia in 1792.

6. Jeremiah Wadsworth, also a member of the 1st, 2d, and 3d Congresses (1789–95), and a Federalist. JT painted a miniature of him (on copper, instead of the usual mahogany; now owned by a Wadsworth descendant at Utica, N.Y.) in 1790 or 1792 at Philadelphia. He also made a replica (property of the Wadsworth family, Geneseo, N.Y.) of the statesman from the "Jeremiah Wadsworth and His Son Daniel Wadsworth," the "bent-tin" portrait painted in 1784 at London, 54 years later (see p. 388).

gress, which was to meet in New York early in December.[7] With them I returned to New York, for the purpose of pursuing my work of the Revolution; all the world was assembled there, and I obtained many portraits for the Declaration of Independence, Surrender of Cornwallis, and also that of General Washington in the battles of Trenton and Princeton, and in April, 1790, I offered my subscription for the two first engravings from the pictures of Bunker's Hill and Quebec, which had at last been contracted for with Mr. Müller of Stutgard in Germany, and Mr. Clements [8] of Denmark. I obtained the names of the president, vice president, ministers, seventeen senators, twenty-seven representatives, and a number of the citizens of New York.[9]

7. JT's numerous letters from this period to 1839 at the New-York Historical Society cover a great variety of subjects. JT kept a vast amount of "paper work." It passed from the hands of Prof. Benjamin Silliman to his son and grandson, both of the same name, and was dispersed at the "Silliman Sales," held at Philadelphia (Stan. V. Henkels) in 1897.

8. Johann Friedrich Clemens, 1749–1835, of Copenhagen.

9. There are many of JT's subscription lists extant, in both public and private hands: "Proposals by John Trumbull, for publishing by subscription, two prints from original pictures, painted by himself, representing the death of Gen. Warren, at the Battle of Bunker's Hill, and the death of Gen. Montgomery, in the attack of Quebec . . . The price to subscribers, three guineas for each print . . ." See *Autobiography* (1841), App., pp. 339–345.

On 6 February 1799 Washington wrote from Mount Vernon to JT's brother Jonathan informing him that "by the ship Nancy, from London, just arrived at Alexandria, I have received four copies of the Prints of the Deaths of Montgomery & Warren (the number of Setts I presume I subscribed for) sent me by your brother." Elizabeth Bryant Johnston, *Original Portraits of Washington* (Boston, J. R. Osgood, 1882), pp. 72–73. Washington waited, therefore, 9 years for his prints. Three sets are accounted for in the inventory of Mount Vernon during the life of the general; one hung in the "New Room," another at the "foot of the Stair case to the Second floor," and the third "In the Study." Today one set (one of the 3 originals owned by the general from the deLancey Kountze Collection, lent to the Mount Vernon Ladies' Association by the Yale University Art Gallery) now hangs in the banquet hall, and a second set (from the collection of the late R. T. H. Halsey) in the central hall.

Advertisements for the publication of these prints from the *General Advertiser* (Philadelphia) for 15 December 1790 and 24 October 1791 are reprinted by Alfred Coxe Prime, *The Arts and Crafts in Philadelphia, Maryland and South Carolina, Gleanings from Newspapers, 1786–1800*, Ser. 2 (Topsfield, Mass., Walpole Society 1932).

Washington, at JT's request, wrote to Lafayette, from Philadelphia, 21 November 1791: ". . . I have taken peculiar satisfaction in giving every proper aid in my

In May, I went to Philadelphia,[10] where I obtained some portraits for my great work, and a number of subscribers. I returned
in July to New York, where I was requested to paint for the corporation a full length portrait of the President.[11] I represented him

power, to a subscription here supporting this work . . . Mr. Trumbull informs me
that he has ordered a subscription to be opened in Paris: and the object of this letter
is, to engage you to support the subscription in that city, and in other parts of the
nation, where it may be offered. . . . He [Trumbull] has spared no pains in obtaining from life, the likenesses of those characters, French as well as American, who
bore a conspicuous part in our Revolution; and the success with which his efforts
have been crowned, will form no small part of the value of the pieces . . ." (Pp.
345–346.)

JT, the ex-Revolutionist, referred to the French Revolution as "a curse and not a
blessing to the human race, utterly destructive to all the arts of peace . . . from that
time to 1815, Europe was a field of blood, and America a scene of discord, fatal to
the enterprise [of publishing prints after his work]. . . ." (P. 345.)

10. JT was probably the architect of the elegantly proportioned classical Georgian
First Presbyterian Church, Philadelphia, built 1794 and demolished 1821 (see William Birch's engraving of 1799). It was listed in Stephens's Philadelphia Directory,
1796, as "The first Presbyterian Church by Mr. Trumbul." Joseph Jackson (Development of American Architecture, 1783–1830 [Philadelphia, McKay, 1926], pp.
15–16) says of it: "designed by an amateur, it was the first classical structure in
Philadelphia." The Corinthian façade recalled the then recently completed Panthéon,
finished in 1781, which JT greatly admired. It also had a strong suggestion of St.
Martin-in-the-Fields, London—which one might expect from the French-speaking,
London-trained artist. When JT was collecting "heads" while the Continental Congress was sitting at Philadelphia (his brother Jonathan was a member from Connecticut) and drawing plans for Yale for another member, James Hillhouse, it is
quite possible that he would have been asked to prepare the plans, as an architectur-
ally minded, God-fearing expert from afar, conversant with the latest European
styles. If this is the case, JT deserves credit for introducing the neoclassic style by
designing the "first classical structure in Philadelphia." See Sizer, "Philadelphia's
First Presbyterian Church by 'Mr. Trumbul,'" Journal of the Society of Architectural Historians, 9 (October 1950), 20–22, and "Again Philadelphia's First Presbyterian Church," 10 (May 1951), 27–28. JT designed the neoclassical Congregational
Church at his home town, Lebanon, Conn., in 1804, which still stands. JT was a fine
architectural draftsman; a number of his drawings made during 1794–96, in the
style of the architecture of his London contemporary Robert Adam, are in the
Alexander Jackson Davis Collection in the New-York Historical Society.

11. There are a dozen references in the Washington Diary to this and other
sittings. JT painted his old commander in chief in his military uniform, first in small
scale, and from that the larger replica (108 by 72 inches), which still hangs in the
governor's room at City Hall. The original study (30 by 20 inches) he gave to
Martha Washington; it is still owned by the Custis family at Reunion, Lutherville,
Md. See "A Note of Trumbull's Eyesight, a Letter to Benjamin West," App., p.

in full uniform, standing by a white horse, leaning his arm upon the saddle; in the background, a view of Broadway in ruins, as it then was, the old fort at the termination; British ships and boats leaving the shore, with the last of the officers and troops of the evacuating army, and Staten Island in the distance. The picture is now in the common council room of the city hall. Every part of the detail of the dress, horse, furniture, &c., as well as the scenery, was accurately copied from the real objects.

At this time, a numerous deputation from the Creek nation of Indians [12] was in New York, and when this painting was finished, the President was curious to see the effect it would produce on their untutored minds. He therefore directed me to place the picture in an advantageous light, facing the door of entrance of the room where it was, and having invited several of the principal chiefs to dine with him, he, after dinner, proposed to them a walk. He was dressed in full uniform, and led the way to the painting-room, and when the door was thrown open, they started at seeing another "Great Father" standing in the room. One was certainly with them, and they were for a time mute with astonishment. At length one of the chiefs advanced towards the picture, and slowly stretched out his hand to touch it, and was still more astonished to feel, instead of a round object, a flat surface, cold to the touch. He started back with an exclamation of astonishment—"Ugh!" Another then approached, and placing one hand on the surface and

---

326. Richard Varick, 1753–1831, mayor of the City of New York (whom JT painted in 1805; the portrait hangs in City Hall), wrote to Tobias Lear, secretary to the President of the United States, on 19 July 1790: "The Corporation of this City have this Day resolved to request the favor of the President to permit Mr. Trumbull to take his picture to be placed in the Hall, as a Monument of the Respect of the Inhabitants of this City for him"; Washington's compliance was immediate—the same day. On 24 August 1790 the compliment was returned, "The President of the United States requests the Mayor, Recorder, Aldermen and Common-council men of the City of New York to dine with him on Saturday next at four o'clock." (Tomlinson Collection, New-York Historical Society).

12. Abigail Adams, referring to American Indians, wrote to her sister Mary (Mrs. Richard Cranch of Braintree, Mass.) from New York, 8 August 1790: "They are very fine looking Men, placid countenances & fine shape. Mr. Trumble says, they are many of them perfect models." See Stewart Mitchell, ed., *New Letters of Abigail Adams, 1788–1801* (Boston, Houghton Mifflin, 1947), pp. 56–57.

the other behind, was still more astounded to perceive that his hands almost met. I had been desirous of obtaining portraits of some of these principal men, who possessed a dignity of manner, form, countenance and expression, worthy of Roman senators, but after this I found it impracticable; they had received the impression, that there must be magic in an art which could render a smooth flat surface so like to a real man; I however succeeded in obtaining drawings of several by stealth.[13]

In September I went into the country, passed some time with my family, then went on to Boston and New Hampshire, obtained heads of several statesmen and military officers for my great work, and in Boston received a handsome addition to my list of subscribers.[14] I returned through Connecticut to Philadelphia, to which place Congress had adjourned from New York. In February I went to Charleston,[15] S. C., and there obtained portraits of the

13. JT was always interested in the aboriginal Americans. See pp. 7–8. He painted "Col. Joseph Lewis," an Oneida, in the "Attack on Quebec," before 1786. In 1790 he made pencil sketches of "Hopothle-Mico," a Creek (now at Fordham University); "Hysac" (now lost); "John," a Creek (Yale); "Stimafutchke," a Creek (lost); and "Tuskatche-Mico" or "Bird Tail," a Cusitah (Yale). Later, in 1792 at Philadelphia, he painted the miniatures of "The Infant," a Seneca (Yale); of "Good Peter," an Oneida (Yale); and of "The Young Sachem," of the Six Nations (Yale). The five drawings are reproduced in John R. Swanton, *The Indians of the Southwestern United States* (Washington, U.S. Government Printing Office, 1946, Pls. 26, 32, and 33), with the modern equivalent of JT's spelling of their names. A contemporary description (as of 1798–99) of two is to be found in Col. Benjamin Hawkins, "The Creek Confederation," *Collections of the Georgia Historical Society, 3*, Pt. 1 (1848), 26–27 and 60.

14. Benjamin West wrote from London on 14 October 1790 to JT: ". . . Mr. Sharp is attentive to the plate from your picture of Gibraltar, and promises to be successfull in that production . . ." (Yale Library.)

15. JT wrote to Harriet Wadsworth of Hartford, Conn., the daughter of Jeremiah Wadsworth, from Charleston on 7 April 1790: "I have just returned from a short excursion into the Country, my *dear Cousin*, . . . I went first to Middleton place, which is a very handsome house in the style of the old English country seats on the River side, where much Labour has been employ'd to distort nature, & to transform a very pleasing variety of Ground into regular terraces adorn'd with straight Rows of Trees:—I here found the picture of W. A. Middleton (my young friend's Father), painted by Mr. West,—& while I waited for a Boat to take me across the River to the House where the family live since the Death of Mrs. Manigault, I had time to make the copy I wish'd . . .

"I have hop'd for the arrival of a packet—but my time has not been idly spent:—

Rutledges,[16] Pinckneys,[17] Middleton,[18] Laurens,[19] Heyward,[20] &c., and a handsome addition to my list of subscribers. On the 17th of April, I sailed for Yorktown in Virginia, and there made a drawing of the spot where the British army, commanded by Lord Cornwallis, surrendered in 1781; [21] thence rode to Williamsburg, and obtained a drawing of Mr. Wythe [22] for the Declaration; thence to Richmond; thence to Fredericksburg, and obtained a drawing of General Weedon [23] for the battle of Trenton; thence to Georgetown,

---

in addition to the pictures which I wanted, I have been painting Mrs. Rutledge, her daughter & youngest son. I was distress'd by their extreme civility to me & have happily hit upon this method of making them a return which to them is the most valuable possible:—including these I have painted or drawn about 20 heads since I have been here . . . I hope soon to meet you in Hartford . . ." (Yale Library.)

Although the letter is plainly dated 1790 that is a mistake. It should read 1791, as an examination of JT's correspondence for these two years clearly indicates, which is in accordance with the text of the *Autobiography*.

16. JT painted miniatures (in oil on mahogany) of John Rutledge, 1739–1800, statesman and jurist (now at Yale); his wife Elizabeth Grimké Rutledge, married in 1763 (lost); their son States Rutledge (lost); daughter Eliza Rutledge, later Mrs. Henry Laurens, Junior (a replica? owned by Lamar Garmany, Stony Creek, Conn.); and a sketch (?) of Edward Rutledge, 1749–1800, signer of the Declaration of Independence, governor of South Carolina (lost).

17. Brig. Gen. Charles Cotesworth Pinckney, 1746–1825, Revolutionary officer, statesman and diplomat, brother-in-law of Edward Rutledge (Yale); and of Maj. Thomas Pinckney, 1750–1828, Revolutionary officer, diplomat, governor of South Carolina (Yale).

18. JT copied the portrait of Arthur Middleton, 1742–87, signer of the Declaration of Independence and Revolutionary leader, of Middleton Place, from Benjamin West's group portrait of 1771.

19. Henry Laurens, Senior, 1724–92, merchant, planter, president of the Continental Congress (Yale).

20. Thomas Heyward, Junior, 1746–1809, of White Hall, signer of the Declaration of Independence, Revolutionary officer, jurist (sketch or miniature now lost).

In many instances JT made replicas of his miniatures; those for the above are listed in the *Works of Trumbull*.

21. This drawing, a panorama in sepia on three cards, entitled "Yorktown, in Virginia—as seen from the point the British army entered between the lines of the allied troops . . . ," is now at Fordham University.

22. George Wythe, 1726–1806, signer of the Declaration of Independence, professor of law, chancellor of Virginia; pencil drawing labeled "Geo. Wythe, 25th April '91," now lost.

23. Brig. Gen. George Weedon, *ca.* 1730–93, who was a colonel of the 3d Virginia Regiment at the Battle of Trenton (No. 15 in the Key), a pencil drawing (Yale). While at Fredericksburg JT made pencil sketches of the sons of deceased Brig. Gen.

where I found Major L'Enfant [24] drawing his plan of the city of Washington; rode with him over the ground on which the city has since been built—where the Capitol now stands was then (May, 1791) a thick wood; delayed a few days in Philadelphia, and the same in New York, and in June was again among my friends in Connecticut.

After a few days' stay, I returned to New York, where I painted for the corporation the whole length portrait of General George Clinton,[25] which is now in the common council-room of the City Hall. The background of this picture represents British troops storming Fort Montgomery in the Highlands, (where the general commanded,) and the burning of two frigates in the North River; this background is one of my favorite compositions.[26]

In 1792 I was again in Philadelphia,[27] and there painted the por-

---

Hugh Mercer, studies for "The Death of Gen. Mercer at the Battle of Princeton." These are now at the Metropolitan Museum of Art and Fordham University. See Sizer "Sketches by Trumbull," *The Metropolitan Museum of Art Bulletin*, 6 (June 1948), 261–263, and "Trumbull's 'The Battle of Princeton,'" *The Princeton University Library Chronicle*, 12 (Autumn 1950), 1–5.

24. Pierre Charles L'Enfant, 1754–1825, soldier, engineer, and architect.

25. 1739–1812, seven times governor of New York, vice-president of the United States. In 1802 Clinton was one of the founders of the American Academy of the Fine Arts. The portrait still hangs in the governor's room at City Hall.

26. On 24 August 1791 JT was elected a fellow of the American Academy of Arts and Sciences (Boston, founded in 1780); he subsequently painted 32 of his fellow members. He was also elected to the American Philosophical Society (Philadelphia, founded 1743), of which he was member No. 570 (he painted 37 of the members); and an honorary member of the Pennsylvania Academy of the Fine Arts on 20 April 1808. He became a member of the Connecticut Academy of Arts and Sciences (New Haven, 1799) the year of its founding, and was one of their 5 councilors from 1813 to some time after 1821; he painted 14 of its members. JT always made the most of his opportunities. In 1819 he was elected to the Accademia Reale di Belle Arti (founded in 1741) of Naples and in 1820 made an honorary member of the 16th-century Accademia Romana di San Luca, of which in 1817 Canova was the "Principe Perpetua." JT was elected a corresponding member of the Massachusetts Historical Society but declined the honor. See record of the monthly meeting, 28 May 1835, *Proceedings* of the Society, 2, 11. Stewart Mitchell, director of the society, writes: "It is an interesting fact that since our founding in August 1790 (although the Society wears the date of 1791 erroneously) only six or seven persons have refused election."

27. In 1792 James Hillhouse, treasurer of Yale College, then a member of Congress meeting at Philadelphia, employed JT to draw up a comprehensive plan for a

trait of General Washington,[28] which is now placed in the gallery at New Haven, the best certainly of those which I painted, and the best, in my estimation, which exists, in his heroic military character. The city of Charleston, S. C. instructed William R. Smith,[29] one of the representatives of South Carolina, to employ me to paint for them a portrait of the *great man,* and I undertook it *con amore,* (as the commission was unlimited,) meaning to give his military character, in the most sublime moment of its exertion—the evening previous to the battle of Princeton; when viewing the vast superiority of his approaching enemy, and the impossibility of again crossing the Delaware, or retreating down the river, he conceives the plan of returning by a night march into the country from which he had just been driven, thus cutting off the enemy's communication, and destroying his depot of stores and provisions at Bruns-

series of buildings (subsequently the Brick Row) for the college. He wrote Ezra Stiles, the president, on 24 December 1792: "I have procured Mr. John Trumbull to draw from the result of all our information . . . and indeed I pay great deference to the opinion of Mr. Trumbull who appears to be perfect master of the subject . . ." (Letter and JT's drawings for elevation and plan for the grounds, now at Yale.) JT accompanied his plans by detailed, comprehensive description: "Projected Building . . . the Gambol Roof . . . is an inconvenient & expensive Gothicism & in whose place is substituted a low Story & flat Roof . . . ;" "Present Building;" and "Buildings which may be erected hereafter." He even went into such matters as latrines: "Temples of Cloacina, (which it is too much the custom of New England to place conspicuously) I would wish to have concealed as much as possible, by planting of a variety of Shrubs, such as Laburnums, Lilacs, Roses, Snowballs, Laurel, etc.— a gravel walk should lead thro the Shrubbery to these buildings." Although these plans were never executed "a study of the documents reveals the importance of Trumbull's influence on the architecture of Yale for a century." See Anne S. Pratt, "John Trumbull and the Brick Row," *Yale University Library Gazette,* 9 (July 1934), 11–20; Jean Lambert Brockway, "John Trumbull as Architect at Yale," *Antiques, 28* (September 1935), 114–115; and Sizer, "John Trumbull, Amateur Architect," *Journal of the Society of Architectural Historians,* 8 (July–December 1949), 1–6.

28. This celebrated portrait (92½ by 63 inches) came to Yale in 1806. It is still considered the best portrait of Washington the *general,* as Gilbert Stuart's "Athenaeum" portrait (now at the Museum of Fine Arts, Boston) is unquestionably the finest of him as *president.* JT made at least 4 replicas of his portrait.

In May 1793 JT again painted Washington (bust size), in civilian clothes, as president. It was not particularly successful; original at Yale, replicas at Harvard and at Bedford House (John Jay's home), Katonah, N.Y.

29. William Loughton Smith, *ca.* 1758–1812, congressman from South Carolina, elected 5 times, served until 1797, United States minister to Portugal, 1797–1801. JT painted his miniature that year, 1792, at Philadelphia (Yale).

wick. I told the President my object; he entered into it warmly, and, as the work advanced, we talked of the scene, its dangers, its almost desperation. He *looked* the scene again, and I happily transferred to the canvass, the lofty expression of his animated countenance, the high resolve to conquer or to perish. The result was in my own opinion eminently successful, and the general was satisfied. But it did not meet the views of Mr. Smith. He admired, he was personally pleased, but he thought the city would be better satisfied with a more matter-of-fact likeness, such as they had recently seen him—calm, tranquil, peaceful.

Oppressed as the President was with business, I was reluctant to ask him to sit again. I however waited upon him, stated Mr. Smith's objection, and he cheerfully submitted to a second penance, adding, "Keep this picture for yourself, Mr. Trumbull, and finish it to your own taste." I did so—another was painted for Charleston,[30] agreeable to their taste—a view of the city in the background, a horse, with scenery, and plants of the climate; and when the state society of Cincinnati of Connecticut dissolved themselves, the first picture, at the expense of some of the members, was presented to Yale College.

In 1793 I again went to Boston by the way of Newport and Providence, and there obtained drawings of Mr. Ellery,[31] Col. Olney,[32] Judge Howel,[33] &c. Wherever I went I offered my subscrip-

---

30. In the Charleston City Hall.

Washington wrote to William Moultrie on 5 May 1792 from Philadelphia: "I am much pleased to hear, that the picture by Colonel Trumbull gives so much satisfaction. The merit of this artist cannot fail to give much pleasure to those of his countrymen, who possess a taste for the fine arts; and I know of no part of the United States, where it would be put to stronger test than in South Carolina." William Spohn Baker, *Washington after the Revolution* (Philadelphia, Lippincott 1898), p. 236. JT painted the miniature of Maj. Gen. William Moultrie, 1730–1805, governor of South Carolina, in 1791 at Charleston (Yale).

31. William Ellery, 1727–1820, signer of the Declaration of Independence, pencil sketch (lost), used in the "Declaration" (No. 24 in the Key) and "Resignation of Gen. Washington" (No. 18).

32. Lieut. Col. Jeremiah Olney, 1750–1812, Revolutionary officer, collector of customs at Providence, R.I., pencil sketch (lost).

33. David Howell, 1747–1824, educator, professor at Brown University (then Rhode Island College), jurist, member Continental Congress, commissioner under the Jay Treaty. This pencil drawing and a miniature are both lost.

tion book, but wretched was now the success, and rapidly decreasing the enthusiasm for my national work.[34]

The progress of the French revolution was blasting to my hopes; for in four years which had elapsed since my interview and conversation with M. de La Fayette, in Paris, recorded in the preceding chapter, all the evils which he had there anticipated, had been realized. The money of that bad man, *the Citizen Égalité*,[35] had been successfully applied to the nefarious purposes which he (the Marquis) had foretold—the elections had been corrupted—the worst of men had been introduced into the National Assembly—the beautiful theory of those estimable men, the early leaders of the revolution, had been subverted—France had been overwhelmed in crime, and deluged with blood—the king had been beheaded, Lafayette himself had been exiled, and the author of all these calamities had expiated his crimes under the same axe which had fallen on so many virtuous men.[36]

In America, the artful intrigues of French diplomatists, and the blunders of the British government, united to convert the whole American people into violent partisans of one or the other;—to such a degree did this insanity prevail, that the whole country seemed to be changed into one vast arena, on which the two parties, forgetting their national character, were wasting their time, their thoughts their energy, on this foreign quarrel. The calm splendor of our own Revolution, comparatively rational and beneficial as it had been, was eclipsed in the meteoric glare and horrible blaze of glory of republican France; and we, who in our own case, had scarcely stained the sacred robe of rational liberty with a single drop of blood unnecessarily shed, learned to admire that hideous frenzy which made the very streets of Paris flow with blood. And worse, some of our people, or of those who called themselves Americans, even hurraed when the head of Louis XVI, our real

34. Lack of the hoped for subscriptions plagued JT's later life. Perhaps this was due to protracted delay; the engraving for "Attack on Quebec" did not appear before 1792, 17 years after the event.

35. Duc d'Orléans, called Philippe Égalité, supported the Revolution.

36. Many of JT's friends, former officers under Rochambeau, were guillotined during the Terror. There are a number of letters written by JT to his brother, Jonathan Trumbull, about the French Revolution, at the Yale University Library.

benefactor, was submitted to that instrument of wholesale butchery, the guillotine.[37] Still worse, when the National Assembly of France, the elected rulers of a great nation, formed a procession to the metropolitan church of Nôtre Dame, which had been consecrated during long ages to the worship of God, and there in mock solemnity bowed their knees before a common courtezan, basely worshiping her as the goddess of reason, still there were those, and not a few in America, who threw up their caps, and cried, "glorious, glorious, sister republic!" The spirit of discord which thus distracted the people of America, pervaded also the very cabinet of the President, and Mr. Jefferson, the secretary of state, became the apologist of France, and was pitted against Mr. Hamilton, the secretary of the treasury.

In such a state of things, what hope remained for the arts? None, —my great enterprise was blighted.

In the mean time, the aggressions of Great Britain upon our commerce became intolerable, and the question of peace or war with her, came to be seriously agitated. The President, unawed by popular clamor, determined to try the effect of negotiation; and John Jay,[38] chief justice of the United States, was appointed envoy extraordinary to Great Britain. He did me the honor to offer me the situation of secretary, and I accepted the proposal with pleasure.

It has been seen, that in Europe I had been on terms of confidence with Mr. Jefferson; this continued for some time, so that in America, when the first mission to the states of Barbary [39] was determined on, it was, through him, offered to me, and declined; but as the French revolution advanced, my whole soul revolted from the atrocities of France, while he approved or apologized for all. He opposed Washington—I revered him—and a coldness gradually

37. 21 January 1793.
38. 1745–1829, jurist, statesman, diplomat, whose home, Bedford House, Katonah, N.Y., is still intact. JT painted the justice in 1793 at Philadelphia in miniature (Yale), a bust, now at Bedford House, a year or two later, and a full-length portrait in 1805 for the New York City Hall. A half-length portrait exhibited at the American Academy of the Fine Arts in 1824 is lost.
39. See Ray W. Irwin, *The Diplomatic Relations of the United States with the Barbary Powers, 1776–1816* (Chapel Hill, University of North Carolina Press, 1931), ch. 3. Jefferson apparently thought well of JT's diplomatic ability.

succeeded, until in 1793, he invited me to dine. A few days before, I had offended his friend, Mr. Giles,[40] senator from Virginia, by rendering him ridiculous in the eyes of a lady, to whose favorable opinion he aspired. On entering the drawing-room at Mr. Jefferson's, on the day of the dinner, I found a part of the company already assembled, and among them Mr. Giles. I was scarcely seated, when Giles began to rally me upon the puritanical ancestry and character of New England. I saw there was no other person from New England present, and therefore, although conscious that I was in no degree qualified to manage a religious discussion, yet I felt myself bound to make the attempt, and defend my country on this delicate point, as well as I could.

Whether it had been pre-arranged that a discussion on the Christian religion,[41] in which it should be powerfully ridiculed on the one side, and weakly defended on the other, should be brought forward, as promising amusement to a rather freethinking dinner party, I will not determine; but it had that appearance, and Mr. Giles pushed his raillery, to my no small annoyance, if not to my discomfiture, until dinner was announced. That I hoped would relieve me, by giving a new turn to the conversation, but such was not the case; the company was hardly seated at table, when he renewed his attack with increased asperity, and proceeded so far at last, as to ridicule the character, conduct, and doctrines of the divine founder of our religion—Jefferson in the mean time, smiling and nodding approbation on Mr. Giles, while the rest of the company silently left me and my defense to our fate; until at length my friend, David Franks,[42] (first cashier of the bank of the United States,) took up the argument on my side. Thinking this a fair opportunity for evading further conversation on this subject, I turned to Mr. Jefferson and said, "Sir, this is a strange situation in which I find myself; in a country professing Christianity, and at a table with Christians, as I supposed, I find my religion and myself

40. William Branch Giles, 1762–1830, an opponent of Hamilton, at the time a member of the House of Representatives, later senator and governor of Virginia.

41. Trumbull was a devout Congregationalist.

42. David Salisbury Franks, an English-Jewish merchant from Canada who served with distinction as an officer in the Revolutionary army, later as vice consul and American agent abroad.

attacked with severe and almost irresistible wit and raillery, and not a person to aid me in my defense, but my friend Mr. Franks, *who is himself a Jew.*" For a moment, this attempt to parry the discussion appeared to have some effect; but Giles soon returned to the attack, with renewed virulence, and burst out with—"It is all a miserable delusion and priestcraft; I do not believe one word of all they say about a future state of existence, and retribution for actions done here. I do not believe one word of a Supreme Being who takes cognizance of the paltry affairs of this world, and to whom we are responsible for what we do."

I had never before heard, or seen in writing, such a broad and unqualified avowal of atheism. I was at first shocked, and remained a moment silent; but soon rallied and replied, "Mr. Giles, I admire your frankness, and it is but just that I should be equally frank in avowing my sentiments. Sir, in my opinion, the man who can with sincerity make the declaration which you have just made, is perfectly prepared for the commission of every atrocious action, by which he can promise himself the advancement of his own interest, or the gratification of his impure passions, provided he can commit it secretly, and with a reasonable probability of escaping detection by his fellow men. Sir, I would not trust such a man with the honor of a wife, a sister, or a daughter—with my own purse or reputation, or with any thing which I thought valuable. Our acquaintance, sir, is at an end." I rose and left the company, and never after spoke to Mr. Giles.

I have thought it proper to relate this conversation, as helping to elucidate the character of Mr. Jefferson, on the disputed point of *want of credulity*, as he would call it. In nodding and smiling assent to all the virulence of his friend, Mr. Giles, he appeared to me to avow most distinctly, his entire approbation. From this time my acquaintance with Mr. Jefferson became cold and distant.

During this period, recurred to my remembrance, in all its force, the wise advice of Mr. Burke, which I had so absurdly neglected to follow, "*to study architecture.*" [43] The government of the United

43. Edmund Burke, see p. 71. Shortly after JT's return he wrote Burke, who had helped him when he was in prison, soliciting his "protection once more" in the matter of subscription for his engravings: JT's letter, dated New York 2 December

States, having been insulted by a mob in Philadelphia, which they had not power to repress, had felt the necessity of possessing a territory under their own exclusive jurisdiction, where state authorities or mobs should have no power to influence or overawe the deliberations of Congress, and of there erecting permanent buildings for national purposes. The District of Columbia had been selected and ceded for that purpose, and Major L'Enfant, a French officer of engineers, who had served in the army of the Revolution, was chosen to survey the ground, and plan the future city of Washington. At the same time, an English gentleman, Dr. Thornton,[44] assisted by a Russian officer of engineers,[45] and the Vitruvius Britannicus,[46] had made a drawing and plan for the Capitol or house of government. The doctor requested me to show these drawings to the President, and commend them to his attention, which I did. The plan was generally adopted, and the erection of the building was commenced and proceeded under several superintendents, until in ——, being then in London, I received a letter from the commissioners of the public buildings, (of whom Dr. Thornton

---

1790, in the Sheffield Central Library, Sheffield, England. "The advice was not neglected and great attention was paid by him to that very important & beautiful art . . . Col. Trumbull . . . had knowledge, judgment & taste in architecture, as well as consummate skill in delineation . . ." (From Benjamin Silliman's "Note Book," Garvan Collection, Yale University Art Gallery, p. 19 of the typed transcript.)

During the 18th century familiarity with architecture was regarded as one of the accomplishments of a man of birth and breeding. The best collection of JT's architectural drawings is at the New-York Historical Society. See Sizer, "John Trumbull, Amateur Architect," p. 238, n. 6.

44. William Thornton, 1759–1828, born in the British Virgin Islands, came to the United States in 1787, architect of the Capitol and of a number of residences at Washington, including the Tayloe house, now known as the Octogon, the present headquarters of the American Institute of Architects.

45. Possibly one DeMiroth, who was in Washington at this time. He was the inventor of a supposedly waterproof cement which unfortunately was not. Latrobe mentions him and his product several times in 1808.

46. Colen Campbell (d. 1729), *Vitruvius Britannicus or the British Architect,* London, 1717–25 (3 vols.), continued 1767–71 (2 vols.) and into the 19th century, among the most influential of 18th-century architectural publications (largely engraved plans and elevations of English mansions); not to be confused with the works of the Roman architect, Vitruvius, whose celebrated *De architectura libri decem,* published during the Renaissance (1st ed. 1486), was one of the most important sources for the revival of classical architecture.

was one,) requesting me to select, contract with, and send out a young architect, qualified to conduct and superintend the work. I consulted my friend, Mr. West,[47] and Mr. Wyatt,[48] (then the principal architect in London,) and they united in recommending George Hatfield,[49] a brother of Mrs. Cosway, who had been a fellow student with me in the Royal Academy, from which he had received all the academical prizes, and who had recently returned from a three years' residence in Italy, where he had completed his architectural studies, under the patronage and at the expense of the Academy. He accepted the proffered terms, and came out; but his services were soon dispensed with, not because his knowledge was not eminent, but because his integrity compelled him to say, that parts of the original plan *could not be executed.* Poor Hatfield languished many years in obscurity at Washington, where however, towards the close of his life, he had the opportunity of erecting a noble monument to himself in the city hall, a beautiful building, in which is no waste of space or materials.

I have always felt as if I had been instrumental in causing the ruin of this most admirable artist, and excellent friend; for if I had not been the means of inducing him to leave London, his con-

47. Benjamin West, P.R.A.

48. James Wyatt, R.A., 1746–1813, surveyor general of the Board of Works (1796), a neoclassical architect who became a champion of the Gothic revival, P.R.A. (1805).

49. George Hadfield, *ca.* 1764–1826, born at Leghorn, son of Charles Hadfield, an English or Irish hotel keeper, worked at London under James Wyatt. See Fiske Kimball's article in the *D.A.B.* for the life of this talented, irritable, frustrated architect.

The young man arrived with a letter of introduction to Lear from JT, dated London, 9 March 1795: "I . . . recommend him to your particular Civilities, as a Gentleman, whose professional Talents and knowledge do not render him more worthy of Attention, than does his Personal Character of Esteem . . ." (Avery Library, Columbia University.) JT wrote from London on 8 March 1795 to Tobias Lear: ". . . The Letter which you enclosed from the Commissioners at Wash.tn gave me much pleasure as it authorizes me at once to serve my Country and a friend. M. Hatfield complies with the proposals . . . and will embark as soon as he can make the arrangements necessary on quitting this Country, & provide himself with such additional books, instruments, and information as will be necessary. I presume he will be ready to sail within a month . . . you will permit me to say here, that I have found him in an acquaintance of Ten Years, a man of modesty and amiable qualities as well as of Talents . . ." (Yale Library.)

nexions there, who had some influence with the late king, George IV, might have procured him the execution of those extensive and splendid works, which were committed to Mr. Nash.[50]

50. John Nash, 1752–1835, city planner and architect, planned Regent's Park, Regent Street, remodeled Buckingham Palace—a favorite of the prince regent, later George IV—initiated the neoclassic Regency style. JT had the planning of the Capitol very much on his mind. His brother Jonathan, governor of Connecticut, wrote to him on 12 December 1794: "Your letter, respecting a proposed Architect for the City of Washington, I gave to the President, who seemed much pleased with your attention." (State Library, Hartford.)

For these years see "A Note of Trumbull's Eyesight, a Letter to Benjamin West," and "Trumbull's Troubles: an Omitted Chapter of the Artist's Life," concerning JT's illegitimate son, John Trumbull Ray, App., pp. 325–327 and 332–350.

6

Diplomacy and Distraction 1794–1804 [1]

ON THE 12th of May, 1794, Mr. Jay [2] embarked in New York on his mission to Great Britain, amidst the acclamations of his fellow citizens. The passage across the Atlantic was pleasant, and on the 1st of June, we must have been near, almost within hearing, of the decisive naval battle which was fought on that day, between the British and French fleets; [3] for on our arrival at Falmouth, a few days after, we found there a sloop of war just arrived with dispatches from Lord Howe. [4] Nothing was suffered to transpire relating to the news she brought, and we met the note of triumph at Bath, on our way to London. [5]

1. JT at the very height of his creative ability suddenly abandoned painting for diplomacy—to the great detriment of his work. He never painted as well after 1794, or to take a more convenient though less accurate date, 1800, as he did before. He once (in 1840) told a young aspiring painter: "I would have been a beggar had I wholly relied on painting for my support." *Selections from the Works of the Late Sylvester Genin, Esq., in Poetry, Prose, Historical Design* (New York, Maigne & Hall, 1855), p. 37.

2. Jay's request for JT to be his secretary was transmitted through Jonathan Trumbull, Junior, see the latter's letters to JT, dated Philadelphia, 20 April 1794. (Connecticut State Library.) JT's salary as secretary to Jay was £25 a month. See "Account of Expenses, 1794–1795," Henrietta W. Hubbard Collection, Connecticut State Library.

3. The French fleet under Rear Admiral Villaret-Joyeuse set sail on 16 May to protect provision ships coming from America. On 28 and 29 May there were partial actions with the British fleet under Lord Howe; on 1 June the French fleet was crippled and fled, the British gave chase and captured 7 French vessels; the grain fleet from America, however, reached Brest safely as a result.

4. Richard Howe, Earl Howe, 1726–99, naval commander during the American Revolution, 1776–77, admiral and commander in chief in the Channel, 1782, first lord of the Admiralty 1783, admiral of the fleet and general of marines, 1796.

5. There are many references to JT scattered through the pages of *The Farington*

The reception of Mr. Jay by the government, in London, was calm and decorous, and his own conduct quiet and conciliatory; soon after the presentation of his credentials, it was determined by the British administration to meet the proposed negotiation, and Lord Grenville,[6] then secretary of state, was appointed, with full powers to confer and conclude with Mr. Jay.

The negotiation [7] was difficult, complicated, and intricate in the extreme; for not one cause of complaint only, but many, various, and mutual, were to be discussed, and if possible adjusted. For,

1st. Great Britain had infringed the treaty of peace of 1783, by retaining the military posts on the western frontier.

2d. She had not given up, or made compensation for the negro slaves, which had been carried away by her officers.

3d. Several of the American states had withheld the settlement and payment of debts, contracted before the Revolution.

4th. The geography of the western frontier was still unexplored, the true situation of the Lake of the Woods, as well as the course and extent of the Mississippi, were unknown, and of course the boundary of the United States on that side was unsettled.

5th. The boundary of the United States on the northeast was also unsettled, in consequence of the imperfect geographical knowledge of the real river St. Croix.

6th. Great Britain complained of damage done to her commerce, by French privateers fitted out in the ports of the United States.

Diary, 1793–1802 (by Joseph Farington, R.A., 1747–1821, the landscape painter), James Greig, ed. (8 vols., London, Hutchinson, 1922).

6. William Wyndham, Baron Grenville, 1759–1834, secretary of state for the Home Department, 1789; created baron of Wotton-under-Bernewood in the county of Buckingham, 1790, Pitt's foreign secretary, 1791–1801; not to be confused with another, contemporary Lord Grenville, George Nugent-Temple-Grenville, marquess of Buckingham, 1753–1813, lord lieutenant of Ireland, whose portrait JT painted (Yale).

7. There is a large packet entitled: "Papers of John Trumbull, one of the Commissioners under the 7th article of Treaty with Great Britain, 1796–1804, Claims under the Jay Treaty," at the New-York Historical Society. See Samuel Flagg Bemis, *Jay's Treaty, a Study in Commerce and Diplomacy* (New York, Macmillan, 1923), and, for some additional details, his *John Quincy Adams and the Foundations of American Foreign Policy* (New York, Knopf, 1949); and Charles R. King, M.D., ed., *The Life and Correspondence of Rufus King* (6 vols., New York, Putnam, 1895.)

7th. The United States complained of damage done to her commerce, by irregular or illegal captures on the ocean by British cruisers, to a great extent.

It was easy to foresee, that all these causes of mutual complaint must lead to interminable discussion, with little hope of a favorable result, if treated in the usual form, by diplomatic notes; and therefore, at his first official meeting with Lord Grenville, Mr. Jay proposed, "that they should meet, and discuss in conversation the several involved and intricate subjects of mutual complaint, (avoiding in the outset all written communications,) that they should continue so to meet and converse, until there should appear a probability of coming to some amicable mutual understanding; that then only, each should commit to paper informally, the conclusions at which he might have arrived—that these informal papers should be exchanged; that neither party should be considered as bound by any expression contained in these preliminary papers; that both should be at perfect liberty to change, or to retract entirely, whatever upon more deliberate consideration, might appear to be unadvisable; that in all this, they should avoid employing secretaries, or copyists, in order to escape the possibility of public opinion, or national feeling, coming in to influence that perfect calmness of discussion, which alone could lead to an amicable settlement; both parties always bearing in mind, that this was not a trial of skill in the science of diplomatic fencing, but a solemn question of peace or war between two people, in whose veins flowed the blood of a common ancestry, and on whose continued good understanding might perhaps depend the future freedom and happiness of the human race."

Lord Grenville being very much struck with the wisdom of this novel proposition, without hesitation gave it his entire approbation and assent; and on this plan the negotiation proceeded. Frequently meetings were held by the two ministers, at which no other person was permitted to be present; and the secretaries, Sir James Bland Burgess [8] and myself, had a real holiday for a month.

8. Sir James Bland Burges, 1752–1824, politician, poet, and playwright, member of Parliament, under-secretary of state in the Foreign Office, 1789–95; assumed the name of Sir James Lamb in 1821.

At length the work approached to an amicable termination, and then, secretaries and copyists had ample occupation. The treaty was signed on the 19th of November, 1794, and copies were immediately prepared and sent by several ships of both nations, to the government of the United States. None arrived, however, until after the 4th of March, on which day the session of Congress closed; and when the senate was afterwards convened to consider the treaty, the opposition made to its ratification was violent in the extreme. It was, however, ratified, with the exception of the twelfth article, which was rejected, among other reasons because it forbade the exportation of cotton from ports of the United States. At the time of signing the treaty, very little cotton, if any, grown in the country, had been exported—the first exportation took place in 1796, it was uncleaned from the seed, and packed in casks—and Mr. Jay believed that the admission, even of small vessels, to the trade of the British West India islands on free and equal terms, would prove to be a very important benefit to the commerce of the United States, while he was willing to trust the enlargement of the privilege to the wisdom of futurity.

I cannot forbear a digression here. Before the culture of cotton had made any considerable progress in the southern states, silk had received great attention in the north, and especially in Connecticut, my native state. Before the mission of Mr. Jay, almost all the dry, sandy, unproductive soil in the state, had been planted with mulberry trees, particularly the vicinity of New Haven, Mansfield, &c., and not only was the quantity of the silk produced considerable, but attempts had been made, with some success, to manufacture silk goods,[9] particularly at Hartford; so that in 1793, an agent from that city presented himself to President Washington, at Philadelphia, offering for sale, specimens of silk manufactured there, of so good a quality, that the President purchased some yards, as did many other persons, friends of domestic industry. I also bought a pattern for a vest and small clothes, of a fabric resembling a coarse

9. President Stiles of Yale was much interested in the silk industry in Connecticut. He refers to his experiences in silk culture in his diary (MS at the Yale University Library) between the years 1763 and 1790. See Franklin Bowditch Dexter, ed., *The Literary Diary of Ezra Stiles*, and Linus Pierpont Brockett, *The Silk Industry in America* (New York, Silk Association of America, 1876).

black satin. I had this made up, took the clothes with me when I went to London with Mr. Jay, and there I became acquainted with Mr. Titford,[10] a considerable silk manufacturer in Spitalfields. I asked his opinion of the quality of this silk, and, after examining it carefully, he pronounced the quality to be excellent, although it was rudely manufactured. He expressed great surprise, when told that the silk was both grown and manufactured in Connecticut, and assured me that if the people there would raise silk of such quality and ship it to London in its raw state, as cotton is now generally shipped, they might rely upon receiving the highest market price, for that there was none of a superior quality received from Italy or France.

Now mark the miserable effect of that *auri sacra fames*—that hurry to become rich—which is becoming the disgrace and the curse of this country! No sooner did the northern people hear of the sudden wealth acquired at the south by the culture of cotton, which gives its result in one season, than silk, and its mulberry trees, which are of slower production, though not less certain, were neglected; so that, at this time, the trees have generally perished, and little silk is produced in Connecticut, except at Mansfield, where the inhabitants have been more wise, and now receive an annual income of about $50,000 from labor done principally by their children. If this culture had been pursued with proper industry and perseverance, silk would have become, at this time, an important and productive branch of national income, and we should not be seen, at this hour, relying upon the labor of slaves for almost the only article of direct remittance to Europe!

I must not omit to remark the admirable conduct of General Thomas Pinckney,[11] then minister of the United States at the court of St. James. The appointment of Mr. Jay, as envoy extraordinary, might have been regarded by him as an affront, but his patriotism

10. Probably William Titford, London. Spitalfields is now a part of that city. The *Post Office London Directory* (London, Critchett & Woods, 1819) gives: "Titford, W. C. silk-manf. 2, Windsor-terrace, City-road." Both Trumbull and William Titford are listed as subscribers to William Jowitt Titford, *Sketches towards a Hortus Botanicus Americanus* (London, Stower, Hackney, 1811).

11. JT painted 3 miniatures of Thomas Pinckney at Charleston, S.C. in 1791; one is at Yale and the other 2 in private hands.

took no offense, and the greatest cordiality prevailed between Mr. Jay and him to the end of the negotiation.

Soon after the arrival of Mr. Jay in London, Mr. Monroe [12] arrived in Paris, having been appointed minister of the United States to the government of France. He was received by the Convention with marked distinction, and in a speech which he delivered upon that occasion, he made a most unfortunate promise "to communicate to the authorities of France all the information which he might obtain of the progress and character of the negotiation which was conducting between Mr. Jay and the government of Great Britain;" and further, in pursuance of such promise, he wrote a letter to Mr. Jay, requesting him to keep him informed of the progress he made, for the purpose of enabling him (Monroe) to fulfill his promise by communicating the same to the French rulers. This strange proposal met, of course, the most decided disapprobation of Mr. Jay, and all intercourse on the subject ceased until the treaty was signed, and copies had been dispatched to the government of the United States.

My official duty having then ceased, I was anxious to know the progress of the engraving from my picture of Bunker's Hill, which was in the hands of Mr. Müller [13] at Stutgard in Wirtemberg. I

12. James Monroe, 1758–1831, the 5th president of the United States. JT included his portrait in the "Battle of Trenton" (No. 4 in the Key) and "Resignation of Gen. Washington" (No. 15).

13. Goethe, visiting the studio of Johann Gotthard von Müller at Stuttgart, saw JT's "Battle of Bunker's Hill" in the process of being engraved. In a long letter to his friend Schiller, dated Stuttgart, 30 August 1797, he set forth his opinion of the work: "The engraving is well on the way toward an excellent outcome. Meanwhile he [Müller] is occupying himself also ['also' is stressed here because Schiller was at the time working on his *Wallenstein*] with the death of a general, an American in fact, a young man who was killed at Bunker's Hill. The picture is by an American, Trumbul; it brings out the artist's talent, but also the connoisseur's faults. His talent shows itself particularly in the character portraits brought out in bold strokes. The faults concentrate themselves upon the disproportion of the figures in respect to each other and the disproportion in the bodies themselves. Within its own genre it is well composed, and for a picture in which so many red uniforms must be introduced, the color scheme is well managed. At first glance it produces a garish reaction which lasts until one becomes reconciled to it through an understanding of its real deserts. The engraving is pleasing to the eye and is exquisitely executed throughout." *Goethes Werke* (Weimar, 1893), *4*, 12, p. 278; later incorporated in the *Reise in die Schweiz*. A framed impression of the engraving hung in the reception room

determined to visit the engraver, and to take the shortest route, which was through Paris. Mr. Jay now requested me to commit the treaty, verbatim, to memory; to wait on Mr. Monroe, and deliver to him a letter from Mr. Jay, in which it would be stated, that I was authorized to repeat to him the treaty, on condition that he would first promise me that he would not make any communication of the same to any person whatever, especially not to the French government.

I waited on Mr. Monroe as soon as I reached Paris, delivered the letter of Mr. Jay, and declared my readiness to proceed to the rehearsal of the treaty so soon as the condition proposed in the letter should be complied with. After a moment's hesitation, Mr. Monroe declined making the promise required, as involving a breach of his antecedent engagement to the Convention. The communication was therefore withheld on my part, and I became obnoxious to the French rulers.

Very soon after, I received an informal notice from Mr. Monroe, through Mr. B. Hichborn [14] of Boston, that he had reason to know, from hints which he had received from a member of the French government, that my remaining in Paris gave great dissatisfaction, and advising me to leave the country without delay. I replied, that I had not acquired the habit of paying attention to hints, but had been taught to obey commands; that I would ask leave to take breakfast with the minister the next morning. I did so—went into a long explanation, which ended with the assurance, that my visit to France was purely on individual, personal and pacific business; that I was an artist by profession, and had been made a politician by accident; that I could be governed in my conduct by *no hints*, from whatever quarter, but would obey the *orders* of the French authorities the moment they should be officially signified to me; that therefore I would, without delay, prepare for pursuing my journey to Stutgard, and, in the mean time, I begged leave to claim from him the protection of the minister of the United States.

---

of the poet Schiller's house at Weimar before World War II and presumably is still there.

14. Benjamin Hichborn, 1746–1817, Harvard, A.M. 1768, lawyer, owned a large brick house on Marlboro Street, Boston.

I, of course, made my preparations, but receiving no order to quit the country, and having learned, that in the confusion of the time, and the consequent ruin of ancient and opulent families, paintings by the old masters might be advantageously purchased, I entered upon that speculation, with the advice of my friend, M. Le Brun,[15] the most experienced judge on that subject then in Europe. With his advice and assistance I purchased more than an hundred valuable paintings, and leaving them in his hands to be packed for removal, I proceeded to Stutgard, through Basle in Switzerland, where, having examined the work of Mr. Müller with great satisfaction, I commenced my return to Paris, by way of Schaffhausen, Landshut, Basle, &c.

At Basle I was advised, on account of the ruined state of the other road, to take that which led down the banks of the Rhine for some distance, and when I arrived at Mulhausen, near sunset of the first day, I found the village full of French troops, and the yard and entrance of the inn crowded with officers. To my demand of horses for Schlestadt, the innkeeper said that it was not in his power to furnish them, and if he could, it would be useless for me to attempt to proceed, for that, before I could possibly reach the town, the gates would be shut, (it is the first fortified place on the old French frontier, in that quarter,) and I should be under the necessity of passing the night outside of the walls, in my carriage. "Can you, then, give me a bed?" "I am afraid that too will be impossible— hostilities are about to be renewed; the head-quarters of the commanding general are established at my house, and it is entirely occupied by him and his suite; but come with me, and I will do as well as I can." I followed, through a crowd of young officers, and at the door met the old general coming out. The veteran looked at me keenly, and asked bluntly, "Who are you?—an Englishman?" "No, general, I am an American, of the United States." "Ah! do you know Connecticut?" "Yes, sir, it is my native state." "You know then the good Governor Trumbull." "Yes, general, he is my father." "Oh! *mon Dieu! que je suis charmé;* I am delighted to see a son

15. The art dealer, Jean Baptiste Pierre LeBrun. For an interesting reference to JT and LeBrun at this time, see Mabel Munson Swan, *The Athenaeum Gallery, 1827–1873,* pp. 156–157.

of Governor Trumbull; *entrez, entrez;* you shall have supper, bed, every thing in the house." I soon learned that the old man had been in America, an officer in the legion of the Duke de Lauzun, who had been quartered in my native village, during the winter which I passed in prison in London, and had heard me much spoken of there. Of course, I found myself in excellent quarters. The old general kept me up almost all night, inquiring of every body and every thing in America, especially of the people in Lebanon, and above all, the family of Huntington,[16] with whom he had been quartered. In the course of the evening, some official paper was brought to him, for his signature, and observing that he wrote with his left hand, I glanced my eye at his right, and saw that it was disabled, useless. I remarked upon this. "Yes," said he, "last year, in Belgium, the Austrians cut me to pieces, and left me for dead, but I recovered, and finding my right hand ruined, I have learned to use my left, and I can write and fence with it tolerably." "But sir," said I, "why did not you retire from service?" "Retire!" exclaimed he, "ha!—I was born in a camp, have passed all my life in the service, and will die in a camp, or on the field." This is a faithful picture of the military enthusiasm of the time, 1795.

Next day I proceeded on my journey to Paris. On my arrival there, heard no more of being ordered to quit the country; remained a few days, completed my business of pictures,[17]—sent them on to Guernsey, and followed at my leisure.

The island of Guernsey is beautiful and fertile, and has a very extraordinary harbor—at high tide, perfectly safe, with a good depth of water—at low, entirely dry, with a bottom of solid rock; the entrance almost perfect by nature, and the defect supplied by a fine pier. The roadstead is surrounded by reefs of rock, with deep water, and perfect safety from almost all winds, but exposed to others. I remained here a few days, saw my paintings safe, gave orders to ship them for London, and make insurance. I then crossed

16. Of Norwich, Conn. Jedediah Huntington, 1743–1818, married Faith Trumbull, the artist's sister. JT painted 3 generations of Huntingtons.

17. There is a vast amount of correspondence, bills, and accounts at the Yale Library covering this long, complicated, and partially disastrous transaction; more is to be found in the New York Public Library.

the channel to Weymouth, and went up to London, where the pictures soon followed me, and arrived in safety.

The London docks were not then built, and goods were generally landed by the help of lighters. Orders were very thoughtlessly given by the broker, to get my pictures to the custom-house as soon as possible; and they were obeyed to the letter, without my reflecting that the next day was the 12th of August, the birth-day of the Prince of Wales,[18] and of course a holiday at all public offices. The lighter-men brought my cases safely to the custom-house quay, when finding no one to receive them, the custom-house closed, no business doing, and all the porters, watermen, &c. making merry, they thought they might as well join. It was near low water, so they made the lighter fast with a chain to one of the posts, for perfect security, and then went their way for a frolic. In the evening, when the tide came in, the bow of the boat being held down by the chain, she gradually filled with water, and my cases being light, floated out. The watchmen on the wharves, who had paid some attention to their duty, observed cases floating in the river, gave the alarm, and the cases were all saved, and got on to the quay. The next morning I went to the custom-house, to have my cases opened, the pictures examined, and duties settled. To my astonishment, I found the cases already on the quay, dripping with water, and upon opening them, the paintings all water soaked, (for the cases were by no means water-tight,) and apparently all irretrievably damaged. My first impression was, to abandon the whole to the underwriters. With this view, I first consulted mercantile friends, and finally obtained the opinion of the celebrated Mr. Erskine; [19] his answer was, that the underwriters were not holden. In the mean time, the paintings had all been removed by permission, to the extensive rooms of my friend, Mr. West, and there I passed the remainder of the season in repairing, as well as I could, the damage they had sustained.[20]

18. 1762–1830, prince regent, 1811, and George IV, 1820, an honorary member of the American Academy of the Fine Arts in 1819.

19. Thomas Erskine, 1st baron Erskine, 1750–1823, Whig member of the House of Commons, 1790–1806, celebrated trial lawyer.

20. There were two auction sales. The earlier was at Christie's; see *A Catalogue of the most Superb and Distinguished Collection of Italian, French, Flemish, and Dutch Pictures, a selection formed with peculiar Taste and Judgment by JOHN*

In the following autumn, another speculation was contemplated by three considerable mercantile houses in London, founded on

---

TRUMBULL, Esq., during his late Residence in Paris, from some of the most CELE-BRATED CABINETS in FRANCE . . . which will be Sold at Auction by Mr. CHRISTIE, at his Great Room in Pall Mall, on Friday, February 17th, 1797, and the following Day (JT's own copy of this with prices, estimated and actual, is in the Yale Library). The second was at Peter Coxe, Burrell & Foster on 17 May 1798; see Frits Lugt, Répertoire des catalogues de ventes publiques . . . 1600–1825, and William Buchanan, "The Trumbull Collection," Memoirs of Painting, with a Chronological History of the Importation of Pictures by the Great Masters into England since the French Revolution (2 vols., London, R. Ackermann, 1824), 1, 257–270; buyers' names and prices noted. The Times, London, for 16 February 1797, carried a notice of the sale and on 20 February 1797 noted: "The sale of Mr. Trumbull's collection of pictures closed on Saturday, and it sold extremely well. The highest priced pictures were bought by Mr. West, supposed to be for the King. Among these were Deijenara and the Centaur, 588/. A Landscape, with figures and cattle, by Berghem, 945/. and the Virgin, Christ and St. John, by RAPHAEL, 892/. The whole collection, containing 91 pictures sold for 8217L. 17s." The Morning Herald, London, for this last date noted: "The sale of Mr. Trumbull's elegant Collection of Pictures, at Christie's, has commenced with more advantage to the Connoisseurs than to the proprietor. Many of the most celebrated pieces have been knocked down at very moderate prices." The True Britain for 21 February 1797 repeated much the same story. Even in the United States the event was reported. The Connecticut Journal (New Haven) for 26 April 1797 stated: "The sale of Mr. Trumbull's pictures, says a London paper, has greatly excited the attention of connoisseurs, and with good reason they have chiefly been collected during the unhappy troubles and distresses of France, and the knowledge of Mr. Trumbull, he being himself an artist of high eminence, enabled him to select pictures that were highly valuable, the whole number in the catalogue, including two drawings by LeBrun, was 91, and the sum they produced was seven thousand, seven hundred and eighty odd pounds. There were several specimens of Teniers, and some of them were excellent, particularly the Concert, with portraits of himself and family, and the Chymist. The First sold for one hundred and thirty-five guineas, and the other for one hundred and seventy-five. The Pordenone, or as some of the connoisseurs affirm, the Padnanino, was knocked down at five hundred and eighty guineas. The Berghem at nine hundred, and the Raphael at eight hundred and fifty." And in a subsequent paragraph: "Mr. Trumbull's collection of 91 pictures produced the comfortable sum of 8217 £. 17s." JT's friend, the sculptor Joseph Nollekens, wrote: "My friend Mr. Robertson [Andrew Robertson], the justly-admired Miniature-painter, upon receiving an exquisitely beautiful picture by Raffaelle, consigned to him by Mr. Trumbold, invited Mr. Nollekens, among many other artists of eminence, to see it: but, with all its excellence, it appeared to make no impression upon him whatever; and the only observation he made upon leaving the house, was 'Well, as you are pleased with it, I am glad you have got it.'" John Thomas Smith, Nollekens and His Times (London, Lane, 1920), 1, 323. Benjamin West's interest in the sale amounted to an estimated £2,900.

apparently the soundest calculations.[21] The crops of corn had fallen short to such a degree, that the distillation of spirits from corn was prohibited in all the British dominions. The crops had also failed in the West India islands, so that very little rum could be expected; the stock on hand in the market was trifling, yet the navy and army must have their rations of liquor. Brandy, in the mean time, was plenty in France, but could be obtained only by the aid of a neutral, as not every one could be entrusted with such an important and extensive concern. I was offered a fourth part of the expected profits, on condition that I should go to France, purchase the brandy, ship it in my own name, the merchant partners agreeing to furnish the necessary funds, and bear all loss. The temptation was irresistible;[22] I undertook the business, and immediately went over to Rochefort, where I soon found myself involved in all the intricacies of a great commercial operation. As assignats were expiring, it became necessary to draw bills of exchange to a large amount, on foreign neutral houses; to negotiate those bills for cash (*metallique*) in Paris; to transport this coin across La Vendee, then in the most horrible state of civil war; to purchase brandy; to see it prepared (cut) for the particular market; to see it shipped, &c.; and all this was done advantageously, yet our speculation failed. For, in the first place, a severe loss, to the extent of twenty or thirty thousand pounds, was incurred by the well intended temerity of a bold Irish captain, commanding one of my ships, loaded with more than four hundred and twenty-nine pipes of Cogniac brandy, of very superior quality. He arrived in Guernsey Roads one fine summer afternoon, came to anchor, and, according to orders, sent letters on shore to my correspondent and the harbor master, who both happened to be in the country. The captain looked at the entrance of the port, and at the sky; the wind was fair, the sea was smooth, the tide favorable, and nothing visible to prevent his running the ship safely into the harbor. There was some risk in lying all night in the open road—the mind might change—but he could

21. JT's detailed correspondence, accompanied by invoices, shipping declarations, and so on, fully covering the brandy episode (from the collection of Col. Ralph H. Isham, a Trumbull descendant), is at the Yale Library.

22. To the great detriment of his painting.

see no danger or difficulty in going in. He therefore hoisted his anchor, set his sails, ran the ship in, with perfect security, and in the most gallant style. He then made her fast to another large ship, and thought that all was well. But he did not know that the ebbtide left the harbor absolutely dry, nor that he had moored his ship over a part of the bottom where the rock sloped outward, like the bottom of a basin. In the night, with the turn of the tide, the ship touched the rock; as it continued to ebb she heeled outward, and at length fell over on her side, with a heavy crash, which stove every cask of brandy, and the ship herself, producing thus a total loss of ship and cargo, for which the underwriters could not be held responsible, inasmuch as the policy was violated by having gone into port without a pilot, and as the ship was considered by the captain, to have been safely moored.

An additional evil, and definitely ruinous, was that my partners in the concern, dazzled by the probability of splendid success, pushed the purchases too far, so that when the article began to arrive in the port of London, they found it difficult to meet the payment of the duties, which amounted to nearly as much as the first cost, (and I had by their instructions expended in my purchase nearly £80,000, or $400,000 cash.) The moment it was discovered that they were pressed for money, purchasers held back, when they were at length under the necessity of selling at a reduced price; and they were happy at last to wind up the account without much loss, instead of having made a splendid profit. By the agreement, I was not answerable for any loss, but I had gained nothing, and had thrown away eight months of precious time, to say nothing of the risk I had run.

Having closed all my accounts in France, I returned to London, by the way of Guernsey, and arrived early in August, 1796, having in little more than two years passed through the several varieties of a political secretary, a picture dealer, and a brandy merchant. A new scene now opened, which must be the subject of another chapter.

On my arrival in London,[23] early in August, I received from

23. In 1797 JT lived at 29 Berners Street just around the corner from Benjamin West's on Newman Street. "Berners Street . . . was built about the middle of the

Mr. Pickering,[24] then secretary of state of the United States, through Mr. King,[25] a commission and instructions, appointing me agent for the relief and recovery of American seamen impressed by Great Britain; [26] and before I had an opportunity of returning an answer, I received notice from the commissioners who had been appointed by the two nations to carry into execution the seventh article of the late treaty, that they had appointed me the fifth commissioner.

The vast importance of the latter situation left no room for hesitation as to accepting it, and the probable difficulties of this duty, forbade the attempt to execute those of the other also, which, although inferior, were still too important to be exposed to any risk

---

eighteenth century, and has always been celebrated as the 'home and haunt' of artists, painters and sculptors. In this street Sir William Chambers dwelt in 1773; Fuseli in 1804; and Opie from 1792 to 1808. (Thornbury's 'Old and New London', IV, p. 464)." Quoted from Lilian and Ashmore Russan, *Historic Streets of London* (New York, Crowell, 1927), p. 30. For some years before his marriage in 1800 JT lived in the next block, at 72 Welbeck Street. Both streets begin at Oxford Street, not far from Oxford Circus, and run north as far as Mortimer Street.

24. Timothy Pickering, 1745–1829, of Salem, Mass., Harvard 1763, Revolutionary general and statesman, secretary of state, 1795–1800. JT included his portrait in the "Surrender at Yorktown" (No. 30 in the Key).

25. Rufus King, minister to Great Britain, 1796–1803, JT's lifelong friend and patron. JT painted his miniature in 1792 at Philadelphia (Yale); during their stay at London he painted Rufus King twice, bust size (Yale and a descendant, Charles King Lennig, Junior, of Chestnut Hill, Philadelphia), Mrs. Rufus (Mary Alsop) King (plus a posthumous replica), and their four sons, John Alsop, Charles, James Gore, and Edward—all of these between 1800 and 1801.

In 1796 the versatile JT designed 3 Indian Peace Medals (which were struck at Birmingham, England, in 1797), on the order of James McHenry, secretary of war, through Rufus King. The medals had considerable distribution in the west during the presidencies of Adams and Jefferson. See Bauman Lowe Belden, *Indian Peace Medals Issued in the United States* (New York, American Numismatic Society, 1927), pp. 22–24.

26. JT's commission as agent of the United States, dated 10 June 1796, signed by President Washington and Secretary of State Timothy Pickering, is to be found in the General Records of the Department of State, Record Group 59, National Archives, pp. 86–87, and the accompanying Instructions, from the secretary of state, on pp. 163–166. The latter contains the following information: "You will be allowed for your services and for your personal and travelling expenses, a compensation at the rate of two thousand five hundred dollars a year."

of neglect. I therefore wrote the following answers, which are copied from my letter-book of the time.[27]

London, August 26th, 1796.

To John Nickoll,[28] John Anstey,[29] Christopher Gore,[30] and Wm. Pinckney,[31] Esqrs.

GENTLEMEN—I have received your note of yesterday's date, in which you inform me, that, "pursuant to the authority vested in you by the treaty of amity, commerce and navigation, between his Britannic Majesty and the United States of America, you have appointed me fifth commissioner for the execution of the seventh article of said treaty."

Having determined to return to America in a few weeks, and having taken my arrangements in part for that purpose, I was not prepared to give you an immediate answer to a proposition as unexpected as it is honorable; but the reflection, that the duty which I owe to my country, and the satisfaction which I shall have in cooperating with you, gentlemen, (by removing an unfortunate ground of discontent,) to restore and confirm the harmony and good understanding which are equally the interest of the two nations, induces me to accept the honor which you have been pleased to confer upon me,—in the hope, however, that it may be in our power to fulfil the intentions of the treaty by an accomplishment

27. JT started a large and beautifully kept letter book in August 1796, which he continued until July 1802 (New-York Historical Society). The drafts of most of the later correspondence are on separate sheets—often on odd bits of paper.

Another letter book, in the Library of Congress, contains much information about the Jay Treaty negotiations.

28. John Nicholl, 1759–1838, king's advocate, 1798; knighted that year; Privy Council, 1809; judge of the High Court of the Admiralty, 1833.

29. John Anstey, barrister and poet, came to the United States to settle Loyalist claims before serving on the mixed commission; while here probably met John Jay.

30. JT painted 5 portraits of his lifelong, influential friend (Christopher Gore), 2 of which were done in 1800 at London (Yale, and Massachusetts Historical Society, Boston). He also painted Mrs. Gore (Rebecca Amory Payne) at the same time.

31. William Pinkney, 1764–1822, lawyer, statesman; painted by JT *ca.* 1800 at London (portrait in the hands of a descendant).

of our duty so prompt, as shall not too seriously interfere with my wish for an early return to my country.

I shall have the honor to meet you at nine o'clock, as you request, at the house of Doctor Nickoll, in Lincoln's Inn Fields. I am, gentlemen, &c. &c.

JOHN TRUMBULL.

London, August 27th, 1796.

To the Hon. Timothy Pickering, Esq.,
secretary of state of the United States of America.

SIR—On my arrival here from the continent, a few days ago, I had the honor to receive from Mr. King, your letter of the 9th of June, enclosing a commission from the President of the United States, appointing me to act in this country, as agent for the relief of American seamen; accompanied with a copy of the law instituting that office, and your instructions relative to the manner of its execution.

During the time I was with Mr. Jay, my private affairs had been very much neglected; they now require my attention. I saw under this commission no opportunity to render any very essential service to our countrymen, nor any obligation to attempt it, from a probability that the humane and interesting object of the appointment could be better attained by my agency, than by that of many of our countrymen to whom it might be less inconvenient; and, for these reasons, as well as from an aversion to public employments, I had determined to beg you to return my thanks to the President, for the honor done me by this mark of his remembrance, and to request that another person might be named. An unexpected and more weighty reason is now added, which at once renders it unfit that I should hold this office, or persist in the resolution which I had formed to avoid public life.

Mr. Gore will have informed you of the manner adopted for naming the fifth commissioner, under the seventh article of the late treaty, and that the lot has fallen upon me. I am to add, that I have thought it to be my duty to accept the employment so singularly conferred, and have, with the other commissioners, taken the oath prescribed by the treaty.

In doing this, I feel that I have taken upon myself a situation of much responsibility, and which, on some occasions, may prove peculiarly delicate; being placed in it in some sense, by the joint choice of the two nations, the strongest obligation is imposed upon me to obtain accurate information of the law of nations, and scrupulously to regard that and the great principles of justice and equity in the discharge of this trust. A sincere desire that justice may be done speedily, impartially, and in the most conciliatory manner, will govern my conduct, and if on any occasion I should be thought by either party to err, I must rely upon the candor of both to believe that my errors will be those of judgment only, from which none of us are free. I have the honor to be, &c.

JOHN TRUMBULL.

[EXTRACT]

London, Sept. 7th, 1796.

To John Jay, Esq., &c. &c.

"You will know that I have most unexpectedly become once more an agent in the business of the treaty, having been, by the concurrence of chance and destiny, named the fifth commissioner, under the seventh article. I could hardly have been called to a situation more unlooked for than this. I feel its delicacy and importance, and the imperfect preparation for its duties which I derive from the general nature of my pursuits, for many years past. But the general principles of justice and equity, I hope, are sufficiently established in my mind, to prevent the danger of any gross errors; and the law of nations, so far as it relates to this subject, is neither so voluminous, nor so intricate, but that the degree of attention which I have sometimes given to other subjects, applied to this, will I trust, render me sufficiently master of it. It will, however, be almost impossible so to conduct, as not to offend alternately, some of both parties; and I must trust to the candor of the dispassionate, to do me justice in believing, that if I should be thought to err, my errors will at worst be those of judgment only, from which the best and the wisest can claim no exemption."

JOHN TRUMBULL.

[EXTRACT]

London, Sept. 7th, 1796.

To Oliver Wolcott, Esq.,
secretary of the treasury, United States.

"You will know, from the secretary of state's office, that I am placed by the singular concurrence of choice and destiny, in a state of the most absolute neutrality. I shall sometimes find it difficult perhaps to distinguish the precise point of justice and equity, and my endeavors to ascertain it, may possibly give offense alternately to both the interested parties; *but, as I neither sought this situation, nor shall ever seek any other of public responsibility,* it may at least be relied upon by both, that what I do will be the true result of my best knowledge and judgment, imperfect doubtless, but at least honest in intention."

JOHN TRUMBULL.

The commissioners having taken the oath dictated by the treaty, proceeded immediately to hold meetings, for the purpose of making the necessary arrangements for entering upon their important duties; such as naming a secretary and other necessary officers, establishing an office, rules of business, &c. In the course of these preliminary discussions, it soon became manifest that the difficulties which I had apprehended in my situation of fifth commissioner, were by no means imaginary or exaggerated; it was easy to foresee, that the commissioners of each nation were likely to regard the conduct of their own government as right and just, and that they were bound to support and defend its acts and measures, and that therefore, the decision of almost every important question must devolve upon the fifth commissioner.

Upon the very threshhold of business, we were met by a question, which bid fair to occasion the most serious disagreement. "What are the cases which are to be entertained and examined by this board?"

The treaty requires that the complainant shall state, "that he has suffered loss and damage, for which he cannot obtain just and adequate compensation, in the regular course of judicial proceedings.

He cannot assert this until he shall have gone through the entire course of regular judicial proceedings. The last step of regular judical proceeding in England, is the ultimate decision of the high court of appeal, that is to say, of the king in council. Does any one suppose that this board has power to examine, revise, and reverse the decisions of this supreme tribunal?" asked the British members of the board. "Certainly," replied the American members, "if it should appear to us, that in any case the high court of appeal had decided, rather in conformity with *the laws and usages of England,* than in consonance *with the law of nations, and the principles of equity and justice,* it will become our duty, as it is clearly within our power, to examine the case, and to make such decision as shall be in conformity with the law of nations, and the principles of justice and equity. If this be not the true construction of our powers, it does appear to us that this article of the treaty is little better than a nullity."

Such was the outline of the agreement, placing the commission in a state of helpless inactivity, between the two horns of a dilemma. It remained for me to decide.

My opinion was decidedly with the American members. But I saw distinctly, that in the eyes of the British gentlemen, the question was of the deepest importance, and that a decision contradictory to their reverential estimate of the sanctity of the high court of appeal, would be submitted to by them with extreme reluctance, if it did not produce a remonstrance against our abuse of authority—a refusal to proceed in the business—ultimately a dissolution of the commission;—and thus, a renewal of angry discussion between the two nations. I therefore took time to consider, and finally suggested, that the question should be submitted to the lord chancellor (Loughborough) [32] for his decision. He had taken a deep interest in the negotiations of the treaty, and undoubtedly, must know the intentions of the parties. The British members of the commission readily acceded to this proposal; an audience was asked of the lord chancellor and obtained, at which all the members of the board were present. The question was stated by the senior

32. Alexander Wedderburn, 1st baron Loughborough and 1st earl of Rosslyn, 1733–1805; lord chancellor, 1793–1801, under Pitt.

British commissioner, on which the board requested his lordship's opinion, and the answer was immediate and frank.

"The construction of the American gentlemen is correct. It was the intention of the high contracting parties to the treaty, to clothe this commission with power paramount to all the maritime courts of both nations—a power to review, and (if in their opinion it should appear just) to reverse the decisions of any or of all the maritime courts of both. Gentlemen, you are invested with august and solemn authority; I trust that you will use it wisely."

This decision of the chancellor terminated the difficulty, relieved me from a situation of extreme delicacy, and the board immediately proceeded in its duties.

In July, 1797, I found myself under the necessity of deciding the very important question of general blockade, and the detention of neutral vessels, laden in part or entirely with provisions, bound from neutral to hostile ports. From the beginning, I had made it a rule to give my opinion in writing in all cases where questions were to be decided by my voice. This question was highly important, and I endeavored to study it carefully. The elaborate opinion which I gave, will form the following chapter.

This was an American vessel,[33] bound to a port in France, with a cargo consisting of rice, tobacco, indigo, &c., American property, captured in June, 1795, by one of his Britannic Majesty's frigates, acting under the general order of April, 1795, which directed the bringing into British ports of all neutral vessels laden in whole or in part with provisions, and bound to ports of the enemies of Great Britain.

Proceedings were had, in this case, in the form which was adopted on that occasion, and which commenced with an order of the judge of the high court of admiralty, that the cargo should be sold to his

33. The case of the *Neptune,* James Jeffries, master, chartered by William Harrison and John Price & Co., claim preferred by Thomas Mullet & Co.; see *International Adjudications,* Modern Ser., 4, "Compensation for Losses and Damages Caused by the Violation of Neutral Right and by Failure to Perform Neutral Duties" (New York, Oxford University Press, 1931), pp. 372–442; JT's opinions of the question of provision as contraband, pp. 427–433, and of judicial remedies, pp. 433–439. The case was tried before the commission under Art. 7 of the Jay Treaty.

majesty's government, and resulted in a decree of the same court, that both vessel and cargo belonged as claimed to neutrals,—an order of the court to restore the vessel, with freight, demurrage, and expenses—costs, both of captor and claimant, to be paid by his majesty's government, and the value of the cargo to be paid by the same to the neutral owner.

The vessel was, of course, restored as ordered, and the value of the cargo ascertained in the manner following, viz. The registrar and merchants proceeded, under an order of the court, to make their report under the usual form, in which they stated the invoice-price, and ten per cent. thereon as the value of the cargo, to be paid by his majesty's government to the neutral owners. Against this *ex parte* mode of sale, as well as against the measure of value, the claimant, by his agent, remonstrated to the registrar and merchants, while making up their report, as inadequate and unjust, inasmuch as the sum resulting from this mode of estimation was much below what would be the result at the current market-price at the port of destination, or even at the port of London; requesting at the same time permission to sell the cargo himself, under bonds that it should be sold and delivered in England. To this application and remonstrance he received for answer, from the registrar and merchants, "that, although his case was doubtless a hard one, yet, as they acted by the express order of government, they could give no more, being bound by instructions officially received, to give, in all such cases, ten per cent. on the invoice price, as a fair mercantile profit." The agent for the claimant, however, not satisfied with this answer, pursued his inquiries further, until he received from a high official character (as stated to us in his affidavit) the same answer, and an absolute refusal of his request for permission to sell the property himself, under bonds that it should be sold in England. Concluding then, as it was natural for one of his majesty's subjects to do, that information so obtained was true and correct, and perceiving it to be useless and presumptuous for an individual to struggle further against an order of his majesty's government, he abandoned any further attempt to obtain a remedy in the ordinary course of judicial proceedings, and being pressed by the necessity of meeting bills which had been drawn in America, on the expected proceeds of this cargo, and which otherwise must have gone back, subject to such heavy damages as might prove ruinous to his correspondent there—but protesting at the same time against the injustice of the mode of sale, and the inadequacy of the sum ordered to be paid, according to the report of the registrar and merchants—he received the same, and now comes before this board, claiming such further sum as shall appear to the board a full and adequate compensation for the loss and damage which he has sustained.

A memorial, in the usual form, has been preferred to the board in this case, accompanied by sundry papers. Copies of this memorial, and of these papers, have been submitted to the agency of his Britannic majesty, in the usual manner, and the usual time has been allowed to him to lay before the board his objections in writing to the prayer of the memorial. Those objections have been received, and without offering any reasons exclusively applicable to this particular case, or arising out of any peculiar circumstances attending it, we find them to be general against the powers of the commissioners as extending to cases of this description; and they appear to rest, for much of their force, on the construction of the eighteenth article of the existing treaty between Great Britain and America. On the correctness of this general objection, a difference of opinion exists at the board, which leaves the decision of the question to me.

A just sense of the very high responsibility which devolves upon me, under such circumstances, induced me to form an early determination to give my opinion in writing on all such occasions—and that determination is strengthened by the painful and unfortunate frequency with which such occasions have hitherto recurred—in order that, in discharging this arduous and unpleasant part of my duty, I might impartially give their just weight to the arguments of each of the commissioners, (all of whom, from the nature of their education and studies, must, unquestionably, possess a degree of knowledge far superior to what I can pretend to on subjects of this nature.) It was further my wish to have been indulged, on all such occasions, with the sight of the written opinion of each member of the board previous to giving my own. I should then have seen the precise and meditated arguments of learned men reduced to point, and divested of that looseness and inaccuracy of expression which too generally accompany verbal discussions; and those arguments thus correctly and visibly before me, would neither have been subject to be weakened by the incorrectness of memory, nor to be distorted by any misunderstanding arising from the rapidity of conversation. I have requested this indulgence in the present case; and if it should seem from my decision, that I have been less influenced by any of the arguments which I have heard, than those gentlemen who have made use of them may feel that they deserved, I hope to be forgiven.

The numerous and concurring authorities which the gentlemen with whom I agree in opinion, have, in the course of their written arguments on this case, quoted from the writings of the most eminent men, appear to me so clear and conclusive, as to render it equally unnecessary, as it would be presumptuous in me to follow them in that mode of examining the subject. I shall therefore confine myself to such views of it as might naturally offer themselves to men of no extensive reading or profound reflection, and such as may appear, perhaps, more particularly to affect the equity than the law of the case.

The subject, obviously, divides itself into two leading questions:

First. Has the neutral claimant, in this case, sustained loss or damage, by reason of an irregular or illegal capture or condemnation of his property?

Second. Could the neutral claimant actually have obtained, had and received, full and adequate compensation for such loss and damage, in the *ordinary course* of judicial proceedings?

If the ship had been taken in the act of entering, or attempting to enter, a port or place actually besieged, blockaded or invested, and known to the neutral master to be so, I believe there is little doubt but the capture, considered under the existing law of nations, would have been regular and legal.

But if, with his majesty's agent, we admit that the existing treaty between Great Britain and America, was in operation at the time of this seizure, (although not then ratified,) it will then follow undeniably, that even if the ship had been stopped in the act of entering, or attempting to enter, a port or place actually besieged, blockaded or invested, yet if the neutral master was ignorant of that fact, he could not, regularly and legally, have been seized as prize, nor even detained. His case would have fallen under the provision of the third section of the eighteenth article of the treaty, and it would have been the duty of the captor to have notified to the neutral the state of the place, and (having prevented his entering such port) to have permitted him to proceed to any other port or place without interruption. If then, even in attempting to enter a port or place actually besieged, blockaded or invested, (the neutral master not knowing it to be so,) it was inconsistent with this eighteenth article to seize or even to detain the ship; much less must such seizure or detention appear to be justifiable under that article, the ship being bound to a port not besieged, blockaded or invested, for it is not pretended that Bordeaux, (the port of destination in this case,) or even any particular port of France, much less the whole country, was at the period in question in such a state.

But it is held that cases other than those of actual siege, blockade or investiture, are evidently alluded to in the eighteenth article of the existing treaty, as justifying "the seizure of provisions, or other articles going to the enemy, in certain cases." This, however, does not appear to me to be correct. There is, indeed, an evident allusion to, or rather declaration of, a difference of opinion on this subject, on which the two negotiators finding it difficult to agree," all decision appears to have been therefore intentionally waived; and in order that "this difficulty of agreeing on the precise cases in which alone provisions, and other articles, not generally contraband, may be regarded as such," might not become a source of future contention between the two nations, in consequence of the possible continuation of contrary opinions on this subject of special contraband, it was wisely stipulated, "that when provisions, or any such articles, so becoming contraband, according to the existing law of nations, shall for that reason be seized, the same shall not be confiscated, but the owners thereof shall be speedily and completely indemnified." The stipulation extends only to cases where provisions, &c. shall become contraband, "according to the existing law of nations." Those appear to be limited in all the books, to cases of actual siege, blockade or investiture. It is however further alledged, that "every case where there exists a reasonable hope of reducing the enemy to terms of peace by famine," is also within "the spirit of the law." But such a description must necessarily remain vague and indefinite, because it may always be questioned by the one party whether the hope entertained by the other was reasonable or not. No new cases or descriptions of contraband, are either established or admitted by this eighteenth article, which, on the contrary, instead of increasing the restrictions and inconveniences of neutral commerce, and thus opening new sources of dispute and misunderstanding, I do conceive to have been intended, (as several other articles of this treaty evidently were,) to remove the grounds and lessen the probabilities of future mutual complaints; to extend, rather than to narrow, the benefits of the state of neutrality, and thus to diminish to mankind in general, those inconveniences which are necessarily and unavoidably consequent upon every extensive war between great maritime nations. This article provides only for cases "where provisions, or other articles not generally contraband, may become so, according to the existing law of nations." What is the universally acknowledged consequence of an attempt to carry contraband goods to an enemy, according to those existing laws?—An unequivocal right not merely to seize, but *to confiscate without reserve*. But this eighteenth article stipulates that provisions, &c., "*so becoming contraband*," shall not be confiscated. How then does this article vary the law? Not by enlarging the description of contraband beyond what shall be consistent with the existing law of nations, and to the prejudice of the state of neutrality, but by stipulating, to the benefit of neutral commerce and of mankind at large, that even "in certain cases where provisions and other articles not generally contraband, *may become so, according to the existing law of nations,* and for that reason be seized," yet "the same *shall not be confiscated,* but" (on the contrary) "the owners thereof shall be speedily and completely indemnified."

The tenth article of the treaty appears to have been suggested by the same principle, which I believe to have animated the two eminent negotiators on other occasions—a sincere desire to diminish rather than to extend those evils which inevitably accompany the state of war; and this article which is here I believe for the first time made part of a solemn engagement between two nations, will do honor to those who have here introduced it, in proportion as the long neglect of a stipulation so obviously just, is unworthy of praise in the negotiations of past ages. Let me suppose that some metaphysical head should undertake to derive a right, under that article, to confiscate property in the public funds, or debts due from individuals, in the event of peace and good understanding, because such confiscation is prohibited only, "in any event of war or national difference." The odd ingenuity of such an argument would excite our surprise, and perhaps call up a smile; yet would not this logic be nearly as sound as that, which, from a stipulation to pay for goods "become contraband in certain cases, according to the existing law of nations," would infer a right to seize as contraband, provisions, &c., in cases where they are manifestly not so according to that law?

The argument in justification of the present seizure, is then reduced to this, "that the right of the belligerent to seize as contraband, provisions going to the enemy, extends to all cases where there exists a reasonable hope or expectation of reducing an enemy to terms of peace by famine." I willingly waive all those objections to this vague and indefinite principle, which arise in general from the difficulty of ascertaining what are cases in which a hope of this nature may reasonably be entertained; because I do not think it difficult to demonstrate, that the case before us was not of that description.

In Coxe's View of America, published in 1793, will be found a correct and official statement of the exports of the United States for the preceding year, 1792; from which we learn, that the whole quantity of bread-stuff exported from that country, during that year, was as follows, viz.

Of flour,   824,464 barrels, at 190 lbs. each, is 156,648,160 lbs.
" wheat,   853,790 bushels, "   60 "   "   51,227,400 "
" maize, 1,964,973   "   "   60 "   "   117,898,380 "
" rice,   141,762 tierces, " 300 "   "   42,528,600 "
And in all other articles of a nature convert-
   ible into bread, including ship-bread and } 31,697,460 "
   biscuit,

Total of exports, pounds,   400,000,000 "
To this add for increase of weight by } 100,000,000 "
   making into bread, one fourth,

And we shall have, pounds of bread,   500,000,000 :

being all that could be made from the whole exports of America for the year 1792.

In a work published in France in 1775, "Sur le Legislation et le commerce de Grains," regarded as one of the most estimable and correct works of the kind extant, may be found a note, at page fifty nine of the first Paris edition, Chap. xiii, in which the author states his opinion of the quantity of corn or bread, annually and daily consumed by the inhabitants of France, and a very correct detail of the principles and inductions, on which this opinion is grounded; from which it appears, that the inhabitants of France were then estimated at twenty four millions, and that each inhabitant was estimated to require for food, about two septiers or eight and two thirds Winchester bushels of corn each year, equal to one and a half pounds of bread daily. In his estimate of the quantity of bread, this author has been followed by Neckar [33a] and others, but almost all agree that the actual number of inhabitants in France exceeds his estimate. I will however follow him entirely, and by his estimate, we shall have thirty six millions of pounds of bread, as the daily consumption of the French nation.

We have before seen that all the corn, &c. exported from the United States of America in the year 1792, would have produced five hundred million pounds of bread. Dividing this sum by thirty six million pounds, the amount of the daily consumption of France, we have as the result, nearly fourteen days' bread for the people

33a. Jacques Necker, 1732–1804, director-general of finances under Louis XVI.

of that country. Fourteen days are the twenty sixth part of the
year: supposing then, that each person in France should prudently
economize, each day, one twenty sixth part of his customary allowance of bread, and instead of twenty four ounces, eat somewhat
more than twenty three; and the same effect would be produced, as
by the importation of all that America could export.

I am well aware that in a case of sudden alarm, or apprehension
of scarcity, (in a country habituated to ease and plenty,) where
the actual evil is magnified ten-fold by the united operation of
fear and avarice; the importation of such a proportion of foreign
corn would be of vast importance, by dispelling the fears of the
timid, and by opposing the dread of a falling market to a disposition to monopolize. Such was lately the state of England; the alarm
(which is now known to have had little true foundation,) was too
sudden and universal, to be remedied by the slow but certain operation of a system of economy only, and government wisely had recourse to the same passion which was the principal cause of the
evil—a bounty on foreign corn was offered, and the importation of
a quantity comparatively very trifling, produced the most salutary
and important effects. The public sale of this small quantity in the
London market, produced a reduction of price, and of course from
every part of the country, corn was hurried to market by those who
before had been busily employed in hoarding and withholding it.
But such was not the state of France at the period in question.
There the people had long apprehended and sometimes felt a real
degree of scarcity; the attempt to reduce them to terms of peace
by famine, had already been made in 1793, without success, although under circumstances much more favorable to the hopes of
her enemies. The people had of course been trained to habits of
economy, and had learned to rely on that resource, whose operation when once generally adopted, is infinitely more effectual than
any aid which may be hoped for from foreign supplies. I must be
permitted to observe, that in the foregoing statement I have given
the most unlimited extent to the argument against me, for in
truth, almost all the wheat which is exported from the United States
goes to Portugal, where, for the benefit of the manufactures, the
importation of flour is prohibited, and almost all the maize or In-

dian corn is sent to the West Indies, and there forms a principal part of the food of the blacks; so that deducting these two great articles from the account, it can scarcely be possible that even on extraordinary occasions, more than one half of the exports of America can find their way to France. Thus, in fact, this hope of reducing the French nation to terms of peace by famine, (so far as the interruption of American commerce would influence,) is founded on the supposition that the people of France may be reduced to the necessity of eating one fifty second part less than their usual allowance of bread.

But it may fairly be objected to the whole of this argument, that it is altogether hypothetical, and that I have considered only the resources drawn from America, whereas, I ought to consider that all supplies from abroad were intended to be intercepted by the entire interruption of neutral commerce. I am happy to have it in my power to give more correctness to this part of my argument, and to state from official documents, what real effect was produced both by the orders of 1793, and by those of 1795.

An important paper, (No. 23 of the appendix to the third report of the committee of secrecy, printed in April, 1797,) showing the amount in value of the corn imported into, and exported from Great Britain, in the years 1793, '4, '5, '6, and '7, gives us correct and unquestionable information on this subject. It is there stated, that the corn of all nations either detained, or brought into ports of Great Britain as prize, amounted to the following value, viz.

In 1793 and '4, to	. . .	£232,771 12s. 5d.
" 1795,	"	. . . .	129,063 03s. 7d.
" 1796,	"	. . . .	20,384 13s. 8d.

I will suppose this entire quantity to have consisted in wheat, which, in the paper referred to, (No. 23,) is stated to be valued at 32s. the quarter, or 4s. the bushel; at that rate of value, the above several sums will give us the following quantities of wheat, viz.

1793 and '4, bushels,	1,163,860	at 60 lbs. each, is	69,831,600 lbs.
1795,	"	645,316	" 60 "	" 38,718,960 "
1796,	"	101,923	" 60 "	" 6,115,380 "

Let it next be understood that the whole of this corn so captured or detained, at those several periods, was destined to ports of France, then we shall find that, by their capture, the French nation was actually deprived of the following part of their bread, viz.

In 1793 and '4, of almost two days' bread.
In 1795, of something more than one day's bread; and that
In 1796, they did not lose one breakfast.

Such was the real effect produced by the operation of the orders of 1793 and 1795.

At the time of the transaction which gave rise to the present discussion, the trivial effect of the order of 1793 must have been known; and it is palpable, therefore, that the order of 1795 could not have been founded in any *reasonable* hope or expectation, of thereby reducing the French nation to terms of peace by famine. An ardent and enthusiastic enemy cannot *reasonably* be expected to make any considerable sacrifice of his animosities, his prejudices or his pursuits, in consequence of such very trifling inconveniences as we see were the consequence of the orders in question.

From the foregoing observations I trust it sufficiently appears, that the capture in question cannot be justified by the law of nations, under the description of goods attempted to be carried to a place actually besieged, blockaded or invested; nor yet under the eighteenth article of the existing treaty; nor yet under the broad idea of a reasonable hope of reducing the enemy by famine. It only remains to inquire, whether there existed at the time any necessity on the part of the captor, so pressing as to justify the act.

The necessity which can be admitted to supersede all laws, and to dissolve the distinctions of property and right, must be absolute and irresistible; and we cannot, until all other means of self-preservation shall have been exhausted, justify, by the plea of necessity, the seizure and application to our own use, of that which belongs to others. Did any such state of things exist in Great Britain in April, 1795? Were any means employed to guard against an apprehended, rather than an existing scarcity, before the measure in question was adopted? And when a degree of scarcity really was felt, a few months later in the year, was not the obvious and inoffensive measure of offering a bounty on corn imported, effectual, and that speedily? It cannot then be presumed, that the capture in question is any more to be justified by the plea of necessity, than it is by that of right; and I must therefore conclude, that the neutral claimant has in this case suffered loss and damage by reason of an irregular and illegal capture.

I am next to examine the second leading question, viz. Whether, *in the ordinary course of judicial proceedings*, the neutral claimant could actually have obtained, had and received, full and adequate compensation for the loss and damage which he has so sustained.

When in a public instrument of contract between two nations, the ordinary course of judicial proceedings of one of the parties, is made the rule by which the other party is bound to govern his conduct on an important point, we must presume that the meaning of the term *ordinary course*, is easily within the knowledge of the foreigner, whose interests are made so materially to depend upon a correct understanding of the term. In the present case, the most obvious and authoritative source to which a foreigner would naturally look for information on the subject, appears to be the written law, by which proceedings in matters of prize are regulated, commonly known by the name of the prize act: he would naturally conclude that this act was intended by the legislature, to provide and define the *ordinary* course of judicial proceedings in matters of prize.

I have followed this mode of inquiry, and in seeking in that act, for provisions descriptive of, or applicable to, the proceedings which have been had in this and similar cases, I find very few of its provisions which are so applicable. But I observe, that the thirty fifth section of the act reserves authority to his majesty, with the advice of his privy council, to give from time to time, such further rules and directions to his courts of admiralty, as by him shall be thought necessary and proper.

The ordinary course of judicial proceedings, I conceive then to be pointed out in the body of the act; and the thirty-fifth section, I presume, was intended to apply to extraordinary and unforeseen cases which might arise, and which might, in the opinion of his majesty's government, require measures varying from the ordinary course which the act had already defined.

The prize act authorizes all persons acting under commissions or letters of marque, duly granted, to seize and bring into port, &c. all vessels, &c. belonging to *enemies* of Great Britain. The seizure in question is understood to have been made under an order or instruction of his majesty, for seizing and bringing into port, &c. *all neutral vessels,* laden, either in whole or in part, with provisions, and bound to ports of the enemy. It is further understood to have been part of that order and instruction, "that the officers and companies of his majesty's vessels of war, acting in execution thereof, were to be paid a certain sum per ton on the measurement of the neutral vessels which might be so taken in lieu and discharge of all other and customary claims." I say *understood* to have been, because we have not been able to procure a copy of the order itself, which circumstance forms an additional point, in which this business varies *ab initio* from the ordinary course of proceedings, according to which his majesty's orders and instructions (of this nature) to his vessels of war are public, and copies thereof always easily to be obtained, at his courts of admiralty. Thus it appears that the capture, or first step in the business before us, took place in obedience to a particular order of his majesty's government, varying from the ordinary course of proceedings.

The second step in this case, in which a wide deviation from the ordinary course of judicial proceedings is observable, is, that the judge of the high court of admiralty, as soon as the cause was brought within his cognizance, and before any decision or even inquiry was made, whether the property belonged to neutral, friend or enemy, ordered the cargo to be sold to his majesty's government, and afterwards, upon due examination, decreed both vessel and cargo to belong as claimed to neutrals. In this deviation from the ordinary course, it is also understood, that the judge acted in obedience to an express order of his majesty's government.

A third conspicuous deviation from the ordinary course of judicial proceedings observable in this case, is the manner of sale, and the rule by which the value of the cargo, decreed to be paid to the neutral owner, was ascertained. The merchants, by whom the registrar was assisted in this case, are highly respectable and very well informed men. It must have been obvious to them, that the cargoes of different ships are very seldom composed either entirely of similar articles, or of various articles in precisely the same proportion; and that, of course, one rate of compensation could never, with equal justice, be applied to many cases. In cargoes composed principally of articles for which the demand was great, it must have been evident to them, that ten per cent. advance on the foot of the invoice, was not an adequate compensation; and it must have been equally evident, that in other cases of cargoes composed principally of articles not in demand, ten per cent. might be more than an adequate compensation. Those gentlemen acting as in the ordinary course of judicial proceedings, and following the dictates of their own judgments and consciences, would never have thought it their duty to adopt this rule of ten per cent. (which might thus prejudice, in some instances, the interests of their own nation, and in very many those of the neutrals) as a measure of justice, equally applicable to all the variety of cases which the order of April, 1795, might bring before them; and, accordingly, we find them declaring to the claimant, that they (in thus deviating from their ordinary course) acted in obedience to the particular and positive instructions of his majesty's government.

The agent for the neutral owners, (a respectable merchant of the city of London, and a British subject,) states to us, in an affidavit in due form, that after remonstrating in vain with the registrar and merchants, while making up their report, on the injustice of applying the rule of ten per cent. in this case, he (being so referred by them for further information) made personal application to Mr. Long,[34] one of the secretaries of his majesty's treasury, that having repeated to him the hardships of this case, and having solicited permission to take the sale of this cargo into his own hands, giving bond that it should be sold in England, he received for answer from Mr. Long, "that the whole business had been conducted, and the registrar and merchants had acted in obedience to

34. Charles Long, Baron Farnborough, 1761–1838, member of Parliament, joint secretary to the Treasury, 1791–1801, amateur, collector, later trustee of the British Museum and of the National Gallery.

the orders of his majesty's government, and that no deviation from the rules established by those orders, could be admitted in any particular case;" and upon the proposal of the said agent to carry his inquiries and remonstrances to a still higher authority, he was answered by Mr. Long, "that all further application would be vain; that the execution of this branch of business was committed expressly to his (Mr. Long's) direction, and no variation from the system which had been adopted by his majesty's government would be admitted."

Thus it appears, that the whole of this transaction, from its commencement to its ultimate stage, was out of the ordinary course of judicial proceedings; and that by the express and repeated orders of his majesty's government.

It is now to be inquired, whether the claimant, by any possible endeavors to pursue the ordinary course of judicial proceedings further than he did, could in the end, actually have obtained, had and received, full and adequate compensation for the loss and damage which he complains to have sustained in this case.

We have been told that an application to the judge of the high court of admiralty, to correct the report of the registrar and merchants, would have been effectual; but I cannot consider this to be presumable; nor can I even regard the claimant as having been under any obligation to attempt that mode, because we have seen that the judge himself had deviated as essentially from the ordinary course of proceedings, in obedience to one order of his majesty's government; and I cannot perceive a shadow of reason for believing that he who had yielded a ready obedience in one stage of the business, would have undertaken, at the next step, to oppose or control another order emanating from the same high authority.

It does not appear to me that the judge could have done so consistently with his duty; nor, in truth, can I comprehend, that the captor, the judge, or the registrar and merchants, have done either more or less than their duty, in the whole course of this transaction. They have acted in their several characters of officers or servants of his majesty, who, by the thirty-fifth section of the prize act, is expressly invested with the power to give them such further instructions, as to him, with the advice of his privy council, shall appear to be necessary; further instructions were given in this case, and these servants of the crown had but one duty—to obey.

It may here, perhaps, be objected, "that it does not appear that the order under which the registrar and merchants acted, was an order of his majesty, with the advice of his privy council, and that neither were they bound to obey an order given by any other authority, nor was the judge bound to confirm their report, unless made in obedience to the order of that particular authority." I beg leave to reply, that neither does the contrary appear; the objection may, with equal justice, be extended (for aught we know) to the orders under which the capture was made, and to that under which the cargo was sold to his majesty's government, since all these orders were in such complete deviation from the ordinary course, as to have been, and to remain at this hour, all and equally invisible to us. It is enough to my argument, that they were thus out of the ordinary course, and (whether rightfully or not is not for us to inquire) that in fact, they have been obeyed by his majesty's officers and servants, and thus have hitherto prevented the actual receipt of full and adequate compensation by the neutral claimant.

One step only remained to have been taken by the claimant, in compliance with the ordinary course, which appears to me to have offered any hope of relief—an appeal to the lords commissioners—and this we understand to have been omitted, in consequence of the answer of Mr. Long to the agent, which has been stated above. We are told that this was not sufficient authority, and that an appeal ought to have been instituted notwithstanding that answer. What authority then would have been sufficient? Is it expected that the prime minister, or the lord president of the council, shall personally answer every question respecting the several departments? Why are secretaries attached to those departments, if faith and credence are not due them? Mr. Long, a member of the house of commons of England, has been for several years one of the confidential and efficient secretaries of the first minister; a character of no light import, whether we consider the very important duties of the employment, or the discriminating talents of that great man, under whose near and constant inspection those duties are performed.

I confess myself so confirmed in habits of subordination, that I should regard the information officially given to me by Mr. Long, relative to a measure actually adopted, or to an order actually given by his majesty's government, to be of exactly equal authority, as if it had been communicated to me by the minister himself.

But here again the objection returns, "that the order of his majesty's government, is not the order of his majesty with the advice of his privy council." Granted; and I will for a moment admit, (what is by no means ascertained by any evidence before us,) that the orders under which the captor and judge acted, were orders of the king and council; and that the orders under which the registrar and merchants acted, were not. What then would have been the course of the business? By his majesty's government, let me be understood to mean, those ministers to whom his majesty is pleased to confide the executive power and business of the government. His majesty's government (in common with the executive branch of every government) must possess an unity of sentiment and action; that is, there must reside somewhere a power to prevent discord, and the struggle of any part against the general will, since these would tend to produce contradictory measures, to introduce confusion, and to obstruct the business of the nation. This controlling power is generally understood to be in the prime minister; where it actually does reside, requires no long investigation. We need only look to the order of council of the 26th of February last. Let it further be remembered, that the ministers composing his majesty's government are also members of his majesty's privy council, and of course have a right to—and on important occasions actually do—sit as lords commissioners of appeal in prize cases. Knowing and remembering these things, are we to believe, in direct contradiction to precedent and to daily practice, that the lords commissioners of appeal, would on this occasion have placed themselves in direct opposition to an important measure of his majesty's government?—that his majesty's government would thus have become "a house divided against itself?" Is it not rather to be believed, that if the lords commissioners had found themselves embarrassed by the supposed informality of the order in question, this embarrassment would have been removed, by a reference to the privy council for the adoption of the necessary forms? I cannot but believe that such would have been the course, and that an appeal would have answered no purpose to the neutral claimant but to create delay, and to increase his expenses; neither can I believe that many Englishmen, of candid minds, can really persuade themselves to entertain a contrary opinion.

I trust that I have thus made manifest at least, a very high degree of improbability of redress having been attainable by the neutral claimant in this case, in the ordinary course of judicial proceedings; but it may be denied that I have demonstrated the absolute impossibility.

I beg leave to refer those who may be disposed to make this objection, to the legal arguments of other gentlemen on this subject, and particularly that of Mr. Pinckney. These appear to me to be fully conclusive, and therefore have my entire assent. I shall content myself with further observing, generally, that the first step of the judge, in ordering the cargo to be sold to his majesty's government, and its consequent delivery out of the custody and control equally of the captor and of the court itself, into the hands of his majesty's government, or its agents, discharged the captor in every view of justice or of equity, that I can comprehend, from any just responsibility thereafter. By what process consistent with the ordinary course of judicial proceedings, the neutral claimant after that step, was to obtain, have and receive, the full compensation which is the object of the treaty, either from the captor, who appears to me to have been thus deprived of that, which, in the ordinary course of judicial proceedings, constitutes the object and the measure of his responsibility, or from his majesty's government, whose responsibility respects only the supreme tribunal of the nation, I confess I cannot comprehend. I have searched in vain that act, which I understand to designate the ordinary course of judicial proceedings in matters of prize, and which is the measure and rule of the claimant's duties; and finding no such process there designated, I cannot but conclude, that it was not possible for the claimant in this case, actually to obtain, have and receive, full and adequate compensation for the loss and damage which he has sustained, in the *ordinary course* of judicial proceedings.

To no extraordinary means had he either the power or the obligation to have recourse, except to that which he has followed by his memorial to this board; and it is clearly my opinion that we are bound carefully to examine his case, and to give therein such award, as shall appear to us to be consistent with equity, justice, and the law of nations.   (Signed)   JOHN TRUMBULL. July 26th, 1797.

The board of commissioners adjourned on the last of July, to meet on the 1st of November, 1797.[35] I had received information from Mr. Müller, the engraver, at Stutgard, that he had finished the engraving of the battle of Bunker's Hill, and waited my final criticism and orders. This recess of the board allowed good time for the journey to Stutgard,[36] and I determined to go, passing through Paris, for the purpose of closing all my business and accounts there.

35. On 12 January 1797, Martha Washington had written to JT: "From the hands of Mr Anthoney, I received a proof print engraved from the whole length Portrait of the President. I received it, Sir, as a mark of your esteem and polite attention, and shall set great store by it accordingly . . . a few weeks now, will place me in the shades of Mount Vernon, under our own vines and fig trees; where, with very sincere assurances I may add, we should be always extremely happy to see you. For the numberless instances of your politeness to me, I pray you to accept my thanks; and to be persuaded of the great esteem and regards. The President has enjoined it upon me to tender you his sincere regards." (Huntington Library, San Marino, Calif.) The print was the stipple engraving, dated 1795, and again in 1796, by Thomas Cheesman of London, after JT's portrait of the general painted at Philadelphia in 1792, and now at Yale. Joseph Anthony, Senior, a cousin of Gilbert Stuart, was a Philadelphia jeweler and silversmith and JT's agent for the sale and distribution of his prints, with a place of business at 76 Market Street. JT wrote to General and to Mrs. Washington on 25 April 1797 (drafts at the New-York Historical Society), in answer to their letters of 12 January.

36. For his trip to Germany, it is interesting to note, JT's traveling wardrobe consisted of the following articles: "3 Coats, 10 Vests (8 Cotton & 2 Silk), 5 d^o Flannel, 1 pr Silk Breeches, 3 d^o Kerseymere d^o, 1 d^o Ribb'd Cotton d^o, 3 d^o Nankeen, 4 pr Flannel Drawers, 10 pr Worsted hose, 6 d^o Cotton d^o, 16 d^o Silk d^o, 9 Shirts, 9 Cravats, 9 Handk's, 4 Night Caps, 1 Silk handk's, 1 pr Conkshell shoe and knee buckles, 1 pr. Silver Shoe latchets, Razors & instruments for Teeth, Sword, Pistol & Ammunition, Flannel Dressing Gown, Writing Desk with Telescope, etc., Dressing Case, Great Coat, 3 pr Shoes, 1 pr Black Slippers, 2 d^o half boots."

He also took "2 Pocketbooks to give to Mrs & Miss Müller," and "2 Doz^n of Pencils to give to Mr. Müller" and "1 Doz^n of best Gravers from Mr. Sharp to D^o." (Yale Library.) English-made engraving tools were evidently preferred to the German.

M. Talleyrand [37] was, at the time, minister of foreign affairs in France. He had been in America, and was there treated with marked civility by my brother, then speaker of the house of representatives of the United States; had there known also, and been treated with the utmost hospitality and kindness by my friends Mr. King and Mr. Gore. I therefore requested letters from them to the minister, and felt myself secure of a kind reception. I crossed to Calais, where I found it necessary to remain, until a passport could be obtained from Paris. I wrote immediately to M. Talleyrand and my bankers, put my letters in the post-office, with my own hand, and in regular time received an answer from the bankers, but none from the minister, nor any passport, and of course I remained in Calais three weeks, in a state of painful surveillance.

It had become a popular notion in France, that the enemies of the republic had adopted a particular color of dress, by which they recognized each other—a sort of freemason sign—a grey coat, with a cape of black velvet. This was a favorite color with me, which I had worn for several years, and, unluckily, one morning I walked to the public square in this suspected dress. I observed on the opposite side of the square, a considerable assemblage of people, apparently in some agitation, and I had hardly entered the square, when I heard the cry, "*à bas, les collets noirs—à bas, les collets noirs.*" (Down with the black collars.) It was fortunate that I understood the language, and caught instantly the cry and its horrible meaning. I hurried back to my hotel, changed my dress, tore off the offending collar, and threw it in the fire. The next day's post explained the irritated state of the people; it brought news of the Revolution,[38] as it was called, of the 18th Fructidor,[39] in which Pichegru,[40] Barthelemy,[41] Barbe Marbois,[42] and others, were ar-

37. Charles Maurice de Talleyrand-Périgord, prince de Bénévent, 1754–1838, minister of foreign affairs, 1797–1807.

38. Coup d'état rather than revolution.

39. 18 Fructidor, an V, is 4 September 1797; Fructidor, the 12th month of the Revolutionary year.

40. Gen. Charles Pichegru, 1761–1804, deported to Cayenne.

41. François, marquis de Barthélemy, 1747–1830, politician, diplomat, member of the Directory in May 1797, deported to Guiana.

42. François, marquis de Barbé-Marbois, 1745–1837, politician, deported to

rested and ordered to be transported to Cayenne. In these days, the feverish symptoms of Paris were propagated, through the affiliations of the Jacobin system, with the velocity of electricity, and the pulse of every village responded to the feverish heat of the great political heart. I received by the post a line from my bankers, advising me to get out of the territory of France as soon as possible.

Finding a vessel about to sail immediately for Rotterdam, I obtained a passage in her, and was soon at the Hague, where I obtained from the resident minister of France, a passport to travel up the Rhine to Stutgard, and thence to return through Paris to Calais. There was an armistice at the moment, and in my journey, my road led me alternately through the military positions of the French and Austrian troops. For instance, at Coblentz, I met the funeral procession of General Hoche,[43] which passed under the walls of Ehrenbretstein, and received the funeral salute of respect and condolence from the Austrian garrison. And on the plains of Schwetzingen, my road carried me through the army of the Archduke Charles,[44] of fifty thousand men, engaged in a mock battle on the last day of a grand review. It was a magnificent representation of the awful reality, and had called together a prodigious multitude of spectators, from all the surrounding country. The neighboring city of Heidelberg was full of strangers, and a bed unattainable; I passed on therefore, and soon reached Stutgard.

I found my plate of Bunker's Hill admirably engraved,[45] and requiring very little additional work. I remained a few days, and was present at a splendid ball given in the theatre, on the occasion of the marriage of the Duke of Wirtemberg with the princess royal of England,[46] and there saw waltzing for the first time,[47] in high style.

Guiana, negotiated the treaty in 1803 by which Louisiana was ceded to the United States; one of the original honorary members of the American Academy of the Fine Arts in 1804.

43. Gen. Lazare Hoche, born 1768, French Revolutionary soldier; promoted from corporal to general (1789); died 19 September 1797 at Wetzlar.

44. Karl Ludwig, 1771–1847, archduke of Austria and duke of Teschen, 3d son of Emperor Leopold II and brother of Francis II.

45. One of the finest engravings after JT's work.

46. The marriage took place on 18 May 1797; the bride was Charlotte, daughter

Having received my picture and copper-plate,[48] and settled with M. Müller, I obtained from the Prussian resident minister, as well as from the government of Wirtemberg, passports for Paris, and set off with the intention of passing through Strasbourg, but was stopped near Rastadt, which had been named as the place for the approaching negotiation, and was obliged to return through Carlsruhe and Baden to Manheim. There I found the military again in motion, and with some difficulty obtained from the Archduke Charles, his passport to pass the military posts on the frontier. I went on, through roads very much broken up by military transportation and neglect, and arrived in Paris about the middle of October.

When I presented myself at the police, *selon les règles*, to obtain

---

of George III, the groom Frederich, duke of Würtemberg, an enormously fat despot with a vile temper; the marriage was not too happy.

47. See Curt Sachs, *Eine Weltgeschichte des Tanzes* (Berlin, D. Reimer, E. Vohsen, 1933), pp. 288–291, and Ethel L. Urlin, *Dancing, Ancient and Modern* (London, Simpkin, Marshall, Hamilton, Kent [1914?]), p. 127: "The Waltz . . . is a German modification of the Italian Volta . . . the first German Waltz-tune was . . . written in 1770. . . . It was first danced at the Paris Opera in 1793 . . . In 1812 it was introduced into English ballrooms and roused a perfect storm of ridicule and protest."

48. The time lag in the receipt of the plate should be noted as it goes far to explain the failure of sale of the engravings. The battle was fought in June 1775; JT finished his picture 11 years later in March 1786; he delivered the painting to Herr Müller in September 1786; the engraving was offered to the public in April 1790; the plate was delivered in late August or early September 1797, and the engravings from it published in 1798, 23 years or a generation after the battle. The same story was repeated, with but slight variations, in regard to the other engraved plates.

When the capital was at Philadelphia framed impressions of the engravings of "Bunker's Hill" and "Quebec" flanked the speaker's chair. JT wrote the speaker of the House of Representatives from his London quarters at 72 Welbeck Street on 20 September 1798: "I beg leave, through you, to offer to the House . . . impressions of the two prints of the American Revolution, which I have lately caused to be published." The House adopted the resolution: "Resolved, That the two elegant prints offered by Mr. Trumbull, be accepted; and that the Speaker be instructed to write an answer, expressive of the pleasure with which this House has observed his genius and talents exerted in the patriotic task of celebrating the events which led to his country's independence, and dedicated to the memory of those heroes who fell in its defence." See *Proceedings and Debates of the House of Representatives of the United States*, at the 1st session of the 6th Congress begun at the City of Philadelphia, Monday, 2 December 1799. (Library of Congress.)

my *carte de residence,* I first offered a German passport; as soon as the clerk observed my name, he asked sharply, *"N'étiez vous pas à Calais, il y a quelques semaines?"* (Was you not at Calais, a few weeks ago?)

"Oui, citoyen." (Yes, citizen.)

"Et, au nom du diable, comment est ce que vous êtes içi?" (And in the devil's name, how did you get here?)

"En vertu de ce passeport, de votre ministre à la Hague"—(by virtue of this passport of your minister at the Hague)—producing it. He looked at it carefully, and then turning to the clerk on his right, and shewing it to him, he said, *"Le bête, il fait toujours des sottises."* (The blockhead, he is always committing blunders.)

I obtained, however, my *carte de residence,* but it was evident that I was remembered, and that the suspicions of 1795 and '6, were not done away.

I immediately set about concluding my commercial affairs, and visited the American X, Y, Z [49] negotiators, Pinckney,[50] Marshall [51] and Gerry.[52] The next morning I was surprised to receive a visit from a French gentleman, M. D'Hauteval,[53] whom I had known some years before as consul at Boston. After the first compliments of recognition, he asked if I had yet seen the minister.

"What minister, sir?"

"Oh, M. Talleyrand, to be sure."

"No, sir; I wrote to him some weeks since, and having received no answer, I concluded that he did not wish to recognize me, and that it would be thought impertinent in me to visit him."

49. See Carl Ludwig Lokke, "The Trumbull Episode, a Prelude to the 'XYZ' Affair," *The New England Quarterly,* 7 (March, 1934), 100–114, which covers JT's part in the event thoroughly.

50. Charles Cotesworth Pinckney.

51. John Marshall, 1755–1835, of Richmond, Va., chief justice of the United States Supreme Court, 1801–35.

52. Elbridge Gerry, 1744–1814, signer of the Declaration of Independence, governor of Massachusetts, and vice-president of the United States, 1813–14; JT included his portrait in the "Declaration" (No. 20 in the Key) and "Resignation of Gen. Washington" (No. 3). JT's cipher with the note "Gerry, Marshall, and Pinckney have the counterpart" is at the New-York Historical Society.

53. Lucien Hauteval, a Swiss, was "Z." See Stewart Mitchell, ed., *New Letters of Abigail Adams,* p. xxxvii.

"Oh, no; on the contrary, he will be happy to see you; I have just been with him, and he told me so."

"In that case, I will wait upon him without delay."

I went therefore, was admitted, received with great civility, and invited to dine. I accepted the invitation, went, found the company small—among them Madame de Stael,[54] Lucien Buonaparte,[55] Count Lorigey,[56] &c. During the dinner, Madame de Stael attempted to engage me in a conversation on the subject of American affairs, but the minister cut her short with, "*Mais, Madame de Stael, on ne politique pas içi.*" (But, Madame de Stael, nobody talks politics here.)

I conversed with Lucien Buonaparte, at whose right hand I was seated, on the subject of his brother's wonderful success—the bridges of Lodi,[57] Arcola, &c. Towards the close of the dinner, a continued regular firing of cannon was heard; all were anxious to know the cause. The minister coolly replied, "*On annonce le traité de Campo Formio.*" (To announce the treaty of Campo Formio.) [58]

I hurried the settlement of my business, occasionally seeing the American ministers, and learning from them the strange state of their affairs. I also occasionally saw the ministers of several small German states, all trembling for their future existence, and endeavoring to avert the impending danger, and learned from them all, that the permission even to speak of negotiation, could be obtained only by the previous payment of sums proportioned to their ability to pay. Such was then the general system—not confined to us, but universal.

Having closed my financial and commercial concerns, I applied at the police for a passport, to leave Paris and France, but met with

54. Germaine de Staël, 1766–1817, French-Swiss woman of letters whose full name was Anne Louise Germaine Necker, baronne de Staël-Holstein.

55. Lucien Bonaparte, prince of Canino, 1775–1840, who became, in 1825, an honorary member of the American Academy of the Fine Arts, New York, of which Trumbull was then president.

56. JT possibly refers to Jean Nicolas Loriquet, 1760–1845, theologian and historian.

57. In Lombardy near Milan, where, on 10 May 1796, Napoleon defeated the Austrians after storming the bridge over the Adda.

58. Between France and Austria, signed 17 October 1797, news of which reached Paris on the 27th.

delays, which satisfied me, that my first reception was but the omen of coming evil. I was referred from day to day, and from office to office, until I began to be alarmed. The 1st of November was at hand, on which day I ought to be in London. In this embarrassment, I applied to the American ministers for advice and protection, and was answered by Gen. Pinckney, "My friend, I know not what to advise; we have no means of aiding you, we cannot even protect ourselves; so far from it, indeed, that I shall not be at all surprised, if within thirty six hours, we should all meet in the temple."

Having nothing further to hope here, I resolved on trying the influence of M. Talleyrand. I went at once to his office—he was there —and I was immediately admitted to a *tête-a-tête* interview, in his private bureau. He received me with great politeness, and immediately began to talk of the American negotiation, as if I was intimately connected with it. This I denied, assuring him that I had no manner of connection with it, nor any other knowledge of its progress or state than was common to the public. He next alluded very distinctly to the necessity of *the employment of money,* to which I replied, "Sir, you have been in America, and know the constitution of the United States, probably better than I do. You must know, that the ministers can take no important step which is not prescribed by their instructions, and I can hardly imagine that the government of the United States could have anticipated the necessity of employing money to facilitate this negotiation." The minister listened to this answer with evident impatience, and exclaimed, (striking the table violently at the same time,) *"Mais, il le faut, Monsieur."* (But they must, sir.) I endeavored to keep my countenance, and replied with a smile, "That is their affair; I am happy to repeat, that it is no concern of mine."

From the strange turn and result of this conversation, it was manifest that I had nothing to hope from that quarter, and therefore I rose to take my leave. The minister resumed his usual calm, cold manner, accompanied me to the door, and as I was about to open it, said, in his softest tone, *"Mais, comment se porte Hamilton?"* (But, how is Hamilton?) This was the only inquiry he made for any of those from whom he had received such unbounded civilities in the United States.

I withdrew, and with a heavy heart went again to the police, where I was told, with an air of solemn politeness, "*Si le citoyen veut bien monter le grand escalier, en entrant la premiere porte à droite, il trouvera l'homme qui fera son affaire.*" (If the citizen will be so good as to walk up the grand staircase, and enter the first door on his right hand, he will there find the man who will do his business.)

I mounted the grand staircase, entered the first door on my right, and there, in a large low *entresol,* found one old man sitting at a desk, in a corner of the room, whose appearance at once suggested the idea of a solitary spider watching for flies. As I entered, he looked up from the desk before him, and accosted me with "*Que veux-tu, citoyen?*" (What would you, citizen?)

My reply was, "*Un passeport, pour aller à Calais, et m'y embarquer pour Hambourg.*" (A passport to go to Calais, and there to embark for Hamburg.)

"*Et ton nom?*" (And thy name?)

I told him. He looked carefully at a paper before him, and with a look, and in a snuffling, sneering tone of voice, which it is impossible ever to forget, returned, "*Ah, on te connait très bien içi*"—(ah, you are very well known here)—and resumed his pen.

I had now my definitive answer from the police; it was manifest that this man had before him the list of those, who, in the phraseology of the day, were to be *garde à vûe,* that is, to be kept always in sight, and that my name was upon that list.

I descended the *grand escalier,* (great staircase,) with heart and foot heavier than when I mounted it. I endeavored to recollect some one whom I had formerly known, to whom I could look for aid in this extremity. The name of David flashed upon my mind. His intimate connection with Robespierre, in the most horrid period of the Revolution, had hitherto deterred me from making any attempt to renew my former acquaintance with him; but now my situation appeared to be desperate, and he the only person of my acquaintance in France, from whom I could flatter myself with any hope of assistance. I therefore went to his apartments in Louvre, found him at home, was instantly recognized, and very cordially received, although many years had elapsed since we had met. He immediately inquired about my picture of Bunker's Hill, Mr. Müller, and the engraving. I told him that I had been at Stutgard, that the plate was finished to my entire satisfaction, that I had both plate and painting with me, and was on my way to London for the purpose of printing and publication, but found very unexpected difficulty in obtaining a passport to proceed, and asked him if he knew the minister of police, and could give me any assistance. He replied that he did not know the present minister— "but I know his secretary, and that may do as well. Go to your hotel, my friend, get the picture, and return with it. In the mean time, I will change my dress and go with you to the police, *et nous verrons, ce tableau-là vaut bien des passeports,*" (and we will see— that picture is worth a multitude of passports.)

I did so, returned, and he entered the carriage with me. In our short drive to the office of the police, the conversation turned naturally upon the strange events which had occurred in Paris since our first acquaintance. "True," said he, "much blood has been shed, but it would have been well for the republic, if five hundred thousand more heads had passed under the guillotine." I shuddered— and this, thought I, is the only man on earth to whom I can now look for assistance in a case which involves the question of imprisonment or death.

We arrived at the police, and, anxious as I was, I could not but be struck with the ludicrous effect produced upon the crowd of clerks, (to whom I was by this time well known,) when they saw me again enter, the Bon Citoyen David [59] leaning familiarly upon my arm—he had broken the *tendo Achillis,* and was lame of one leg.

He asked, in the tone of a master, for the secretary's room; we were shewn in, and he immediately entered upon my cause. "I have known Mr. Trumbull these ten years—I know him to be an American, and opposed to the English in their war. *Je vous en*

59. JT, in a footnote, explained that " 'Bon Citoyen' was, during the revolution, the favorite title of honor."

réponds; il est bon revolutionnaire tout comme nous autres"—(I answer for him; he is as good a revolutionist as we are,)—horrid encomium from such lips. "He saw the battle of Bunker's Hill, and has painted a fine picture of it—here it is. *Il est grand artiste, et on fait mal de le retenir dans ses occupations actuellement paisibles des arts."* (He is a great artist, and it is wrong to interrupt him in his present peaceful occupations of the arts.) This plea from the Sieur David was irresistible; the secretary looked at the painting— admired it—regretted that my character had been so misrepresented and misunderstood—I should have a passport immediately. "But, sir, I must first present you to the minister; he will be pleased to be undeceived—to see you and your picture."

We were shown into the minister's room, and presented to him. The same eulogy from David, the same approbation of the painting, and an immediate order for the passport—the minister adding, with a most courteous smile, "I am half disposed, however, to use the power which I possess, and to retain in the service of the republic, *un artiste de tant de talent,"* (an artist of so much talent.) The passport was immediately prepared, and I left the office of police in triumph, returned the most sincere thanks to my friend David, took leave of him and his family, ordered post-horses, and was instantly upon the road for London.

Here let me pause a moment, upon the character of the man from whom I had just received such an inestimable service. David was naturally a kind and warm-hearted man, but ardent, sometimes even violent, in his feelings; an enthusiastic admirer of the Roman republic, and of all the illustrious characters of Rome, he most admired the elder Brutus, who had sacrificed his two sons for the good of his country. He had painted a fine picture of this subject,[60] and had wrought up his own feelings to the belief that all which was otherwise dear must be sacrificed to our country. When the Revolution commenced in France, he took the popular side, devoted all the energy of his character to the establishment of a

---

60. "Les Licteurs rapportant à Brutus les corps de ses fils" or "Le Retour de Brutus dans sa maison," painted in 1789, collection of Louis XVI, now in the Louvre; a smaller version of the same subject is in the Wadsworth Atheneum, Hartford, Conn.

republic, (that favorite phantom of the age,) and had brought himself to the full belief, that the blood of individuals was of no more value than water, in comparison with the success of his favorite theory. This gave to his public life the imprint of a ferocious monster, while, as a private individual, his primitive character of kindliness resumed its sway. No man could be more kind and amiable in his family; no man could have taken a deeper or more ardent interest in the dangers of another, than he had done in mine, although not otherwise connected with me than as an acquaintance and a brother artist.

The 1st of November was but to-morrow, and I resolved to travel day and night, that I might reach London as little after my time as possible.

At St. Dennis, the first stage from Paris, I stopped to change horses, and as I drove up to the post-house, I observed that the yard was unusually crowded; and among others, a tall, gaunt, Don Quixotte looking man, in cavalry uniform, with a sabre proportioned to himself, whose glittering steel scabbard clanked upon the pavement, as he stalked up to my carriage, and leaning his arm familiarly upon the door, (the glass was down,) he looked in and said, *Le citoyen est seul,*—(citizen, you are alone,)—in the quaint laconic language of the day. *Comme vous voyez, citoyen,*—(as you see, sir,)—was the equally concise reply, while my fears, not fully lulled, from the late scenes, whispered to me,—here is a new trap; this man is posted here to intercept me, and examine my papers, in the hope of finding some important communications relative to the negotiation, from the American ministers to Mr. King in London, or to the government in America.

"Are you going to Chantilly?" was the next question of my spectre neighbor.

"Yes."

"Will you give me the vacant seat in your carriage?"

I glanced my eye at the irresistible sabre, and answered, "Willingly, sir."

As he opened the door to enter, he said, "I have been too abrupt, I should have given the reason for my request. I command a de-

tachment of cavalry, which is stationed at Chantilly, for the protection of public carriages, and of travellers generally, from a
banditti who infest the forest, and have lately committed several
atrocious robberies. I have been into Paris this morning, on business, and have lamed my favorite horse, which will be ruined if I
ride him any further. I must not be absent from my post a night,
and had been watching some time for the arrival of some traveller,
from whom I might ask a ride, when you drove up, and I thank you
for your kindness."

I breathed more freely. He took his seat, and appeared to be a
plain blunt soldier.

"You will stop at Chantilly?" said he.

"It is not my intention; I am in haste, and mean to travel post,
night and day."

"You are going to Calais?"

"Yes."

"You are an Englishman?"

"No, an American of the United States."

"But your carriage is English; you are going to London?"

"True, and impatient to get on."

"You cannot go on to-night; you must stop at Chantilly, and sup
with me, for the forest is dangerous, and my men are harassed, so
that I cannot give you an escort until morning."

Again my heart beat quick. I was completely in the power of
this man—there was no possibility of escape—he would execute
his commission at his leisure, and search me in his own quarters,
surrounded by his troops.

We drove on, and after a short silence he abruptly asked, "Do
you know the Prince de Poix [61] in London?"

"I have seen him."

"He is a great fool," exclaimed he. "He commanded a company
of the royal guard, in which I was a private soldier; he emigrated,
and I command in his place. Was not that folly?"

Again I began to be reassured, and to believe that he was indeed

61. Antoine Claude Dominique Just, comte de Noailles, prince de Poix, 1777–
1846, diplomat.

an honest, blunt, heels-over-head soldier. We rode on, and all his conversation was in the same heedless style; and I recovered my tranquillity, though vexed at the unavoidable delay.

We reached Chantilly early in the evening, and he hurried to his quarters, promising to return in half an hour to supper. This he did, and we supped together most amicably and cheerfully. At length, he asked at what hour I chose to proceed in the morning, and receiving for answer, "at daylight,"

"*Bon, a l'aube du jour vous entendrez sonner le bugle de votre escorte, dessous votre fenêtre.*" (Well, at daybreak we shall sound the bugle for your escort, under your window.)

We separated in mutual good humor. I ordered horses to be put to my carriage at daybreak, retired, and slept with some composure, after the various agitations of the day. With the early dawn, I was up and dressing, when the bugle sounded under my window, as promised. I mounted my carriage and drove off, under the escort of ten as fine hussars as I ever saw. A few hours carried us through the forest, without any adventure, and the subofficer and guard took their leave, *en militaire*, wishing me a pleasant journey.

My object now was to arrive at Calais, if possible, before the post from Paris, for I felt myself on the crater of a volcano, and after the experience of the last few weeks, could not divest myself of the apprehension, that some capricious change of opinion might yet produce an order to arrest me, before I could embark. I therefore hurried on, drove to the hotel *ci-devant de Dessein,* and inquired of Quillac, if there was any packet for Dover in port.

"No, there is one just arrived in the road, but she cannot come into the port this afternoon, as it is low water."

"If she comes in, will it be possible for her to get out to-morrow morning, before the arrival of the post?"

"No."

"Then send on board, and desire the captain not to come in, but to be ready to receive me where he lies, and to sail very early in the morning."

"But, sir, that will cost you dear."

"No matter for the expense, I am in haste; here is my passport from the police at Paris, to embark—engage the vessel at any price."[62]

The bargain was made at seventy guineas, a part of which was however saved, by permitting several passengers, who were waiting, to embark with me. We were on board early, sailed with a fair wind and tide, and in a few hours I found myself safe on British ground. Never, in my long life, have I experienced more heartfelt satisfaction, than I did on feeling that I was out of the reach of such a sanguinary and capricious government, as was that of France at the time of my late visit to the continent.

I reached London the next morning, bade a long farewell to dangerous adventures, and returned to the sober quiet duties of the commission.

Referring to the twelfth chapter [63] of this work, it will be observed, that the third difficulty attending the negotiation of Mr. Jay, was a complaint by the British government, "that several of the American states had withheld the settlement and payment of debts contracted with British subjects before the Revolution, in contradiction to the stipulation of the treaty of peace of 1783."

This subject of complaint was, by the treaty of November, 1794, referred to a commission, to be formed on the same principles as that under the seventh article of the same; and accordingly, the two gentlemen appointed by Great Britain, Mr. McDonald and Mr. Rich,[64] sailed from England for America early in the winter of 1796-7, and soon after their arrival the commission was organized, and commenced their labors in Philadelphia. Differences of opinion on important questions soon manifested themselves in

62. JT was due back at London, as a member of the commission, on 1 November. He did not arrive there until the 11th.

63. In this volume, pp. 179–191.

64. Thomas MacDonald and Henry Pye Rich, commissioners for Great Britain on the settlement of prewar debts under the Jay Treaty, both serving from September 1795 to September 1799. See "Arbitration of Claims for Compensation for Losses and Damages Resulting from Lawful Impediments to the Recovery of the Pre-war Debts," *International Adjudications*, Modern Ser., 3, and Bernard Mays, ed., "Instructions to the British Ministers to the United States, 1791–1812," *Annual Report of the American Historical Association*, 1936, 3 (Washington, United States Government Printing Office, 1941), 126–127.

their case, as they had done in ours, and resulted more seriously; insomuch that the commission, finding it impossible to agree, even upon first principles, dissolved itself, and the question came back to the two nations as a renewed source of dispute and negotiation.

One of the first consequences of this dissolution, was the suspension, by the British government, of the commission acting in execution of the seventh article of the existing treaty; and this produced a request from the minister of the United States in London, Rufus King, Esq., "that the commission would furnish him with a statement of the business before the board." In reply to this request, by the direction of the board, I wrote to him the following letter, which I find recorded in my letter-book of the date.

72 Welbeck Street, London, Nov. 16th, 1799.

Rufus King, Esq., &c. &c.

DEAR SIR—Mr. Gore is so good as to take charge of this packet, which contains statements in detail of all the business which has come before the commissioners acting under the seventh article of the treaty, between the United States of America and the government of Great Britain.

You will find noted therein every case, with its actual state, whether decided or not; together with the amount of sums claimed, whether refused, or pending, or awarded in each; and thinking that these statements would be imperfect, unless they were accompanied with a general abstract of the whole, I have endeavored to prepare one, in such a manner as to place the great outlines of the business under the eye at one glance. From this you will be pleased to observe, that the number and amount of the American claims dismissed by the board, nearly equal those in which favorable awards have been the result of careful examination. You will also observe, that the aggregate sum finally awarded to American claimants, including interest and law expenses, falls very far short of the sums claimed, although neither interest nor expenses are generally included in these claims. You will also please to observe, that on the contrary, in such claims by British subjects against the American government, as the board has hitherto considered as within their cognizance, and in which favorable decisions have been made, the sums awarded considerably exceed the sums claimed; which excess arises from *the interest* (which generally is not included in the claim) having been allowed in the awards.

In that paper which contains the details of cases dismissed, you will also find noted, in many instances, the reasons which the board were pleased to assign for such dismissals, and which will show how very different the principles which have governed many of those decisions are, from those which appear to have been adopted in Philadelphia.

In some important cases of award, as well as of dismissal, the different opinions filed by the several members of the board, are referred to; and I trust that the plain result of the whole will be, that the business, as far as it has been suffered to proceed, has not been conducted with negligence or with partiality.

Abstract of claims decided by, or depending upon the decision of the board of commissioners, acting under the seventh article of the treaty between the United States of America, and his Britannic Majesty; collected from the detailed official statements.

AMERICAN CLAIMS.

	Cases.	Amount of claims.	Amount of awards.
Dismissed,	37	£72,864 12s. 0d.	
Withdrawn,	7		
Depending,	393	1,307,497 12 3	
Awarded,	41	129,968 16 2	91,358 17s. 11¾d.
	478	£1,510,331 0 5	£91,358 17 11¾

BRITISH CLAIMS.

	Cases.	Amount of claims.	Amount of awards.
Dismissed,	10	£107,993 14s. 2½d.	
Depending,	43	256,531 00 0	
Awarded,	5	6,733 9 2	£7,558 15s. 9d.
	58	£371,258 3 4½	£7,558 15 9

Total, 536 cases.

From which it appears, that the American claims which have been decided,

Amount to	£72,864 12s. 0d.	
And	129,968 16 2	
		£202,833 8s. 2d.
Of which were granted,	£91,358 17s. 11¾d.	
Dismissed,	111,474 10 2¼	
		£202,833 8s. 2d.

Copy sent to Mr. King, the American minister, enclosed in the foregoing letter; and also copies to Mr. Gore and Mr. Pinckney, the American commissioners.

JOHN TRUMBULL.

November 16th, 1799.

At the close of the second volume of opinions, recorded by members of the board on various questions, which is in my possession, I find also a statement, of which the following is a copy.

"Mr. Samuel Cabot,[65] who was one of the assessors of the board, and who, from his other relations to the claims of American citizens for compensation, on account of captures by British cruisers, previous to the treaty of 1794, had an intimate knowledge of all that was claimed and paid, states the amount awarded by the board, and paid by the British government, to have been in pounds sterling,   £1,350,000

"Amounts recovered from the captors, on what were called Martinique cases, meaning captures in the West Indies,   100,000

"Amounts produced to claimants from other cases of restitution,   160,000

"That the vessels captured, under what were called *"provision orders,"* viz. orders to capture vessels bound to France, and laden with provisions, were in number one hundred and twenty, and that there must have been received from the British government, at least £6,000 each,   720,000

£2,330,000

Amount in dollars, allowing five dollars to the pound sterling, $11,650,000

65. 1758–1819, see Briggs, *History and Genealogy of the Cabot Family, 1,* 198–199, and ch. 13, "Samuel Cabot, Commercial Agent of United States in matter of British Spoliation Claims," *1,* 230–265.

This was the statement of Mr. Cabot, whose accuracy and knowledge on this subject, were beyond all doubt. This amount of money may be justly considered as some of the fruits of Mr. Jay's treaty, and this was the result of my voice, for I do not recollect that a single case of American claims was favorably decided, without the vote of the fifth commissioner.

From the foregoing statement it appears, that the large sum of eleven millions six hundred and fifty thousand dollars, was recovered by American citizens from the hands of British captors, by, or in consequence of, the abused treaty of 1794, negotiated by Mr. Jay. The whole of this sum was promptly and punctually paid to each complainant, or his assignee; for, after a careful and accurate examination of the merits of every case of complaint, the awards of the board were made in favor of each individual, in the form of an order to pay, and payable at the treasury of Great Britain; nor do I recollect even to have heard a single complaint, of the delay of an hour, in any instance of an award presented for payment.

We all remember the parade and triumph which took place, a few years since, when the president whom the people delighted to honor as the greatest and best, succeeded in obtaining from the government of France, the reluctant payment of five millions of dollars. But John Jay was not Andrew Jackson; [66] nor was Great Britain like our great and good ally, the republican kingdom of France. Let those who have eyes to see, and ears to hear, both see, and hear, and understand; and let the blind continue to lead the blind, until they fall into the ditch of ruin and disgrace together.

The commission proceeded to this result, with no farther important interruption, until its termination in the spring of 1804, at which time the business was concluded, and the commission, having fulfilled all its duties, was dissolved.

The commissioners of each nation made a full report of the proceedings and acts of the board to the respective governments by which they had been appointed, accompanied by copies of the journal, and of all important written documents. It is to be hoped, that those which were deposited in the hands of the British government,

66. 1767–1845, 7th president of the United States, was serving, from 1798 to 1804, as a judge in the Tennessee superior court.

have been carefully preserved, and still exist; for, it is known, on the other hand, that those which were placed by the American commissioners in the hands of the secretary of state, were deposited by him in one of those public offices of the government, at the city of Washington, which, soon after, was destroyed by fire; and it is understood, that thus, all official records of the proceedings of this very important commission (in America) have been swept into oblivion.

Nor, can I find that any notice of the closing of this commission, or of the very important extent and happy result of its labors, was ever made to the government and people by the president of the United States, whether in his annual message to Congress, or in any special one; for, it did not consist with the political views and principles of an administration which openly avowed its hostility to the treaty which had been negotiated by Mr. Jay, to publish to the world the result of an article so important to the commercial prosperity, and to the honor of the nation, and the decisions under which had such an important bearing upon the future construction of maritime international law.

It therefore appeared to me proper, that the only American who survives, of those who were employed on that important occasion, should endeavor to redeem such transactions, in some degree, from utter oblivion; and I have been fortunate after so many years, in finding, in my possession, such a mass of manuscripts, of the time, as have enabled me to make the foregoing statements, not as random assertions, depending for their authenticity upon the correctness of memory, but from existing documents.

It is a fact of public notoriety, that one of the commissioners, who received his legal education from the care and bounty of Judge Chase [67] of Baltimore, whose talents and success in life did honor to the discrimination and kindness of the Judge, and who for a time boasted to have derived his learning and his political as well as legal principles from that source, did not assist in the defense of the Judge, when, immediately after the conclusion of the labors of

67. Samuel Chase, 1741–1811, Revolutionary leader, signer of the Declaration of Independence, justice of the United States Supreme Court in 1796.

the commission, he (the Judge) fell under the wrath of the administration, and was brought to trial on the accusation of high treason, for having, in his judicial character, carried into execution, in certain cases, the provisions of the Alien and Sedition law.[68] The trial of the Judge took place before the senate of the United States, the highest tribunal of the nation, and the audience consisted of all that was learned and eminent, thus offering the finest imaginable opportunity for the display of that eloquence, in which it was the just object of that gentleman's ambition to shine. This act, or rather this declining to act, according to the dictates of gratitude, met the approbation of the existing powers, and the gentleman received eminent proofs of that approbation, in successive appointments to the embassy to Great Britain, to Naples, and to Russia, each accompanied by the usual gratuity of nine thousand dollars for outfit, and nine thousand a year salary.

Perhaps no brighter example can be produced of the application of that admirable rule of modern republican policy, which teaches "to reward your friends, and punish your enemies;" a rule, the neglect of which, more perhaps than any other one cause, occasioned the downfall of the administration of John Q. Adams; a rule which, from the days of Washington and of the first Adams, and since, (with the solitary exception of his son,) has been regularly practiced, until it has resolved itself into a still more simple aphorism, which has been formally announced in the senate of the United States, "that to the victors belong the spoils."

The other American commissioner, as well as the fifth, was too deeply steeped in the unpardonable sin of federalism, to be smiled upon by the ruling powers of that day. Mr. Gore's conduct, however, met the approbation of his native state, (Massachusetts,) of which he became, for a short time, governor. Not such however was my fate; my political glory, as well as my military, was departed—to rise no more.

---

68. The first of these, 6 July 1798, to restrict the political activities of aliens; the Sedition Act, 14 July 1798, to deal with civilians or aliens who too severely criticized the government. See John Spencer Bassett, *The American Nation, a History* (New York and London, Harpers, 1906), *11*, 252–264.

7

The New-York Experiment 1804–8

IT HAD been my intention to have embarked in London for Boston, but circumstances prevented my being prepared in time;—I therefore took passage on board a fine ship bound to New York, and sailed on the 25th of April.[1] This delay was unfortunate, since the easterly winds which prevail in that climate, in early spring, were already beginning to yield their dominion to the western; while we lay at anchor in the Downs, and during our passage down the Channel, we met frequent westerly squalls, which retarded our way, and when we had fairly cleared the Channel, we encountered the full force of the western gales, in such a degree, that at the end

1. It is always interesting to note what books an artist reads. When JT packed up his library in July 1803 for shipment to America he had 725 volumes. Nearly all were English classics—Sir Philip Sidney, Samuel Butler, Milton, Bunyan, Swift, Richardson, Johnson, Pope, Addison, Smollett, Goldsmith, and so on; among his histories there was Gibbon's *Decline* in 12 volumes; Adam Smith's *Wealth of Nations* and Blackstone's *Commentaries* were the only two of their kind. Curiously, there was but one art book, Jonathan Richardson's *An Account of Some of the Statues, Bas-reliefs, Drawings and Pictures in Italy, Etc., with Remarks* (London, 1722), the first and, for some time, the best English guidebook to works of art in Italy. Did he, remembering his refusal—to his regret—of Jefferson's once generous offer, intend to go to Italy?

When he returned to England in 1808 he packed up 134 volumes for transportation to London. He stored his household furnishings and books—65 boxes and trunks—at the warehouse of John Murray & Sons. Among the latter were Hogarth's *Analysis of Beauty,* Walpole's *Anecdotes of Painting,* Sir Joshua Reynolds' *Discourses,* Roger de Piles' *Principles of Painting,* du Fresnoy's *Art of Painting,* Vasari's *Lives* (in Italian), J. J. Winckelman's *History of Ancient Art,* Matthew Pilkington's *General Dictionary of Painters,* and Stubbs' *Anatomy of the Horse.* There were books on architecture, including the Gothic, on Palmyra, Balbec, and Herculaneum; books of travel; a portion of his library was in French, a small number in Italian and Spanish. (Check list of 23 June 1808 in the New-York Historical Society.)

236

of twenty days, during which we were contending with the elements in their most angry mood, our captain assured us that we had not advanced a single league, so that it would have been better at the beginning of the gale, to have put into Cork, and there to have lain quietly until it was over. At length, however, we began to go ahead, but the result was a very tedious passage of sixty three days, and we did not land in New York [2] until the 27th of June.

I had not resided much in New York, and of course had there but few connections; our reception, however, by the few friends I had, was cordial and pleasant. On the 4th of July, I dined with the society of the Cincinnati,[3] my old military comrades, and then met, among others, Gen. Hamilton [4] and Col. Burr.[5] The singu-

2. In a portion of an imperfect letter of the late 1820's or early 1830's JT explained his course of action: "Returning to America in June 1804, the Artist found a new Scene of Change. The Demon of discord had Sunk the Character of Americans, in the contemptible distinction of French or British partisans. It was useless in this absence of all national feeling, to persevere in his work of the Revolution—and two other courses lay before him—the pursuit of his profession as a Portrait painter, by which he might hope to obtain in Subsistence—or following the general Example, to swim with the Current, and take his chance (then not a bad one) for his Share of the good things which were liberally distributed to all true believers in the political Creed of the day. He chose to retain his principles, and to rely for Subsistence, on the more humble branch of his profession. From this time his great project slept . . ." (New-York Historical Society.) JT, like his master, West, always considered himself a historical painter—portraiture being regarded as a little below his dignity.

3. Founded in May 1783, a few weeks before the army's disbandment. JT's certificate of membership for the Society of the Cincinnati, signed by G. Washington, president, and H. Knox, secretary, dated 4 July 1786, is at Yale. He subsequently drew or painted 95 of the original members of the society, among them George Washington, Alexander Hamilton, Charles Cotesworth Pinckney, Thomas Pinckney, and Morgan Lewis, all presidents general; Horatio Gates, Thomas Mifflin, Henry Knox, and John Brooks, vice-presidents general, and Otho Holland Williams, assistant secretary general. He was himself an original member.

4. Alexander Hamilton, 1757–1804, Federalist champion of the aristocratic republic, was greatly admired by JT, who painted him from life in 1792 for John Jay (still in the Jay home, Bedford House, Katonah, N.Y.) and made 6 replicas. Shortly after Hamilton's dramatic death he painted another portrait, for the New York City Hall, after the marble bust by the visiting Italian sculptor, Giuseppe Ceracchi (ca. 1751–1802). He made at least 9 replicas of this later version. See Sizer, Works of Trumbull, pp. 28–30. Hamilton's death was a financial godsend to the artist, who had returned from England just 2 weeks earlier. JT was kept in comfortable employment for some years in turning out replicas of his 2 portraits.

5. Aaron Burr, 1756–1836, was born the same year as JT. The famous and fatal

larity of their manner was observed by all, but few had any suspicion of the cause. Burr, contrary to his wont, was silent, gloomy, sour; while Hamilton entered with glee into all the gaiety of a convivial party, and even sung an old military song. A few days only passed, when the wonder was solved by that unhappy event which deprived the United States of two of their most distinguished citizens. Hamilton was killed—and Burr was first expatriated, and then sunk into obscurity for life, in consequence of their compliance with a senseless custom, which ought not to have outlived the dark ages in which it had its origin. It always appeared to me, that the obvious and honorable reply of Gen. Hamilton might have been: "Sir, a duel proves nothing, but that the parties do not shrink from the smell of gunpowder, or the whistling of a ball; on this subject you and I have given too many proofs, to leave any necessity for another, and therefore, as well as for higher reasons, I decline your proposal."

It was still my intention to make Boston my future home, and therefore, having landed our effects, and stored them, we [5a] set off for Boston, passing through Connecticut, and making our visits to all branches of my family, at Hartford, Lebanon [6] and Norwich.[7]

---

duel took place at Weehawken, on the banks of the Hudson, on 11 July 1804. Dr. David Hosack, JT's close friend and patron, was the physician in attendance.

5a. "We," that is the Colonel and his wife, Sarah Hope Harvey Trumbull, whom he scarcely mentions in the *Autobiography*. See pp. 350 ff.

6. JT makes no mention of the designs he prepared at this time (1804) for the Congregational Meetinghouse at his home town, Lebanon. This elegantly proportioned church building was finished in 1806, partially ruined by remodeling of the interior, in the "General Grant" style in 1875, and largely destroyed in the great hurricane of 1938. It has been rebuilt according to the original designs under the expert supervision of the late J. Frederick Kelly and his brother, Henry Schraub Kelly, of New Haven. See *High Winds & High Hopes, a Patriotic Effort to Restore the Hurricane-stricken Meeting House at Historic Lebanon, Connecticut*, foreword by the Hon. Wilbur L. Cross (n.d.); J. Frederick Kelly, *Early Connecticut Meetinghouses* (2 vols., New York, Columbia University Press, 1948); Rev. Robert G. Armstrong, D.D., *John Trumbull Returns*, an address before the Connecticut Society of the Colonial Dames of America, 1948; Sizer, "John Trumbull, Amateur Architect," *Journal of the Society of Architectural Historians*, 8, 1–6; and, Sizer, review of J. Frederick Kelly's "Early Connecticut Meetinghouses," *The New England Quarterly*, 22 (December 1949), 534–540.

7. The cost of travel at this period (1804) is interesting; from JT's accounts (Yale): carriage from New York to New Haven $35, New Haven to Hartford $12,

On our arrival at Boston, I was received by my old friends with great kindness and cordiality, but I soon observed that whenever I alluded to the idea of settling in Boston, and there pursuing my profession as a portrait painter, a cloud seemed to pass over and to chill the conversation. I could not, for a long time, account for this, but at length I learned that my old friend and fellow student, Stewart,[8] who having pursued that branch of the profession for more than twenty years, had established a very highly merited reputation, and who had for some years resided in Washington, had lately received an invitation from Mr. Jonathan Mason,[9] one of the members of Congress, to come and settle at Boston. He had been promised the patronage of Mr. Mason and his friends, (who were the rich and fashionable of the city,) and Mr. Stewart having accordingly accepted the invitation, was preparing to quit Washington and to establish himself in Boston. This was enough. Boston was then a small town,[10] compared with its present importance, and did by no means offer an adequate field of success for two rival artists. I therefore immediately returned to New York, took a furnished house for the winter,[11] and began my course as a portrait painter.

I was immediately employed by the government of the city, to paint whole length portraits of Mr. Jay,[12] and of Gen. Hamilton,[13]

Hartford to Lebanon $12, Lebanon to Boston $50, Lebanon to New Haven $50, and passage (by steamer) New Haven to New York $10. In 1805 he recorded: "coach from New Haven to New York $40, expenses on road $10." For the same year Mrs. Trumbull paid her "female servant" $10 a month.

8. Gilbert Stuart moved to Boston in the summer of 1805 and lived there the rest of his life. He was elected an honorary member of the American Academy of the Fine Arts in 1825.

9. Jonathan Mason, 1756–1831, United States senator from Massachusetts, was like JT, a strong Federalist.

10. In 1810 Boston was a city of 33,250 and New York 96,373; 30 years later—near the time of JT's death—it was Boston 93,383 and New York 312,710.

11. He first stopped at 108 Broadway; settled for the winter at 74 Broad Street. JT is listed in *Jones's New York Mercantile and General Directory* for 1805/6 under "Learned Professions and Public Officers": "Trumbull Col. John, artist, 108 Broadway, corner Pine." For these years see Sizer, "Trumbull's New-York" (Walpole Society *Note Book*, 1949), pp. 15–20.

12. John Jay's portrait hangs in the governor's room at the New York City Hall.

13. Alexander Hamilton's well-known portrait (frequently used on Federal cur-

(from the bust by Cerracchi,) [13a] and to put in order those of Gen. Washington [14] and Gov. Clinton,[15] which I had painted in 1791 and '2. The four now hang in the common council room in the city hall.[16] I had also a good share of occupation from private families, and at this period were painted two portraits which are now in the Gallery at New Haven, viz. those of President Dwight [17] and Stephen Van Rensselaer;[18] from which may be seen what was my style of portrait painting at that period. In short, my success was satisfactory.[19]

In the mean time, the French revolution and the war between Great Britain and France raged furiously, the political feelings of Mr. Jefferson [20] leaning entirely in favor of France. Asperities towards England increased, and at length, in the autumn of 1808, issued in the unlimited embargo system, which threatened the

---

rency; on the reverse of the current $10 bill) hangs in the governor's room, New York City Hall.

13a. Giuseppe Ceracchi, 1751–1802, visiting Italian sculptor; see Sizer, *Works*, p. 29.

14. The full-length portrait of Washington probably required revarnishing.

15. The full-length of George Clinton.

16. There are 12 portraits by JT in City Hall: George Washington (acquired in 1790), George Clinton (1791), John Jay (1805), Alexander Hamilton (1805), James Duane (1805), Richard Varick (1805), Edward Livingston (1805), Marinus Willett (1808), Morgan Lewis (1808), Daniel D. Thompkins (1808), Peter Stuyvesant (1808), and Jacob Radcliff (1816). Much information is to be found scattered through the *Minutes of the Common Council of the City of New York, 1784–1831* (19 vols., New York, City of New York, 1917), through the means of the *Analytical Index*, Vol. 2, prepared by David Maypole Matteson, and published under the same auspices in 1930.

17. Rev. Timothy Dwight, 1752–1817, president of Yale College, 1795–1817. JT also painted a full-length portrait, posthumously, in 1817; both portraits are at Yale.

18. Stephen Van Rensselaer, 1764–1839, Harvard 1782, of Albany, Federalist; the half-length portrait is at Yale.

19. In spite of the commercial depression engendered by the Jeffersonian embargo, JT was kept reasonably busy for a time painting portraits of New York merchants and their wives—James Codwise, Robert Lenox, Francis Bayard Winthrop; of John Vernet, merchant of Norwich, Conn.; Stephen Minot and Nathaniel Prime, merchants of Boston, and so on. They are mostly perfunctory performances.

20. JT, at this period, had no love for Jefferson. Again, all of this constituted a digression from the serious business of painting.

entire destruction of commerce, and of the prosperity of those friends from whom I derived my subsistence.

Independently of the immediate effect upon my professional prosperity, which threatened to be the result of this political measure, it has been seen that I had, for years, taken such an interest in, and been so connected with the public affairs of my country, and had foreseen so much and so nearly the drift of the French revolution, as to render it impossible that I should feel indifferent to such a course. I therefore, always in conversation, and occasionally with the pen took an open and undiguised part with those who opposed the government and its measures.

In the autumn of 1807, the message of President Jefferson announced, and recommended to Congress for adoption, his system of naval defense by gun-boats. This appeared to me so utterly absurd and inefficient, that I could not refrain from publishing in Coleman's paper,[21] a short examination of its merits, the effect of which was to dissolve that illusion, and to show to his admirers, that however great Mr. Jefferson's philosophical and political reputation might be, he was, in the year 1807, no more qualified to lead in naval defense, than he was in warfare on land, in 1781, when, as governor of Virginia, his conduct demonstrated that he possessed no military talents.

FROM THE NEW YORK EVENING POST, DEC. 12TH, 1807.

GUN-BOATS

"As Congress has once more got on board the gunboats, we take the liberty of recommending to their perusal the following piece, written by an officer of our revolutionary army."

MR. COLEMAN—The various opinions and singular doctrines which have lately been advanced, both in the national legislature and in private conversation, on the system of naval defense by gun-boats, have induced me to examine with some attention, both the efficiency and the economy of that system. The result of my

21. William Coleman, 1766–1829, a Federalist, editor and proprietor of the New York *Evening Post* in 1800.

examination has completely satisfied my mind, that the system is incomparably less efficient, less economical, and of course more absurd, than it had previously appeared to me; and, as the course of inquiry which has satisfied me, appears to be well calculated to convey the same conviction to the minds of others, I beg leave, through the medium of your useful paper, to address some observations to my countrymen.

I have examined one of the gun-boats of the latest construction, which I presume is regarded by government as built upon the most approved plan. It is of the following dimensions: length, fifty feet; breadth, eighteen feet; height, four feet nearly, between deck and keel, for the accommodation of the crew. These boats are schooner rigged, and intended to carry one heavy gun, working on a circle, between the two masts; each boat to be manned with fifty men, officers included.

Fifty of these boats are regarded by the President of the United States, as adequate to the protection of this harbor, the Sound, and the coast, as far as Cape Cod; and two hundred are by him considered as sufficient for the defense of the entire coast of the Union.

We will first consider the efficiency of the system. The usual mode of estimating the relative importance of artillery is, to compare the weight of shot which can be thrown in a given time. A heavy gun cannot be loaded and discharged with the same celerity as a light one, and therefore, the ratio of power does not correspond with the size of the calibre. I will however consider the fifty thirty-two pounders, on which we are to rely for safety, as carrying as great a weight of balls, as the eighty guns which are borne by what is usually called a seventy-four gun ship,—and this will be regarded by every artillerist, as a large concession.

The *essential* damage which can be done to vessels of war, is in a great degree confined to the water-line, and near it. Ships have fought until four port-holes were beat into one, and yet were neither sunk nor taken, but returned into port. Shot striking between wind and waters, as it is called, i. e. on the water-line, are more dangerous. Now the seventy-four gun ship, in the extreme length of her water-line, exposes something less than two hundred feet. Supposing the fifty gun-boats in action with her, to lie *bow on*, the shortest possible line exposed by each is *eighteen* feet, amounting in the whole to *nine hundred* feet; and whenever they present their broadsides, as they must sometimes, their water-line will amount to two thousand five hundred feet—ten times the extent of line exposed by the ship.

Again, the disproportion in the relative strength of the two machines, is obviously much greater than that in the size of their guns; a twelve pound shot will more entirely penetrate a gun-boat, than a thirty-two pound shot will a ship of the line.

I allow that, in a calm, the gun-boats, possessing the power in some measure of choosing their position, by means of oars, will have an advantage over a heavy ship. In deep water, this advantage may prove irresistible, but in a harbor, where the ship could anchor with springs on her cables, it would be trifling. In a breeze, the seventy-four gun ship will outsail the gun-boats, and, unless they take shelter in shallow water, will have no more difficulty in running down a squadron of them, than a ship of three hundred tons would have in running down a squadron of birch canoes. It results then, that, in a calm, the fifty gun-boats may be considered as equal in efficiency to one ship of seventy-four guns; but in rough water, or a fresh breeze, utterly inferior.

I ought, however, to state one additional consideration, which gives to the ship, in every circumstance, an immense advantage; it is, that her force is compact, her crew disciplined, and under the eye and absolute command of one man; whereas, the fifty gun-boats must have fifty commanders, a number which can never be expected to act in concert, even if there existed on board each separate boat, the most perfect discipline.

Let us next consider the economy of the gun-boat system, with respect to human life—a consideration which ought not to have been overlooked by *the friends of the people*. A seventy-four gun ship in the British service, is regarded as fully manned with six hundred men. The fifty gun-boats, with which we are to oppose them, require two thousand, five hundred men. The six hundred men on board the ship are sheltered in a great measure, from the fire of an enemy. But the two thousand five hundred men on board the gun-boats, must all be upon deck in action, completely exposed, the waist of the gun-boat being neither high enough, nor strong enough, to shelter even their legs; the boats, of course, must never approach within the range of musketry or grape. In addition to this lavish exposure of life and limbs, there is no provision made on board for the comfort or relief of the wounded,—*there is no cock-pit;* while on board the ship, both the wounded and the surgeons in attendance are out of further danger, the cock-pit being deep below the water-line, and secure from the enemy's shot. So much for the humanity of the system.

Next, let us consider the economy of the first expense. Each gun-boat of the dimensions before described, has cost in this port, for the naked hull, three thousand dollars. To rig and equip her, (as I am informed by men of skill and experience,) will cost four thousand dollars more, making a total for each gun, which is water-borne, of seven thousand dollars, or one thousand, five hundred and seventy five pounds sterling. In the British service, some years ago, the estimate was one thousand pounds for a gun, for ships of the line. Allow a rise of fifty per cent. on the expense of ship-building, the first cost of their ships, will then be the same, per gun, as ours.

But the expense of a navy does not arise so much from the first cost of the machinery, as from the annual waste in manning, victualling, and pay; and here, the wisdom of our legislature shines with superior splendor, for while in the British service eight men to a gun are considered as a full complement, even for distant expeditions, they would, even for harbor duty, *economically* employ fifty men to each gun. Hence it results, that the two hundred gun-boats, which, by the transcendent wisdom of our rulers, are destined to guard this happy country, will require ten thousand men to man them, while in the British service, ten thousand men would be a full complement for *fifteen ships of eighty guns each.*

It is not necessary to compare the immense disparity of pay, victualling, and wear and tear of the two systems; I will merely state the number of officers and men, which must stand nearly as follows:

In the two hundred gun-boats, divided into six flotillas—

Six flotillas,	each 1,	6 commanders.
Two hundred boats	each 1,	200 captains.
" "	each 2,	400 lieutenants.
	Total,	606 comm'd officers.

In fifteen ships, of eighty guns each—

Three squadrons,	each 1,	3 admirals.
Fifteen ships,	each 1,	15 captains.
" "	each 4,	60 lieutenants.
	Total,	78 comm'd officers.

Our economists then, in order to put afloat two hundred guns, propose to employ six hundred and six commissioned officers, and nine thousand, three hundred and ninety four warrant officers and seamen; while the prodigal Britons, in *fifteen ships*, of eighty guns each, put afloat twelve hundred guns, and employ seventy eight commissioned officers, and nine thousand, nine hundred and twenty two warrant officers and seamen. Thus, the annual expense of our two hundred guns, which are destined to lurk in mud-holes, will be equal to that of twelve hundred British cannon, a force sufficient to command the respect of mankind in every quarter of the ocean; for it is conceded in that model of naval, military and economical wisdom, the late presidential message on the subject of gun-boats, "that this species of naval armament can have but little effect towards protecting our commerce, *in the open seas,* even upon our own coasts."

If I am answered, that there is no intention of manning all the gun-boats, except in case of war, I admit it; neither are British ships of war manned except in case of war. But both boats and ships, when manned, and to whatever extent, must be victualled and paid, and the disparity of expense will be in exact proportion to the disparity of numbers above stated.

I presume that the same sublime strain of wisdom will pervade the whole system, and be displayed in the means of procuring men, as in devising and constructing the machines. The law which was passed some years since, will render useless the slow and old fashioned and exploded forms of enlistment, and guard the liberties of the dear people from the abomination of impressment. According to that law, whenever danger shall menace any harbor, or any foreign ship shall insult us, somebody is to inform the governor, and the governor is to desire the marshall to call upon the captains of militia, to call upon the drummers to beat to arms, and call the militia-men together, from whom are to be *draughted* (not impressed) a sufficient number to go on board the *gun-boats,* and drive the hostile stranger away, unless during this long ceremonial he should have taken himself off.

My friends of the militia must permit me to describe the accommodations which they will find on board. As the height below deck is not quite *four feet,* they will not only not be able to stand upright under cover, but cannot even sit upright, unless they squat upon the floor, like puppies in a dog-kennel—a most elegant position, in which we are all, in our turns, liable to be placed, by *those most admirable friends of the people,* our sagacious rulers.

Such is the gun-boat system. Yet there are legislators, who call this prodigality, this wasteful imbecility, by the name of economy! —and men in the community, who, for want of reflection, suffer themselves to be the dupes of such palpable nonsense and falsehood.

After the publication of this piece, the debates in Congress on the subject of defense by gun-boats ceased, and this display of presidential wisdom slept in peace.

8

England and a Second American War 1808–15

ON THE 15th of December, 1808, I embarked at New York on board the British packet-ship Chesterfield, Capt. Gibbons, and sailed for Falmouth.[1] This was almost the last ship that was permitted to sail for Great Britain, under this self-denying ordinance—the embargo. The season was severe, but the wind was generally fair, and the passage safe and short. We arrived in Falmouth on the 7th of January, 1809. The officers of the customs were obliging, and having landed our effects, and seen them on board a waggon bound for London, we set off for that city, and arrived without accident or delay.[2] We were kindly received by our old friends, Mr. and Mrs. West,[3] as well as by many others;—and I again commenced painting.

1. On 30 November 1808, before sailing for England, JT drew up an account of his worth (Yale Library), figuring his assets amounted to $95,977 including an item of $10,000 for his lands in western New York. In spite of this, he found it necessary to continue to borrow large sums of ready cash from his banker, Samuel Williams of Finsbury Square, London.

2. The Trumbulls lived at 31 Argyle Street for which they paid £100 quarterly to Lady Hort (lease at Yale Library), later at 33 Argyle Street and 29 Leicester Square. Fashionable Argyle Street, a short distance from Hanover Square, runs off Oxford Street, near Oxford Circus and Regent Street; it is but a 5-minute walk from Benjamin West's at Newman Street. See J. Heneage Jesse, *London: Its Celebrated Characters and Remarkable Places* (3 vols., London, Richard Bentley, 1871), 1, 50–51.

3. Benjamin West married Elizabeth Shewell, daughter of the Philadelphia merchant Stephen Shewell, at St. Martin-in-the-Fields, London, about a year after his arrival, on 2 September 1764. Of their 2 sons, Raphael Lamar and Benjamin, Junior, JT saw much of the elder, "Raph."

Benjamin West was president of the Royal Academy from 1792 until his death in 1820—with the exception of one troubled year—and had written to his former pupil giving him an intimate account of his temporary unseating. The letter, dated

247

The uncertain state of political relations between the United States and Great Britain, and the manifest inclination of the head of the American government in favor of France, naturally produced a coldness in the minds of Englishmen towards the people of the United States, and increased the unavoidable jealousy of the members of a profession which is seldom overloaded with any superfluity of patronage. I had no family connections—few personal friends, and all the unfavorable passages of my preceding life now came up to view, to my serious disadvantage. No wonder then, if in my new character of a painter, many were disposed to see rather the mask of a concealed public (probably hostile) agent, than the honest and fair competition of an individual for his share of professional reputation.

Large pictures were not, however, the only works which I executed during these four years. I painted also a number of portraits,[4] for which good prices were paid, but not to an amount suf-

6 February 1805, addressed to JT at 74 Broad Street, New York, is at the Yale Library. See Sizer, "Benjamin West to His Former Pupil, John Trumbull," *Yale University Library Gazette*, 25 (January 1951), 104–109.

West wrote JT from London on 8 September 1805: "I am happy to hear so good an Account of your Pencil being employed at New York . . ." (Historical Society of Pennsylvania, Philadelphia.)

In 1808 West was 70. Benjamin Robert Haydon wrote in his *Autobiography* (p. 192) in 1814: "It is extraordinary how men of the worst taste get on—Mengs, Battoni, West, Dance . . . all were believed divinities in their lifetimes. And where are they now?" Nonetheless, his old master continued (unfortunately) to exert a lasting and powerful influence on JT, as a comparison of the former's "Ophelia and Laertes," dated 1792, and similar productions, with JT's "Angus Conferring Knighthood on deWilton," signed (rare for JT) and dated 1810, now hanging in the Linonia and Brothers Library at Yale, will bear out. "Ophelia's Madness" was once the property of the painter-inventor, Robert Fulton, 1765–1815, a student of Benjamin West until 1793. It was exhibited as a loan from his widow at JT's American Academy of the Fine Arts annually from 1816 to 1828, and since 1882 has been at the Cincinnati Art Museum. Other interesting comparisons can be made between JT's "Christ and the Woman Taken in Adultery" of 1811 (Yale) and West's "Chryseis Returned to Her Father Chyses," signed and dated 1777 (New-York Historical Society); JT's many "Holy Families" of his later period and West's "Apotheosis of Princes Octavius and Alfred" in the Royal Collection at Windsor. Both West and his pupil JT could be exceedingly dull.

4. These were lean years financially, and the portraits were few: Edward Ellice of London; John Luxmore, bishop of Hereford; a Mrs. Mitchell, "wife of an English clergyman"; a Mr. and Mrs. Sanderson, likewise unidentified (all unlocated—prob-

ficient to defray my expenses. I was thus placed under the necessity of borrowing, and was constantly drifting upon the fatal lee-shore of debt. Finding this to be unavoidable, I at length gave up the fruitless struggle, and determined to return to America, and had

---

ably still in England). He posed for himself and painted his wife (this fine pair of portraits now at Geneva, Switzerland). The ex-Revolutionist (who had little liking for the French Republic or Empire) painted 3 portraits of the British hero, Wellington (who never sat for him), twice using the marble bust by his friend Joseph Nollekens, the sculptor (Hyde Hall, Cooperstown, N.Y., and Yale), and once a portrait by another friend, Sir Thomas Lawrence (Wadsworth Atheneum). JT also continued to exhibit at both the Royal Academy and at the British Institution. At the former, for the year 1809, there were "The Holy Family with Saint John and His Parents" (No. 9, now at the Connecticut Historical Society, Hartford); 2 landscapes, each entitled "View of the Falls of the Yantick, a Branch of the River Thames near Norwich, in North America" (Nos. 85 and 198—pictures, painted in 1806, referred to on pp. 308 and 392; and a "Portrait of a Gentleman" (No. 356, unidentified). In 1811: "Mrs. Sanderson" (No. 87); "Lady of the Lake" (No. 237; inspired by Scott's contemporary poem published in 1810; JT painted 2 versions of this subject, both unlocated); "Mr. Hamilton" (No. 427, probably one of the many replicas of his Alexander Hamilton); and "Portrait of a Lady" (No. 457, unidentified). In 1812: "Suffer Little Children," listed as by "Colonel Trumbull, President of the Academy of Arts, New York" (No. 331, reminiscent of West at his worst; Yale). And in 1818: "The Portrait of D. Hosack, M.D., F.R.S. of London and Edinburgh, First Vice-President of the Literary and Philosophical Society of New York, and Professor of the Theory and Practice of Medicine, etc., etc." (No. 275; now at the New York Hospital). At the British Institution he exhibited, in 1810: "Lamderg and Gelchassa" (inspired by Macpherson's *Ossian;* No. 93); "The Holy Family with Saint John and His Parents" (exhibited the year before at the Royal Academy; No. 134). In 1811: "The Knighting of De Wilton by the Earl of Angus in Tantallon Chapel" (No. 147; inspired by Scott's poem *Marmion,* which appeared in 1808; Yale). For 1812: "The Sortie Made by the Garrison of Gibraltar in November, 1781, under the Command of the Late Lord Heathfield, then Sir George Augustus Elliott" (No. 26; one of the several versions of this spirited composition) and "The Woman Taken in Adultery" (No. 84; a small version of this picture is unlocated; the large exhibition picture, in the artist's most unfortunate manner, is at Yale). And in 1813: "Peter the Great of Russia" (No. 34; inspired by Voltaire's life of that monarch; Yale) and "Suffer Little Children" (No. 80, a heavyhanded affair, based upon a picture by Correggio, exhibited the previous year at the Royal Academy). See Algernon Graves, *The Royal Academy of Arts* (London, Henry Graves, 1906), 8, 24, and the same author's *The British Institution, 1806–1867* (London, George Bell and Sons and Algernon Graves, 1908), p. 542. Also during these financially unproductive years he painted a copy (now lost) of Van Dyck's "Madonna and Infant Saviour" (which he once owned and sold in 1797; this picture is now in the Dulwich Gallery, London). In 1811 he painted "Susannah and the Elders" or "The Chastity of Susannah," frequently exhibited at the American Academy of the Fine Arts and

written to Liverpool, to engage a passage on board a ship which was about to sail from that port, when we were confounded by the news, that the United States had, on the 18th of May, 1812, declared war against Great Britain, and that all mutual intercourse was at an end.[5]

Ever since the commencement of the revolution in France, bitter recriminations had been passing between Great Britain and the United States, and for several years, the great subject of contention had been the orders in council, (encroaching severely upon the

---

at the Apollo Association, New York, sold in the 1844 auction (No. 3), now lost.

JT was interested in the Old Masters which were then passing through the London auction rooms. The sale of the Bryan pictures by Peter Coxe, Burrell, and Foster on 17 May 1798 included (No. 51) Van Dyck's "celebrated portrait of Govartius. This wonderful head is sufficiently known to render any account of it unnecessary. Indeed it beggars all description, and it is beyond all praise." See F. Lugt, *Répertoire des catalogues de ventes,* No. 5764. To while away his time JT copied the portrait long known as "Gervartius" (actually of Cornelius van der Geest, 1577–1647). The Van Dyck portrait was purchased by the Russian-born London merchant and celebrated amateur of the fine arts, John Julius Angerstein, and since 1824 has been in the National Gallery (No. 52). JT must have seen the picture in the 1815 exhibition at the British Institution (No. 9), for his copy, now at the New-York Historical Society, was made that year. The 59-year-old Colonel, in making such copies, was repeating what he had done years before in Smibert's Boston painting room at the age of 22.

During these years JT purchased his pigments from the firm of Thomas Brown of High Holborn; see William T. Whitley, *Artists and Their Friends in England, 1700–1799* (London and Boston, Medici Society, 1928), pp. 335–336, and Sizer, "Trumbull's Painting Procedure," *Works of Trumbull,* pp. 100–105.

JT's book of recipes (undated) at the New-York Historical Society contains interesting formula and observations for the preparation of varnishes, oils, drying agents, and the like, the composition of pigments, a method of "cleaning Silk, Cotton or Woolen cloths," "Rev. Mr. Finch's remedy for the Ague," and "Dr. Hosack's prescription for Enuresis," a "Recept for Dropsy" and one "for the Gout."

5. JT's feeling about the War of 1812 is expressed in a letter to Mrs. Julia K. Wheeler, a daughter of General Hull: "The declaration and conduct of that war I have always regarded as one of the least honorable passages of the American history, but I now view it with increased disgust, as a most disgraceful period of the grossest ignorance and misconduct; and, what is worse, a vile endeavor to divert public indignation from its authors and conductors by a sacrifice of the reputation and even life of one of the bravest officers of the Revolution." James Freeman Clarke, *William Hull and the Surrender of Detroit, a Biographical Sketch* (Boston, Geo. H. Ellis, 1912), p. 31. JT wrote to Rufus King constantly about the political situation in Europe. These letters, chiefly from 1809 to 1822, are at the New-York Historical Society.

American commerce,) which Great Britain had passed in retaliation for the Berlin and Milan decrees, antecedently promulgated
by Buonaparte. The commerce of America was, in truth, crushed
beween the two, as between the upper and nether millstones, until
at length the patience of the American government was exhausted,
and this definitive step was taken, unhappily, almost on the very
day on which the British government repealed the oppressive
order.

Thus all hope of a speedy return to America was destroyed, and
of necessity I was driven to continue the wretched resource of
borrowing [6] the means of subsistence. I did not, however, sink fee-
bly under this new blow; I endeavored, on the contrary, to revive
the acquaintance of men in power, to whom I had formerly been
known. I wrote to several, but although I was on all hands treated
with great personal civilty, yet all the answer I could get, was, "that
since the United States had chosen to take the step she had, the war
must proceed, and could not, on the part of Great Britain, be a
sentimental war. Events must take their course, and no exceptions
could be made in favor of individuals, however otherwise respected or esteemed." The only indulgence I was able to obtain,
was permission to reside at Bath or Cheltenham,[7] in preference to
London.

6. On 25 July 1815 his balance due his London banker, Samuel Williams, was
£7,695 15s.

7. On 31 January 1814 the ex-Colonel wrote the home secretary, Lord Sidmouth
(Henry Addington, 1st viscount Sidmouth, 1757–1844): "Mr. Trumbull presents
his most respectful Compliments . . . & begs leave to request the renewal of the
enclosed License with permission to reside at Bath, Clyton or Cheltenham." He went
to Bath. It was there that JT painted a number of landscapes in watercolor.

Drafts of JT's numerous letters to Lord Sidmouth are at the New-York Historical Society. On 22 November 1814 he asked for permission "for an early return
to America" and noted that he received "a verbal answer of Virtual refusal and
evasion." Earlier he had written to his young friend, Charles King (1789–1867),
then in England, of Lord Sidmouth: "that the order for the Detention of all Americans now resident in this Kingdom is absolute and no exception can be made, but
in respect of Prisoners of War" (31 August 1813) and later: "I have again seen your
noble friend . . . I am explicitly told that no exception can be made" (2 September
1813).

There is a long memorandum in JT's hand, possibly written in September 1814,
at the New York Public Library, in which he records his correspondence and audi-

Of the letters which I wrote at this time, I insert one, as a specimen, and the answer, as being highly honorable to the great and good nobleman to whom it was addressed.

London, 29 Leicester Square, Nov. 19, 1814.
To the Right Hon. Lord Grenville.

My Lord—I trust to your lordship's candor, to forgive this intrusion, when you shall have seen its object.

Misrepresentation, ever the fruitful source of mischief, has been but too active and successful, not merely in producing and prolonging the present calamitous contest between Great Britain and the United States, but also in giving to the military operations in that country, a character of ferocity seldom seen in modern times; and it has even been so triumphant, as to produce in the minds of Englishmen, approbation of measures from which they would recoil with abhorrence when not under the influence of delusion. Even I, though an American, did not doubt that my countrymen were the aggressors in the incendiary system which has been too long pursued, until I saw the extraordinary letter of Admiral Cochrane,[8] dated August 16, 1814, and the answer of Mr. Monroe. I then felt it to be my duty to examine the question, dispassionately and carefully, and in doing this, I determined to take the London gazettes alone as authority, and to rest the question on them.

I have done so, my lord; I have twice carefully examined the gazettes for the years 1812 and 1813, and have extracted with care,

---

ence with Lord Sidmouth over his detention in England during the War of 1812 (of which JT did not approve): ". . . I had given the strongest possible evidence [of good will to Britain] in permitting my only Son to enter into the British Army as a volunteer in the Peninsula; where his good conduct had gained him a Commission & where He had been twice wounded . . . that I conceived such circumstances gave me reason to hope that the Govt. would not insist upon my detention . . . since I had already expended too much time & Mony in a fruitless attempt to establish myself here in a profession which was in a great measure ruined by the circumstances of the pressure of the times, & too great numbers of those who pursued it . . . ." It is interesting to note that the ex-Revolutionary War Colonel used his son, who joined the British army against his father's wishes, as an excuse to leave England. See App., pp. 340 ff.

8. Sir Alexander Forrester Inglis Cochrane, 1758–1832, younger son of Thomas Cochrane, 8th earl of Dundonald.

and I hope with accuracy, every article which speaks of *burning*. I have the honor to enclose a copy of these extracts, and beg leave to request your lordship's attention, particularly, to the contrast between the third article of capitulation of York on the 27th of April, 1813, and the almost contemporaneous despatches of Amiral Cockburne,[9] as well as to that between the fourth article of the same capitulation, and the wanton and studied destruction of papers of all kinds which took place at Washington.

The war between the two nations becomes daily more important, and every man of humanity must wish to see its future operations divested, as far as possible, of all unnecessary ferocity.

Your lordship, I know, will contribute to this end with delight, and if the statement which I have the honor to lay before you, should in any degree lead to the same purpose, it will afford durable satisfaction to me.

I have the honor to be, &c. &c.   J. TRUMBULL.

To this letter I received the following answer:

Dropemore, Nov. 23d, 1814.

To John Trumbull, Esq., &c. &c.

SIR—No apology whatever could be necessary for your letter, conveying information on a subject in which I take so deep an interest.

Among the circumstances to which I look back with most pleasure, in the close of a long and I hope not wholly useless public life, is that of the uniform, though frequently ineffectual, efforts which I have made, for the maintenance of peace and friendship between my own country and the United States. How much the conduct of both governments has contributed to disappoint those wishes, I need not say, to a person so well informed on the subject as you are.

Lamenting deeply the existence and continuance of the war, I felt additional grief when I saw it assuming a shape of unusual and revolting ferocity, unnecessarily aggravating the public and general evils of such a state, by the wanton infliction of private and individual calamity. To do all in his power to check the progress of

9. Sir George Cockburn, 1772–1853, 2d son of Sir James Cockburn, bart.

such a system, seemed to me the duty of every man, and I took the very first opportunity of expressing my abhorrence of it, (on whichever side it originated,) and of calling for official measures to prevent its continuance. Had this claim been resisted, I was prepared and resolved to pursue the subject further, nor did I desist from that intention, until I received public and solemn assurances, that orders had already been sent out to America for the discontinuance of such measures, and for a return to the practice of modern and civilized war, provided the same course shall in future be adhered to by those whom I lament to call our enemies.

This was the only practical result that could be hoped for from pursuing the subject further. An inquiry which party first resorted to practices which both now equally disclaim on principle, and justify only on the ground of retaliation, could now only produce fruitless recrimination, tending more to irritation than to peace.

I therefore let the matter rest there, but with the full purpose of renewing it, should the expectations now held out be ultimately disappointed.

I am, with great truth and regard, sir,
Your most faithful, humble servant,
GRENVILLE.

9

Painting for the Nation's Capitol 1815–28

THE restoration of peace gave me the opportunity of returning to America. I lost no time, but embarked for New York, on board the Illinois, a fine American ship, and sailed August 18th, 1815.[1] Our passage was pleasant and rapid, until, in September, we had found soundings, and concluded ourselves to be near Montauk point; a heavy gale from the southeast, then overtook us in the morning, and increased in fury until, in the afternoon, our maintop-mast went overboard, and hanging by the backstay and other rigging, dragged alongside, beating heavily, from time to time, under our quarter, with a violence which threatened to start a butt, or stave a hole in the ship's side. Our situation was, for some time, truly dangerous; we knew that we were near land, with a disabled ship, the gale increasing in fury, and driving us irresistibly toward the beach. The wreck was however cut clear, the wind suddenly changed, and in a moment, when we almost despaired, we were out of danger. Two days after we were safe in the harbor of New York.

I immediately took a house in Broadway, (now the Globe hotel,)[2] at $1,200 per year, and commenced my labors, with good

1. The Trumbulls shipped on the *Illinois*, Captain Noyes, 9 boxes, 4 crates, 21 trunks. His inventory included such items as 9 large table clothes, 18 middle sized, 4 small, 24 breakfast cloths, 47 napkins, and 36 "D'Oyleys."

2. Francis Blancard's Globe Hotel is listed at 61 Broadway in the New York City directories for 1836–39, and at 66 Broadway—on the opposite side of the thoroughfare—in the directories for 1839–42. It is to the former that JT must refer.

JT is listed in *Longworth's American Almanac, New York Register & City Directory* from 1816 to 1835. His addresses, in expanded form, are given below: 1816–17, Beach Street, corner of Hudson Street; 1817–20, 26 Park-place; 1819–24, 27 Park-place, corner of Church Street; 1824–25, Park-place house; 1825–32, Academy of Arts, Chambers Street; 1832–35, Academy of Arts, 8½ Barclay Street.

Much information for these years may be found scattered through the pages of

prospect of success. On the 1st of February, a lodging-house keeper offered $2,200, which the executor was bound to accept, and I was turned adrift.

I removed, in May, to Hudson square, to a good house, at a reasonable rent, and in a beautiful situation; but I soon found myself too far out of town for success in portrait painting, and business languished.

My friend, Mr. Charles Wilkes,[3] informed me, that the city of Baltimore had resolved to procure two paintings, one representing the death of Gen. Ross at North point,[4] the other, the attack on Fort McHenry by the British ships, and had advertised for proposals. He advised me to visit Baltimore, to carry with me some of my studies of national subjects, and offer to paint these pictures; to aid my plans, gave me an introduction to Judge Nicholson.[5] I went accordingly, in December, was well received, conducted with some ceremony to the two scenes of action, which were carefully and intelligently described, and made proposals.[6] After some days' deliberation, the government of the city decided not to incur the expense.

the *Letters from John Pintard to his Daughter, 1816–1833,* Dorothy C. Barck, ed. (4 vols., New York, New-York Historical Society, 1940–41). Pintard was the founder, in 1804, of the New-York Historical Society and was an active member of the American Academy. JT painted his portrait for the Society in 1817.

JT was elected a vice-president of the Society in January 1818, continuing in office until January 1827. References to his activities are to be found in the minutes, the most interesting of which is 9 June 1818: "Col. Trumbull presented an account, in Mss., of the action between the Bonhomme Richard and the Seraphis . . . written by Paul Jones and given to Colonel Trumbull in Paris in 1789 . . ."

3. Collector of pictures, treasurer of the New-York Historical Society. See App., p. 364.

4. The British general, Robert Ross, 1766–1814, was killed by a rifle bullet; again the subject of dramatic death upon the field of battle.

5. Joseph Hopper Nicholson, 1770–1817, judge of the Maryland Court of Appeals, 1806–17, was present at the battle of Fort McHenry. It was he who caused Francis Scott Key's "Star Spangled Banner" to be published (Key married the sister of Nicholson's wife).

6. To paint several large compositions "in memory of the defense of Baltimore" for that city, at "$5,000 for each painting—to be finished within three years—one fourth to be paid on signing the contract, and one fourth at the end of each succeeding year." JT to William Patterson, 13 January 1817. (New-York Historical Society.)

2. The "Patriot-Artist," with his palette, brushes and Revolutionary sword, at the age of sixty-five, by Samuel Lovett Waldo and William Jewett. (*Courtesy of the Yale University Art Gallery*)

Congress was in session, and my friend, Judge Nicholson, advised me to go on to Washington,[7] and there offer my great, but long suspended, project of national paintings of subjects from the Revolution. The Judge went with me, introduced me to his friends in both houses, and the plan was favorably received. Several gentlemen, (particularly Mr. Timothy Pitkin,[8] of the house of representatives,) were zealous to see my plan executed in its full extent.[9] Some of the studies were put up in the hall of the house; and in one of the debates on the subject, Mr. John Randolph [10] was ardently eloquent in his commendation of the work, and insisted that I should be employed to execute the whole. The result was, that a resolution finally passed both houses, giving authority to the president, "to employ me to compose and execute *four* paintings, commemorative of the most important events of the American revolution, to be placed, when finished, in the Capitol of the United States." [11]

The choice of the subjects, and the size of each picture, was left to the president, Mr. Madison.[12] I immediately waited upon the president to receive his orders. The size was first discussed.[13] I pro-

7. Much information about JT's long connection with the Capitol is to be found in Charles E. Fairman, *Art and Artists of the Capitol of the United States of America* (Washington, Government Printing Office, 1927), especially pp. 32–35.

8. Timothy Pitkin, 1766–1847, of Connecticut, Federalist, statesman, historian, served in the House from 1805 to 1819.

9. The Capitol was burned by the British on 24 August 1814.

10. John Randolph of Roanoke, Virginia, 1773–1833, a Jeffersonian, statesman. It was he who declared in the House of Representatives (9 January 1828) that "in his opinion, the picture of the Declaration of Independence should be called the 'Shin-piece,' for surely, never was there, before, such a collection of legs submitted to the eyes of man." See *Registry of Debates in Congress, 4* (Washington, Gales & Seaton, 1828), Pt. 1, 1827–28. The name has stuck.

11. The resolution was initiated in the Senate on 13 January 1817 and approved 6 February 1817. See *Annals of the Congress of the United States: Debates and Proceedings . . . Fourteenth Congress, Second Session . . .* (Washington, Gales & Seaton, 1854), pp. 64, 67, 69, 79, 704, 746, 761–763, 1041, and 1348.

12. James Madison, 4th president, 1809–17, wrote JT from "Montpelier" on 1 March 1835, reviewing the reasons for the choice of the four events depicted. (Yale Library.)

13. In reality JT's four "murals" are but enlarged easel pictures. Most of his large-scale work, due to his monocular vision, is unfortunate. It is tragic that much of his fame rests on these pictorial failures, executed when the artist was three score

posed that they should be six feet high by nine long, which would give to the figures half the size of life. The president at once over-ruled me. "Consider, sir," said he, "the vast size of the apartment in which these works are to be placed—the rotunda, one hundred feet in diameter, and the same in height—paintings of the size which you propose, will be lost in such a space; they must be of dimensions to admit the figures to be the size of life."

This was so settled, and when we came to speak of the subjects, the president first mentioned the battle of Bunker's Hill. Observing me to be silent, Mr. Madison asked if I did not approve that. My reply was, "that if the order had been (as I had hoped) for eight paintings, I should have named that first; but as there were only four commanded, I thought otherwise. It appeared to me, that there were two military subjects paramount to all others. We had, in the course of the Revolution, made prisoners of two entire armies, a circumstance almost without a parallel, and of course the surrender of General Burgoyne at Saratoga, and that of Lord Cornwallis at Yorktown, seemed to me indispensable." "True," replied he, "you are right; and what for the civil subjects?" "The declaration of independence, of course." "What would you have for the fourth?" "Sir," I replied, "I have thought that one of the highest moral lessons ever given to the world, was that presented by the conduct of the commander-in-chief, in resigning his power and commission as he did, when the army, perhaps, would have been unanimously with him, and few of the people disposed to resist his retaining the power which he had used with such happy success, and such irreproachable moderation. I would recommend, then, the resignation of Washington." After a momentary silent reflec-

---

years or more. The notes on the four pictures are to be found together in the Appendix, p. 309. There is an undated fragmentary draft of JT's defense of his choice of subject for the pictures at the New York Public Library.

Benjamin Robert Haydon's passionate pleading for the public employment of artists—a new and then unpalatable doctrine—written from a debtors' prison in 1823 and addressed in the form of a petition to the House of Commons, has much the same ring as JT's numerous letters. (Haydon, *Autobiography*, pp. 333–336). JT continually complained of the lack of sustained patronage and the fickleness of taste. Haydon committed suicide, but JT lived on and on.

tion, the president said, "I believe you are right; it was a glorious action."

The price was settled, at eight thousand dollars for each painting, and, as soon as the new administration was formed under Mr. Monroe, the secretary of state was charged to prepare a contract on these principles, which was done, and was in the following form, viz.

"Articles of agreement, made and executed this fifteenth day of March, one thousand eight hundred and seventeen, between Richard Rush,[14] acting secretary of state for the United States, of the one part, and John Trumbull of Connecticut, of the other part.

"Whereas, a resolution was passed on the sixth day of February, one thousand eight hundred and seventeen, by the senate and house of representatives of the United States, authorizing the president of the United States to employ the aforesaid John Trumbull, to compose and execute four paintings, commemorative of the most important events of the American revolution, to be placed, when finished, in the capitol of the United States; now, therefore, I, Richard Rush, acting secretary of state as aforesaid, in virtue of authority vested in me by the president of the United States, do hereby employ the said John Trumbull, to compose and execute four paintings as aforesaid, the subjects of which, in pursuance of the spirit of the said resolution, to be as follows, viz.

"1st. The Declaration of Independence; 2d. Surrender of the British to the American forces at Saratoga; 3d. The Surrender of the British to the American forces at Yorktown; 4th. The Resignation of General Washington at Annapolis.

"And the said John Trumbull engages, that each of the aforesaid paintings shall have a surface of not less than eighteen feet by twelve feet, with figures as large as life; that they shall be executed with all reasonable dispatch, and in a manner (as far as may be attainable by the skill of the said John Trumbull) worthy the dig-

14. Richard Rush, 1780–1859, statesman, son of Benjamin Rush, the Philadelphia physician and political leader. The original of the articles of agreement signed by Rush is to be found in the General Records of the Department of State, Record Group 59, National Archives.

nity of the subjects, and the destination of the paintings when finished. And the said Richard Rush, acting secretary of state as aforesaid, engages to pay, or cause to be paid, to the said John Trumbull, the sum of thirty-two thousand dollars, in manner following, and not otherwise; that is to say, the sum of eight thousand dollars upon the execution of this instrument; the sum of six thousand dollars upon the completion and delivery of the first of the aforesaid paintings; the like sum of six thousand dollars upon the completion and delivery of the second of the aforesaid paintings; the like sum of six thousand dollars upon the completion and delivery of the third of the aforesaid paintings; and the like sum of six thousand dollars upon the completion and delivery of the fourth of the aforesaid paintings.

"And it is moreover understood and agreed by the said John Trumbull, that, in the case of his death before the completion or commencement of the first of the aforesaid paintings, or his inability occasioned by any other means to enter upon or complete it, the aforesaid sum of eight thousand dollars to be paid on the execution of this instrument as above mentioned, or such portion thereof as shall be just and reasonable, shall be by him refunded.

"In witness of which the parties have hereunto set their hands, the day and year above written, the party of the first part causing the seal of the department of state to be also hereunto affixed.

RICHARD RUSH, *Acting Sec. State.*

JOHN TRUMBULL."

Witnesses, 'DANIEL BRENT.[15]

JOHN H. PURVIANCE.[16]

I had hardly commenced my first painting, when I received a letter from Charles Bulfinch,[17] Esq., who had been recently ap-

15. Daniel Brent, 1774–1841, chief clerk of the Department of State, later United States consul at Paris 1834–41.

16. Possibly John Purviance, 1773?–1854, one of the leading counsel in the federal courts at Baltimore during the War of 1812, appointed associate justice of the Sixth Judicial District of Maryland 1833.

17. Charles Bulfinch, whom JT first met at Paris in 1786; architect of the National Capitol 1817–30. JT wrote to Charles Bulfinch from New York on 12 January 1824 about the frames for the 4 pictures, giving his preference for "simple architectural

pointed to succeed Mr. Latrobe [18] as architect of the public buildings at Washington—(this letter was lost at the fire that partly consumed the Academy of Fine Arts [19] in Barclay street, New York, in 1836,)—to which, the following is my answer, transcribed from my letterbook of that period.

New York, January 25, 1818.
Charles Bulfinch, Esq., Architect of the Capitol, Washington.

DEAR SIR—Your favor of the 19th came duly to my hands, and the subject has entirely occupied my attention since. I will at pres-

---

foliage" and accompanying this with a sketch. "I deprecate Eagles and all those cumbrous ornaments which call the Eye from its proper object and by their massy projection cast heavy and false Shadows on the Painting." (New-York Historical Society.) A letter from Bulfinch to JT dated Washington, 12 August 1824, contains that architect's sketch for the frames of the 4 pictures for the Rotunda. (Yale Library.)

18. Benjamin Henry Latrobe, 1764–1820, appointed by Jefferson a surveyor of public buildings at Washington in 1803, designed the south wing of the Capitol, engaged to rebuild the Capitol after its destruction 1815–17; an honorary member of the American Academy of the Fine Arts.

19. It is, indeed, curious that JT only made two rather unimportant references to the Academy (this and on p. 268) in his *Autobiography*, considering that he was among the original members in 1802, that he was its dictatorial president from 18 January 1817 to 12 January 1836—for 19 long years—and continued to be associated with it until it passed out of existence in 1839–40, three years before his death. He painted the portraits of many members of the Academy and their wives. A dispute between him and the younger artists, led by S. F. B. Morse, at the Academy, culminated in November/December 1825, and led to the establishment of the National Academy of Design in January 1826.

It was at this time that he relinquished the direction of the American Academy of the Fine Arts. It is recorded, 12 January 1836: " 'Col. Trumbull presented himself to the Board and tendered his resignation, and declines being re-elected President of this Academy. The President requested permission of the Board to retain the rooms now in his possession until 1st of April next. Moved and seconded that the President's request be granted.' That is all there was to it; there was no fanfare, no accolade, no vote of thanks for his nineteen years of presidency—nothing but 'the President's request be granted.' It must have hurt—even though he merited the injury. Rembrandt Peale was elected president, Ithiel Town, Trumbull's architectural friend, vice president, and Alexander Jackson Davis, Town's partner, secretary, at the same meeting." From the editor's article (p. 58) in Mary Bartlett Cowdrey, *American Academy of Fine Arts and American Art Union, Exhibition Record, 1816–1852, with an Introduction on the American Academy by Theodore Sizer and a Foreword by James Thomas Flexner* (New York, New-York Historical Society, 1953), pp. 3–94.

ent beg leave to state two difficulties, which to my mind appear formidable.

If you adopt a staircase similar to that in the city hall here, it will be imperfect without a dome light; this will not come in the centre of the building. How then can you have the grand dome, even for show?

To the saloon which you propose for the gallery of paintings, there is this insurmountable objection,—the pictures must hang opposite to the windows, which is the worst possible light; besides which, the columns and projection of the portico will darken the room in some degree, and render what light there may be, partial and unsteady.

These objections occurred to me at once, and with the reluctance which I feel at the idea of abandoning the original plan of the capitol, so totally as to give up the circular room, and the grand dome, conspired to stimulate my imagination. An idea has occurred to me, which I think will preserve both, and unite originality, utility, simplicity, and grandeur, with economy. It is difficult to explain my meaning fully, without drawings; I am, therefore, endeavoring to put my plan upon paper.

A young gentleman whom I employ to open a subscription for me at Washington, will leave this in two or three days, and will be with you about this day week; by him I will send you the detailed descriptions and drawings of what has occurred to me, and I shall be truly happy if they should be of any use to you.

I heartily wish we were near each other, that I might have the pleasure of discussing with you, in conversation, the objections which will naturally occur to you. I am, &c.

New York, Jan. 28th, 1818.
Charles Bulfinch, Esq., Washington.[20]

DEAR SIR—Your letter of the 19th, paints to me precisely, the situation in which I imagined you would find yourself, on your ar-

20. The original letters of 25 and 28 January are in the Library of Congress. Bulfinch wrote JT on 17 April 1818 "respecting the temples of Congress" and his difficulties "to convey correct ideas" to the Congressional committee. His idea of the appearance of the façade is further conveyed by a sketch at the bottom of the letter, also in the Library of Congress.

rival at Washington, surrounded by every diversity of opinions, interests and prejudices. That, under such circumstances, you should have felt the want of some friend, conversant with the arts, to advise with, was natural, although in any other situation the resources of your own mind would have been amply equal to any professional difficulties which you might have to encounter. It gives me great satisfaction, that in such a moment you should have thought of consulting me; for, thirty years of personal acquaintance and esteem, have rendered your good opinion peculiarly valuable to me.

I am glad to know that so much is done, and magnificently done, at the Capitol; but I feel the deepest regret at the idea of abandoning the great circular room and dome. I have never seen paintings so advantageously placed in respect to light and space, as I think mine would be, in the proposed circular room, illuminated from above. The boasted gallery of the Louvre is execrable for paintings —windows on each side, and opposite to each other, and the pictures hanging not only between them but opposite to them. The governor's room here is subject, in part, to the same objection—the pictures being hung generally opposite to the windows, and in two instances between them. The same objection applies in its full force, to the proposed saloon or gallery in the Capitol; and I should be deeply mortified, if, after having devoted my life to recording the great events of the Revolution, my paintings, when finished, should be placed in a disadvantageous light. In truth, my dear friend, it would paralyze my exertions, for bad pictures are nearly equal to good, when both are placed in a bad light. These considerations must be my apology for presuming to offer any idea on the subject of architecture, of which I profess to have no other than a very superficial knowledge, and which I have studied only as connected with the picturesque of my own profession.

You state two objections to this favorite situation; first, that the room is so vast, that paintings of whatever size will appear small in it; and secondly, that, being open to the public, the paintings will be exposed to danger from damp, from the familiarity of friends, and from the malice of enemies.

In the plan which I venture to submit to you, I have endeavored to obviate these difficulties. I proceed to the necessary details with diffidence, but with the hope that I may suggest to you some ideas which may be ripened to maturity.

Referring to plan No. 1, I propose then to enclose the basement story of the two porticos, in the same style of piers and arches, as in the wings, and to enter, under each portico, a hall forty five feet by twenty, with apartments for door-keepers adjoining—to open a passage through the centre of the building, similar in style and dimensions to those already existing in the wings, which I also continue so as to meet each other, thus forming a simple and obvious communication to all parts of the ground plan. I suppose the inner diameter of the grand circular dome to be ninety feet, and the thickness of the wall five. Nine feet within this wall, I carry up a concentric circular wall of equal thickness to the height of the basement story. Between these two walls I place grand quadruple stairs, beginning at the doors of the two halls, and mounting on the right and left, to the floor of the dome vestibule. Twenty feet within this inner wall of the stairs, I raise a third concentric circular wall, of equal, or (if required) greater solidity. At the meeting of the two passages I thus obtain some variety of form, without any diminution of the requisite solidity, and the spaces contained within this central wall, the inner wall of the staircase, and the passages, will form four large, or eight small rooms, for the deposit of papers, &c. These rooms will be fire-proof, illuminated and aired by semicircular windows, secured by iron gratings, and pierced through the inner wall of the staircase, and will be entered by doors from the passages. The spaces under the stairs I devote to vaults for coal, &c., and in one (or two if necessary) of the triangular spaces left between the circle and the space, I place the fires necessary to warm the great room above, by means of flues conducted round the whole and over the two inner circular walls, as in the house of representatives. The corresponding plan will clearly explain this intricate description.

Plan No. 2, represents the grand staircased vestibule; entering from the two walls, stairs nine feet and lighted from the dome, mount on the right and left of the vestibule, and land at the entrances to the apartments of the senate and of the house of representatives. Around the inner wall of the stairs, I propose a bronze railing five feet high, with gates at the four entrances; by this means the floor of the vestibule is diminished to seventy feet diameter, and the spectator cannot approach nearer to the wall on which the paintings hang than ten feet, nor view them at a greater distance than eighty, which being a little more than three diagonals of the surface, is not by any means too great. Thus, my dear sir, two objections are removed.

Again, the room being warmed by flues, no danger is to be feared from dampness; where it will answer the essential purpose of an entrance to both houses, and a place where members and their friends may meet and converse at ease, in cold or warm weather. The warm air will equally affect the stairs and the record-rooms below, to which it will be admitted freely, through the grated openings on the staircase.

During the hours that the houses are in session, one of their door-keepers ought, for obvious reasons, to be in this room, and at all other times the gates at the four entrances of the railing should be kept locked, by which means the public will have access here, only as you propose, to the saloon, under the eye of a proper guardian; while the members of the government will possess a splendid entrance to their several apartments, and the present entrances and stairs will become secondary in their destination, as they will be in their dimensions.

No. 3, is a slight ideal view of the grand vestibule and staircase, as seen at entering from the hall of either portico. In the centre, the passage is seen in front, the stairs are shown in their ascent, and the solid wall of the record-rooms, with their semicircular windows. The railing is also shown, with the general proportions and decorations of the grand room.

Perhaps I am wrong, for we are all partial to the offspring of our own minds; yet I cannot but believe, that the effect of such a room would be peculiarly grand and imposing, from the union of vastness of dimensions with simplicity of form and decoration. The uses of the room have already been spoken of. I have only omitted to observe the manner in which it is connected with the two porticos, which, in fine weather, and on occasions of great national solemnities, such as inaugurations, &c., would form magnificent accompaniments.

Having thus explained my ideas, (I hope intelligibly, with the aid of the drawings,) permit me to add a few words on the important subject of economy, where I am persuaded there is strong ground of recommendation. I want not a column nor a capital; plain solid walls, embellished only by four splendid door-casings of white marble and elegant workmanship; a fascia of white marble running around the room, with an ornament somewhat like that which surmounts the basement story on the outside; and a frieze crowning the top of the wall, where, either now or at some future time, basso-relievos may be introduced; these are all the decorations which I propose, except the paintings.

Compare now, my dear friend, the expenses of this with the sum which will be necessary to introduce merely a staircase, like that in the city hall here, which can be distinguished from its prototype only by greater dimensions, and more exquisite decorations. Twenty-four Corinthian columns, at least, with their capitals, entablature, and sculptured dome, all in the purest white marble and choicest workmanship, will be necessary, and after all it will be but a copy.

Permit me to add, that the great circular room and dome, made a part of the earliest idea of the Capitol, as projected by Major L'Enfant, drawn by Dr. Thornton, and adopted by General Washington. You will see it so marked on the plan of the city engraved by Thackera & Vallence,[21] in Philadelphia, in 1792. If there be a dislike to M. Latrobe's plans, that dislike cannot apply to this part of the building; here he only followed the original intentions.

I believe that my plan differs from that finally adopted by him, essentially, in carrying up the grand staircase *within* the room, thus rendering it a guard to the paintings, and leaving the basement of the two porticos, and the whole substructure, free and applicable to economical purposes. I also omit the grand niches which M.

21. James Thackara, 1767–1848, and John Vallance, 1770?–1823, engravers; after 1826 the former became keeper of the Pennsylvania Academy of the Fine Arts, where JT occasionally exhibited.

Latrobe had devised, I presume for the purpose of sculpture. It appears to me, that the uninterrupted simplicity of the room will add to its grandeur, and that ample scope is left for sculpture, either now or hereafter, in the frieze, while abundant space is thus acquired upon the walls for other paintings than mine.

I hope, my dear sir, that I have made myself understood, and I shall rejoice if, either upon my plan or some other, you can succeed to preserve the great central circular room. Indeed, I must entreat you to preserve it if possible; and I repeat, that the loss of that, in my opinion, unrivalled situation and light for my pictures, I shall lose half my zeal.

Forgive the earnestness with which I write, for I consider my future fame involved in this question, and excuse the inaccuracies which may have escaped me.

I am, &c. &c.   J. T.

New York, July 25th, 1818.

Charles Bulfinch, Esq., Washington.

DEAR SIR—I received your favor of April 17th, in proper time, and it relieved my mind from no slight anxiety, inasmuch as your plan has saved the grand room, and gives at the same time all those various conveniences which were indispensably necessary.

It appears to me, that you have extricated yourself most happily from the multitude of contradictory projects with which you was surrounded. The granite basement is, I presume, original; I cannot recollect any example of the kind, nor do I find any among a collection of views of country seats in England, which I have. I believe the effect will prove as you anticipate, useful to the perspective; but if it should prove otherwise, the necessity of the case justifies the novelty; and nothing can be easier than to disguise it by what the English call *planting it out,* that is, screening it from distant view by shrubs.

My first painting approaches its completion. Is there any place in the building where it can be put up in a proper light? I should regret to have it seen in a bad one, and wish not to have it removed too often. It is so large, that few doors will admit it when stretched, its shortest diameter being twelve feet, and I should not be willing to have it rolled, unless I am present? Will you think of this, and inform me how and where it can be placed?

You will forgive my long delay in answering yours; I had nothing to suggest, and we were both too busy to write or read unnecessary letters.

I hope Mrs. Bulfinch [21a] and all your family are well, and Mrs. Trumbull [22] unites with me in best wishes for them and you.

I am, &c.   J. T.

The foregoing letter [23] was in answer to one in which Mr. Bulfinch gave me a detailed description of his plan for the present western front of the Capitol, by which he gained space for the library, &c., and saved the dome.[24] This letter itself was lost (I presume) in the fire which consumed the upper floor of the Academy of Fine Arts, in Barclay street.[25]

21a. Hannah Apthorp.

22. The first of three references to the artist's beautiful English wife, Sarah Hope Harvey, whom he married at London in 1800. He painted her portrait more than a dozen times (three of the portraits are at Yale). She must have modeled for some of her husband's allegorical, literary, and religious subjects; many of these paintings are unfortunate aesthetically.

Sometime after her death JT wrote to Daniel Wadsworth of Hartford on 2 February 1825 from New York: ". . . I have gone to my former bachelor quarters, Park Place House, where I have the society of your friend, Mr. Bull, and the advantage of a very quiet house. I have a Room at the Academy where I intend to paint portraits . . ." (Yale Library.)

Among the vast Trumbull correspondence still preserved the editor has not found a single letter of Sarah's—not a scrap, not even a signature. She could not have been illiterate, as he wrote her constantly. The Colonel kept correspondence of the most intimate—and damning—nature (that concerning his illegitimate son, John Trumbull Ray, for instance) but apparently not his wife's. Could it be that he destroyed Sarah's letters lest her background, revealed by her hand and prose style, might prove embarrassing?

23. This letter is at the Library of Congress, where much Bulfinch-Trumbull correspondence is located; other letters are to be found at the New-York Historical Society and at the Yale Library.

24. For the intimate relationship of artist and architect see Christopher Tunnard, *The City of Man* (New York, Scribner, 1953), ch. 12, "An Artist in the Streets."

25. The correct appellation, according to the articles of incorporation, is "American Academy of *the* Fine Arts." It was 8½ Barclay Street (in the rear of Dr. David Hosack's residence, 14 Vesey Street), a plain 3-story brick building designed by JT himself (plans completed on 6 June 1831), in consultation with his friend, Ithiel Town (1784-1844). These plans are still preserved among the papers of Alexander

New York, June 29th, 1818.

John Q. Adams,[26] Esq., Secretary of State.

Dear Sir—I take the liberty to enclose to your care a letter for Mr. Cardelli,[27] which I have just received from his friends in Europe.

You will permit me to avail myself of this occasion, to speak to you of my painting. It is so far advanced, that I may safely promise, that the large work will be superior to the small—a result of which I was by no means secure in the beginning. It would be finished in two months more, but for the numerous and daily interruptions which arise from the increasing curiosity of friends and strangers.

Jackson Davis (Ithiel Town's partner) at the New-York Historical Society. The gallery was opened on 7 October 1831.

Accounts of both disastrous fires—that of March 1837 and that of April 1839—may be found in the editor's article in Cowdrey, *American Academy* . . . , pp. 59–60.

26. John Quincy Adams wrote JT from Washington 4 December 1817: "I have this morning received your Letter of the first instant, which reached me too late, the Office in question having previously been assigned to Charles Bulfinch Esq. Cardelli is now employed and has hitherto given satisfaction. There will probably be constant employment for him, for a considerable time . . ." (New-York Historical Society.)

The original of the following letter is to be found in the General Records of the Department of State, Record Group 59, National Archives.

27. Pietro Cardelli, an Italian sculptor from Rome, employed 1806–10 on the Vendôme column at Paris, London 1815–16, Washington 1817. There are copies of JT's letters of introduction, all dated September 1817, to James Monroe, Benjamin H. Latrobe, and Sir Charles Bagot, British minister to the United States, 1815–20, at the Huntington Library, San Marino, Calif. Cardelli returned the compliment by making busts of the Colonel and his wife. The *Catalogue of Permanent Collection, National Academy of Design, 1826–1910*, contains the items: "761. Bust of John Trumbull" and "762. Bust of Mrs. John Trumbull." The former is in plaster, painted a dull gray, about 17½ inches high—a handsome affair. It was presumably executed in 1817 at New York and is now to be seen at the National Academy of Design's new quarters at 1083 Fifth Avenue, New York. The bust of Mrs. Trumbull, "damaged beyond repair or misplaced," has disappeared. In H. W. French, *Art and Artists in Connecticut* (Boston, Lee & Shepard, New York, Charles T. Dillingham, 1879), p. 49, he is called Georgio Cardelli, "who came to New York in 1816. His patronage was not extensive at the first; but in a year he received the distinguished honor of an order from Mr. Trumbull for a bust of himself and Mrs. Trumbull. The casts were prepared; but, finding fault with them, Mr. Trumbull refused to take them. The sculptor became excited. Mr. Trumbull in turn remarked, 'But you cannot be a popular sculptor in New York if I refuse to indorse you.'" The cast at the National Academy of Design is signed "P. Cardelli."

It is difficult to refuse to my countrymen, whether personally known to me or not, a view of a painting in which all are deeply interested, and for which all must contribute to pay; but the tax upon my time becomes daily more severe, and the delay of the work is painful.

This has determined me to request from the President, permission to exhibit it publicly to the view of the citizens, previous to its removal to Washington. I shall then be justified in not showing it during its progress. Many are anxious to see it, and few will have an opportunity after it shall have gone to its destination. At the same time that public curiosity will thus be gratified, I trust that the exhibition will prove a source of some legitimate advantage to myself.

I trust the President will not object to this. You must recollect that Mr. Copley exhibited his Gibraltar,[28] which was painted for the city of London, previously to its being put up in Guildhall. Will you, my dear sir, have the goodness to make this request known to the President, and solicit for me his consent. I do not write to him on the subject, because I would not add to his labors. Have the goodness to assure him that I lose no time, and spare no labor, to render this work worthy of its ultimate destination, and of the national patronage.

Please to accept the assurance of Mrs. Trumbull and myself, of our best wishes for the health and happiness of Mrs. Adams,[29] yourself, and your family. I am, &c.

The work went on without interruption, and was finished in 1824. The following is a copy of the final settlement of my account at the treasury of the United States.

28. Copley painted 2 versions of "The Siege and Relief of Gibraltar," the first, 4⅓ by 6⅙ feet, in 1783, now in the Tate Gallery, London, and an enlargement, 25 by 20 feet, completed in 1791, for Guildhall. See James Thomas Flexner, *John Singleton Copley* (Boston, Houghton Mifflin, 1948), pp. 93–94. JT probably derived the portrait of Lieut. Col. Ernst August von Hugo, No. 4 in the key of his "Sortie from Gibraltar," from this picture.

29. Louisa Catherine, daughter of Joshua Johnson of Maryland, married 1797, died 1852.

[No. 1546.]

Treasury Department, fifth Auditor's office, }
December 27th, 1824. }

I hereby certify, that I have examined and adjusted an account between the United States and John Trumbull, relative to paintings for the Capitol, and find that he is chargeable as follows, viz.
To treasury warrants, as by register's certificate herewith,

For No.	476,	dated	March	15th, 1817,	for	$8,000
"	234,	"	"	4th, 1819,	"	6,000
"	9267,	"	Nov.	13th, 1820,	"	6,000
"	67,	"	May	1st, 1822,	"	6,000
"	5584,	"	Dec.	24th, 1824,	"	6,000
						$32,000

I also find that he is entitled to credit, for the following historical paintings, executed agreeably to his contract with Richard Rush, Esq., acting secretary of state, entered into with him in pursuance of a resolution of Congress, passed on the 6th day of February, 1817.[30]

Declaration of Independence, as by voucher No.	1,	$8,000
Surrender of Lord Cornwallis,	"	" 2,	8,000
Surrender of Gen. Burgoyne,	"	" 3,	8,000
Resignation by Gen. Washington of } his commission to Congress, }	"	" 4,	8,000
			$32,000

It appears from the statement and vouchers herewith transmitted, for the decision of the comptroller of the treasury, therein.

STEPHEN PLEASONTON,[31] *Auditor.*

30. Some were delivered before that date. There is a note in the Library of Congress, dated 4 August 1820, signed by Daniel D. Tompkins, vice-president of the United States, 1817–25: "I approve of placing Col. Trumbull's paintings, designed ultimately for the saloon of the Capitol in the Senate chamber; and advise the Architect to put them there."
31. Stephen Pleasonton, for several administrations first auditor of the Treasury.

To Joseph Anderson, Esq. Comptroller of the treasury.
Treasury Department, Comptroller's office, ⎤
December, 29th, 1824.   ⎦
Admitted and certified,

JOSEPH ANDERSON,[32] *Comptroller.*

To Joseph Nourse, Esq., Register.
Treasury Department, Register's office, ⎤
December, 29th, 1824.   ⎦

I hereby certify that the foregoing report is a true copy of the original on file in this office, and that the account on which the foregoing advances were made is finally closed in the books of this office.

JOSEPH NOURSE,[33] *Register.*

The last picture was scarcely finished in April, 1824, when I had the misfortune to lose my wife,[34] who had been the faithful and beloved companion of all the vicissitudes of twenty four years. She was the perfect personification of truth and sincerity—wise to counsel, kind to console—by far the more important and better *moral* half of me, and withal, beautiful beyond the usual beauty of women! And as if this calamity was not sufficient, the friend who had kindly advanced money for me during my last unfortunate residence in Europe, found it necessary from the state of his own affairs, to ask a settlement. It was made, and it required all my means to meet the demand. Every thing however which could be converted into money was disposed of, at whatever sacrifice, and among other things, land was placed in the account at ten thousand dollars, which would now sell for one hundred thousand.[35]

32. Joseph Anderson, 1757–1837, Revolutionary officer, jurist, senator from Tennessee, appointed comptroller of the Treasury by President Madison, served from 1815 to 1836.

33. Joseph Nourse, 1754–1841, born at London, emigrated 1769, military secretary to Gen. Charles Lee 1776, secretary of ordinance and paymaster of the Board of War 1778, register of the Treasury 1781–1829.

34. See "Who was the Colonel's Lady? The Strange Case of Mrs. John Trumbull," App., pp. 350–365.

35. This is the only reference JT makes to his 1280 acre Mount Morris estate. These lands are described by Lockwood L. Doty, *A History of Livingston County,*

I had assisted in saving the dome and central grandeur of the Capitol, but whim and caprice ruled in the execution of the details. A notion had long prevailed, that a statue of Washington [36] must

---

New York (Geneseo, Edward E. Doty, 1876), pp. 619–621: "Mount Morris is one of the larger towns and lies on the western border of the county. It takes its name from Robert Morris of Revolutionary memory who in the spring of 1792, purchased the great farm of Ebenezer Allen, which embraced the village site and many broad acres of the flats . . . That city was then the seat of the general government, and Colonel Trumbull, an officer of the personal staff of Washington, whose artist brush has preserved some of the most interesting subjects of Revolutionary history, formed the half romantic notion of establishing his home in these beautiful wilds. He purchased a section of land, planted an orchard, made some preparation for building a residence near the site of the late Judge Hastings' house, and changed the name of the spot to Richmond Hill. For some reason the purpose was abandoned by him and the property passed from Allen into the hands of Robert Morris . . ." Judge Hastings' house at Mount Morris still stands and is (in 1952) the property of Sam and Joseph Cipriano. Now known as Oak Grove, it is located on Grove Street, a short distance from the junction of Routes 36 and 408. The site, on a bluff, commands a fine view of the Genesee Valley. With the winding river in the distance, the romantically inclined JT must have had Richmond Hill on the Thames, 10 miles from London, in mind when naming what he intended to be his country seat.

In the Trumbull records at the New-York Historical Society there are orders for fruit trees and the like for Mount Morris. Samuel Miles Hopkins, who acted as land agent for JT, wrote from Leicester, Genesee County, 16 April 1816: ". . . Mrs. Hopkins & myself shall look for you and Mrs. Trumbull with Solicitude, till you come. You will make our house your Home. Mean time we beg you to accept our best respects. Mrs. H's in particular to Mrs. Trumbull." JT was at Geneseo in August 1816, if not before—probably leaving his wife in New York City. In that month he lists the value of his holdings as $35,018.16.

"A few men unwilling to move to the Genesee attempted absentee landlordism. Notable among them was John Trumbull of Hartford, Connecticut, for whom James Wadsworth acted as agent. Because of difficulties of supervision this system broke down. A few persons migrated and settled on their holdings in the Genesee Valley. Yet the problem of gaining a return from unsold acres still persisted." Neil Adams McNall, *An Agricultural History of the Genesee Valley, 1790–1860* (Philadelphia, University of Pennsylvania Press, 1952), p. 52.

JT was hard pressed (in 1824) by his banker, Samuel Williams of London, for the repayment of the extended loans incurred during his protracted stay in England at the time of the War of 1812. See especially JT to Williams 7 December 1823, Yale Library. He was finally forced to sell—to one T. Williams, on 12 May 1824, for $10,000. This was a year before the completion of the Erie Canal, the opening of which JT believed would greatly enhance the value of the property.

36. JT's advice was sought, naturally, concerning a number of proposed statues for New York, Washington, and Raleigh, N.C. Antonio Canova, 1757–1822, of Rome, Houdon of Paris, and Francis Legatt Chantry, 1781–1842, R.A. (knighted in 1835),

be placed in the Capitol—and where so well as under the centre of the dome, on the ground floor, where it would be always accessible to and under the eye of the people; the ground floor might then become a magnificent *crypt*, and the monument of the father of his country, surrounded by those of her illustrious sons, might there seem still to watch over and to guard the interests of the nation which they had founded. The idea was poetical, grand, and captivating.

The statue being there, must be lighted, and as the projection of the porticos must necessarily screen all the light which might otherwise have been obtained from the arches between the piers of the ground floor, it was evident that the object could only be attained by letting down light from the summit of the dome; and to effect this, it would be necessary also to pierce the floor of the grand room, with an opening large enough for the purpose, say twenty feet diameter, at least. These whims prevailed, and the project was adopted. Of course, the staircaise which I had recommended, together with the fire-proof rooms for the preservation of important records, &c., were sacrificed, and instead of the concentric walls and simple arches of my plan, to support the floor of the great room, a wilderness of truncated columns and groined arches were employed for that purpose, and this wilderness, called the crypt, very soon degenerated into a stand for a crowd of female dealers in apples, nuts, cakes, liquors, &c., for the accommodation of hackney coachmen, servants, negroes, &c., and becoming an intolerable nuisance, was ultimately denounced as such by Mr. John Randolph, and abated.

In the mean time, I was in New York, busily employed in finishing my picture of the Declaration of Independence, and knew nothing of the architectural department, and the intrigues which perpetually controlled the good intentions and pure taste of Mr. Bulfinch,

---

come into the picture. The prices and conditions asked by these artists are interesting. See the Rufus King and John C. Calhoun correspondence with JT at the New-York Historical Society and especially Canova's letter (with a translation by JT) owned by Henry Woodhouse of New York; also *Minutes of the Common Council of the City of New York, 12, 37*, for 1 October 1821. Canova was elected an honorary member of the American Academy of the Fine Arts in 1817.

until I arrived at Washington with that picture. It was placed temporarily in a room of the north wing, then used for the sittings of the supreme court; this part of the building had been first erected, and was believed to be perfectly dry; yet this room proved to be damp to such a degree, that I thought it to be my duty to write the following letter to the secretary of state.

Washington, Feb. 18th, 1819.

To J. Q. Adams, Esq., &c.

SIR—Having carefully examined the room in the Capitol, in which the picture which I have painted for the government of the United States is at present placed, I feel it to be my duty to state to you, for the information of the President, my opinion, that, in consequence of the dampness of the walls and vaulting of that room, it is by no means advisable that the painting should remain there longer than may be thought necessary for the satisfaction of the members of the government, and the immediate gratification of public curiosity.

The cloth on which this work is executed, was prepared in the most approved and perfect manner, by the same person who is employed by Mr. West, to prepare those which are the basis of his admirable works. In this preparation, *size* is necessarily employed, which in damp situations is subject to contract mildew, and of course to decay; and no dampness is found to be so fatal to paintings, as the exhalations from newly erected masonry, where the corrosive quality of lime is added to the pernicious effect of mere moisture. I am, &c.[37]

When, in 1823, the last of the four paintings approached its termination,[38] I wrote to Mr. Bulfinch, the architect, the following letter.

New York, Dec. 15th, 1823.

Charles Bulfinch, Esq., &c. &c.

DEAR SIR—My last painting for the Capitol, the Resignation of Washington, although far advanced, will not be ready to deliver

37. The original of this letter is to be found in the General Records of the Department of State, Record Group 59, National Archives.

38. This was the "Resignation of General Washington." At its exhibition in New York in June 1824, JT netted $406.75.

during the present session; but, trusting from your last letter, that the great room will be quite finished, dry, and ready to receive them all at some time during the approaching summer, and before the next session, I wish to arrange with you, the time when all will be prepared and dry, that I may come on and see them all put in their places.

It will be necessary that the pannels on which they are to be strained, should be prepared in the mean time, of perfectly seasoned mahogany or cedar, and also the gilt frames.

Two young men of this town, whom I have employed for some time, and regard as excellent workmen, Messrs. Parker and Clover,[39] are desirous of being employed to execute the gilt frames, and should there be no other arrangement, I beg leave to recommend them strongly to you, and to the commissioner of the public buildings.

Mrs. Trumbull joins me in best wishes for the health and happiness of Mrs. Bulfinch, yourself, and family.

I am, &c. &c.   J. T.

When, in 1824, I went to Washington, to place all the paintings in their ultimate destination, I found the grand room finished indeed, but so very damp that I felt great reluctance in placing them there, and insisted most strenuously upon having the great opening in the centre of the room, which had been left for the purpose of lighting the crypt, closed; for, as the arches behind and under the porticos were closed only by iron grilles, the external air was freely admitted into the crypt, in all varieties of weather, as well by night as by day, and thence, by means of this unfortunate and ill judged opening, distributed through the great room, to every part of the principal floor of the building, rendering the atmosphere of all the apartments equally damp and cold as the weather in the open square. My remonstrances, however, were all in vain; and in this situation the four paintings were placed and remained, until, in 1828, the change on their surfaces became obvious and conspicuous to all who saw them, and occasioned the resolution of the house

39. L. Peter Clover and John Parker, both listed as gilders in the New York City Directory, 1823–24.

of representatives alluded to in the following report, which I addressed to the speaker of the house on the 9th of December, 1828.

Twentieth Congress, } [Doc. No. 10.] Ho. of Reps.
Second Session.

NATIONAL PAINTINGS

Letter from JOHN TRUMBULL, *to the Speaker* [40] *of the House of Representatives, on the subject of the national paintings in the rotunda of the Capitol, Dec. 9th, 1828, read, and laid upon the table.*

To the Honorable, the Speaker of the House of Representatives, United States.

SIR—On the 30th of May last, I received from the commissioner of the public buildings, a copy of the resolution of the honorable the house of representatives, dated the 26th of May, authorizing him to take, under my direction, the proper measures for securing the paintings in the rotunda from the effect of dampness.

I had always regarded the perpetual admission of damp air into the rotunda from the crypt below, as the great cause of the evil required to be remedied, and of course considered the effectual closing of the aperture which had been left in the centre of the floor as an indispensable part of the remedy. I had communicated my opinions on this subject to the chairman of the committee on public buildings, and had been informed that this had been ordered to be done.

So soon, therefore, as I received information from the commissioner that this work was completed, (as well as an alteration in the sky-light, which I had suggested,) and that the workmen and incumbrances were removed out of the room, I came on and proceeded to take the several measures for the preservation of the paintings, which are stated in detail in the following report, which I beg leave to submit to the house.

1st. All the paintings were taken down, removed from their frames, taken off from the pannels over which they are strained, removed to a dry warm room, and there separately and carefully

40. Andrew Stevenson, 1784–1857, representative from Virginia, served as speaker from 1827 to 1834, minister to Great Britain, 1836–41.

examined. The material which forms the basis of these paintings is a linen cloth, whose strength and texture is very similar to that used for the topgallant-sails of a ship of war. The substances employed to form a proper surface for the artist, together with the colors, oils, &c., employed by him in his work, form a sufficient protection for the threads of the canvass on this face, but the back remains bare, and of course exposed to the deleterious influence of damp air. The effect of this is first seen in the form of mildew—it was this which I dreaded; and the examination showed that mildew was already commenced, to an extent which rendered it manifest that the continuance of the same exposure which they had hitherto undergone, for a very few years longer, would have accomplished the complete decomposition or rotting of the canvass, and the consequent destruction of the paintings. The first thing to be done was to dry the canvass perfectly, which was done by laying down each picture successively on its face, upon a clean dry carpet, and exposing the back to the influence of the warmth of a dry and well aired room. The next thing was to devise and apply some substance, which would act permanently as a preservative against future possible exposure.

I had learned that a few years ago, some of the eminent chemists of France had examined with great care, several of the ancient mummies of Egypt, with a view to ascertain the nature of the materials employed by the embalmers, which the lapse of so many ages had proved to possess the power of protecting from decay a substance otherwise so perishable as the human body. This examination had proved, that after the application of liquid asphaltum to the cavities of the head and body, the whole had been wrapped carefully in many envelopes or bandages of *linen prepared with wax*. The committee of chemists decided further, after a careful examination and analysis of the hieroglyphic paintings with which the cases, &c. are covered, that the colors employed, and still retaining their vivid brightness, had also been prepared and applied with the same substance.

I also knew, that towards the close of the last century, the Antiquarian Society of England had been permitted to open and examine the stone coffin deposited in one of the vaults of Westminster

Abbey, and said to contain the body of King Edward I.[40a] who died in July, 1307. On removing the stone lid of the coffin, its contents were found to be closely enveloped in a strong linen cloth waxed; within this envelope were found splendid robes of silk, enriched with various ornaments, covering the body, which was found to be entire, and to have been wrapped carefully in all its parts, even to each separate finger, in bandages of fine linen, which had been dipped in melted *wax;* and not only was the body not decomposed, but the various parts of the dress, such as a scarlet satin mantle, and a scarlet piece of sarsnet,[40b] which was placed over the face, were in perfect preservation, even to their colors. The knowledge of these facts, persuaded me that *wax,* applied to the back of the paintings, would form the best defense hitherto known to exist against the destructive effects of damp and stagnant air; and therefore,

2dly. Common bees' wax was melted over a fire, with an equal quantity (in bulk) of oil of turpentine, and this mixture, by the help of large brushes, was applied hot to the back of each cloth, and was afterwards rubbed in, with hot irons, until the cloths were perfectly saturated.

3dly. In the mean time, the niches in the solid wall, in which the paintings are placed, were carefully plastered with hydraulic cement, to prevent the possible exudation of any moisture from the wall; and, as there is a space from two to eight inches deep between the surface of the wall and the pannels on which the cloths are strained, I caused small openings to be cut in the wall, above and under the edge of the frames, and communicating with those vacant spaces, for the purpose of admitting the air of the room behind the paintings, and thus keeping up a constant ventilation, by means of which the same temperature of air will be maintained at the back of the paintings as on their face.

4thly. The cloths were finally strained upon pannels, for the purpose of guarding against injury from careless or intentional blows

40a. See Sir Joseph Ayloffe, Bart., "An Account of the Body of King Edward the First, as it appeared on opening his Tomb in the year 1774," *Archaeologia* . . . , London, The Society of Antiquarians of London, 1775, 3, 376–413.

40b. Sarsenet, a fine, soft silk material.

of sticks, canes, &c., or from children's missiles. These pannels are perforated with many holes, to admit the air freely to the back of the cloths; and being dried, were carefully painted, to prevent the wood from absorbing or transmitting any humidity. The whole being then restored to their places, were finally cleaned with care, and slightly re-varnished.

5thly. As the accumulation of dust, arising from sweeping so large a room, and what is much worse, the filth of flies, (the most destructive enemies of painting,) if not carefully guarded against, renders necessary the frequent washing and cleaning of the surface of pictures, every repetition of which is injurious, I have directed curtains to be placed, which can be drawn in front of the whole, whenever the room is to be swept, as well as in the recess of the legislature during the summer months, when flies are most pernicious.

6thly. As nothing is more obvious than the impossibility of keeping a room warm and dry by means of fire, so long as doors are left open for the admission of the external air, I have further directed self-closing baize doors to be prepared, and placed so that they will unavoidably close behind every one who shall either enter or leave the room.

When the doors are kept closed, and fires are lighted in the furnaces below to supply warm air; I find that the temperature of this vast apartment is easily maintained at about sixty-three degrees Fahrenheit; and the simple precaution of closed doors being observed, in addition to the others which I have employed, I entertain no doubt, that these paintings are now perfectly and permanently secured against the deleterious effects of dampness.

I regret that I was not authorized to provide against the danger of damage by violence, whether intended or accidental. Curiosity naturally leads men to touch as well as to look at objects of this kind, and placed as low as they are, not only the gilded frames and curtains, but the paintings, are within the reach of spectators; repeated handling, even by the best intentioned and most careful, will in the course of time produce essential damage. But one of the paintings testifies to the possibility of their being approached for the very purpose of doing injury; the right foot of General Morgan, in the picture of Saratoga, was cut off with a sharp instrument, apparently a penknife. I have repaired the wound, but the scar remains visible. If I had possessed the authority, I should have placed in front, and at the distance of not less than ten feet from the wall, an iron railing, of such strength and elevation as should form a complete guard against injury by ill-disposed persons, unless they should employ missiles of some force.

I beg leave to commend to the attention of the house, this further precaution.

All which is most respectfully submitted to the house, by

JOHN TRUMBULL.[41]

41. Original draft in the Library of Congress; the same letter was printed in the *American Journal of Science*, 16 (1829), 163–168, of which Prof. Benjamin Silliman of Yale was editor.

JT sent a bill to the government "for services performed in obedience to a Resolution of the House of Representatives bearing the date of 26th of May 1828, from Octo. 6th to Decr. 15, Ten Weeks at $100 pr. week, $1000, travelling Expenses from and to New York $50," and so on, making a total of $1,153. (Huntington Library.)

The 72-year-old JT wrote to Daniel Wadsworth from Washington on 27 November 1828: "I have been employed in a laborious, troublesome and dangerous task— clambering for days on Scaffolds & Stepladders high above a stone floor. Thank God, it is done. I have got down safely & can think of other things." (Faneuil Adams, Boston.)

IO

New Haven Interlude: the Trumbull Gallery and the Autobiography *1828–40*

My contract with the government was thus honorably fulfilled; the paintings were placed in the Capitol, and so far as my skill extended, they were secured from ruin by dampness. My debts were paid, but I had the world before me to begin anew. I had passed the term of three-score years and ten, the allotted period of human life. My best friend was removed from me, and I had no child.[1] A sense of loneliness began to creep over my mind, yet my hand was steady, and my sight good, and I felt the *vis vitæ* strong within me. Why then sink down into premature imbecility?

I was strongly impressed with a sense of the importance of those great events which had brought into existence a mighty empire and a new world, and although the actual government had stopped short and forgotten (if indeed they ever knew) the beautiful language of our Savior, in his last conversation with his disciples, as recorded by St. John, *"that greater love hath no man than this, that a man lay down his life for his friends,"* [2] and had omitted to shew the gratitude of the nation to those eminent patriots who had given their lives for their country at Bunker's Hill, at Quebec, and at Princeton, still I doubted not, that at some future period sentiments more just and more dignified would prevail, nor that future generations would thank me for what I had done to preserve the remembrance of the great and good men of that memorable period.

I resolved, therefore, to begin a new series of my paintings of revolutionary subjects, of a smaller size than those in the Capitol,

1. Technically untrue. The last letter Trumbull wrote to his bastard son, John Trumbull Ray, was on 16 March 1829. See "Trumbull's Troubles: an Omitted Chapter of the Artist's Life." App., pp. 332–350.
2. John 15:13.

and to solace my heavy hours by working on them. I chose the size of six feet by nine,[3] and began.

The cholera made its appearance in New York,[4] soon after I commenced, and was peculiarly fatal in the sixth ward, in which I

3. These heavyhanded performances, the battles of "Bunker's Hill," "Trenton," and "Princeton," the "Attack on Quebec," and the "Declaration of Independence," a part of the artist's estate at the time of his death, were acquired by the Wadsworth Atheneum, Hartford, a year later, in 1844. Two of the series, with figures painted half the size of life, were begun in 1830, and the other 3 in 1832; they were executed at JT's painting rooms at the American Academy of the Fine Arts at New York; all were completed by 1834; there were no more than these 5.

On 15 February 1840 JT wrote from New Haven to his old friend Ithiel Town, who was one of the Committee of Selection for the design of the Ohio State Capitol at Columbus (built 1838–58 by Henry Walters and several other architects; see Roger Hale Newton, *Town & Davis, Architects*, New York, Columbia University Press, 1942). ". . . Your friend has probably been in Washington, & seen, in the Rotunda of the Capitol my paintings of four Subjects, from the History of the Revolution—they form but one half of a Series of Compositions recording great Events of that immortal Period, which I had prepared many years ago. Among them were four Military Subjects of the deepest Interest & Importance (in my own opinion,) & certainly my finest Compositions. I was not a little mortified at not being employ'd to execute the whole for that magnificent Apartment which might then have been called with propriety *the Hall of the Revolution*. What the Government of the U.S. thus omitted I have always hoped to see corrected by some individual State & looking to such a probability I have been preparing a Second Sett of this Historical Series (of which the small originals have all been deposited in the Gallery of Yale College) —differing from those at Washington principally in Size, their dimensions being 6 feet by 9: and thus better adapted to an apartment less vast. Of these Five are finished, & in my estimation are better than those in the Capitol (especially the Declaration of Independence) and I shall go on to finish the other three, without delay:—and hope to have them all finished before the State house in Ohio, can be made ready to receive them. My price for each painting will be $8,000.—to be paid in Bonds of the State, bearing an Interest of 6 per C and redeemable in Fifty years. The Government of the U.S. are now paying for works to complete the Rotunda to Junior Artists, and for Subjects of inferior Importance $12,000 each. The Pictures which are finished are—1st the Battle of Bunker's Hill, 2 The Death of Gen¹. Montgomery before Quebec, 3 The Declaration of Independence, 4 The Battle at Trenton, 5 The Battle at Princeton. The Three to be finished are 6 The Surrender of Burgoyne, 7 The Surrender of Lord Cornwallis, 8 The Resignation of Washington. A Military whole length Portrait of Washington shall be added." (Wadsworth Atheneum, Hartford.) Thus to the very end of his long life JT was involved with his "historical series"—which he began 55 years before.

4. This "passage . . . is indeed confusing. Asiatic cholera appeared in India on the banks of the Ganges in 1817; but since there was little travel in those days, it remained confined for nearly twelve years in that local geographical area. It reached Persia probably in 1829, having been transmitted thither by caravan. It was rife

lived. I was busily employed upon the Declaration of Independence, when I was attacked by this deadly disease, but, by the blessing of Providence or the kind care of my friends, it passed away in a few days, and without any serious consequences.

Funds, however, began to diminish, and I sold scraps of furniture, fragments of plate, &c. Many pictures remained in my hands unsold, and to all appearance unsaleable. At length the thought occurred to me, that although the hope of a sale to the nation, or to a state, became more and more desperate from day to day, yet, in an age of speculation, it might be possible, that some society might be willing to possess these paintings, on condition of pay by a life annuity. I first thought of Harvard College,[5] my alma mater, but she was rich, and amply endowed. I then thought of Yale—although not my alma, yet she was within my native state, and poor.

---

in Russia, France, and England in the early thirties and it appeared in epidemic form in New York in October 1832. The name was introduced at the same time . . . Colonel Trumbull . . . would not have recovered in a matter of days. What I suspect happened is that he had a severe attack of dysentery which was rife on the North American continent in the late eighteenth century and of course throughout the nineteenth. Thus he probably had an acute attack of diarrhoea while painting the Declaration of Independence, and later when the word 'cholera' became current put this tag on his indisposition. Beyond this I don't think one can safely speculate." Dr. John F. Fulton of the Yale University School of Medicine.

5. JT's draft of his letter to President Josiah Quincy of Harvard is in the Yale Library: "I have conveyed my Original paintings of subjects of the Revolution, with others, to the President and Fellows of Yale College—burthened with payment of an annuity to me during my life:—and afterwards the income which may be derived from the Exhibition of them to be applied forever to the Education of Poor Scholars—to guard against the possibility of a perversion to any other purpose in any future time I wish to insert a clause in virtue of which (in case of such perversion) the whole may pass into the possession of my alma mater, Harvard, to whom I should have offered the Donation in the first instance had not she been very rich and Yale very poor. It is necessary to know accurately the Legal Style and Title or Appellation of Harvard for the purpose. May I beg you to give me as soon as may be this information." George Parker Winship, late of the Harvard College Library, states: "We have in the files the original of Trumbull's letter to Quincy, duly docketed in the President's hand; 'Trumbull 20 Oct 1831. Ansd in letter book.' We also have a scant score of letters in a folder, showing evident signs of having been torn out of a binding, with a note stating that Miss Quincy turned these over, with more of the same sort, saying that most of his papers had been destroyed before he died. So I fear we will never know what words the President used to correct Trumbull's notion that Harvard is richer than Yale—perish the thought."

I hinted this idea to a friend, (Mr. Alfred Smith,[6] of Hartford,)—
it took—was followed up, and resulted in a contract, of which the
following is a copy.

"This indenture, made the nineteenth day of December, in the
year of our Lord one thousand eight hundred and thirty one, between John Trumbull, of the city and state of New York, Esquire,
of the first part, and the President and Fellows of Yale College in
New Haven, of the second part, witnesseth, that the said John
Trumbull, in consideration that the said parties of the second part
have executed a bond or obligation, whereby they have bound
themselves to pay to him during his natural life an annuity of one
thousand dollars a year, in the manner and at the times specified
in the condition of the said bond; and also in consideration of his
good will towards Yale College, and his desire to promote its
prosperity, hath granted, bargained, sold and conveyed, and
hereby doth grant, bargain, sell and convey, to the parties of the
second part and their successors, all the pictures or paintings mentioned in the schedule to this indenture, annexed, to have and to
hold the same upon the conditions and for the purposes herein
mentioned, provided always and nevertheless, and these presents
are upon condition, that if the said annuity, or any part thereof,
shall be behind or unpaid by the space of fifteen days next after
any of the days of payment whereon the same ought to be paid,
pursuant to the condition of the said bond, or if default shall be
made in any of the covenants or agreements herein contained, on
the part and behalf of the parties of the second part, or their successors, to be kept and performed then and from thenceforth, it shall
and may be lawful for the said John Trumbull, his executors, administrators or assigns, to retake and repossess the said paintings,
and the same to have again, repossess and enjoy, as in his first and
former estate, any thing herein contained to the contrary notwithstanding. And it is covenanted and agreed by and between the
parties to these presents, in manner following, that is to say, that
the parties of the second part shall erect upon land belonging to

6. Alfred Smith, 1789–1868, prominent lawyer, member of the Connecticut Historical Society, 1840, trustee of the Wadsworth Atheneum, 1842, and president,
1856.

them in New Haven, a fire-proof building for the reception of the said paintings, which building shall be finished on or before the first day of October, in the year of our Lord one thousand eight hundred and thirty two, and shall be of such form and dimensions as shall be approved of by the said John Trumbull, and the said paintings shall be placed and arranged in the said building, under the directions and superintendence of the said John Trumbull. The said paintings, after they shall be so placed and arranged, shall be exhibited, and the profits of such exhibition shall be received by the parties of the second part, and applied in the first place towards the payment of the said annuity during the life of the said John Trumbull, and the whole of such profits after his death, (except in the case hereafter mentioned,) shall be perpetually appropriated towards defraying the expense of educating poor scholars in Yale College, under such regulations as the said President and Fellows, and their successors, shall from time to time see fit to make. And if the profits of such exhibition shall not, during the life of the said John Trumbull, be sufficient to discharge the said annuity, then the said parties of the second part may borrow as much money as may be necessary for that purpose, and the profits of the said exhibition, after the decease of the said John Trumbull, shall be applied to discharge the principal and interest of the debt which shall thus have been incurred, and after the said debt shall be extinguished, then the whole profits of the said exhibition shall be applied towards defraying the expense of the education of poor scholars, in manner aforesaid. *And it is further expressly agreed, that the said paintings shall never be sold, alienated, divided or dispersed, but shall always be kept together, and exhibited* [7] as aforesaid, by the said parties of the second part, and their successors, and that the profits of such exhibition shall be sacredly applied to the purposes before mentioned, and to no other.

7. These words are italicized for the benefit of the directors, past, present, and future, of the Yale University Art Gallery, as requests are constantly received—which cannot be granted—for the loan of pictures listed in this agreement. (The injunction does not, however, apply to those examples of JT's work belonging to the university and not included in the Indenture.) Only once has the agreement been broken, and that on the advice of counsel. At the outbreak of World War II, the editor, then director of the Gallery, took a number of the most precious pictures, as a safety precaution, to points in the Midwest, where they remained for the duration.

"In witness whereof, the parties to these presents have interchangeably executed the same, that is to say, the said John Trumbull hath to one part of these presents set his hand and seal, and the said President and Fellows of Yale College, in New Haven, have to another part of these presents caused their corporate seal to be affixed, on the day and year first above written.[8]

JEREMIAH DAY,[9] *President of Yale College.*

"Signed by the President of the College, in my presence. Witness the seal of the College.

ELIZUR GOODRICH,[10] *Secretary of Yale College.*"

Schedule referred to in the annexed instrument, being a list of the paintings thereby conveyed to the President and Fellows of Yale College, in New Haven.[11]

Eight original paintings of subjects from the American revolution, viz.

1. The Battle of Bunker's Hill,   size 2 by 3 feet
2. The Death of Gen. Montgomery at Quebec,   do. do.
3. The Declaration of Independence,   20 by 30 inches.
4. The Battle of Trenton,   do. do.
5. The Battle of Princeton,   do. do.
6. The Surrender of Gen. Burgoyne,   do. do.
7. The Surrender of Lord Cornwallis,   do. do.
8. Washington resigning his Commission, do.   do.[12]
   Our Savior with little children.[13]

8. See "John Trumbull, Museum Architect," App., pp. 371–378.

9. Jeremiah Day, 1773–1867, Yale 1795, president 1817–46, known as a conservative but an extremely popular president.

10. Elizur Goodrich, 1761–1849, Yale 1779, secretary 1818–46, a Federalist, active in city and state government, mayor of New Haven 1802–22.

11. The "Catalogue of Paintings by Colonel Trumbull . . . now exhibited in the Gallery of Yale College . . ." was reprinted at the end of the *Autobiography* (1841), App., pp. 405–439.

12. These are the eight originals of the celebrated "national history" series, begun in 1785 and finished in 1822.

13. Or "Suffer Little Children" was painted at London in 1812. This and the following, "in West's worst style." See Samuel Isham, *The History of American Painting* (New York, Macmillan, 1910), p. 187.

The woman accused of adultery.[14]
Peter the Great at Narva.[15]
Madonna and Children, copied from Raphael.[16]
St. Jerome, Madonna, &c., copied from Correggio.[17]
Infant Savior, St. John and Lamb.[18]
Holy Family.[19]
St. John and Lamb.[20]
Maternal Tenderness.[21]
Portrait of President Washington.[22]
    Do. of Alexander Hamilton.[23]
    Do. of Rufus King.[24]
    Do. of Christopher Gore.[25]

Six frames, each containing five miniature portraits of persons distinguished during the Revolution.

JEREMIAH DAY, *President of Yale College.*

"Know all men by these presents, that we, the President and Fellows of Yale College in New Haven, are held and firmly bound unto John Trumbull, of the city and state of New York, Esquire, in the sum of twenty thousand dollars lawful money of the United

14. Or, to give it its more polite title, "The Woman Accused by the Scribes and Pharisees," was painted in 1811 at London.

15. Inspired by Voltaire's *Histoire de l'Empire de Russie sous Pierre le Grand;* executed in 1812 at London.

16. "Madonna and Child with St. John the Baptist" after a copy of Raphael's "Madonna au Corset Rouge," painted in 1801 at London.

17. The "St. Jerome" after West's copy, done in prison, 1780; see p. 70.

18. 1801 at London.

19. "Madonna and Child with Saint Joseph, John the Baptist, Elizabeth, and Zacharias," begun in 1802 at London and finished in 1806 at New York.

20. "The Infant Saviour with St. John the Baptist and the Lamb," painted in 1801 at London.

21. Or "Maternal Affection" (or Love), painted in 1809 at London.

22. Painted at Philadelphia May 1793, bust, exhibited at the American Academy 1831 (No. 13); see John Hill Morgan and Mantle Fielding, *The Life Portraits of Washington and Their Replicas* (Philadelphia, privately printed, 1931), No. 8 (illustrated), p. 170.

23. Painted in 1832 at New York, one of the half dozen replicas of the 1792 portrait for John Jay.

24. Painted in 1800 at London.

25. Painted in 1800 at London.

States of America, to be paid to the said John Trumbull, his certain attorney, executors, administrators or assigns, for which payment we bind ourselves and our successors firmly by these presents, sealed with our corporate seal, and dated the nineteenth day of December, in the year of our Lord one thousand eight hundred and thirty one.

"The condition of the above obligation is such, that if the above bounden obligors shall and do yearly and every year for and during the natural life of the said John Trumbull, well and truly pay or cause to be paid to him or to his certain attorney or assigns, an annuity or clear yearly sum of one thousand dollars lawful money of the United States of America, in even quarterly payments to be made on the four following days in the year, that is to say, on the first day of October, the first day of January, the first day of April, and the first day of July in every year, by even and equal portions, the first payment thereof to begin and be made on the first day of October, in the year of our Lord one thousand eight hundred and thirty two,—then the above obligations to be void, else to remain in full force and virtue.

JEREMIAH DAY, *President of Yale College.*

"Signed by the President of the College, in my presence. Witness the seal of the College. Certified,

ELIZUR GOODRICH, *Secretary of Yale College.*"

Should any one take the trouble of comparing the foregoing schedule with the catalogue of the paintings now in the Gallery, it will be found that the actual number exceeds the schedule by nearly one half. Several of these additions have been painted and added to the Gallery since the date of the original agreement.[26] The last of these, viz. the Deluge,[27] and the two copies of the Trans-

26. As JT aged he seems to have become increasingly concerned with those pictures which had fired his youth; he probably saw Jacques Louis David's "Death of Socrates" of 1787 (now at the Metropolitan Museum of Art) in the artist's Paris studio and had it, or a similar subject and composition, in mind when he painted his large oil "I Was in Prison and Ye Came unto Me," from Matthew 25:36, in 1834 (Yale).

27. "The Last Family Who Perished in the Deluge" painted at New Haven from a pencil sketch (now at Fordham University) made in 1781 at London. It is one of Trumbull's poorest pictures.

figuration [28] and the Communion of St. Jerome,[29] were painted during the years 1838 and 1839.

The Gallery now contains fifty five pictures by my own hand, painted at various periods, from my earliest essay of the Battle of Cannæ,[30] to my last composition, the Deluge, including the eight small original pictures of the American revolution, which contain the portraits painted from life.

Thus I derive present subsistence principally from this source, and have besides the happy reflection, that when I shall have gone to my rest, these works will remain a source of good to many a poor, perhaps meritorious and excellent man.

The large set of Revolutionary paintings was not included in this contract, and indeed, at its date, they did not exist, having been painted since. Five of the series are finished, and should my long life be still further prolonged, I trust they will all be completed, and they will remain a legacy for posterity.[31]

28. A copy after a copy after Raphael, at New Haven, in the same class as the preceding.

29. "The Last Communion of St. Jerome" after a copy after Domenichino.

30. "The Death of Paulus Aemilius at the Battle of Cannae," of 1774, see p. 15.

31. A rather weak note on which to end the account of an extraordinarily interesting life. The author, however, was 85. JT wrote to Daniel Webster, secretary of state, from New Haven on 29 January 1841: ". . . I am printing a Volume of Reminiscences & in which I state some facts of that important period [of the Jay Treaty Commission] & shall take the liberty of offering to your acceptance a Copy of the work, so soon as it shall be completed. . . ." General Records of the Department of State, Record Group 59, National Archives. To the end of his long life, JT knew the "Very Important People."

Notes on Trumbull's Later Years and Additional Information

Colonel Trumbull simply omitted mention in the *Autobiography* of the period in his life between November 1799 and April 1804. London society ignored him, at least professionally; he continued to paint members of the American colony at London: Gores and Kings, Bartholomew Dandridge, Maurice Swabey, a British associate on the Jay Commission, the French Count de Mosloy and his wife, and a few others, including his visiting nephew, John M. Trumbull. He took refuge in painting religious subjects (all of these paintings are poor) and water color landscapes, which are nicely executed, in Sussex, Wiltshire and South Wales during a pleasure trip in 1803.

Much information about these and later years, about JT's death, about his paintings, especially those in the Capitol at Washington, and the Trumbull Gallery is to be found in his correspondence and papers and in the writings of his contemporaries.

JOHN BLAKE WHITE

John Blake White, 1781– *ca.*1859, artist, dramatist, and lawyer, of Charleston, S.C., a pupil of Benjamin West, 1800–03, called on JT in May 1800, shortly after his arrival at London. The young man noted: "As soon as I could I waited on Coln. Trumbull. He resided No. 27 Wardor Street. He invited me to breakfast with him the next morning. I informed the Colonel of my design in visiting England, and spoke as I felt, inthusiastically and rapturously in favor of painting, the profession from which I anticipated so much glory and happiness in pursuing. The Coln. had trodden the road before me, he knew of the many gilded prospects it afforded, and knew also of the many vexations, mortifications and disappointments which were common to the way: 'Were I twenty years younger than I am, I would this moment commence the study of the Law. Be advised by me, and return to that study (the Law) (in) which you say you have been engaged. By all means relinquish that of painting. It will never repay you for your pains. Painting is a profession, the encouragement of which depends alone upon *Fashion* which is the caprice and whim of mankind. It is not *necessary*, it cannot therefore meet with certain encouragement. You have left the study of the Law for Painting, a certainty, for an uncertainty: so long as there are vices and passions in the world the Law will be certain; vices and passions will be found where Taste is not heard of; the Law is therefore the more certain profession. I would sooner make a Son of mine a Butcher or a shoemaker, than a Painter. Take my advice as a Friend, return & prosecute the study of the Law.' All this only made me smile." [1] JT wrote from London to Thomas Pinckney of Charleston (and a similar letter to Henry William DeSaussure) concerning the aspiring painter, on 5 September 1800: "I have a real pleasure in giving him the best advice & assistance I can, but in truth I regard my profession, in these times of Tumult, as little worth the attention of a man of Talent. No human pursuit is more uncertain of success whether we regard real excellence, or that protection without which even excellence is fruitless to the possessor." (Yale Library.) JT's advice was valid; after a short struggle White took up law and painted as an amateur.

MRS. SULLY'S PORTRAIT

In 1806 JT painted the portrait of Mrs. Thomas (Sarah Annis) Sully, wife of the painter. Dunlap recounts: "Trumbull and Jarvis were both painting in New York; and at that time the first was the best portrait painter, though he did not continue long so; his art was without feeling or nature . . . to derive advantage from the older artist was not so easy of attainment. Sully sacrificed one hundred dollars . . . for the purpose, and carried his wife to Trumbull's rooms, as a sitter, that he might see his mode of painting, and have a specimen from his pencil. He gained some knowledge for his money, and probably learned to imitate the neatness with which palette and pencils and oils and varnishes were used and preserved . . . he gained a model, which served him as a beacon, warning him of that which it was necessary to avoid." [2] The portrait, which is charmingly painted, hangs in the Amherst College Art Gallery. No love was lost between Dunlap and JT.

TRUMBULL'S POSITION AT LONDON

It was curious that JT, the "patriot-artist," should attempt to set himself up as a fashionable portrait painter in London. West and Copley had

1. "Journal of John Blake White," *South Carolina Historical and Genealogical Magazine*, 42 (April 1941), 63–64.
2. William Dunlap, *Arts of Design*, 2, 246.

done so before him, but they were settled before the final break with the mother country. It should be remembered, too, that Mrs. Trumbull was anything but a social asset.

JT noted: "During several years of my residence in London, I had the happiness to live on terms of intimacy with Mr. Nollekens, the sculptor . . ."[3] Joseph Nollekens, 1737–1823, British sculptor of Dutch descent, was highly successful, financially, receiving 150 gn. apiece for his portrait busts, and being paid, for instance, £4,000 for his statue of William Pitt (in 1812), erected in the Senate House, Cambridge. He left a fortune of £200,000 when he died in his 86th year. All of this is in marked contrast to JT's want of profitable commissions. Intimacy between the Nollekens and Trumbull families may be inferred by the sculptor's small legacy left to Mrs. John Trumbull Ray, the obscure English wife of JT's worthless natural son. In the 7th codicil of his will, dated 27 September 1819, he stated: "It is my desire that my executors do give as a present from me to Mrs. Elizabeth Gee widow of No. 4, King-street, Golden-square the sum of fifty pounds, as a token of my regard for her. And it is my desire that my executors do give, in the same manner as above, the wife of Lieut. Ray as a token of my regard for her and her family like of my friend Mr. Trumbold in America."[4]

The painter Morse wrote, in 1813, while at London: "The American character stands high in this country as to the production of artists . . . Mr. West now stands at the head . . . Mr. Copley next, then Colonel Trumbull. Stuart in America has no rival here. As these are now old men and going off the stage, Mr. Allston succeeds in the prime of life . . . After him is a young man from Philadelphia by the name of Leslie, who is my room-mate."[5] Charles Robert Leslie, 1794–1859, became a Royal Academician (an honor JT, undoubtedly, would have liked) and later professor at the R.A. JT was elected an honorary member of the Society of Artists of the United States (which was merged with the Pennsylvania Academy) in 1810.[6]

The painter Thomas Sully wrote to the art collector, Daniel Wadsworth of Hartford, from Philadelphia on 17 June 1820: "Whilst in Lon-

3. *Autobiography* (1841), App., p. 313. See also John Thomas Smith (1766–1833, keeper of prints and drawings in the British Museum), *Nollekens and His Times* (London, H. Colburn, 1828), later edition, edited and annotated by Wilfred Whitten (2 vols., London and New York, John Lane, 1920).

4. J. T. Smith, *op. cit.*, 1, 357. See App., p. 345.

5. Edward Lind Morse, ed., *Samuel F. B. Morse, His Letters and Journals* (2 vols., Boston and New York, Houghton Mifflin, 1914), 1, 102–103.

6. See "Society of Artists," *The Port Folio*, 8 (1812), 28.

don I had frequent opportunity of seeing Col. Trumbull, who, as well as Mrs. T., showed much kindness. I do not think this excellent Painter is duly appreciated in London. His merit is neither generally understood, nor valued . . . the English taste is in favor of strong effect, & brilliant colouring; whilst the higher excellencies of painting, which are design, and composition, are unvalued . . . I think France would be a more favorable theatre for a display of Mr. Trumbull's powers and am surprised he has not given that country a trial." (Connecticut State Library.)

JT, like Washington Allston, was a member of the short-lived "British School," founded in 1802, under the patronage of the Prince of Wales.[7] A Trumbull descendant recently presented the Yale University Art Gallery with a small golden palette—the Colonel's certificate of membership: "BRITISH SCHOOL" and the badge of the Prince of Wales (3 ostrich plumes) are on the obverse and the membership, "No. 96," is engraved on the reverse. Trumbull exhibited at the society's gallery at Berners Street, which is but a stone's throw from Benjamin West's studio on adjacent Newman Street.

PICTURE DEALING

JT became involved once more in picture dealing. Some of the "Old Masters," which he purchased in Paris in the spring of 1795, through J. B. P. LeBrun (Vigée-LeBrun's husband) and which were possibly bought in at the earlier auction by JT, or, more probably, by West, were again put up for sale. See "A Catalogue of Eight most Valuable Pictures, the property of John Trumbull, Esq., Purchased by him at Paris, in the Spring of 1795 . . . will be Sold by Auction by PETER COXE, in Maddox Street, Hanover Square, on Friday, the 12th of June, at Two o'Clock precisely" and the "Trumbull Collection," Lugt, *Répertoire des catalogues de ventes*, No. 8202. The catalogue bears no year date; the sale occurred in 1812 (and not in 1808; there was no sale on Friday, 12 June 1808, as recorded by Lugt No. 7122; the day of the week and month correspond to 1812 and not to 1808; the paper on which the "1808 sale" is printed is watermarked with the date 1811).[8]

7. See William T. Whitley, *Art in England, 1800–1820* (Cambridge, Cambridge University Press, 1928), pp. 45–48.

8. See W. Buchanan, *Memoirs of Painting with a Chronological History of the Importation of Pictures by the Great Masters into England since the French Revolution, 1*, 257 ff.

BOSTON ATHENAEUM

In 1827 the Boston Athenaeum held its first art exhibition, in which JT was represented by a "Scene from Fingal" (No. 77), the large, dull "exhibition piece" he had painted at London in 1809, exhibited at the British Institution the following year and at the American Academy of the Fine Arts almost annually from 1816 to 1824, and again in 1831, just before it came to Yale. In the 2d exhibition, of 1828, he exhibited No. 168, "The Saviour and St. John with the Lamb," painted in 1801 at London, exhibited at the American Academy in 1816, 1824, 1831, and now at Yale; No. 190, "Our Saviour with Little Children," painted in 1812 at London, exhibited at the Royal Academy that year and at the American Academy, now at Yale; No. 201, "The Woman Accused of Adultery," of 1811, exhibited at the British Institution and seven times at the annual exhibitions of the American Academy, now at Yale; No. 217, "Preparation for the Tomb," recently completed (1827) at New York, shown that year at the American Academy, now at Yale; No. 225, "Saviour Sinking under the Weight of the Cross," painted in 1826 at New York, American Academy, 1827, now at Yale; No. 237, "Lady of the Lake," painted in 1811 at London, exhibited at the Royal, Pennsylvania and American Academies, now lost; and, what is far more interesting, two pictures that were "a part of the Collection formed by the late President Jefferson; No. 310, 'Surrender of Ld. Cornwallis at Yorktown' (original sketch)," painted in 1787 at London, size 10 by 20 inches, and now unhappily lost; and No. 316, "Thomas Paine, (an original) on Wood," also lost. In 1828 the Athenaeum, after prolonged negotiations, purchased JT's "Sortie from Gibraltar" for $2,000, painted in 1789 at London, in the artist's most brilliant manner; this large canvas is now deposited with the Museum of Fine Arts, Boston.[9]

THE SWEET SINGER OF HARTFORD

In 1835 Mrs. Charles (Lydia Huntley) Sigourney, "the Sweet Singer of Hartford," wrote a poem entitled "The Birth-day of Col. John Trumbull," the manuscript of which is at the Yale Library. So far as the editor can find the poem has never been published.

9. For JT's long connection with this institution see Mabel Munson Swan, *The Athenaeum Gallery, 1827–1873* (Boston, Athenaeum, 1940).

THE BIRTH-DAY OF COL. JOHN TRUMBULL
JUNE 6TH 1835

Son of an ancient name!
Whom Genius early found,
Musing amid the rural bound,
And touch'd thy young heart with her lightning-flame,
Perchance, that sparkling light
Gleam'd on thy mother's sight,
As by thy cradle-side she pass'd the watchful night,
Unwearied, bending o'er her suffering son,
Long cradled in her arms, her youngest, fondest one.

Where Harvard's classick walls,
Sprang up in answer to the Pilgrim's prayer,
Amid those studious halls,
Thy mind with bolder fancies wrought
Than Metaphysicks taught,
Or plodding Logick told,
Such as impassion'd Raphael's thought,
Beneath Italia's skies of gold,
And lo! a daring hand the canvas spread,
Nor shrank to dip the brush in Cannae's carnage red.

Then War swept by,
With all his pageantry,
And summon'd by his trumpet-tones,
Thou, to fields of blood hadst gone,
Sharing the darken'd strife till Freedom's glorious dawn,
But Genius held thee fast,
And bore thee in his arms, above that clarion-blast.

Changes o'er manhood roll,
Proud England spreads that scenery fair
Which oft had fir'd the artist's soul,
Why art thou *prison'd* there?
Yet thou art not alone,
Palace, nor regal throne,
May boast such radiant groups as throng thy cell,
O'er History's magick glass
Embodied phantoms pass,

And while thy thoughts with high conceptions swell,
St. Jerome's features glow,
And the calm martyr's smile, consoles the prisoner's woe.

Thee, Themis sought,
Vaunting her ponderous tomes, with high ambition fraught,
While urgent by her side,
Thy honour'd parent-guide,
To aid her suit, his prudent counsels brought,
But thy lov'd art, with her enrapturing eye
Gaz'd deeply on thy soul & won the victory.

Sire of the pencil, in thy native vales,
Thou art remember'd by warm hearts & true,
We count thy birth-days in that father-land,
We point the mansion where thy boyhood grew,
While side by side, with venerated Yale,
We see thy glory stand,
To claim with dignity sublime,
The signet-seal of Fame, the lasting praise of Time.

"Cannae" in the second verse refers to JT's "The Death of Paulus
Aemilius at the Battle of Cannae," painted by the artist at Lebanon, at
the age of 18, then hanging in the Trumbull Gallery (and still at Yale).
"St. Jerome" in the third verse refers to JT's copy (at Yale) of Benjamin
West's copy after Correggio's celebrated canvas, a large oil, painted in
1780 by the colonel during his imprisonment at the Bridewell, London.

Mrs. Sigourney wrote JT a birthday letter, dated Hartford 15 June
1839 (in the possession of Henry Woodhouse of New York). JT painted
her portrait (Wadsworth Atheneum) in July/August 1838 at New
Haven; details of this are to be found in the Silliman family correspondence at Yale. This portrait has often been considered JT's "last work"—
but he kept on painting as long as he stayed in New Haven. His group
portrait of the Oliver Payson Hubbard family (now belonging to Mrs.
James M. Kennedy of Superior, Wis.) was painted in 1839.

TRUMBULL'S "LIFE"

JT's life appeared in 1834 in *National Portrait Gallery of Distinguished
Americans,* edited by James B. Longacre, Philadelphia, and James Herring, New York, under the superintendence of the American Academy

of the Fine Arts (Philadelphia, Henry Perkins, 1836), Vol. 1. The sponsorship of the publication did credit to the Academy.

PROFESSOR SILLIMAN

When JT came to live with Professor Silliman in 1837 the Silliman home stood on Hillhouse Avenue. How far the professor (who made science respectable in Victorian America) was prepared to go to make his uncle-in-law comfortable may be gathered from his letter to his daughters Maria and Faith, dated New Haven, 30 January 1836: "If every thing should go well, I have some thought of raising a story on the wood house for a library and miscellaneous room and for a repository and painting room for Uncle Trumbull who now appears very well and in very good spirits and most pleased with the prospect of coming to us. We can enter the painting and library gallery at the window where the clock stands and light the passage from the roof. The gallery will be 50 feet long, 13½ wide—9 or 10 high at the sides and arched to 12 or 13 in the middle, to be lighted and with side windows for ventilation. If divided, it will give a room 18 feet long at the north end—with a chimney between the rooms and ample closets and leave a gallery 30 feet long. I think Uncle Trumbull can never paint in peace in the gallery at college." (Yale Library.) On 9 March 1836 Mrs. Silliman wrote to her daughter Faith: "Your Papa is making arrangements for the wing and expects to commence operations as soon as the weather will permit, and I think we shall soon be in a bustling season. He wrote Uncle John to make him acquainted with what he was about to do in order to give him opportunity to make any suggestions and received an answer yesterday which made me feel sad, as from the hand writing and general tenor of the sentiments it showed more infirmity and consciousness of age than I have seen before." (Yale Library.)

The Silliman house, although badly mauled by further and less fortunate additions, still stands on a new and adjacent site—on Trumbull Street—and is now used as the residence of the Dean of Yale College.

Mrs. Silliman wrote her daughters, 19 July 1837: "We had heard the day before that Uncle Trumbull would come up. Your Papa went down to the boat to meet and bring him up and we waited dinner for him . . . There were seven truck loads of boxes and he brought no articles of apparel and his bed has not yet come. He has many boxes of books . . . You see he now seems to be in earnest about making this his home. But he looks too feeble to remain in it long."

It was in this house, as noted in the Preface, that the *Autobiography* was written. The first indication of JT's desire to write it is to be found in his letter of 19 February 1835 from New York to Professor Silliman at New Haven: "I have been so worried by Mr. Dunlap & the foolish people at Washington, that I have really resolved to commence something in the shape of a Biography & have gone to some extent in hunting up materials . . . I find it is the fashion to make up a man's history from his own letter book and I rather think it is the best method, for letters written long since, and on various occasions, certainly give a juster portrait of Character than memory can produce—and if faithfully transcribed cannot flatter: in this way, I find I have ample & various materials which will require little more than arrangement . . . I shall want your advice & assistance . . ." (Yale Library.) Mrs. Silliman wrote on 20 November 1837: "Uncle Trumbull commenced reading a memoir of himself about which he has been occupied part of last year. It is elegantly written and very interesting" and on 23 December 1838 Faith Wadsworth Silliman (Mrs. Oliver Payson Hubbard) wrote to her sister Maria (Mrs. John Barker Church): "Have we ever told you that Uncle is reading again to some friends his manuscript. The Hillhouses, Skinners, Whitneys, Mrs. Pritchard, Susan, Mr. Bakewell come here Saturday evenings. Uncle reads till about nine o'clock and then he furnishes grapes and champagne and we a basket of cake. They are very pleasant little meetings."

Professor Silliman induced JT to lecture to the college students "on the subject of his pictures." "He meets the Senior Class on Saturday, the Sophomore on Wednesday next. He laughs a good deal at his having taken up the trade." Silliman family correspondence (at the Yale Library) 16 October 1839. After his return to New York in 1840 the solicitous Sillimans reported: "He walks out when the weather will admit, his eyes are better, tho he does not allow himself to use them much as all their strength is required to correct the proofs of his book which is now printing, and the interest and excitement caused by its progress will help keep up his spirits and energy" (18 May 1841).[10]

JT's address for these years was given in *Patten's New Haven Directory:* 1840–41, no listing; 1841–42, "Trumbull, John, colonel revolution-

10. For the Silliman-Trumbull relationship see George P. Fisher, *Life of Benjamin Silliman, M.D., LL.D.* (2 vols., Philadelphia, Porter & Coates, 1866), and especially Fulton and Thompson, *Benjamin Silliman,* which contains an admirable account (ch. 10) of "The First College Gallery of Art." For New Haven of this period see Rollin G. Osterweis, *Three Centuries of New Haven* (New Haven, Yale University Press, 1953), Pt. V.

ary army, historical painter, at Prof. Silliman's, Hillhouse Ave."; 1842–43, "Trumbull, John, historical painter, at Professor Silliman's"; 1843–44, no listing.

NEW YORK

Late in 1840 when the aged and infirm JT returned to New York to be near his physician Dr. James Augustus Washington, he lived at Mrs. Lentner's at 21 Amity Street (now West Third Street, a block south of Washington Square). His appearance at that time may be observed from the small, full-length portrait, painted in 1833 by George W. Twibill, which hangs, curiously enough, in the council room of the National Academy of Design, New York, and by a little miniature (owned by Col. Ralph H. Isham of New York), painted shortly after his arrival in the city by Anne Hall. It is the last picture of the old colonel.

Sylvester Genin wrote in December 1840: "I have visited Col. Trumbull two or three times since I have been here: he is very frail, and has painted none for a year. He is a very agreeable man in his conversation. He has a large library, which he has collected during his long life, composed principally of French, Italian, and Spanish works. He employs himself in reading; and is getting engravings made of drawings executed at different periods of life, for the purpose, as I understood him, of publishing them in a history of his life. He advised me to pursue the law for a livelihood, and if I followed painting, to draw for a few weeks from the antique statues in the Academy of Arts, in New York, or Philadelphia, and as far as colors are concerned, to use only in the flesh tints, no brighter red than Indian red; no yellow, brighter than Roman ocher, burnt umber, Prussian blue, black and white." [11]

LAST EXHIBITION

The last picture to be exhibited in JT's lifetime was the "Gibraltar" (the Boston Athenaeum version) at the Apollo Association at New York in October 1841 (No. 65. "This is the Picture from which the admirable print of Sharp was engraved, and is generally esteemed the master piece of the Artist"). It is certainly JT's finest large-scale historical composition.

DEATH

JT died at the age of 87½, at New York, on 10 November 1843. There is a good description of the funeral at New Haven in the New Haven

11. *Selections from . . . Sylvester Genin*, p. 39.

Morning Courier for 13 November 1843 and the *New-York Spectator* of 18 November 1843. The funeral was held at New Haven on the 13th.[12]

Thomas Seir Cummings, who had much ill to say of JT in his *Historic Annals of the National Academy of Design* (Philadelphia, George W. Childs, 1865), stated (p. 175) under the date of 13 November 1843: "Departed this life, the venerable Colonel Trumbull, aged eighty-seven years—an artist and a gentleman. Whatever differences of opinion may have existed as to his policy as President of the old American Academy —however he may have proved deficient in his estimate of the rising generation of artists in his day—there is no doubt he acted in the full belief in the wisdom of his views. He was of the old school; his courtesy and urbanity of manner were worthy of imitation; his want of heartfelt-ness for the professional was severely felt by the youngest artist. On the 14th Mr. Morse communicated the fact to the Council [of the National Academy of Design], as follows: . . . it is my melancholy duty once more to convene you, to announce to you the death of Colonel John Trumbull, . . . whose name and works are amongst the earliest associa-tions of our childhood, and whose fame is interwoven, not merely with the history of the arts of design, but also with the political history of the country. Although not enrolled as a member of this Academy, yet I be-lieve I express your sentiments, gentlemen, when I assert that we render a sincere, willing homage to the character of Trumbull, as one of the brightest ornaments of his country in the arts of design. On numerous paintings connected with our Revolutionary history, Colonel Trumbull's fame as an artist may securely rest. . . ."

"Colonel Trumbull's will, courage, independence, self-reliance, and enterprise are fully apparent . . . ; something more is necessary to com-plete our idea of him as a man. While Colonel Trumbull was sensitive, proud, of perfect integrity, a man of honor in the highest sense of the term, it must be also admitted that he was of an excitable and even pas-sionate temperament, which often rendered him arbitrary and dictatorial in certain public relations. Never, however, was he uncourteous or un-forgiving with anybody. These traits, as well as his urbanity and benevo-lence, can be demonstrated by many who knew him and still survive. Of superior intelligence, wide experience, noble in aspiration, and con-scientious, he would defer only to those whom he knew to surpass him

12. Sizer, "The Reinterments of Colonel Trumbull," App., pp. 379–382. Many references will be found to JT's death in the *Proceedings* of the New-York Historical Society for the year 1843, pp. 15, 106–107, 122–124, and for 1845, pp. 106–108.

in these qualities." John Durand, "John Trumbull," *American Art Review* (1881), p. 23.

Philip Hone recorded in his diary for 13 November 1843: "Col. John Trumbull died in this city, on Friday last, aged eighty-seven years. He has been a distinguished man during the whole of his long life, a patriot of the Revolution, a chevalier 'sans peur et sans reproche,' a gallant soldier, one of the aides of Washington, a statesman and diplomatist intrusted with important concerns in Great Britain at the close of the Revolutionary war. As a painter, his pencil has chronicled some of the great events of the fearful struggle, the issue of which was the liberty and independence of a great nation." [13]

Silliman noted in his *American Journal of Science, 66* (1843-44): "Death of Col. Trumbull—The venerable patriot, artist, and friend of Washington—the father of American historical painting—died at New York, Nov. 10, 1843, and was interred at New Haven in his own stone tomb, beneath the Trumbull Gallery of pictures. [See Vol. 39 of this Journal.] His autobiography was published two years ago in a beautiful illustrated volume. He was nearly half through his 88th year."

On 17 March 1846 Professor Silliman wrote to C. Edwards Lester of New York: ". . . Col. Trumbull wrote most of his auto-biography in my house, to which he was invited by Mrs. Silliman who was his niece, and myself. He came to us in 1837 and remained four years in our family. He then returned to New York to be near his favorite physician, Dr. Washington, and there he remained until his death Nov. 10, 1843. By his own request his remains were brought to my house, whence his funeral proceeded, Saturday, Nov. 13. His remains were borne to the College Chapel, where an appropriate and feeling historical discourse was delivered by the Rev. Prof. Fitch—from Gen. XXV. V. 8, 9, and 10. Eight of our principal citizens were bearers—the students and citizens formed a procession to the stone tomb beneath the Trumbull Gallery, where his remains were laid beside those of his wife. His pictures he called his children and the Gallery he wished to be his monument. The vault was kept open under a proper guard through the night and the next day that the citizens might have the opportunity of looking into it. After the massy lid—a single stone of 8 feet by 5 was let down . . ." This letter is printed in full in Lester's *Artist of America* (New York, Baker & Scribner, 1846), pp. 168–171. The original letter is the property of Dr. John F. Fulton of Yale.

13. *Diary of Philip Hone*, Bayard Tuckerman, ed. (New York, Dodd, Mead, 1889), 2, 200–201.

That sensitive art critic, James Jackson Jarves, 1818–88 (whose collection of early Italian paintings came to Yale in 1871 and was deposited in the gallery founded by JT), observed: 'Trumbull, Sully, and Peale are Americans in feeling and expression, although their education, of necessity, was more or less foreign. Trumbull resembles Copley in his general style, but he was a man of finer taste, warmer color, and wider ideas. He was our first historical painter, much the best we have had in composition, truthful and natural in portraiture, avoiding exaggeration, faithful to his principles of art, and too honest to rely on technical artifices for effect. Above all, we see the gentleman and patriot of the old school in his paintings. There is a high-toned sense of character and individuality in his portraits. Our forefathers are better represented in the portraiture of their day than the distinguished men of ours in theirs. His historical compositions are graphic, well-balanced, well-composed. Fond of spirited action, he equally understands the value of aesthetic repose and the subordination of minor to principal parts. The American school of historical painting and portraiture has a respectable parentage in Trumbull." [14]

John Ferguson Weir, dean of the Yale School of the Fine Arts from 1869 to 1913, "prepared for the Committee on the Bi-Centennial Celebration of the Founding of Yale College," *John Trumbull, a Brief Sketch of His Life, to Which Is Added a Catalogue of His Works* (New York, Scribner, 1901). The editor finds in Professor Weir's hand the following unpublished note: "If any name, distinguished in the annals of American art, is worthy of being placed in a so-called 'Hall of Fame,' that name is John Trumbull; whose three or four principal works, executed when his powers were at their best, should be accorded a higher rank for excellence than those of any other American artist of his time. And if there is added to their artistic quality, historic interest and national repute, their claims in the estimate of professional judges, outrank the claims of the artist chosen in his place." (Yale Library.)

WILL

JT's will, dated 19 December 1842, is to be found in the Probate Court, New Haven City Hall, 55, 491–494. The will, with the exception of the

14. *The Art-Idea* (New York and Boston, Hurd & Houghton, 1864; 2d ed., 1865; 3d ed., 1866; 4th ed., 1877. For Jarves and the Trumbull Gallery see Sizer, "James Jackson Jarves, a Forgotten New Englander," *The New England Quarterly*, 6 (June 1933), 328–352, and Francis Steegmuller, *The Two Lives of James Jackson Jarves* (New Haven, Yale University Press, 1951).

insertions in brackets, is as follows: "I John Trumbull of the City of New York make this my last will [copy at Yale] and testament as follows. I bequeath to my Physician, Doctor James A. Washington, to whose care and skill, I am greatly indebted, my breast pin which was given to me by General and Mrs. Washington, and which contains a lock of the hair of that illustrious man, set with pearls [now the property of Herbert A. Washington of Seattle, Washington]. I bequeath to John T. Ray. a Lieutenant in the British army, a miniature likeness of himself painted by Robertson [Yale]. I bequeath to Joseph Lanman, now in the Navy of the United States, the cane presented to me by commodore Hull, made of wood of the frigate Constitution, the ship which under his command captured the British Frigate La Guerriere [Trumbull College, Yale University]. I bequeath to Mrs. Bull, wife of Frederick Bull and eldest daughter of Mr. Lanman, the portrait of my wife dressed in black, and a lace cap, which has hung in my bedroom [Mrs. Frederic Bull of New Canaan, Connecticut]. I bequeath to Miss Catharine Lentner the picture containing portraits of her sister, Mrs. Sewell, and of Mrs. Sewell's two sons [unlocated], the portrait of myself in a blue coat and buff vest, and also the four proof engravings which hang in the dining room of her mother's house, of the battle of Bunker's hill, the attack on Quebeck, the declaration of independence, and the Sortie from Gibralter, and also a proof print of Washington framed to correspond, and also a print from Vandyke. I also bequeath to her the Syrop antihydropique which she has prepared for me, and of which she knows the composition. [Dr. John F. Fulton writes: ". . . evidently some concoction which the old gentleman used to help his swollen ankles—a condition . . . which was referred to in those days as the 'dropsy.' . . . James Thacher's *Materia Medica* of 1810 . . . lists all sorts of syrops among the folk remedies of the day, but he does not specifically mention one with antihydropique qualities. I suspect, however, that Colonel Trumbull's was probably a strong purgative which tended to remove fluid, and hence prevent its accumulation in the pendant parts of the body . . ."] I bequeath to the children of Professor Benjamin Silliman the copy right of my autobiography, also my notes on painting,[15] and of experiments to discover the vehecle employed by Venetian artists, and also the copper plates of the battles of Bunkerhill, and Quebeck, Small Size [Yale], and also all the engravings of those battles both great and small, which remain undisposed of, and also the copper plate engraved by Durand [unlocated], from the portrait of Judge Jonas Platt [unlocated] painted by me. All

15. See Sizer, "Trumbull's Painting Procedure," *Works*, pp. 100–105.

the Residue of my estate whatsoever and wheresoever, I give and bequeath to the said Catharine Lentner and to Abby Lanman [Abigail Trumbull Lanman] share and share alike. I appoint Benjamin Silliman of New Haven, and Joseph Trumbull of Hartford Executors of this will."

The appraisers were the deceased's friends, Nathaniel Jocelyn, painter and engraver, and Edward Claudius Herrick, then librarian, later treasurer of Yale; the active executor was Professor Silliman; and the probate judge Alfred Blackman. The estate was appraised at $13,452.63 (inventory, property of Alfred Duveen of New York), which, after debts and expenses, came to $11,782.44 (Executor's accounting of the estate in Vol. 56, 165–168). It is interesting to note that JT died leaving a library of 537 volumes.

Much correspondence concerning the liquidation of the Colonel's estate is in the possession of the Connecticut State Library, Maria Trumbull Dana of New Haven, and Mrs. Thomas D. (Henrietta Dana) Hewitt of Greenwich, Conn. Miss Lentner's ideas appear to have been extravagant. Abby Trumbull Lanman's were more reasonable. Professor Silliman was patient, efficient, and expeditious.

TISDALE MINIATURES

William Dunlap noted in his *Diary* that Elkanah "Tisdale, a man of wit and genius . . . in New York painted Miniatures during Trumbull's first visit to America *with his wife*. Painted their miniatures . . ." [16] This would be 1804. That of the Colonel is the property of Jonathan Trumbull Lanman of New York; the companion miniature of his wife is unlocated.

PEALE PORTRAIT

Charles Coleman Sellers, author of *Charles Willson Peale, Early Life*, Hebron, Conn. (Feather & Good, 1939), *Later Life* (Philadelphia, American Philosophical Society, 1947), and *Portraits and Miniatures by Charles Willson Peale* (Philadelphia, American Philosophical Society, 1952), calls my attention to the Peale Diary. On 28 May 1817 Peale requested JT to sit for his portrait (for Peale's Museum at Philadelphia), which, at that time, JT did not find convenient. On 10 February 1819, at Baltimore, Peale noted: "I began a portrait of Col. Trumbull but he has left this place sooner than I expected and of course I must wait some other opportunity of finishing it." The unfinished portrait is unlocated (see p. 212, item 880, in the last-mentioned publica-

16. New York, New-York Historical Society, 1931, 3, 811.

tion). JT was no great admirer of Peale's work, though in 1778 he had copied the head of Washington (Yale) from Peale's three-quarter portrait of 1776 (Brooklyn Museum).

STUART PORTRAIT

Washington Allston, at Boston, noted: "Stuart has painted an admirable portrait of Trumbull . . ."[17] The portrait, used here as frontispiece, was painted at Boston in December 1818. In 1828 JT gave the portrait (now at Yale) to his physician and close friend, Dr. David Hosack, who died in 1835.

OTHER PORTRAITS OF TRUMBULL

The Yale University Portrait Index, 1701–1951 (New Haven, Yale University Press, 1951) lists the 1818 portrait by Gilbert Stuart, the two, jointly, by Samuel Lovett Waldo and William Jewett, ca. 1821 (illustrated) and 1832, and the marble bust by JT's young English friend, Ball Hughes, of 1839. JT painted the sculptor and his wife that year (see Works of Trumbull, p. 33).

LANDS IN NORTHWESTERN NEW YORK STATE

JT's land operations in northwestern New York State, though not to be classed entirely as a speculation, had their inception in 1796. (See note on p. 86.) Jeremiah Wadsworth's extensive holdings on the Genesee River were taken up (in 1790) by his cousin, James Wadsworth, 1768–1844, who acted as agent for their sale. Young Wadsworth was in Europe from February 1796 to November 1798, during which time he saw much of the American colony at London. Benjamin West was induced to purchase a block of land; possibly JT did so at the same time, as Dunlap states. (See note on pp. 272–273.)

The landscape painter and diarist, Joseph Farington, 1747–1821, noted on 8 December 1798: "West, Trumbull, R. [Raphael] West and a Mr. Wroughton were at Fonthill last summer, and induced Beckford to purchase an estate (covered with wood) of 25,000 acres at the price of 10 shillings an acre. It is considered a monstrous price."[18] William Beckford, 1759–1844, a man of letters, art critic, and early enthusiast for the Gothic, built Fonthill Abbey in Wiltshire, a pseudo-Gothic pile with a 260-foot tower. A copy of an agreement with James Wadsworth,

17. Flagg, Washington Allston, p. 145.
18. The Farington Diary.

involving a township of some 23,340 acres, dated 15 September 1798, in JT's hand, is at the New-York Historical Society.

JT wrote to Jeremiah Wadsworth on 20 September: ". . . This goes by your cousin James Wadsworth, who notwithstanding the very unfavorable nature of the times has by great prudence and perseverance managed to have some Success, a Connexion to which I have had the pleasure to introduce, promises to be a very valuable one. It is Mr Wm Beckford the only Son of the famous Patriot and Friend of Lord Chatham. He has immense wealth principally in Jamaica, and has the good Sense to look forward to those changes which must probably extend to that quarter of the World, in this Age of Change. He has therefore . . . begun by purchasing a Township in the Genesee, . . . Should the confusion of Europe encrease much farther I should not be surprised to see Mr. Beckford establish himself in the U.S. I was one day describing to him your West Mountain, as a place more formed by nature to make a delightful and magnificent Country residence . . . He was struck with the Description and desired to know whether it could be bought, and at how much an Acre . . . about 8 or 10,000 Acres . . . to comprehend the Lake, the Mountains South and North of it, to the precipice on the Farmington side . . . (Yale Library). West or Talcott Mountain, near Hartford, was the Wadsworth country seat, known as Monte Video. JT made a sketch of the mountain in 1791 (Yale) and painted several views of it, one of which is the property of Marion Cruger Coffin of New Haven, Conn.[19]

While JT was busily engaged in diplomacy his young friend "Raph," son of his master, Benjamin West, went to America to inspect his father's landholdings in Genesee. Dunlap tells a good story: "In the year 1800 this gentleman, my old and intimate companion in London, most unexpectedly appeared in New York with his wife. Benjamin West and John Trumbull had made purchases from Mr. Wadsworth, of Genesee, of tracts of land on that paradise . . . The elder West wished his son to visit his purchase, and as we Yankees say, improve it. But of all creatures my friend Raphael was the least fitted for the task of a pioneer in America. Born and educated in London, he had never been out of its neighborhood; and though he had studied the noble oaks of Windsor forest

19. The editor has discovered no reference to Beckford's purchase of a township in America in any of his biographies. A rather general letter about the United States from Beckford to James Wadsworth, written from Fonthill on 7 September 1798, is printed in full in Lewis Melville, *The Life and Letters of William Beckford of Fonthill* (London, William Heineman, 1910), pp. 252–255.

. . . he was a stranger to the appearance of the untamed forest, where only the Indian footpath gave token of the presence of man . . . Disappointed, discouraged, and homesick, Raphael gladly broke from the Big Tree prison, to return to the paternal home on Newman Street. On his way he visited me in New York. His anger was kindled against Wadsworth, who, like a true American, saw in the wilderness the paradise which was to grow up and bloom there, but which was invisible to the London painter, and if possible, still more so to his London wife. 'Would you believe it, Dunlap, as I sat drawing by a lower window, up marched a bear, as if to take a lesson!' . . ." [20] Dunlap might have mistaken the exact year. JT wrote from London on 20 September 1798 to his brother, Jonathan, then governor of Connecticut: ". . . This letter goes by Mr. James Wadsworth, who is accompanied by a Son of my excellent friend, Mr. West. He goes with the intention of purchasing some Land in our Woods, and settling down there as a Farmer. He will probably go to the Genesee under Wadsworth's wing . . ." (Yale Library).

JT must have had these lands in western New York in mind later when his close friend, James Wadsworth of Geneseo, N.Y., published a broadside description of "A Township of New Land for Sale, or to be Exchanged for Improved Farms" (copy at the New Haven Colony Historical Society). On 7 February 1806 JT purchased from one Isaac Bronson of Greenfield, Conn., 1,280 acres, west of the Genesee River, at Mount Morris for the sum of $3,660.80 (copy of the deed at the New-York Historical Society; the deed is at the Genesee County Clerk's Office at Batavia, N.Y.). In a "Schedule of property in my possession, this 30th November 1808," JT lists "Lands at Mountmorriss, 1200 Acres, Dollars 10,000." (Yale Library.) Before he left for England, on 30 November 1808, JT drew up a will leaving to "a Youth now in my Family and Known by the name of John Trumbull Ray" certain of his landholdings at Mount Morris, hoping that Ray might become a farmer and settle there.

LANDSCAPE PAINTING

Possibly the lack of hoped-for portrait commissions drove JT to paint landscapes, the most notable of which are of "Norwich Falls" in Connecticut (one at the Slater Memorial Museum, Norwich, and the other at Yale) and of "Niagara Falls." It is curious that JT made no mention in the *Autobiography* of his extended stay at Niagara in 1807 or his trip to Canada. He painted four pictures of the Falls; two of these are at

20. Dunlap, *Arts of Design*, 2, 286–289.

the Wadsworth Atheneum, Hartford (having been purchased in 1828 by Daniel Wadsworth for $400) and two enormous panoramas (14½ feet long) at the New-York Historical Society. These romantic views of Niagara, depicting the grandeur of America, were taken to England in the hope of sale. JT wrote to his London banker, Samuel Williams, from New York on 11 November 1808, "I shall also bring with me two panoramas Views of the falls of Niagara, and Surrounding Objects. The Scene is magnificent and novel. I have copied it with all the fidelity in my power, and am not without a hope that it will at once excite and in some measure gratify the public curiosity." (Yale.) However, strained feelings, culminating in the War of 1812, brought the scheme to naught. Dunlap notes in his gossipy *Diary* that JT quarreled with his master West "about the panorama." [21]

JT's "Niagara Falls" of 1808 were among the earliest, large representations of this romantic and awe-inspiring scene. Young John Vanderlyn, 1775–1852, painted small-scale pictures of the Falls in 1796–1801. Frederick Edwin Church, 1826–1900, painted his celebrated picture of Niagara Falls (at the Corcoran Gallery, Washington, D.C.) in 1857—nearly a half century after JT's initial efforts.

For his excursion to Canada JT drew $750. He noted, 23 August 1808: "Duke of Gloucester, a fine topsail Schooner of 120 tons . . . sailed from Niagara for Kingston . . . to Montreal 160 miles . . ."

THE CAPITOL PICTURES

(Thomas Jefferson)

JT wrote to Thomas Jefferson on 26 December 1816: "Twenty eight years have elapsed, since under the kind protection of your hospitable roof at Chaillot, I painted your portrait in my picture of the Declaration of Independance, the composition of which had been planned two years before in your Library. The long period of War and Tumult which succeeded, palsied & suspended my work, and threw me as you know into other pursuits . . . The Government of the U.S. are restoring to more than their original Splender, the Buildings devoted to National purposes at Washington, which were barbarously sacrificed to the Rage of War. I have thought this a proper opportunity to make my first application for public patronage, and to request to be employed in decorating the walls of their buildings with the paintings which have employed

21. Dunlap, *Diary* (3 vols., New York, New-York Historical Society, 1929–31), 3, 684 and 799.

so many [years] of my life . . . The Memory of your kindness & of the interest which you formerly took in this work is too strongly in my memory, to suffer a doubt to intrude of your powerful protection at this time, —again, the work has been carried thus far by my own unaided exertions, *and can be finished only by me:*—future Artists may arise with far Superior Talents, but time has already withdrawn almost all their Models; and I who was one of the youngest Actors in the early scenes of the War, passed the Age of Sixty:—no time remains therefore for hesitation. Hoping that my application will meet your approbation, & support, & that you will honor me with an Answer addressed to me at Washington—Poste restante." (Draft of letter at Yale Library.)

There is an interesting letter from Thomas Jefferson to James Barbour, U.S. senator from Virginia, 1815–25, dated Monticello, 19 January 1817, at the New York Public Library: "I have been very long and intimately acquainted with Col. Trumbull, have had the best opportunity of knowing him thoroughly, and can therefore bear witness of my own knolege [sic] to his high degree of worth as a man. For his merit as a painter I can quote higher authorities, and assure you that on the continent of Europe, when I was there, he was considered as superior to West—Baron Grimm [the Prussian ambassador to Paris], who was the oracle of taste at Paris in sculpture, painting and the other fine arts generally, gave him the decided preference, and came often to my house in Paris, while Mr. Trumbull was with me, to see his paintings. I pretended not to be a connoisseur in the art myself, but comparing him with others of that day I thought him superior to any historical painter of the time except David: it is in the historical line only that I am acquainted with his painting. In England West was preferred by the King to whom all others followed suit. The subjects on which Col. Trumbull has employed his pencil are honorable to us, and it would be extremely desirable that they should be retained in this country as monuments of the taste as well as of the great revolutionary scenes of our country." [22] Of the 33 presidents of the United States, the modest Jefferson certainly had the best aesthetic discrimination and judgment. Jefferson, however, was thinking of the Trumbull of 30 years previous. He apparently had no idea how far JT had slipped.

On 3 March 1817 JT wrote Jefferson from Washington: "You will I trust forgive my having so long delayed to answer your very kind letter . . . I did not feel I could write with certainty, until by passing the Ap-

22. Printed in Andrew A. Lipscomb, ed., *The Writings of Thomas Jefferson*, 5, 242–243.

propriation bill, the House of Representatives had sanctioned the agreement which was made with me by the President. I have now the pleasure to say that unexpected Success has attended me, and that I am authorized to paint four of the great Events of the Revolution, the Declaration of Independence, the Surrender of Burgoyne, the Surrender of Cornwallis, and the Resignation of Washington; the pictures are to be 12 feet high by 18 feet long, which will give to the principal figures the Size of life. I shall begin with the Declaration of Independence, and shall exert all my talent to produce a work worthy of the Event, and of the high patronage which I enjoy. The kind approbation which you was so good as to express contributed powerfully to my Success—and I beg you to accept my cordial thanks . . ." (Yale Library). And on 28 November 1817: ". . . I cannot refrain from informing you that I have made considerable progress in the large picture of the Declaration of Independence for the Capitol. . . . You recollect the Composition, which you kindly assisted me to sketch at Chaillot . . . I, at first, dreaded the Size of my Work—but I have proceeded far enough to have conquered my timidity, and to be satisfied that this Picture as a mere work of Art will be superior to those which have been heretofore engraved . . ." (Library of Congress.)

(John Adams)

The 82-year-old John Adams wrote JT from Quincy on 1 January 1817: "Your kind letter . . . has given me more pleasure than it would be prudent or decent for me to express. Your design has my cordial approbation and best wishes. But you will please to remember that the Burin and the Pencil, the Chisel and the Trowell, have in all ages and Countries of which we have any Information, been enlisted on the side of Despotism and Superstition. I should have Said of Superstition and Despotism, for Superstition is the first and Universal Cause of Despotism. Characters and Counsels and Action merely Social merely civil, merely political, merely moral are always neglected and forgotten. Architecture, Sculpture, Painting, and Poetry have conspir'd against the Rights of Mankind: and the Protestant Religion is now unpopular and Odious because it is not friendly to the Fine Arts. I am not, however, a Disciple of Rousseau. Your Country ought to acknowledge itself more indebted to you than to any other Artist who ever existed; and I there fore heartily wish you success. But I must beg Pardon of my Country, when I say that I See no disposition to celebrate or remember, or even Curiosity to enquire into the Characters Actions or Events of the Revolution. I am therefore more inclined to despair, than to hope for your Success in Congress: though I wish it with all my heart. I should be glad to be informed of your progress, being with Sincere Esteem and real affection, Your Friend." JT replied from Washington on 3 March 1817: "You will forgive my having so long delayed to reply to your very kind letter of the 1st of January . . . I have the Satisfaction therefore to acquaint you that unexpected Success has crowned my wishes (to which your cordial approbation not a little contributed) . . ." (Yale Library.)

(Benjamin Henry Latrobe)

Latrobe wrote on 22 January 1817 to JT "at Mrs. Wadsworth's, Capitol Hill": "I am also honored in having my Walls destined to support your paintings." On 11 July 1817 he addressed the Colonel at New York: "You know how I am obliged to fight my way along in compleating the Capitol. I have now arrived, not without a hard struggle, at the commencement of the only apartment in this enormous piece of patch work, the Central Hall" (note at side of page, "in which there is room for your pictures"). He explained "the circular form of the room" and suggested, with the aid of sketches, how the paintings could be installed on a concave surface. Again, on 10 October 1817, he wrote to New York: "I have continued to make the spaces devoted to them [the pictures] 19 feet long by 14 feet 7½ high. Therefore they should be raised to the hight by 5 feet 7½ inches from the floor, which would protect them against touch and an iron railing in front at 3 feet distance would protect them even against the reach of a cane." (Yale Library.) In order to meet JT's objections Latrobe suggested, with an accompanying sketch, a flat surface in a recess, instead of the concave. Complete cooperation between architect and painter and due provision for mutual requirements was thus achieved at the inception of a project. JT was extraordinarily fortunate in his relations with both Latrobe and Bulfinch.

(King-Gore)

Rufus King wrote from Georgetown on 17 January 1817 to his friend Christopher Gore at Gore Place, Waltham, Mass.: "Col. & Mrs. Trumbull arrived last night; the Col. has just left me; they are at Queens near the House where Congress meet. His object is to adorn the Capitol with pictures which shall perpetuate the great events & the glories of the Revolution, as the Ducal Palace of Venice, and the State House at Amsterdam, by the talents of the great painters of the day, have commemorated those of these Republics. He has with him the small Pictures which exhibit the Portraits of the Statesmen & Heroes, and the principal incidents of the Revolution. By inviting the Members to see and admire them, he may awaken a spirit and desire of possessing these sketches, in the form of enlarged and more perfect works. I have advised him to wait on Mr. Monroe and to endeavour to engage him & his influence in favor of his being employed. He finds the Capitol a ruin . . ." Gore answered on 26 January 1817: "I shall rejoice if Trumbull succeeds in his Endeavors to adorn the Capitol . . ." and again, Gore to King, 23 February 1817: ". . . Trumbull's bargain with the Pr. [President] is completed. For the four Pictures he is to receive thirty two thousand Dollars, eight of which are to be in advance. I am to move an amendment in the appropriation Bill tomorrow for the 8000 in advance & the residue as the Pictures are finished." [23]

(John Quincy Adams)

The Secretary of State, John Quincy Adams, noted when at New York on 14 August 1817: "Called on Mr. Trumbull, and found him with the frame for his large picture of the Declaration of Independence, upon which he is just preparing to begin . . ." [24] Again at New York, he noted on 1 September 1818: "Called . . . at Mr. Trumbull's house, and saw his picture of the Declaration of Independence, which is now nearly finished. I cannot say I was disappointed in the execution of it, because my expectations were very low; but the picture is immeasurably below the dignity of the subject. It may be said of Trumbull's talent as the Spaniards say of heroes who were brave on a certain day: he has painted good pictures. I think the old small picture far superior to this large new one. He himself thinks otherwise . . ." [25]

JT wrote Secretary Adams from New York on 29 December 1817: "I feel it my Duty to report to you the progress which I have made in the work which was so honorably assigned to me at the last Session of Congress. I could not procure Clothes of the proper Size and Texture, in this Country, and was therefore unavoidably delayed until . . . I received them of excellent quality from London. From that day I have been constantly occupied on the Declaration of Independence . . ." (National Archives.) It is interesting that the pictorial record of Amer-

23. C. R. King, ed., *The Life and Correspondence of Rufus King*, 6, 45–48, 63.
24. Charles Francis Adams, ed., *Memoirs of John Quincy Adams* (12 vols., Philadelphia, Lippincott, 1874–77), 4, 4.
25. *Ibid.*, 4, 128.

ica's political independence was necessarily conditioned by her economic dependence on the mother country!

JT informed the Secretary on 5 January 1819, that his "Father did me the honor to look at my work [the Declaration of Independence] in Faneuil Hall, and I was delighted to find him in good health & in the perfect enjoyment of all his faculties to a degree I scarcely ever witnessed at his advanced age. I left him well." (National Archives.) John Adams died in 1826 at the age of 91.

JT wrote again on 16 February 1819: "Mr. Trumbull begs leave to inform the Secretary of State that the picture [the Declaration of Independence] which He had painted for the Government of the United States, is ready for inspection in one of the Committee Rooms of the Senate. . . ."; on 19 July 1820 he reported: "I have great satisfaction in acquainting you for the information of the President of the United States, that my painting of the Surrender of YorkTown is finished. . . ." (This was the second of the series to be painted.) And on 16 October 1821: "I beg leave to inform you the third painting . . . the Surrender of General Burgoyne, is nearly completed, and will be delivered . . . before the close of the approaching Session of Congress . . ." [26] "Gen. Washington Resigning His Commission" was the fourth and last composition undertaken.

Other references to JT may be found in the *Memoirs of John Quincy Adams*, 7, 188–189, for 28 November 1826: "At noon I rode up to the Capitol, and met Colonel Trumbull in the Rotunda. His four pictures are placed, and in such a favorable light that they appear far better than they had ever done before. There are four other spaces to be filled with pictures of the same size, for which the Colonel is very desirous of being employed." (8, 27 and 81 for 1828.) Further correspondence between the two is to be found at the Huntington Library and at Yale.

(Charles Bulfinch)

JT wrote to Charles Bulfinch from New York on 17 January 1822: "I have the pleasure to inform you that I have finished my third picture [of the four] of the Surrender of Burgoyne and mean to deliver it at Washington before Congress adjourn. I am anxious to know if in the new parts of the Capitol, any Room of proper size is sufficiently finished and dry to receive it . . ." On 5 July 1824 he wrote from New York advising the architect that "the last [Resignation of Gen. Washington] is finished." (New-York Historical Society.)

26. General Records of the Department of State, Record Group 59, National Archives.

(John Holmes)

Among the colonel's papers at Yale is a 17-page memorandum (the first draft of which belongs to Mrs. Robert F. Jefferys of Faulcon Farm, Spring House, Montgomery County, Penn.) entitled, "Corrected Copy of an intended Answer to the abusive Speach of Mr. John Holmes, Senator from Maine, made in the Senate of the United States in March 1825. Prepared in June 1825 under the irritated feelings of the moment, but reconsidered and never published. J.T." The stature of the querulous, impetuous JT would not have been increased had the letter been sent.

(Charles Tait)

JT wrote to Charles Tait, 1768–1835, of Claiborne, Ala., former U.S. senator from Georgia, then judge of the U.S. District Court for Alabama, from New York on 25 October 1825: "I hope to be summoned to Washington in a short time to put up my paintings in their permanent places in the great Hall, and as the Hall is calculated by the Architect for *Eight* paintings, the *four* will of course leave it with a very unfinished appearance. I intend therefore to take with me my original Studies (two of which you have seen) of Bunker's Hill, Quebec, Trenton & Princeton and place them for a few days in view of the Members of Congress, in the vacant Niches, with the hope that when it is seen that the Eight will form a connected Series of the principal Events of the Revolution, the government may be induced to order me to execute them on the same scale as the four which I have done. Should they do this, & should I live to complete them, I may venture to say that the *Hall of the Revolution* would be one of [the] most magnificent & interesting Rooms in the World." (New-York Historical Society.) Other Tait-Trumbull correspondence is to be found at the Historical Society of Pennsylvania, Philadelphia.

(Hugh Mercer)

The 71-year-old JT wrote to Hugh Mercer of Fredericksburg, Va., from Washington on 4 December 1827: ". . . I have remained quietly at work upon the two pictures of Princeton & Trenton: they are both so far advanced as to shew in some measure what they are intended ultimately to be. Whether Congress will find leisure during this Session to think of such small things as paintings, or if they do, whether they may not think other subjects more worthy of a place in the Rotunda, than those of the Revolution, & whether they may not think more favorable of other artists than me, are all questions perfectly uncertain. But whatever determination may be taken by them, I feel it my duty to persevere in my course. My success in your portrait, & in other parts of the picture since has convinced me that notwithstanding my eyes,—yet with the aid of the Optician I can still execute such small work, as well as formerly, and I shall therefore devote myself without intermission to finishing the entire Series of small paintings which were begun Forty years ago, confident that they will have their value hereafter and constitute a more important legacy to those who are to follow me, than I could hope to acquire by any other pursuit to which I could devote the few remaining years, to say nothing of the pleasure I have in the recollection of past Scenes, in the tranquil society of my old friends, & in the belief that I am performing a duty in thus commemorating their Service & Virtues, for which posterity will thank me." (New-York Historical Society.)

(Comments and Appraisals)

It is curious that JT's "great national work" should be noticed in *The American Journal of Science,* dedicated more especially to "Mineralogy, Geology and of the other branches of Natural History," but so it was: *1* (1818), 200–201, and *16* (July 1829), 163–168: "The four great pictures, painted by order of the General Government, are at length placed securely in their destined situations . . ." The fact that Benjamin Silliman was the founder and for long editor of the journal may explain the matter.

There is a contemporary and derogatory account in the magazine, *The Port Folio* (Philadelphia, Harrison Hall, 7 [February 1819], 84–86), signed "Detector," of the first four pictures to be completed: "It may, perhaps, be a *very pretty picture,* but is certainly no representation of Declaration of Independence. The errors in point of fact, with which it abounds, ought to exclude it from the walls of the capitol . . ." The picture had been exhibited in the 4th exhibition of the American Academy of the Fine Arts, at New York in September 1818. JT replied in kind (pp. 86–88).

JT wrote to Theodore Dwight (Senior or Junior?) of New York from Washington on 13 January 1828: "The newspapers will have shewn you that in the memorable battle of the 9th the mangled bodies of all the painters strewed the bloody field: Allston, & Morse and myself all fell; but we fell gloriously, in the Company of the immortal Hero of the day. You will see that I, in particular, was most barbarously tomahawk'd & scalp'd by the relentless hand of the *half breed Chief* of Roanoke— and saddest of all to say, by the faithless hand of him who had once been my friend. To speak seriously, it was my fate to be selected on that occasion by the Hon. John Randolph of Roanoak (who is said to boast his descent from the Indian princess Pocahontus), as the butt of his merciless sarcasms . . . It ought also to be remembered that the professional reputation of an Artist, like the fair fame of woman is a delicate plant easily blighted by any pestilent blast—and that altho it may be sport to some to indulge in ribald witticisms at our expence, yet, it is Death to us . . ." (New-York Historical Society.)

There is much pertinent criticism of JT and his work to be found in Harold Edward Dickson, ed., *Observations of American Art, Selections from the Writings of John Neal, 1793–1876* (State College, Pa.), The Pennsylvania State College Studies, No. 12, 1943. Neal wrote of the 4 pictures in the Rotunda: "I have now done with Trumbull, lamenting that a man of such strength, when young, should be, in his dotage, or, if not in his dotage, that he should be content with such labour" (p. 15), that the "Declaration" "is only a respectable picture," that the 4 "are among the greatest and most unaccountable failures of the age. The President [Monroe, who was then 67] may not be superannuated, but the pictures are," and that they are "valuable only as a collection of tolerably well-arranged portraits." (P. 28.) Neal considered JT's "Gibraltar" "his best picture . . . so vigorous, and so full of action, as it is." (P. 14.)

Alexander Jackson Davis, JT's friend, architectural pupil, and former fellow officer of the American Academy of the Fine Arts, wrote the old colonel suggesting a joint visit to Washington, to see, among other things, JT's pictures—"your children"—in the Capitol, which he termed as "the only *constant* and unchanging record of a Nation's history!" A. J. Davis Letter Book (p. 337—probably spring of 1841), New York Public Library.

In describing the cultural possessions of New York City, Fitz-Greene Halleck wrote:

> In painting, we have Trumbull's proud *chef d'oeuvre*,
> Blending in one the funny and the fine;
> His "Independence" will endure forever,
> And so will Mr. Allen's lottery sign;
> And all that grace the Academy of Arts,
> From Dr. Hosack's face to Bonaparte's.[27]

27. *Fanny* (New York, Harper, 1839), verse LI, p. 22.

It is JT's large "Declaration of Independence," painted at New York in 1818 and now at Washington, and his portrait of the celebrated Dr. David Hosack, now in the New York Hospital, to which the poet refers.

Philip Hone, the diarist, years later noted: "Tuesday, 20 Oct. 1846. I went last evening to a gathering of the members of the National Academy of Design as their invited guest, where I partook of oysters and champagne . . . I took advantage . . . to visit Vanderlyn's picture of 'The Landing of Columbus,' which he painted in Europe to fill one of the panels in the rotunda of the Capitol at Washington. It is a striking picture, . . . though it has many faults and is not better than Col. Trumbull's pictures in the same place, which have been rather severely criticised. John Randolph's epithet of 'shin piece' was a hasty 'plate of soup' to Trumbull's 'Declaration of Independence.' " [28] Hone, mayor of the City of New York, was one of the chief supporters of the American Academy of the Fine Arts, serving as a director for years.

Charles Sumner, U.S. senator from Massachusetts, 1851–74, is quoted by Richard Henry Stoddard in the *Anecdote Biographies of Thackeray and Dickens* (New York, Scribner, Armstrong, 1874), p. xiv: "When Thackeray was in this city (Washington), [in 1853] we visited, among the earlier places, the capitol rotunda. Thackeray was an artist by birthright, and his judgment was beyond chance or question. He took a quiet turn around the rotunda, and in a few words gave each picture its perfectly correct rank and art valuation. 'Trumbull is your painter;' he said, 'never neglect Trumbull.' "

A conversation taking place in 1873 between Professor Morse and Rembrandt Peale is referred to in Samuel Irenaeus Prime, *The Life of Samuel F. B. Morse, LL.D.* (New York, D. Appleton, 1873), pp. 595–596: "Trumbull, as an artist and a man, was not spoken of in terms of admiration . . . They regarded Trumbull's four pictures as works of great intrinsic value, because of the portraits . . ."

Some interesting foreign appraisal is to be found in Jane Louise Mesick, *The English Traveller in America, 1785–1835* (New York, Columbia University Press, 1922), pp. 238–240; and contemporary appraisals may be found in such works as Oliver W. Larkin, *Art and Life in America* (New York, Rinehart, 1949), and Virgil Barker, *American Painting* (New York, Macmillan, 1950).

28. Allan Nevins, ed., *The Diary of Philip Hone* (New York, Dodd, Mead, 1927), 2, 775–776.

(Exhibitions of the Four Pictures)

As each of the pictures for the Capitol was finished it was sent on tour and exhibited, before delivery at Washington.

Washington Allston noted on 14 December 1818: "Trumbull, . . . has had great success here with his picture, having got, in three weeks, seventeen hundred dollars by its exhibition." [29] The "great success" was the enlarged replica of the "Declaration of Independence," destined for the National Capitol. JT actually received $1701.56 from the exhibition (accounts at the Huntington Library, San Marino, California).

JT wrote to Charles Chauncey, Yale 1792, a member of the Pennsylvania bar, at Philadelphia on 5 January 1819 for "permission to use the Room in which the declaration of Independence passed, for the Exhibition of my picture of that subject . . . and that Room is still more appropriate than Faneuil Hall" in Boston, where it had been exhibited. (Yale Library.) The matter must have been arranged promptly as the *Aurora and General Advertiser*, Philadelphia, carried the following advertisement from 11 to 23 January 1819, with the exception of the 16th: "The Public Are respectfully informed, that the PICTURE of the DECLARATION OF INDEPENDENCE, which has been painted by Mr. Trumbull, for the government of the United States, will be exhibited for a few days in this city, at the old State House on Chestnut Street. The exhibition will commence on Tuesday next, the 12th and will be open from 9 o'clock in the morning until dusk, every day except Sundays, until Saturday the 23d. Subscriptions will be received at the Exhibition Room, for a Print which is to be published from this painting."

Like the "Declaration," the "Resignation" was exhibited at Independence Hall. *Poulson's American Daily Advertiser*, 17 November 1824: "Hall of Independence. By permission of the Honourable City Council. The last of the Pictures painted by Col. Trumbull, for the Government of the United States, representing General WASHINGTON, resigning his Commission to Congress, at the close of the Revolution, will be exhibited for a few days in the Hall of Independence, from 9 A.M. until dark. Admittance, 25 cents."

Peter Lanman wrote from New York on 27 July 1824 to his daughter, Abigail Trumbull Lanman, 1806–91: ". . . The Colonel left the City for Albany yesterday and as I did not arrive in the City before nine at night

29. Flagg, *Washington Allston*, p. 145.

I had not the pleasure to see him. I fear that the exhibition *here* did not meet his expectations, & I hope he will be more fortunate at Albany, & Boston. The truth is our City of Gotham, has been the Theatre of so many *shows*. That what with Mermaids, & Mummies, Elephants & Monkeys—& a thousand and one Pictures of no value—the Gothamites are tired of the shows. The Picture has been much admired, & some of the Colonels friends, consider it among his best." (Connecticut State Library, Hartford.) In 1828 JT painted the portraits of Peter Lanman, 1771–1854, and his wife, Abigail Trumbull Lanman, 1781–1861, the daughter of David Trumbull, the artist's brother. Both portraits are at Yale.

JT wrote to Professor Silliman of New Haven from New York on 24 July 1824: "Having learnt from Washington that the Architect will not be prepared to receive & place my picture until November I shall employ the intermediate time in exhibiting it. I go . . . to Albany . . . Boston . . . Hartford & New Haven—travelling by the Steam boats is so convenient that I can do it with ease & safety & expedition. Will it be possible to obtain a Room in N. Haven of proper size & light and at little or no expense?—is there any in the Court House or College?—the picture with its frame measures 14 by 20 feet . . ." (Huntington Library.) This probably refers to "Gen. Washington resigning his Commission" finished at this time.

(Engravings)

JT hoped to repeat Copley's and West's great successes in selling engravings after his work. The "Declaration of Independence," painted between 1786 and 1797, was finally engraved by a young American, Durand, who received $3,000 for the job. Great were JT's expectations. He employed Theodore Dwight, Junior, to solicit subscriptions among the members of the Senate and House at Washington—actually a prospectus was laid "upon the table of each gentleman of the Senate" and "the Subscription book upon the Secretary's table for two days . . . without a single signature." "I thought it my duty," JT stated, "to offer it first to the members of the legislature, because those whose names stand first on the list will receive the finest prints . . ." It was not a success. "I confess I am not only mortified but confounded," he wrote to Rufus King, "the utter failure of Mr. Dwight . . . has given me more vexation than any accident which has befallen me for a long time . . ." The "Proposals . . . for Publishing by Subscription a Print . . . Price to Subscribers, Twenty Dollars; one half to be paid at the

time of Subscribing, the remainder on delivery of the Print . . . ,"
dated New York, 15 January 1818, were steep. A dozen pages of the
Autobiography, 1841, App., pp. 356–367, are devoted to letters, all
written between 17 and 18 February 1818, registering his chagrin and
bitter disappointment; it was yet another print-making failure. This, in
1818, was 32 years after he had finished the original painting. Actually
the print, though dated 1820, was not available until 1823, or 47 years
after the event.

Asher Brown Durand, 1796–1886, born at Jefferson City near New-
ark, N.J., was of Huguenot ancestry. He was elected academician of
the Trumbull-dominated American Academy of the Fine Arts in 1824.
JT painted his portrait, now at the New-York Historical Society, in 1826.

Theodore Dwight, Junior, 1796–1866, author and educator, was the
son of Theodore Dwight, brother of Timothy Dwight, president of
Yale. JT painted Mr. and Mrs. Theodore Dwight (married in 1827) as a
wedding present in 1828. The portraits are with the Misses Ferris of
Bronxville, N.Y.

It should be noted that the "Declaration" was later engraved, in different sizes, by Francis Eugene Prud'homme, 1800–92, and by Water-
man Lilly Ormsby, 1809–83. At the outset JT had had the celebrated
London engraver, James Heath, 1757–1834, in mind.

As to Durand's ability, JT wrote to Francis C. Gray of Boston on
22 March 1820: ". . . with regard to the engravings of Mr. Durand . . .
It gives me much pleasure to state that there is but one opinion of the
remarkable merit of this engraver; & that the ablest judges are most
liberal of their praise . . . Mr. Allston thinks them proofs of singular
talent. Mr. Stuart says that they are specimens of the highest art, & that
he should not hesitate to have any of his works engraved under his own
eye & in conformity with his directions, by this artist." (Boston Public
Library.)

On 20 October 1823 JT wrote to the Marquis de LaFayette, informing him of his forwarding an engraving of the "Declaration of Independence by a young engraver born in this vicinity, and now only
twenty-six years old. This work is wholly American, even to the paper
and printing—a circumstance which renders it popular here, and will
make it a curiosity to you, who knew America when she had neither
printers nor engravers, nor arts of any kind, except those of stern utility.
I beg you to accept this print as a testimony of my respects . . ." [30]

JT presented impressions of the engravings after his works to John

30. *Autobiography* (1841), App., pp. 402–403.

Quincy Adams and to the Library of Congress. "Col. Trumbull presents his respects to the President of the United States & begs him to accept a Port Folio containing Four Prints which have been engraved from his paintings. Washington, 28 November 1826." This and a similar letter to the Library of Congress are in that institution.

In spite of the repeated failures of his print-selling plans, JT wrote in December 1826, to John Quincy Adams, suggesting an elaborate scheme for the painting of pictures of principal historical events and having engravings made of them. The American Academy of the Fine Arts published the letters in 1827 in an 8-page pamphlet, entitled *Letters proposing a Plan for the Permanent Encouragement of the Fine Arts by the National Government addressed to the President of the United States.* JT's original draft of the proposal is the property of Robert Macbeth of New York.

THE TRUMBULL GALLERY

The "Trumbull Gallery," situated on the old Yale Campus, designed by JT with the advice and assistance of his friend Ithiel Town, the architect, contained two 30-by-30 foot, well-lit exhibition rooms on the top floor, with skylights. The treasurer's office, a theological lecture room, and the mineral collection were on the ground floor. There was a heavy Greek Doric column on either side of the entrance.[31]

There is much correspondence concerning the annuity in the Yale Library. According to the Treasurer's reports the receipts (for admission to the Gallery) for the first year amounted to $930, for the second $847.50, for the third, due to the "cold winter," much less.

Professor Silliman submitted a report for July 1862–63 to Edward Claudius Herrick, treasurer of Yale College: ". . . It appears that the gross receipts for 24 years, $12467.78, have exceeded the amount paid for the annuity by 1217.78. The average expenses have been about $189 per annum—for the last 3 years $67.70 annually. The building cost the College nothing. I obtained the money by attending the legislature at Hartford in 1831, namely $7000 as part of the bonus of a bank at Bridgeport and the grant was sought by me for this object and would not have been otherwise obtained. The building cost $5000 and the College gained $2000 in the operation in addition to the building which was in fact a 'gift to the College'—the net average over expenses has been $334.37 per ann. applicable to the wants of poor students . . ." (Yale Library.)

How the affairs of the Gallery prospered and then declined may be

31. Doors opened to public 25 October 1832.

noted from a lengthy report, dated 18 June 1864, written by Professor Silliman five months before his death to President Woolsey of Yale College, in which he stated: ". . . in the autumn of 1832, a building, satisfactory to Col. Trumbull, having been opened . . . the collection was opened for exhibition. For a series of years, it attracted many visitors, and the receipts were considerable, but after it had ceased to be a novelty, the interest declined, and the receipts were much diminished. The average annual receipts of the first 27 years was a little over 500 dollars. At the end of thirty years, a new generation having arisen, the subject had passed into partial oblivion and the artist and his works . . . ceased to command the attention which they had once received. The admission to the gallery by a fee of 25 cents, while every other department of the College was gratuitously exhibited, became increasingly unpopular . . . Strangers were no longer attracted in large numbers, and the students, unjustly regarding the demand of a fee as a hardship, have generally neglected the gallery, and, of course, failed to cultivate a taste for art by the study of the pictures of a great master . . ." (Yale Library.)

The contents of the Gallery were removed to nearby Street Hall (built in the Venetian Gothic style) upon its completion in 1868. The old Gallery survived, as the office of the college treasurer, until its demolition in 1901—leaving but one example of JT's architectural efforts—the Lebanon Meetinghouse—extant.

The Gallery was demolished in 1901, the year of Yale's bicentennial celebration. Arthur Twining Hadley, president, 1899–1921, in the Report for 1900–01 of the President of Yale University noted: "Before the beginning of the next academic year, North College, the Treasury Building, and the Lyceum will be removed, in accordance with plans long ago made for the completion of the quadrangle. What is now known as the Treasury Building was formerly called the 'Trumbull Gallery,' and was erected in 1831 to preserve historical paintings of John Trumbull, which had then recently come into the possession of the College. In addition to the Trumbull pictures, there were exhibited here also the portraits of the officers and benefactors of the College, and the gallery was much frequented by visitors to Yale. On the completion of the Yale Art School in 1867, the Trumbull paintings were transferred to that building and the portraits were placed in Alumni Hall. The rooms of the old Trumbull Gallery have since served chiefly as offices for the Corporation, the President and the Treasurer of the University. These offices will now be transferred to the new Administration Building."

In August 1834 William Dunlap visited the Gallery. His comments are to be found in his *Diary*.[32] He also has a good deal to say about the contents of the Gallery in *The Arts of Design* (2 vols., 1834), published two years after the Gallery opened. His rather scathing—and just—analysis of JT's paintings must have injured the pride of the old Colonel.[33] (Dunlap had New Haven connections. He married Elizabeth Woolsey of Fairfield, Conn., on 10 February 1789, the aunt of Theodore Dwight Woolsey, 1801–89, president of Yale College, 1846–71.) JT's friend Philip Hone, who had been most active in the affairs of the American Academy of the Fine Arts and one of its directors, wrote to JT from New York on 16 March 1835: "I have this moment finished the reading of Mr. Dunlap's Book, in which I have found some entertainment . . . I read the Book through with some degree of pleasure, but vexed and annoyed occasionally by the bad temper which characterizes every page of it . . . I was willing to make some allovance for the irascibility of an old man, who has not always been on the sunny side of the hill; but the ill-natured remarks in which he has indulged, his bad feelings towards you, have excited my Indignation and I cannot refrain from addressing you on the subject, not to excite your animosity against the author, but to tell you frankly what your fellow Citizens think about it . . . you have risen in [their] opinions . . . by the attacks of this Gentleman and some others to which you have been lately exposed . . ." (Letter in the possession of Henry Woodhouse, New York.) A more recent appraisal is to be found in Oral Sumner Coad, *William Dunlap* (New York, Dunlap Society, 1917), p. 260: "This spirit of ill-will & vindictiveness was chiefly displayed toward John Trumbull . . . Dunlap developed a violent dislike for Trumbull, to which he did not fail to give rein in the 'Arts of Design.' For his best work he had nothing but praise, yet it was his poorer work and his faults of character and conduct which he chose to dwell on. He magnified trifles, misconstrued motives, and in general made Trumbull out a much worse person than he really was."

Local accounts of the Gallery are to be found in *The Literary Tablet*, New Haven, *1* (13 October and 1 November 1832), 111, 127. John Warner Barber, *Connecticut Historical Collections* (New Haven, Durrie & Peck and J. W. Barber, 1838), refers to the Trumbull Gallery as "a neat and appropriate building, erected as a repository for the valuable historical and other paintings of Col. Trumbull." The same author's *Antiquities*

32. Dunlap, *Diary*, 3, 808–809.
33. Dunlap, *Arts of Design*, 3, 75–76.

of New Haven, Connecticut, from Its Earliest Settlement to the Present Time (New Haven, J. W. Barber and L. S. Punderson, 1870) contains a description of the Trumbull Collection, pp. 17–18 and 159–161, with a nice wood engraving of the Gallery. Professor Silliman's *American Journal of Science,* 39 (July–September 1840), art. 1, pp. 214–249, contains an "Account of the Trumbull Gallery of Paintings in Yale College, City of New Haven," with a lithograph illustration of the Gallery; and a contemporary account is to be found in *The New Yorker and Weekly Journal of Literature and Politics and General Intelligence* (H. Greely, New York), *10* (17 October 1840), 76.

There is an excellent account of the history of the Trumbull Gallery by Prof. Edward E. Salisbury in *Yale College, a Sketch of Its History,* William L. Kingsley, ed. (New York, Henry Holt, 1879), *2,* 149–159; and James Mason Hoppin, professor of the history of art at Yale, 1879–99, wrote an account of the collection in the *History of the City of New Haven,* Edward E. Atwater, ed. (New York, W. W. Munsell, 1887), pp. 206–207. The *Records of the Yale Corporation* from 1831 to 1838 and the official correspondence (in the Yale Library) of the same period give a full picture of the contractual obligations of both parties.

A NOTE ON TRUMBULL'S EYESIGHT

A Letter to Benjamin West *

John Trumbull, the "Patriot-Painter," not only had his trials and difficulties with women, but with his eyesight as well. The accident which befell him at the age of five, in which he largely lost the sight of his left eye, is described by the artist in his defensive *Autobiography,* published in his eighty-fifth year. Until then he had not referred to his monocular vision. When, however, he and Gilbert Stuart were fellow students under West at London, he brought Stuart a picture for criticism. Stuart, so William Dunlap recounts in his gossipy *Diary,* told Thomas Sully that he "was puzzled by the drawing and after turning it this way and that . . . said . . . this looks as if it was drawn by a man with one eye," [1] at which Trumbull took offense.

It is in consequence of his one-eyed vision, however, that Trumbull's best work is small in scale—his oil miniatures and the early versions of his celebrated historical paintings. When Trumbull visited Jefferson at Paris in 1786 he had with him the small, newly finished, "Battle of Bun-

* Reprinted from the *Yale University Library Gazette,* Vol. 26 (October 1951).
1. New York, 1930, III, p. 692.

ker's Hill" and the "Attack on Quebec"—the finest of his battle series—
(both now at Yale). Jefferson, ever a discriminating judge of the fine
arts, wrote to Ezra Stiles on 1 September 1786 that "another countryman
of yours Mr. Trumbul has paid us a visit here & brought with him two
pictures which are the admiration of the Connoisseurs. His natural talents for this art seem almost unparalleled," [2] which is high praise indeed. Trumbull's small-scale portrait of Jefferson painted in the autumn
of the following year is, by the way, one of his happiest productions.
Jefferson wrote in 1788 to Trumbull's friend, William Stephens Smith,
Secretary of the American Legation at London (of whom the artist in
1785 painted a life-size portrait, now at Amherst College) with respect
to a projected portrait of John Adams, Jefferson urging Mather Brown,
"because Trumbul does not paint of the size of life & could not be asked
to hazard himself on it." [3] Would that Trumbull had confined himself
to miniature scale! (He did paint Adams, however, in bust size, in 1793,
after a miniature of the same year, the former being at Harvard and the
latter at Yale.)

Benjamin West well understood his pupil's shortcomings. There is a
letter from Trumbull to West, dated New York 30 August 1790, in the
Trumbull Collection in the Library, which states, in part, ". . . I have
several small portraits of the President [Washington was then in New
York] one in particular which I have done for Mrs. Washington a full
length about 20 Inches hight [still in the hands of the Custis family at
Lutherville, Maryland] is thought very like—& I have been tempted to
disobey one of your injunctions & to attempt a large Portrait of him for
this City which I am now finishing—the figure is near seven feet high
compos'd with a Horse, & the back ground the evacuation of this Place
by the British at the Peace:—the Harbour & Fleet with a Part of the
fortifications & Ruins of the Town:—How I have succeeded I hardly
dare judge:—the World have approved the resemblance, it is to Hang
in the most elegant Room in America & in a very perfect light." (It still
hangs in the same room, the Governor's, in New York City Hall.) West,
of course, was right. Would that we knew the other injunctions!

Trumbull wrote to his London friend and banker, Samuel Williams,
from New York in 1808 that his return to London was conditioned by
"an alarming decay of [his] sight." The effect of the painter's impaired
eyesight is abundantly evident in the four enlarged easel paintings in

2. Thomas Jefferson, *Writings*, ed. P. L. Ford (New York [etc.], 1894), IV, 299.
3. *Ibid.*, V, 2.

the Rotunda of the Capitol at Washington as with much of his later work. Trumbull had many troubles.

MILITARY CLOTHING

Trumbull's letter to Rufus King,[1] United States minister to Great Britain, dated 72 Welbeck Street, London, 8 March 1798, from the *Autobiography* (1841), App., pp. 368–373.

DEAR SIR—When you requested me to give my opinion of the dress which was most useful and economical for a military establishment, it occurred to me at once that (as my opinions on this subject varied much from those generally entertained) it would be difficult for me to convey them intelligibly by writing, and that there would be but little chance of a fair examination of what at first would naturally strike men as fantastic innovations, unless I could accompany my letter with a complete dress, made up according to the principles which appear to me to be true. I have taken time to do this, and have now the honor to submit to you the dress, and the following observations.

It appears to me that the first object to be considered in clothing troops, is the health and comfort of the men; no one article in the military system is of more importance than this; with it is connected all that vast economy which arises from a diminished recruiting service, and from diminished hospitals—as well as that which flows from the activity and energy of healthy troops.

The second consideration is the direct economy in the clothing contracts; this may be made a very considerable object, though far less important than the indirect economy alluded to above.

1. The many-sided JT was deeply concerned with the problem of the military uniform. During the Revolution there was but one uniform—for parade, garrison, combat, and fatigue duty—one which was particularly impractical for the last two. This condition lasted throughout most of the 19th century, though post–Civil War troops engaged in Indian fighting in the West wore pretty much what suited them and their commanders. Khaki came with the Spanish-American War. Khaki and woolen O.D.'s were the field uniforms of World War I, sometime before which blue denims were issued for work details, but were not described as fatigue uniforms. The Army did not make a thorough attempt to supply uniforms fully adapted to a variety of field service conditions until after Pearl Harbor.

In 1798 JT apparently discussed his ideas of appropriate field uniforms with his friend, Rufus King, and among other things suggested the employment of a leather helmet (like that used by the old Imperial German Army, an ancestor of the "tin hat" of today), as "security . . . against the stroke of a horseman's sword."

The third, but infinitely least important object, is show and appearance.

Under the head of health and comfort, I shall say a few words on two points, which appear to me to be gross errors, in almost all the modern systems of military dress. I mean long hair and tight ligatures, particularly waist-bands. If the life of a soldier were to be passed in warm and comfortable quarters, and he were kept in pay to look at only, it might be excusable to calculate his dress for the parade, as you would that of a lady for the ball room; and a *tête-a-tête* which requires half an hour at the toilet, might be admissible. But when we view the soldier engaged in that actual service for which his country really employs him, in the presence of an active and superior enemy, in cold and stormy weather, his baggage lost, no shelter but the heavens, nor bed but the cold wet earth—then it is that the poor fellow wants comfort, not finery; then it is that long hair becomes not merely an embarrassment, but essentially prejudicial and dangerous; it becomes wet, and being once in that condition, must remain so for days, perhaps for weeks, like a soaked sponge at the back of the neck, loading the nerves, those mainsprings of life and motion, at their very source, with a cold, noisome humidity, vexatious to the immediate feelings, and infinitely baneful in its ultimate consequences to his health. I doubt the possibility of inventing any so simple application by which the human constitution should be more infallibly, irremediably, and seriously injured, than by this.

On questions of beauty, as well as taste, I know it is generally as difficult to decide as it is easy to dispute; however, on this particular subject of long hair, as being unbecoming and disagreeable to the eye in military dress, I have very high authority on my side. I appeal from the arbitrary and fickle laws of modern fashions, which sometimes require us to wear huge clubs, sometimes little pigtails, and sometimes, as a few years ago in the Austrian and Prussian service, decorates military beaux with tails long and large enough to rival monkies—I appeal from all this nonsense to the example of the ancient Greeks and Romans, who were good judges both of war and of manly beauty. Many of their statues and bas-reliefs have come down to us, after being the admiration of ages; among them are many figures of their heroes and demi-gods, but not one example of a long-haired hero. They very well knew that nothing gives so much appearance of lightness, activity and dignity to the human figure as the smallness of the head; unlike the modern inventors of grenadiers' caps, bear skins, huge three cornered hats, &c. who seem to have supposed that the formidable appearance of their troops was increased by giving them heads too big for their bodies to support; as if a man with a basket or bushel on his head, were more fit for athletic action than one without. Notwithstanding, therefore, that most of the young officers of the army, many of the soldiers, and all the sweethearts of both may think me ridiculous, I have no hesitation to say, that I regard very short hair as indispensable to the comfort, health, and elegance of troops; and in my opinion, an order to this purpose ought to form one of the fundamental regulations of the service. With short hair I will not object to powder, because very little will be necessary; it can be applied in a moment, and will give uniformity of appearance. I scarce need add, that the government which should adopt this idea for its troops, ought at the same time most carefully to avoid enacting any law, which should render short hair a part of the dress of those criminals, whom it might be wise to condemn to hard labor or other ignominious punishment.

Tight ligatures are not merely painful at those times when the body is in exercise, but when long continued do, by checking the circulation, produce gradual and rooted debility. The waistband particularly, for the purpose of keeping the small clothes neatly to their place, is usually drawn tight, and binds hard upon that part of the human figure which is least strongly supported by bones; compresses those muscles upon whose free and perfect action the great movements of the body depend, and injures very materially, though imperceptibly at first, the nervous system of the lower extremities. From the compression of this nervous and muscular part, (and the mass of long hair, so often bearing upon the back of the neck, and affecting the nerves almost in their origin,) arise many of those pains in the back and loins, debilities of the lower limbs, and rheumatic complaints, which so much prevail in armies, and which are usually ascribed to cold and fatigue. Tight waistbands are, therefore, as objectionable in my opinion as long hair; and I have endeavored to avoid the use of them entirely, as well as of all other ligatures in every part of my dress.

It is proper also to say a few words on the other errors of modern uniforms, which are useless, and equally inconsistent with show as with economy;—I mean the long skirts of coats, and lappels; these add nothing to the warmth or comfort of the soldier, but they add considerably to the expense of his dress, in cloth, buttons, and making; the lappel injures his appearance, being of one color, the ground of the dress of another, the underdress of a third, and these crossed by belts frequently of a fourth. The modern well dressed soldier is divided into so many scraps and parcels, that when viewed in front, he really has more the appearance of a harlequin, in a patch-work coat, than a man dressed for service and elegance; and this is still more applicable to the music of most regiments, who are rendered perfectly ridiculous by this study of babyish finery. I have, therefore, discarded from my dress both the skirts and lappels. It remains to describe the several parts of the dress which I have the honor to submit to you.

For the hat, I substitute a cap, nearly resembling the ancient Roman helmet, and calculated for convenience, comfort and safety. It is completely weather proof; it has no superfluous parts or size, no awkward projecting corners, to incommode the soldier or his neighbor in their exercises or firings. The small projection in front, is sufficient to protect the eyes from the sun and weather; the bandeau, which in fair weather is an ornament, becomes useful in foul weather; by removing the cockade, it is loosed in front, and turns down in form of a cape, buttons on the shoulders of the jacket, and ties under the chin, so as to shelter the neck and ears from rain, snow and cold; the cap being made of jerked leather, guarded with brass wire, is a perfect security to the head, against the stroke of a horseman's sword.

The jacket is perfectly simple, calculated merely to cover and show the form of the body. The cuff and collar (upright) of a different color from the basis of the dress, may serve and is sufficient to mark the distinctions of brigades or divisions, while regimental distinctions, may be marked by the number on the button. In place of the common epaulet or shoulder strap, I have adopted what is now worn by many of the British regiments, an epaulet composed of brass rings, laid sufficiently close, to resist the stroke of a sword; by this the shoulders, as well as the head, are very much protected. When these want cleaning, the red cloth is easily removed from under the rings, (which are not sewed to it, but to the leather,) and replaced by the soldier himself; the three buttons on the bottom of the collar, (ranging with those for the shoulder straps,) are to secure the cape of the helmet in bad weather, the four button holes in the waist, are to receive the corresponding buttons on the waistband of the overalls, which are supported by these means.

The overalls are in the common form, except that they do not tie in the waistband, being supported by buttoning the four upper buttons of the waistband to the corresponding holes of the jacket. The gaiters are part of the overalls, the lining of which being continued down to the foot, the cloth of the overalls stops at the calf of the leg, and is there met by a black cloth which forms the gaiter. I have made these to fasten by means of a strap, passing under the foot, and a small buckle on the inside of the foot; but as the men may sometimes hurt themselves in marching, by striking these buckles against their ankles, I am disposed to believe that it might be better to have either a loop, where the buckle now is, and to remove the buckle to the top of the foot, or to have two straps, one on each side of the foot, both to pass under the shoe, and long enough to meet and tie on the top of the foot. Both these articles (the jackets and overalls) are lined, throughout, with flannel; stockings and drawers are therefore useless, except in extreme seasons; in general, a sock reaching a few inches above the ankle will be sufficient.

I have nothing to say of the shoe, except that it is easier to the foot and more economical to use strings than buckles, and as both are equally concealed by the gaiter, nothing is gained or lost, in point of appearance, by the adoption of either. I should prefer black leather straps and belts, for the officers and soldiers of the infantry; the cartridge box and sheath for the bayonet being black, the belts should be so likewise, both for the sake of that beauty which is always derived from simplicity, and because I would not have the men encumbered with various materials, and modes of cleaning their dress and accoutrements.

On the straps which I send with my dress, I have run a chain of brass wire, for the purpose of increasing the safety of the soldier, and of adding something of ornament; but now that I come to see it, it is not a thing which I can approve of, at least for the infantry, because it is inconvenient, particularly in firing; yet I have left it, as worth some consideration, perhaps, for the artillery and cavalry.

The color which I have chosen for my dress may be objected to. I certainly did not choose it for beauty, but for utility; it is durable, and less easily soiled than any color that I know. Hair powder does not soil it as it does blue or any dark color; dust or gunpowder do not injure it as they do white, yellow, buff, or other delicate colors; it is sufficiently dark to be little distinguishable in the night; and further, it is a color which we ourselves can make, even in an imperfect state of manufactures, and we shall save all the expense of the blue, scarlet, and other dyes.

However, if more of elegance be insisted upon, give to each of them a second jacket for the parade, of white cloth, with the same cuff and collar, and the dress will be found to be very showy and elegant. This is the custom of the Austrian service, where the dress uniform is white, with an undress of French grey.

I shall be highly gratified if these observations, either in whole or in part, shall be thought to be just and meet the approbation of yourself, and of those to whom they are ultimately to be submitted. I am, &c.

TRUMBULL'S TROUBLES

An Omitted Chapter of the Artist's Life °

Among the John Trumbull papers in the Library there is a box of un-published letters, a recent gift of Morgan Brainard, 1900. Of peculiar poignancy, these concern Colonel Trumbull's illegitimate son, John Trumbull Ray, and reveal the hidden sources which motivated the "patriot-artist's" otherwise inexplicable bellicosity in his later and, un-fortunately, best-remembered years. While he faced the world bravely, a viper was secretly eating at his heart. A few of his friends knew the facts; others, like William Dunlap, the painter-art historian, suspected concealed complications, and still others gossiped in ignorance. Most of Trumbull's contemporaries . . . knew or suspected nothing. The cor-respondence is a key to his behavior.

Three women conditioned the life of handsome John Trumbull, who preserved his good looks and fine military bearing to the end of his long life. The first of these was the frail and beautiful Harriet, daughter of the soldier-statesman Jeremiah Wadsworth of Hartford. She was the sister of Daniel Wadsworth, who in later years founded the Wadsworth Atheneum. Many and intimate were the relations between the Con-necticut families, the Trumbulls of Lebanon and the Wadsworths of Hartford. The towns were but thirty miles apart—a short day's ride. Governor Jonathan Trumbull, Senior's, eldest son Joseph, it will be re-membered, was succeeded by Jeremiah Wadsworth in the exacting task of providing for the Continental Forces as Commissary General. Daniel Wadsworth married Faith Trumbull, the eldest daughter of Governor Jonathan Trumbull, Junior, brother of Joseph and of John, the painter. The latter, thirteen years Harriet's senior, had known her from "the happy days of infant innocence" when she "would hang fondly upon [his] neck . . . and listen with earnest pleasure to his little stories." During his long absence in England while studying under Benjamin West in London, the little girl grew up. When at the age of thirty-three, Trumbull returned to this country in 1789 to gather at first hand the necessary data for his historical pictures—portraits, topographical and architectural details, and such like visual information—he saw, in the natural course of events, much of the Hartford family. Harriet was then twenty, and the busily employed artist fell in love. While traveling up and down the Atlantic seaboard collecting "heads" for the "Declaration of Independence" and other of his celebrated compositions, he poured

° Reprinted from the *Yale University Library Gazette*, 25 (October 1950).

3a. Harriet Wadsworth of Hartford, Connecticut, beloved by the artist; a miniature by Trumbull painted from memory in 1793, the year of her death, at the age of twenty-four at ermuda. (*Courtesy of Mrs. Helen Wadsworth Post Bergen, Utica, New York*)

3b. The artist's son, Lieut. John Trumbull Ray of the British Army, the 45th (Nottinghamshire) Regiment of Foot; miniature painted at London in 1814 by Andrew Robinson. (*Courtesy of the Yale University Art Gallery*)

out his heart to her. In November, 1791, the letters from the "infatuated Uncle" to his "dear country cousin" ceased; the matter came to naught. Harriet, failing in health, was sent to Bermuda—pure sea air was considered the best means of combating consumption—and there she died in 1793. John painted two charming miniatures of his best beloved, posthumously, from memory, one for the Wadsworth family and one (now at Yale) for himself. It must have been shortly after his rejection that the desperately disappointed but eminently successful artist became involved in a sordid affair, the subject of the revealing Brainard letters.

For the second woman to influence the course of the painter's long life—he died in his eighty-eighth year—was a loose-living servant girl named Temperance Ray of Haddam, Connecticut. The facts concerning her are given in letters drafted by Trumbull to James Wadsworth, originally of Durham, Connecticut, a cousin of the Hartford Wadsworths. (It was James who took up Jeremiah Wadsworth's vast holdings in the Genesee Valley in what was then known as Ontario County, New York.) The first draft is dated from London, 26 July 1799, where Trumbull was then living at 72 Welbeck Street, a fifteen-minute walk from the Newman Street studio of his master Benjamin West. It explains the unfortunate situation with all candor.

When I was last in America an accident befel me, to which young Men are often exposed;—I was a little too intimate with a Girl who lived at my brother's, and who had at the same time some other particular friends;—the natural consequence followed, and in due time a fine Boy was born;—the number of Fellow labourers rendered it a little difficult to ascertain precisely who was the Father; but, as I was best able to pay the Bill, the Mother using her legal right, judiciously chose me;—I was absent at the time;—the Business was illmanaged,—became public,—and I had to settle with the Select Men, instead of providing the poor girl with a good husband, and the Child a more *probable* Father because a more able bodied Man.

But, having committed the Folly, and acquired the name of Father, I must now do the Duty of one, by providing for the education of the Child, to whoever He may belong:—I did not mean to have troubled any of my friends with this awkward business;—but as it is very uncertain how long I may be detained in Europe, and the Child who was born in 1792 is now seven years old, an Age when the impression of good or evil habits is deep and lasting, it is necessary that his Education should be attended to without delay; May I then beg of you who are so good a Negotiator, to undertake this

Business for me?—The Mother's Name was Temperance Ray. She
lived at Haddam, not many miles from your Father;—The Select
Man, to whom I paid the Sum due for the maintenance of the Child
in its Infancy, was Edward Selden. I could wish you to see both
Child and Mother, if they are living; I am afraid it is a blackguard
Family, and that the Child will come to no good, if suffered to remain with them much longer;—of this you will judge, and if the
Fact should be as I suspect, I would wish you to take the Boy out of
their hands, and place him in some respectable & moral Family,
where He may have good Examples as well as Instruction;—if, on
the contrary the Mother and Family live and behave decently, He
may remain with them: but in either case I wish him to be kept constantly at a good common School, and taught reading, writing and
Arithmetic, so as to fit him to make a good Farmer, and to become
hereafter a respectable Inhabitant of Ontario County. If after some
time, He should prove to be a Lad of Talents, I shall try to encourage the Natural Genius, & perhaps make something else of
him.

This affair is really interesting to me;—what is past is Folly—but
to neglect the poor little wretch, (who, at all Events is not here by
any fault of his own) would deserve a much severer name. I therefore beg you will have the goodness to attend to it as soon as you
can, and effectually.—Whatever Expence you may think necessary
or proper, you will not Spare, and it shall be cheerfully repaid.—It
is bad enough to be called the Father of a Child whose Mother is
little worth;—but, to be called the Father of a worthless illiterate
profligate wretch (as He may prove, if left uneducated) is a disgrace to which it is criminal to expose oneself, when it may be
avoided by a little Care and Expence.

The third woman to influence Trumbull's life was a good deal better
than Temperance Ray. She was a beautiful but shallow-minded English
girl, Sarah Hope Harvey, who had been born in the vicinity of London
in 1774, the daughter of William Hope of Perthshire. The socially conscious Connecticut aristocrat married her a year after writing the above
letter to James Wadsworth. He was then forty-four and she twenty-six.
. . . We have it from the painter that he informed his bride-to-be of
young Ray, who was eight at the time of the marriage. For years a fiction
was maintained; Ray was the colonel's "nephew." That the boy's "uncle"
was constantly concerned with his upbringing may be inferred from a

letter from his brother, Jonathan Trumbull, (governor of Connecticut from 1797 until his death in 1809), to Capt. Sylvanus Tinker of South Haddam, Connecticut, dated New Haven, 10 October 1800.

I have been desired by my Brother John, now in England, to make some enquiry respecting the situation of a certain *Bye Blow* Boy, which a Temperance Ray of Chatham produced in Lebanon—not knowing where better to apply than to you—I now give you this trouble—If you have it in your power, I will thank you to give me information of the Boys present situation—where placed & with whom, & what are his advantages & prospects—Or if this is not now in your Knowlege—may I beg you to be so good as to make the Inquiry, & give me the best information you can obtain—also what is the Genius & Spirit of the Boy—My Brother says to me, That—as he must set down with the reputation of having had some hand in his introduction into the world—he would not wish to see him brot up & educated—an uninformed ignorant Blackguard—but rather wishes to contribute towards his being placed in some eligible situation, where he may have the advantages of a decent Education, & the prospect of being brot forward to some reputable Employment & Usefulness in Life—

This was answered by Capt. Tinker ten days later.

I Received your favor of 10th Instant duly came to hand, as I was acquainted where this boy was, I wrote to Capt Smith for Inquiry, without making Mention of any persons Name, his letter you have here inclosed, will give all the information that can be had—The boy lived in this place more than a year. I frequently observed him, I thot him to be a verry likely Sprightly boy, and it is Generally said to be the Most forward Child in School of his Age—if any thing further is wanted on this Subject shall with pleasure attend—

There is further correspondence with other worthies of East and South Haddam of but slight interest. The selectmen came down hard for the support of the boy. James Wadsworth's full report dated New York, 1 February 1801, to John Trumbull, with the observation that "on viewing him I have no doubt but he is your son," merits attention.

. . . If I have not written you as frequently as I ought respecting the Boy, it is not because the subject did not engage my early, and has since received my constant attention—

I received your first letter on the subject at Hartford—I requested my Brother in Durham to go to Haddam and make the necessary inquiries—he informed me that the woman had married a sea-faring man, by whom she had several children & was living comfortably— The Boy was put out by the Select men of Haddam to a Mr. Smith who had removed on to the military Tract in The State of N.York. On my moving westward last winter . . . I found Mr. Smith and to my mortification I found also that he was not from Haddam—On my return to Connecticut I desired my Brother to obtain more particular information, he procured it—As I went up last spring I found Mr. Smiths Family living in Cipio most unluckily he had gone from home—The boy was out after cows—I introduced the business and soon found They were acquainted with all the circumstances—The Boy is called after You—and I shall in future mention him by the name which he bears—I found that John was a favorite and tho a lad they thought him of some consequence—John came home with the cows—I viewed him with much attention—His clothes were dirty & ragged & his hair in every direction. I perceived however a fine countenance, hazel eyes, with ruby cheeks—After conversing with him a few minutes I asked him if he would go home with me & go to school—John with some interest asked me if I knew his Father—I waved the question—I proposed to the Family to take John home with me. They replied as I was a stranger & Mr. Smith from home, they would not consent to it—I had only to request them to take good care of John—schooling him in their situation was out of the question. The Family informed me that John was active, fond of play and a little of a Truant—They said he was remarkable for carrying a compass in his head—that he was in the daily habit of going two or three miles in the woods after cows and never got lost—

In the summer my business called me to the salt works, I went to Cipio on my return—unfortunately Mr. Smith had gone to Concut. —he had written me in the summer if I would pay him 50 Dls. I might take the boy—The idea of going to school had taken full possession of John—He received me with a very hearty welcome. I objected to pay the 50 Dls.—The Family urged that they had been at some expence in bringing John into the Country and furnishing him with clothes—his apparel was not worth sixpence—I at length told them, if I could not agree with Mr. Smith as to the price, I would leave it to indifferent Men to decide—On this condition they relinquished their right to John. He took an affectionate leave, and we came on together—

Mr. Penfield was in Canandagua . . . A Mr. Seymour, who saw you in England when I was there, has been acting as Penfields agent the summer past—I called John into a separate Room & told these Gentlemen his history—They both pronounced him yours without hesitation—Mr. Penfield in particular thought him quite your counterpart—I have mentioned this circumstance supposing that your feeling would be not a little interested on this head—for my own part I was not so struck with his resemblance that I should have distinguished him as yours among a number of boys—Tho on viewing him I have no doubt but he is your son—his forehead in particular and the upper part of his face resembles yours—his rosy cheeks indicate the finest health—in short he is an uncommonly fine looking boy—

A Mr. Whally, an English merchant having failed in trade, has settled at Gennessea, he married a Miss Saltonstall of N. London a most amiable woman—Mr. Whally's only fault is that at periods he is a little inclined to drink—He however, makes a very excellent school master—on my return home I procured John warm and decent clothing, furnished him with books and paper & put him to school to Mr. W. who being a particular friend of ours John will receive a full share of his attention.

John now eats & drinks with our work People, and fodders night and morning—Not knowing what his distinction would be I thought best to put him in this situation first where he will become acquainted with business—

On the whole I consider John a fine boy—possessing a very good understanding whether his talents are brilliant I have my doubts—but it ought to be remembered that I have seen him as yet to every possible disadvantage—I took him from a house where his manners morals and education had been totally neglected—

On my return home in March I will write you more fully my opinion respecting his talents and what you may probably expect from them—if you intend him for the lower walks, perhaps it will be best to remove him to some regular Family where he can learn a trade—if for the higher, of course to a good school—I will take care of him till I hear from you,—it will be rather inconvenient for us, nor will it be best for him to continue in our Family—

Presumably all was well, for there is a gap of four or five years in the correspondence. The boy was growing up and receiving a good country education. The Trumbulls were living comfortably in London. In 1804, however, the ten-year term of the painter-turned-diplomat as a commissioner under the Jay Treaty expired. The Trumbulls left for New York in the spring, where portrait painting was resumed. The painter's hand had lost much of its cunning, and though there were commissions, Trumbull returned to London in 1808, the year of the Embargo. Young Ray accompanied his "uncle and aunt."

There are many of Ray's schoolboy letters among the Brainard papers. From New Canaan, Connecticut, on 30 December 1806, he writes: "[I] . . . am very much obliged to Uncle and Aunt for their kindness and care in furnishing me so comfortably with what I stand in need of. the Coatee suits me as well as if the Taylor had measured me for the purpose of Making it, but the pantalons were so short and small that they cannot be so fixed as to do me any service." And from Morriss Town, on 22 February 1808: "Mr. Trigant has done keeping dancing here. I went two months to him, which comes to $5.44 he says $5.50. Mr. Trigant charges $5. a quarter and two $2 entrance, for them who have never ben to dancing school before. I began Geometry last thursday and shal finish it tomorrow, if God will permit"

A month before the family of three sailed for London Trumbull wrote to his banker, Samuel Williams. The letter is dated from New York, 11 November 1808.

> An alarming decay of my Sight has determined me to revisit London, for advice, and I shall embark in the December packet.—Mrs. Trumbull will accompany me and we shall bring with us a Nephew, a Lad of 17. . . .
>
> I shall also bring with me two panoramic Views of the falls of Niagara, & Surrounding Objects—The Scene is magnificent & novel. —I have copied it with all the fidelity in my power, and am not without a hope that it will at once excite and in some measure gratify the public curiosity.—I will thank you to mention to Mr. T. Baring & some of your other opulent friends who have a taste for the fine Arts, that I have prepared such views and that they will soon be in London—. . .

Arriving in London, the painter sought the advice of Sir John Sinclair about Ray's education. A month before he had left New York he had drawn up a new will in which he devised "to a Youth now in my Family and Known by the name of John Trumbull Ray and to his Heirs and assigns for ever all those six certain Lots or Parcels of Land Parcels of a large tract of Ten thousand two hundred and forty acres situated in the County of Genesee and State of New York commonly called Mount Morris." These potential farm lands, which he, as well as old Benjamin West, had purchased some years before from James Wadsworth, were naturally much in mind as he drafted the following letters, dated January 1809—he had only landed at Falmouth on the 7th—to Sir John.

Knowing your disposition to diffuse the knowledge of Agriculture, & Economy in rural Affairs, I beg leave to consult you—
I have brought with me from America a Nephew, a Lad of 17— whom I wish to have instructed in English Farming:—and with that view I beg to consult you, whether it is not practicable to place him in the Family of some respectable practical Farmer.—where his Morals will be attended to while he gains the requisite knowledge— & if this can be done I would wish to know on what terms—whether his Services will be considered an equivalent to his board or whether any premium would be expected—

and

In the conversation with which you honoured me yesterday on the Subject of placing my Nephew in a Situation to acquire a knowledge of farming, you suggested an Opinion that it would be advisable to place him in the Northern part of the country the reasons which you gave for that opinion are satisfactory—My will is that he should be in the Family of a Moral & respectable man, & a thorough practical farmer who will not only—instruct him in the business of agriculture & keep him constantly occupied, but attend to his Conduct, in other respects . . . The youth is uncommonly Full & Strong for his age—tractable & well disposed—& I hope will prove industrious, & faithful.

These letters are followed by correspondence with one John Bailey of Chillingham, Northumberland, who recommended a Mr. Vardy, "a dissenter" (which would be comfortable to the Congregationalist Trumbull). The painter reported to the Alien Office on 28 February 1809, just seven weeks after landing "that thru the kind offices of Sr. John Sinclair, he has succeeded in finding a respectable farmer in Northumberland, Mr. Thos. Vardy of Fenton, who is willing to take him [his nephew John Trumbull Ray] into his Family for [instruction in] Agriculture." Young Ray, like his father, had martial blood in his veins and did not take too kindly to farming.[1] The Colonel thereupon packed his "nephew" off to a cheesemaker. But the Napoleonic struggle was reaching new heights, and Ray wrote on 22 June 1811:

> I am now going to mention something to you which I am doubtful whether it will please you or not, but I thought the best way was to tell you honestly at once what I wish, that is to go into the army. I should rather do that than to go back to America if I had all the land on mount morris: and as I have cost you a large sum of money and must for this two years if I go back again, I wish to make my own living now, and I do not know so honourable a way as going into the army. If you and Mrs. T. are willing for me to go the best way will be for me to write to Mr. Croisdale to get me a commission, I should not by any means wish for you to buy me one if you were ever so willing to let me go.

Several letters were exchanged. On 10 July the Colonel replied:

> I have received your letter of the 6th—and regret that any part of mine to you should have been difficult to understand:—I meant to say, that the Market price of an Ensign's commission is £400.— so that if I were to purchase one for you, it would cost me that sum: —or if any other gentleman should give you one, you ought to consider yourself as receiving a present of that Value; & of course as being under obligations of gratitude, tho' not of money to that Amount:—Mr. Croasdaile further informed me, that the pay of an Ensign is not sufficient to live upon with decency; and that £60 or £70 a year, in addition to his pay & emoluments, is *necessary* to enable a young man to associate with his brother officers, of his own rank:—I thought that this Statement alone would have been sufficient to convince you that you was mistaken in your Idea of being able to get your living honorably by going into the Army, without being any further expence to your friends:—but this and all the other difficulties which I have hitherto stated seem to vanish before the charms of a red coat and the dreams of vanity & self confidence.

1. [This is typical of JT to Ray, at Fenton, dated London, 20 February 1811: ". . . I have sold no pictures and see no shadow of prosperity. I cannot therefore afford to buy you a horse, or pay the expences of your travelling to Scotland. You will therefore remain with Mr. Vardy until the 18th March, when your year expires and will then come up to London." (New-York Historical Society.)]

Permit me to state another objection:—you have chosen, of all times, to enter the British Army at the moment when a war with America is almost inevitable: and when of course your entering the military service of this Country may be regarded, & perhaps justly as an Act of Treason to your native Country:—at the same time remember what the King said upon a former occasion, "that the Man, who did not love his native Country, could never make a *faithful subject in any other*"—this observation is worthy of Trajan, or Marcus Aurelius:—and undoubtedly the same opinion is held by the Prince Regent, and by his counsellors:—it applies directly to your case: and you must see that you would enter this service at this time under a very serious disadvantage of being suspected by the very Prince whom you would serve.—perhaps you are regardless of these consequences to yourself:—but I should hope that you would not willingly expose me to those accusations which Mr. Clinton, & his worthless friends will not fail to ground upon such a step:—you know that my leaving America when I did, was one of the strongest arguments for refusing the favor which was requested for your Aunt:—your present project if persisted in will probably induce them to go greater lengths [see p. 360].

I did hope that your Spirit would have shewn itself by an eager desire to qualify yourself, for aiding me hereafter in opposition to that malignant party who have so deeply injured & insulted your Aunt, and who disgrace our Country.—for America with all her follies & vices is still my Country & yours. we are both *Aliens* in every other:—and that Patriotism which is so striking a feature in the character of your Aunt & binds her so strongly to her *native* country ought also to animate us:—and should lead us not to abandon America because the ruling party of the day is composed of worthless & unjust Men.—but rather to endeavor to deliver her from the Dominion of a profligate & dangerous Faction.

I recommend to you to reconsider your plan, and to write to Mr. Croasdaile, & ask his opinion of its propriety and prudence.

The Cheese came safe—and I dare say will prove excellent.— Offer our thanks to Mrs. Hill and accept my good wishes that you may be able to distinguish *your duty* from the dreams of vanity and imprudence.

Your Aunt will write you
I am *really* your friend

All of this seems to have done no good, for on 1 January 1812 Trumbull received the following from the War Office:

> I am directed to acknowledge the Receipt of your Letter of the 27th Ultimo requesting permission for your Nephew, Mr. J. T. Ray, to serve as a Volunteer in the Army under the Command of Lord Wellington; and to acquaint you that your Application should be addressed to Lt. Colonel Torrens, the Military Secretary of His Royal Highness The Commander in Chief.[2]

Ensign Ray of the 45th (Nottinghamshire) Regiment reported the part he was playing in the Peninsula Campaign, from Madrid, 23 September 1812, in a letter to Mrs. Trumbull:

> I thinck that Bonaparte has got as much as ever he can manage in the north, so that he will not be able to send any more troops here, which will give us an opportunity of driving the enemy out of the

2. There are many letters in JT's letter book (New-York Historical Society), from December 1811 to January 1812, seeking to expedite young Ray's rise in the Army.

JT's letter to his confidant, Rufus King, written from London, 19 August 1812, displays a certain amount of paternal and martial pride: "The Joy which we felt on seeing the official account of the Battle of Salamanca was for a few hours very much dampened by seeing the name of my boy, Ensign Ray of the 45th reported *severely* wounded, but our anxiety was relieved by soon receiving a letter written by himself at Salamanca on the 26th stating his wound to be only a cannister shot in the left arm, which was doing well & gave him the prospect of soon being able to join his Regt. When Mr. Ray learnt the infamous treatment which his Aunt had received from the Senate of the State of New York, he silently took his resolution never to live under a government capable of such baseness. About a year ago he explained himself to me & begged permission to go into the British Army, and make honorable war his profession, rather than return to a Country, where his Origin & connexions would ensure him Enemies & Insults & where his whole life must be a series of petty & disgusting squabbles. I made all the opposition in my power short of absolute prohibition but, finding argument useless, I at length consented to his going to Portugal as a Volunteer. He was thoroughly drilled—went out in March, with letters to Gens. Graham, Hill & Picton—arrived at Badajor on the 5th of April, and on the next night was with the latter officer in the attack of the Castle. He was among the first who reached the top of the Walls, when he met a French bayonet in his face, which struck him from the top of his Ladder, & ended his exertions for that night— but the wound proved slight & he was immediately made an Ensign. To have been wounded at the Storming of Badajor & again at the battle of Salamanca, secures him the respect of his comrades thro' life & from such a beginning I cannot but hope that he will make a distinguished Officer. We had taken the resolution of returning to New York this Autumn, but the madness of the times induces us to hesitate—at any rate Mrs. T. must not return with me. The Fate of the civilized world hangs on the passing moment . . ." (New-York Historical Society).

Peninsula next summer. They show no disposition to fight us like *soldiers,* since the battle of Salamanca, nor do I thinck they will ever face British troops as they ought again. The Victory gained at Salamanca was without doubt the most compleat that ever was known in this country; the action did not last more than three hours, there was not a shot fired untill near five o'clock and it was all over by eight: if we had had two or three hours more day light there would not a single man of them have escaped from us. We had but four divisions engaged, two of them the weakest in the whole army, the other three never fired a shot during the whole of the action. You would have thought some times that a mouse could not have [escaped] from the balls, they were flying so thick; you never saw a fieu-de-joy fired so quick or so regular, as the fireing was from the last hill we took possession of, where they made their last stand. . . .

Madrid is a very fine place, but it is astonishing the misery which presents itself in the streets, the French laid such heavy contrabutions on the Inhabitants whilst they were here that they reduced many families to begery. The Officiers of our regiment have established a fund for supplying *sixty* poor wretches with soup from the Barracks as long as we remain in Madrid.

I am very much obliged to Uncle for the fifteen Pounds he sent me as it could [not] have arrived at a better time [than it] did. I am happy to hear that all old friends remain the same.

Major—now Col. Greenweell who treated me with so much kindness while a volunteer, received a very severe wound at Salamanca the ball went through his right arm—through his body, and lodged in the left   he is doing remarkably well.

Make my best respects to Uncle and all friends in town.

The next letter of consequence from Ray, now a lieutenant, is from London, on 16 August 1814.

I arrived here this morning from Brighton having left the regt. at Blackington, prepearing for their March this morning on their way to Plymouth, supposed for the purpose of handing over the men of the 2nd. Battn. and then reduce the officers. I shall apply to Sir H. Calvert in person in the course of two or three days when I am almost certain I shall get two or three months more leave.

I dine with Mr. S. Williams this afternoon, I have allso seen Mr. Robonson who is to let me know tomorrow morning when I am to sit for my Minature as I shall allmost inevitably be detained here untill the 25th. I should take it as a most particular favour if you could send Me eight or nine pounds as I am entirely destitue at present and shall be untill after the 25th. I am extreemly obliged to Aunt and yourself for your Minatures which I saw to day.

The Colonel replied from Bath—a better place for an enemy alien to be than London:

I have just recd your letter of yesterday dated in London:—our last directed to Portsea, and advising you to go to London & thence to Cheltenham, I suppose has not reached you . . .

I have requested Mr. S. Williams to give you £10—

You will not fail to wait on Mr. Croasdaile—make our best respects to the Ladies & him—

Your Aunt will thank you to call at Apothecaries Hall & buy for her & bring with you a half pint bottle of *Hoffmans* Anodyne Liquor —it will cost 7/6.

I will thank you to call on my Colourman *Brown* in Holborn, opposite the new buildings near Broad Street St. Giles—& desire him to put up for me a pound of Flake white.—a Glass to grind my Colours *with* not *on*—and a pint of *Nut* oil, if He has any really good:—I will thank you to bring them with you—

Make our best respects to Mr. Robertson—& beg to have the picture in your uniform—request him to tell you, how Mr. Wests last great picture succeeds--whether done—whether Sold or not, & for how much—whether fine as was expected—

A few days later, on 24 August, Ray answered:

I received your last letters in due time and should have answered them before this but waited so as to inform you when I should be with you, which I hope will be Saturday or Sunday. I am very much obliged to you for the money which you sent me. Mr. Robertson has nearly finished my Miniature. I call'd upon Mr. West and got your letter, but did not see him, the outside sheet appears to contain some plan. I have seen most of our old acquaintance except at Hammersmith; I dined with Mr. Croasdaile on Sunday. Old Mr. Knollekens wishes very much to hear from you, he thought you had gone to America untill I call'd, the old lady is very much broken. Mrs. Pettingall is very well and as chatty as ever, poor *Tom* is likewise well.

(The miniature of the young officer in his scarlet tunic by Andrew Robertson is now at Yale. In Trumbull's last will, dated 19 December 1842, there is no mention of Ray other than the single sentence "I bequeath to John T. Ray a Lieutenant in the British army a miniature likeness of himself painted by Robertson." There is a similar miniature, by the same hand, in the National Collection of Fine Arts, Smithsonian Institution.)

(The reference to "old Mr. Knollekens" is to Joseph Nollekens, the celebrated sculptor, a good friend of the Colonel's.)

As soon as possible after the cessation of hostilities the Trumbulls returned to New York—his dream of becoming a popular portrait painter in London having come to naught. Heavy debts were incurred during the painter's long periods of idleness. It is not difficult to understand that English portrait commissions did not pour in upon the ex-rebel officer during these years of strained political relations. In desperation he painted his wife many times, used her in some of his unfortunate religious and allegorical compositions, painted his self-portrait, copied a Van Dyck and even painted two portraits of the Duke of Wellington after a marble bust which Nollekens had carved in 1813. But these pictures did not help to pay bills. Three weeks before sailing on the American ship, "Illinois," Trumbull wrote to Ray on 26 July 1815:

We regret that you have not arrived in time to see us before we sail—

The Events which have passed since you left England will astonish you—

We think it probable that you may be able to get into active Service soon, if you proceed discreetly; ask the advice of Mr. Croasdaile He is really disposed to be useful to you—but avoid Mr. McGougan—

It is not in my power to leave any Money at your Command—in truth you made so poor a use of what you had last winter, that it is well you should feel the value of it by privation:—

You are young, I hope healthy—& have your half pay:—if you are industrious & prudent, you will be able to get on very well:—if you are not, nothing we can do will be of any use to you.—

Your Aunt—and best benefactress, is so much dissatisfied with your unkind conduct to her that She has taken her miniature from Mr. Robertson & will keep it until She has reason to believe that you know how to value it—

Tho' offended with your late Conduct, we both most cordially wish you Health and prosperity:—

Write to us directed at New York—We shall write to you, to the Care of Mr. S. Williams 13 Finsbury Square.

Back in New York Trumbull was shocked to learn from his son of his marriage. He wrote from New York on 20 October 1817:

We are not much surprised that you have taken the most important Step in Human Life, without asking our Opinion: for it is not the first instance of your independence. but, we are a little surprised that it did not occur to Mrs. Ray, (who we understand was a Widow) that *Family wants* might arise which would require more than your half pay to provide for.

We do not mean to Say that we fear you have married a Woman unworthy of you:—but the more meritorious & excellent She may be, the more imprudently we think you have both acted, in being married without Some fairer prospect of at least a competency to Subsist upon.

From your last letter dated at Calcutta, I understood that you liked the Sea:—that you stood high in the good opinion of your Captain, and expected to rise a Step on your return & hoped soon to get a Ship.—What has induced you to give up this pursuit, and to throw yourself again upon the World,—with encreased expenses? You knew my situation when I left England:—You know the pictures are not sold:—and you know that uncultivated Land, can not produce Income.—It is true that I am employed to paint pictures, but I shall not be paid for them, until they are finished. I cannot therefore assist you, *even if I thought it to be my duty.* You are both young, and better able to struggle with the World, than I am who am Old.

Your Aunt & I took care of your early years, and gave you a useful education: You possess Youth, Health, Strength, & a considerable knowledge of *Farming*, and of Military & Naval affairs;—these are precious advantages, Ray: and if Adversity should teach you prudence, & make you feel the value of listening to the Opinions of Friends older than yourself, (which you have heretofore so totally neglected,) you cannot fail to do well:—that you may is our earnest wish.

Continue if you please to write either to Mrs. Trumbull or myself. —We shall always feel deeply interested for the Fate of a Man, over whose early life we watched with so much care

Mrs. Trumbull joins me in wishing Health & prosperity to your Wife and yourself—& I am your *real* friend

A year passed. The correspondence is spotty. On 6 September 1818 Trumbull, professing to be his son's "Real Friend," wrote to him in anger informing his "nephew" of the circumstances of his birth:

I have just received your letter dated the 17th of July, in which you say you have written ten Letters to us, since we left London. We have received one announcing your plan of going to India:—One dated Calcutta 10th Nov. 1816.—One August 13th 1817, to notify your Marriage.—One Dec. 6th 1817 to mention the birth of a daughter:—and this last.—

In this letter, you for the first time address me as your Father, and Mrs. Trumbull as your mother:—You cannot be ignorant that your Mother was Temperance Ray of East Haddam, a Servant in my brother's house: where the looseness of her Conduct left it uncertain who might be your father; but She swore according to Law, that I was:—I had no remedy, and paid the legal penalty. When I made my addresses to my wife, I thought it proper to make her acquainted with this circumstance; and, with a generosity of which there are few examples, She insisted upon my engaging to give you a good education; as a preliminary condition of consenting to marry me.

You was therefore placed, first under the care of Mr. Wadsworth, afterwards under Mr. John R. Murray:—and in July 1804 when you was twelve years old, Mrs. Trumbull saw you for the first time, at the Revd. Mr. Mitchell's at Canaan in Connecticut.

How then can She be your Mother:—true her kindness to you was constant and unvarying as if you had really been her Son; but how have you repaid it?—Memory will answer that question.

Sir, your Conduct ought to have proved your gratitude for her kindness; a few misapplied words do not go far to efface the remembrance of unkind Actions. And Mrs. Trumbull and I join in requesting that neither you & much less Mrs. Ray, will hereafter speak or write of her as your Mother.

You appear to believe that Mr. Robertson has prejudiced us against your Wife:—You mistake—Mr. Robertson informed me that he endeavored to dissuade you from marrying:—but He has not mentioned the Subject since: *Your Own Letters* certainly have left no favorable impression upon my mind; it appears from them that you cannot have arrived from India sooner than the middle of March:—that you was married about the 16th of May: & that the Child was born the middle of November.—Now as it is only *Eight* Months from the day of your arrival, and only *Six* from your Marriage to the birth of the Child, while the ordinary period of pregnancy is *Nine*, the inference is obvious and unfavorable

But I will say no more on this painful Subject:—You are married:—have a family:—have contracted debts, and want assistance:—all these are natural consequences of the first most imprudent Step, and ought to have been foreseen by you both:—in this Situation it appears that you send your wife to Mr. Williams:—Sir you know that whilst I was last in England, I contracted a heavy debt with Mr. Williams, part of which was expended upon your education, and which is not yet paid:—How can I, how can you request that gentleman to advance another Shilling until He sees this debt in a course of being extinguished. He is not obligated to maintain me, or you.

Mr. Ray, it cost me to take you to England, & to give you the agricultural education which you have utterly neglected & thrown away, more than Five hundred guineas:—You have despised my advice, and you now feel the consequences, yet you seem still to think it proper that a Man of Sixty three should labour to support in contempt of himself (and apparently in idleness) a youth of twenty Six, possessing Health and knowledge. Do not blame me if you begin to feel the consequences of Obstinacy and disobedience:—I cannot assist you in your present trouble: and if I could I do not feel that it would be my duty.

Recollect that the worthy Mr. Mitchel of Canaan supported and educated his Family upon a Salary not equal to your half-pay;—and that many Gentlemen of the Army and Navy contrive to maintain families upon the Same narrow means as yours, aided by their own industry: Why cannot you?

You say that your Wife is to become a Singer on the Stage. Is She then to maintain you by this very uncertain profession?—You should remember that when you married you came under a Solemn obligation to provide for your Family: and so long as you possess health you are bound to fulfil this first of duties. Industry and Prudence, in addition to £75 a year, can surely accomplish it

Though this Letter may appear to you now to be severe, yet, be assured Mr. Ray, you will one day feel that it is the wholesome severity of a

Real Friend

The remainder of the correspondence need concern us only briefly. On 7 January 1823, Ray wrote his father from London:

I hope that Mrs. Trumbull & yourself will pardon my long silence, & hope that the difference which has existed between us, you will compute to folly & heat of youth; I now see my folly; & feel the want of that protection which you formerly extended to me; I sincearly wish that all animosity between us was buried in oblivion.

I am now shipped onboard of the Honle. East India Compy Ship Waterloo, bound to Bombay & China, & have a most excellent prospect before me after this Voyage. . . .

And from London again on 5 March 1827: "I am still in the Scotch Steam Vessells where I have been for this last three years."

To this letter Trumbull replied on 20 May 1827:

. . . it gives me pleasure to learn . . . that you are and have been for the last three years employed . . . I should be glad to know more particularly, your Situation & prospects—is your Wife living —how many Children have you?—what is the department you occupy in the Steam Vessel—does it enable you to Maintain your Family decently—& what prospect have you of rising in your present pursuit, or in the Army.

Altho it is no longer in my power to render you any assistance, I shall always be glad to hear of your success.

For myself—the Debt which I contracted to Mr. Williams (in contradiction to the wishes of Mrs. Trumbull whose prudence forsaw the consequences) has eaten me up. The pictures which I left in his hands have been Sold for about the *tenth* part of what I believed them to be worth—the Land in Genesee for about a *fourth or fifth* part of its real Value . . . Take warning—& avoid Debt— if you Subsist on bread & Cheese—you are young, be industrious— frugal, and upright—& in whatever Situation you may be placed by providence endeavor to Do Your Duty

Almost two years later, on 16 March 1829, we have a final, cheerless letter from Ray to his father:

It is with shame for my long silence that I attempt to address you again . . . I am only employed about Nine Months out of 12; I was last year employed to ship & lend their Goods at Blackwalls . . . As for the Army there is no prospect of any employment . . . Mrs. R. continues to have very bad health & unable to do anything, but thank God my Children are all better provided for in another World.

And so ends the saga of the illegitimate son of the proud Colonel Trumbull.

WHO WAS THE COLONEL'S LADY?

The Strange Case of Mrs. John Trumbull *

One of the most inexplicable acts in the long life of the proud and impulsive Colonel Trumbull was his quiet—one might almost say, secret—marriage to an obscure English girl, which took place at London on the first day of October of the year 1800. The groom, who for the past half-dozen years had been serving as one of the American Commissioners for the adjustment of claims under the Jay Treaty, was forty-four and the bride twenty-six. Much mystery surrounded the identity of the lady at the time; the riddle is yet to be solved. We shall probably never know much about her or the real and hidden motives which precipitated the Colonel's sudden marriage to the socially unacceptable, strikingly beautiful Sarah. Tongues wagged and evil gossip circulated. The motivating forces and essential facts were concealed—and still are. Their secret remains sealed in their tomb.[1]

It appears somewhat indecent to inquire into an affair, of a private nature, which took place a century and a half ago, but for the fact that Trumbull was a public figure. Events, even of the most personal nature, which conditioned his life and his art, are of interest and concern to the historian. One might be excused, therefore, for reviewing the limited evidence which has survived the passage of time, with the hope that truth, so far as it can be ascertained, might replace scandalous hearsay. And this we shall proceed to do.

The Colonel was married at St. Mary's (Church of England), Parish of Hendon (seven miles northwest of London), County of Middlesex. The Parish Register,[2] kept in that ancient stone edifice, for 1800, page 50, discloses:

* Reprinted from *The New-York Historical Society Quarterly*, 36 (October 1952), 410–429.

1. The mortal remains of the pair are contained in a vault in the basement of the Yale University Art Gallery.

2. I am indebted to my colleague, John Marshall Phillips, Director of the Yale University Art Gallery, for visiting St. Mary's, in July 1952, and copying the record of the marriage for me.

Although eight volumes of *Middlesex Parish Registers, Marriages,* have been published (W. P. W. Phillimore and Thomas Gurney, eds., London, Phillimore & Co., 1909–1927), the series is still incomplete and Hendon is not yet included.

4. The artist's English wife, Sarah Hope Harvey Trumbull, painted by her husband. (*Courtesy of Marshall Hill Clyde, Geneva, Switzerland*)

No. 195, John Trumbull of the Parish of Mary le bone County of Middlesex and Sarah Hope Harvey of the Parish of Hendon on the first October 1800 were married by

Ralph Worseley
Officiating Minister

Witness } C. Gore
Eliz^th Halbrook

The dramatis personae, other than the bride and groom, were: the officiating minister, Ralph Worsley,[3] Christopher Gore,[4] of "Gore Place," Waltham, Massachusetts, an old Harvard friend of Trumbull's, then serving as a fellow-member on the Jay Commission; and Elizabeth Halbrook, presumably a friend of the bride. The gossip, William Dunlap, Trumbull's old fellow-student at Benjamin West's, stated that Rufus King[5] of Boston, then United States Minister to Great Britain, another Harvard friend, was also there.[6] So much for the identification of the principals participating in this little drama. The one-eyed miniaturist, Dunlap, noted long after the event:

Rufus King told [Gulian C.] Verplank the well known story of the marriage, the Lady being handed into church (where T[rumbull] with King & [Christopher] Gore were waiting with ye priest) from a Coach which drove off & that after the immediately performed ceremony (King giving the bride to T.) King asked who is this lady I have given to you & was anser'd "Mrs. Trumbull, Sir." The secret has been kept, but Verplank supposes that Rufus King knew who she was.

This he followed by the observation:

In the Trumbull papers (at the Yale Library) there is a "True Extract from the Register of Marriages belonging to the Parish of Hendon certified by C (Charles?) Barton, Hendon, 30 May 1801, or eight months after the wedding.

3. Ralph Worsley (or Worseley—it is spelled both ways), 1766–1848, appears in *The Clerical Guide or, Ecclesiastic Directory . . . of the Church of England . . .* (London: Printed for F. C. and J. Rivington, 1822) as Rector of Finchley, "pop[ula-tion] 1292; Value in the King's Books, £ 20-0-0; Patron, Bp. of London." Trumbull painted his portrait (listed erroneously by him in 1828 as "Ralph Worley") probably at this time. It is now unlocated.

4. 1758–1827.

5. 1755–1827.

6. *Diary of William Dunlap* (New York: The New-York Historical Society, 1930, 3 vols.), for 3 September 1833, III: 738–739.

Trumbull gave to [the miniature painter] Arch^d Robertson [of New York] the maiden name of his wife as Hope, the daughter of Wm Hope of Perthshire. She was born on 1st of Augt near London: died 12th April 1824.[7]

This last statement of the unreliable Dunlap is confirmed by a note in the Colonel's hand at the Yale Library, which reads:

Sarah, youngest daughter of William Hope of Perthshire in Scotland, was born on the 1st of April 1774 in the vicinity of London, was married there on the 1st of October 1800 to John Trumbull of Connecticut, and died in New York on the 12th of April 1824. She left this painful and wearisome life in the humble hope of enjoying through the Divine Mercy of the merits of the blessed Redeemer a happy immortality.

Life, indeed, must have been wearisome, if not desperate, for poor, uneducated Sarah. She had few friends other than her loyal husband. It is curious that when he wrote her he usually addressed her as "my best friend," "my dearest friend," or a combination of the two.[8]

The first member of the family to visit the newly-weds was a sixteen-year-old nephew, John M. Trumbull, who reported to his family:

I found Mr. Trumbull in the City at his house in Welbeck Street 72, he was very glad to see me and rec'd me as a Nephew, his Lady is a fine woman, he lives in very handsome style for London and Elegant for America, he has a house in the City and at Hammersmith keeps his Coach & servants in proportion. London a large City and Noble in its structure, but in beauty nothing to New York the buildings are very rusty with the smoke of the coles used here. I should prefer the American Cities to London. Mrs. Trumbull has neither Father, Mother, Sister, Brother, Uncle, Aunt, and may almost say Friend but her husband here. I have not yet found her name before married. Will inform you when I do. Be so good as to Excuse errors as I am in a strange place, surrounded by hundreds of People.[9]

7. *Ibid.* for 12 October 1834, III: 828.

8. There are many such letters, mostly written during the year 1819 from Washington, Baltimore, and Philadelphia, preserved at the Library of Congress.

9. Letter to Solomon Williams, dated 1 May 1801, in the possession of Col. Ralph H. Isham of New York, a Trumbull descendant. The writer was the second son of David Trumbull of Norwich, Connecticut. The Colonel, who was able to attract but

Nearly a year after the marriage John wrote his brother, Jonathan Trumbull, from London on 1 May 1801:

. . . In this Country the Education of the Female Sex is said to be highly improved . . . I cannot say, however, that I think the time spent in acquiring this perfection [in music] is well spent . . . [it being rather] a waste of time & trouble upon the accomplishment, which is elegant . . . [with] the more solid acquirements neglected. The Education of Mrs. T. I am happy was not of the fashionable kind: the Orphan daughter of Parents in middle life. She lost her mother at a very early time, before She remembers, and remained for several years in the Country under the Care of a good notable Woman, who regarded reading, writing & Housewifery, as the essentials of Female education. At 15 or 16, she came to Town & spent some years in the Family of a considerable Merch^t. whose wife had been the intimate friend of her mother. Here also, the business of the Family & Economy were regarded as the principal objects of attention. By this means, while she has read as much as most women, She has acquired knowledge of other kinds here little attended to: there are few things relating to the House in Town or Country which She does not pretty well know & no article of her own dress, except Shoes, which she cannot & does not make. Her Parents, as I said, died when she was young; one sister she had who died when she was an infant, and the only brother she lost a few years later: thus She has no near relations living, of her blood: and in this Country still more than ours, other ties are feeble. No attachments therefore bind her strongly here and when the time arrives for leaving this country, I trust she will leave it with little regret, & soon become a good American. You will not therefore expect to see a modern fine Lady.[10]

This gives something of a picture but little explanation of the lady's identity or how long John had known her before his third journey to London (in 1794) in company with John Jay.

few British sitters at this time, painted a portrait of his nephew during the visit (now the property of Colonel Isham).

For further family gossip see George Dudley Seymour, "Colonel John Trumbull and his well-kept Secret" in New Haven (New Haven: Privately Printed for the Author, 1942), 248–249.

10. Ms., Yale Library.

In the Trumbull papers at Yale there is a note that Sarah Harvey lived at Clitter House in Hendon, county of Middlesex, prior to 1 October 1799, in part of an eighteen-room house, with stable, belonging to one John Fisher at 3 Glocester Place, London, from that date, for exactly a year, to the date of the nuptials. Possibly Trumbull paid the £90 rent. The quarterly payments, signed by J. W. Fisher, are noted as "received from Mrs. Hervey." (Hervey and Harvey were often used interchangeably, in this period of many variations of spelling.) But we have it from her husband that her maiden name was Sarah *Hope*.[11] It is possible that she was married to an unidentifiable gentleman named *Harvey*.[12] That her last name at the time of her marriage was Harvey is so stated on the certificate above mentioned. Two days before her second (?) marriage Trumbull rented a furnished house in lower Mall, Hammersmith, from one John Edward Waring. Of the lady's four names, Sarah Hope Harvey Trumbull, there can be no dispute.

Dunlap states, at second hand: "That unhappy Woman, Trumbull's Wife, he [Verplanck] says, there is reason to believe was the illegitimate daughter of Lord Thurlow, who had several children of this description, took no special care of them but left them an annuity of 300 a year for life."[13] As to Lord Thurlow, the *Dictionary of National Biography* has it: "In consequence of an early disappointment, Thurlow, had not married. . . . By his mistress, Mrs. Hervey . . . to whom he was much attached, he had several children, for whom he provided."[14] There are several references to this in the *Gentleman's Magazine*: "His Lordship has left three daughters; two of whom are married."[15] Again: "His Lordship was never married, but has left issue three daughters; to two of whom he has bequeathed 70,000£ each. To the third (Mrs. Brown), who married against his consent . . . he has bequeathed only 50£. . . . He has also left to Mrs. Hervey an annuity of 1,000£."[16] And again: ". . . Thurlow, then idling in the coffee-room or toying with Miss Hervey in the bar . . ."[17]

To complicate the picture further: "He [Lord Thurlow] subsequently

11. Letter 16 July 1803 to William Williams, New-York Historical Society.
12. There are no (published) records of such a marriage having taken place in the Counties of Middlesex or Kent for this period.
13. *Diary, op. cit.*, for 3 September 1833. III: 738.
14. LVI: 384. Edward Thurlow, c. 1730–1806, Baron of Thurlow and of Ashfield, was Lord Chancellor—with one short interruption—from 1778 to 1792.
15. 1806, II: 882.
16. *Ibid.*, 975.
17. *Ibid.*, 974.

transferred his affections to a lady of extraordinary beauty and of an honourable family, by whom he had several daughters. To this connection the Duchess of Kingston imprudently ventured to advert by observing that she could relate 'a Canterbury tale,' " [18] and: "The ecclesiastical Court are come to a resolution that the Duchess of Kingston is Mrs. Hervey; and the sentence will be public in a fortnight." [19]

One can speculate on whether Mrs. Hervey, Duchess of Kingston and alleged mistress of Lord Thurlow, was the mother of the beautiful Sarah Trumbull and responsible for her maiden name of Hervey.[20] The record of this lady's famous trial for bigamy before the House of Lords, occupying nearly three hundred closely printed pages, affords an interesting insight of eighteenth-century morals and manners.[21] Perhaps, after all, Verplanck was correct in believing her to be an illegitimate daughter of Lord Thurlow. On the other hand, if Mrs. Hervey received an annuity of £1,000 in 1806, *that* Mrs. Hervey could not have been the Duchess of Kingston, who died in 1788. Her first husband might possibly have had an illegitimate daughter by a Miss or Mrs. Hope. This would account for Mrs. Trumbull's names of Hope Harvey, and also for the confusion of her mother with the Duchess—but all of this, in the absence of any proof, must remain in the realm of pure conjecture.

The New-York Historical Society, of which Trumbull was long a member and Vice President, in 1843, the year of the Colonel's death, stated that:

There has always hung a mystery over this marriage, and the

18. *Memoires of Sir Nathanial William Wraxall, 1772–1784,* Henry B. Wheatley (ed.), 5 vols. (London: Bickers & Son, 1884), I: 412.

19. *An 18th Century Journal,* John Hampden (compiler) (London: Macmillan, 1940), 116. The reference should have been to the House of Lords instead of to the Ecclesiastical Court.

20. One becomes quickly lost in a maze of illegitmacy. Of Augustus John Hervey, 3rd Earl of Bristol, 1724–1779, Lord of the Admiralty, 1771–1775, the *Encyclopaedia Britannica* (11th ed., IV: 575) states: "In . . . 1744 he had been secretly married to Elizabeth Chudleigh . . . afterwards duchess of Kingston, but this union was dissolved in 1769. The earl died . . . [in] 1779, leaving no legitimate issue. . . ." And again (XV: 822), for Evelyn Pierrepont, Duke of Kingston, 1711–1773: he "was chiefly famous for his connection with Elizabeth Chudleigh, who claimed to be duchess of Kingston. . . ."

21. T. B. Howell, Esq., *A Complete Collection of State Trials and Proceedings for High Treason and Other Crimes and Misdemeanors* . . . (London: for Longman. . . . 1816), XX: 355–651, entitled: "551. The Trial of Elizabeth, calling herself Duchess Dowager of Kingston, for Bigamy, before the Right Hon. the House of Peers, in Westminster-Hall, in full Parliament assembled, . . . Days of April: 16 GEORGE III, A.D. 1776."

family of the lady, which, perhaps the yet unopened papers of Colonel Trumbull may solve. The late governor de Witt Clinton once told us that he believed she was a natural daughter of Lord Thurlow. But no matter; and it is probably enough to say that she was the idol supremely throned in the heart of her husband. She died in this city in the year 1824; and never was a wife more sincerely or deeply mourned by her husband, than she was, down to the last week of his life, by her surviving partner.[22]

To turn, once more, to Dunlap, who relished a good story and heartily disliked Trumbull, we learn:

J. [James] F. [Fenimore] Cooper called on me. He gave me the most rational account of Trumbulls mysterious marriage that I have heard. He says that 7 or 8 years ago, he dined in a company of Gentlemen among whom was my former (perhaps my present) friend Wm Johnson & an English Gentleman. The latter when it happen'd that Trumbull & wife were the subjects of conversation, told this story. There was an old gentleman, formerly a military man, Col¹ or Gen¹ Williams, who had a young Wife, with whom Trumbull became too intimate. Finally Williams had intimation that the lovers intended to elope, either *that,* or knowledge of the shame inflicted on him, induced him to have an interview with the seducer of his wife for a settlement. He told him that he knew of his situation with Mrs. W. & her preference, that he wished to avoid public scandal; and therefore, offered Trumbull the lady & 800£ per year during her life, if he would take her, & to save appearances, marry her. This was accordingly done. Mr. Johnson afterwards said to Cooper, this is a strange story and it reminds me of a circumstance confirmatory. Walking in Company with my Wife Mr. & Mrs. Trumbull & an English gentleman & lady, the latter preceded him & Mrs. Johnson & Mrs Trumbull. Trumbull was with the English folks, & they were talking of acquaintances in London. Suddenly Trumbull looked back & said "Do you hear that Mrs. W.?" and correcting himself added "Mrs. Trumbull." It has often been suggested that Trumbull received this woman from her keeper with an annuity. This is something like it & more probable.[23]

22. *NYHS Proceedings 1843,* 120.
23. *Diary,* for 4 July 1834, III: 800–801. This possibly refers to Gen. Henry Williams, *ca.* 1765–1845, as, according to the Army Lists, no other Williams reached a rank higher than that of lieutenant colonel from 1790 to 1800. This Williams was

This dinner-party conversation was recorded by the far-from-reliable historian, artist, and dramatist thirty-four years after the marriage in question. But, in all fairness to Dunlap, it should be remembered that his private *Diary* was not written for publication. In his *Arts of Design* he observed: "There is every reason to suppose that Mr. Trumbull meant to make England his home. His wife was an Englishwoman, and his only son an officer in the English army; but Mr. Trumbull returned to the United States, bringing Mrs. Trumbull with him, in June 1804." [24] There is not even a hint in this of the illegitimacy of the Colonel's son, John Trumbull Ray. As to Williams and "Mrs. W." Dunlap might have been confused. Before he left England Trumbull wrote to his brother-in-law, William Williams of Lebanon, a Signer of the Declaration of Independence, on 16 July 1803:

> I shall have the pleasure of shewing you your new Sister whose Portrait you are pleased with. . . . Her maiden name was *Hope.* Her Father was a younger son of an old Scotch Family, but Her Mother an English woman of the name of *West;* both her Parents are long since dead, as well as all her near relatives; so that she has no reluctance to go to America, arising from family separation, which I consider as a very happy circumstance. I hope She will find in my Relations a substitute for those of her own Blood—unfortunately we have no appearance of any addition to our Family. [25]

It is remotely possible that Dunlap's "W" came from the name West. Let us be charitable.

Shortly after landing, Trumbull received a letter from his old friend, Gen. David Humphreys, written from Boston on 14 July 1804:

> I congratulate you sincerely on your return to your native land, and hope Mrs. Trumbull will find her adopted Country in every respect grateful & agreeable to her. In the wish for both of your happiness Mrs. Humphreys unites with me, being particularly desirous of forming & cultivating an acquaintance. . . . Do you remember the last evening which we spent together (at Havre in France) & some

---

major and lieutenant colonel in 1794, colonel 1800, major general 1808, lieutenant general 1813, and general 1830. The General's residence, at the time of his death, was at Chalk Farm, near Bromley, Kent, about seven miles from London. Little credence should be given this account.

24. *Arts of Design*, II: 49.
25. Ms., New-York Historical Society.

of the topics on which we then conversed? They are present to my mind, as if the affair of yesterday.[26]

The Trumbull family called on the couple shortly after they were settled. Mrs. Henry Hudson wrote her mother, the Colonel's sister-in-law, Mrs. Jonathan Trumbull, Junior, from New York on 4 November 1804:

> We called immediately on our arrival yesterday to see Uncle and Aunt Trumbull, they are hardly settled yet but appeared very glad to see us, their house is already in tolerable order and looks very well. Uncle has painted one picture and says they have both been extremely busy. Aunt really shows to great advantage in her own house—she is in excellent humour and spirits, treats us with a vast deal of affection and offered of her own accord to assist me to the best of her abilities in all the purchases I wished to make. . . . They insisted upon our taking tea with them yesterday and we have dined there again today.[27]

All did not go well for the super-sensitive colonel and the uneducated, mysterious Sarah during their four-year stay in America. There was some sort of *contretemps* with the Daniel Wadsworths of Hartford. The Colonel wrote to his niece, Mrs. Wadsworth,[28] from New York on 13 December 1806, a letter which, though petty, gives some indication of the new strained feelings then existing in the immediate family circle:

> I enclose to my niece, a Letter from my Wife, of which I have only to say that it is written by my advice, & with my approbation.
> You must permit me to add a few words for myself, on the same Subject.
> I married at the age of Forty-five, in a Country where I had resided Twenty years—where of course I knew & was known—at a moment when from my official situation, *Indiscretion* in my conduct must have produced a termination of the Business with which I was charged, very different from the amicable & honorable one which took place.—under these circumstances I really thought myself capable of choosing a wife, and felt under no obligation to consult any one, on a subject which interested me alone—unless anyone could feel a mercenary interest in the change of my condition,

26. Ms., Boston Public Library.
27. Letter in the possession of Miss Maria Trumbull Dana of New Haven.
28. Faith Trumbull, eldest daughter of Jonathan Trumbull Junior.

which, had I believed, would have exposed them to my contempt.

I had been in the habit of considering myself a favorite with some branches of the Family, on a friendly footing with all, and the hope of enjoying increased satisfaction in their Society was one great motive which determined me to return to this Country. I trusted to the multiplied assurances of undiminished Esteem, which were in my possession, that the woman of my choice, my best friend, my Wife, would have been received affectionately for my sake. I flattered her with high hopes on that subject & consoled her in parting from her country & friends, with the prospect of finding as delightful a Country, & friends as cordial as those whom She was to leave behind. I have not been altogether disappointed in my hopes. Yet, I cannot say that I found in Boston particularly where I thought I had most reason to expect it, that cordiality of reception either for my wife or myself that I had hoped:—some other little things occurred early, which were painful, but which I thought it wise to overlook. . . .

When at the Altar, & in the presence of the Almighty I promised to love & protect the woman of my choice, I felt the Solemnity of the engagements—the coldness of friends is one of the contingencies which peculiarly claim the fulfillment of that sacred promise—and I shall fulfill it—I know her Virtues and I reverence them, and should the absurdity, the pride or the caprice of others render it necessary, I can obey the Command which requires a husband to leave Parents & Friends, & cleave to his Wife.

Far be it from us however to suffer our feelings to mislead us:— as we never have, so we never will intentionally either injure or insult your Husband or yourself. We shall always remember with pleasure the kindness of Mrs. Wadsworth [29] & Mrs. Terry,[30] but we cannot forget the unkindness of those whom we thought our friends.[31]

The turn of events is further illustrated by a letter from Jonathan Trumbull, Junior, to his brother John, dated 25 January 1808:

. . . you will suffer me to observe that I was grieved to notice the State of Mind with which you express yourself respecting the recep-

29. Mrs. Jeremiah (Mehitable Russell) Wadsworth.
30. Mrs. Nathaniel (Catherine Wadsworth) Terry, daughter of Jeremiah and sister of Daniel Wadsworth.
31. Ms., Yale Library.

tion you have met among your Relatives and friends since your last
return from Europe, and the Estimation in which you seem to think
you are now held by them. . . . Since your last return to them you
have not viewed your friends with the same cheerful Eyes you used
to do. . . . I do not wish to cherish disagreeable subjects, nor to
enter into details of imaginary Injuries, or unfounded Jealous-
ies. . . .[32]

In 1808, while living in New York, Trumbull tried, through his friend,
DeWitt Clinton, to obtain nationalization papers for his wife, "Sarah
Trumbull," from the State Legislature, saying that she had been a resident of the State for nearly five years.[33] Trumbull wrote to John Cotton
Smith from London [34] asking that a special bill be passed for Sarah's
citizenship because his lands in the Genesee could not be willed to her
if an alien. No notice of the first request was taken in the session for
1809; in that of 1810 it was rejected. Trumbull excused the near-treason-
able action of his American-born, illegitimate son, John Trumbull Ray,
in joining the British Army during the War of 1812, by the treatment
that the boy's "aunt" had received by the New York State legislature.

The four-year New York experiment came to a close late in 1808. The
Jeffersonian Embargo and the general business depression were the
possible causes for the lack of the many hoped-for portrait commissions
—though the Colonel was far from idle. His wife was certainly anything
but a help in securing desired sitters. Rufus King wrote to George Ham-
mond, who had served as British Peace Commissioner, from New York
on 12 December 1808:

Col. Trumbull, whom you will probably recollect, is the bearer of
this letter; he is going with his wife to England and may there resume his profession. Having lived in friendship with this gentleman
for a great many years, I can with confidence introduce him to you,
as a gentleman of distinguished probity and honour. Going directly
from hence, he is enabled to speak with knowledge concerning the
course and condition of our affairs as connected with those of Europe.[35]

32. Ms., Connecticut State Library, Hartford.
33. See letter dated 14 December 1808, Yale Library and p. 341.
34. Ms., Yale Library.
35. *Life and Correspondence of Rufus King*, Charles R. King (ed.), 6 vols. (New
York: G. P. Putnam's Sons, 1894–1900), V: 123.

How things were going for him in England, so far as his family relations were concerned, is indicated in a letter from the Colonel to Jabez Huntington of Norwich, Connecticut, dated London, 10 July 1812: "The Silence of every branch of my family for nearly four years (except one short letter from my brother) leaves me to suppose that I am quite excommunicated by them." [36]

Time must have hung heavily on the Colonel. Portrait commissions, naturally, did not fall his way during this period of strained international relations, resulting in the War of 1812. The ex-rebel officer found himself a second time in the camp of the enemy during wartime. Official permission was requested—the enemy-alien had to report his movements to the government—and received, to quit London for the pleasant surroundings of Bath. There the artist painted a few landscapes and a portrait of a new friend, James Hewlett (1789–1836), the eminent floral painter. The socially isolated Sarah probably took lessons of this celebrated artist, for some years later, in America, she exhibited several "fruit and flower" pictures. [37]

To make up for the dearth of commissions the restless, officially restrained colonel painted his wife's portrait and even posed for himself. [38] He painted his wife somewhat in the spirit of a Lady Hamilton portrait, as "Sensitivity" and "Innocence." [39] In desperation he even copied portraits after the Old Masters. [40] Some of Trumbull's dullest religious and literary compositions, too, date from this period. [41] His beautiful wife was a handy model.

36. Ms., New-York Historical Society.

37. At the American Academy of the Fine Arts, New York, of which her husband was President; in 1816, No. 165, and 1817, No. 205; and at the 7th Annual Exhibition of the Pennsylvania Academy of the Fine Arts, Philadelphia, in 1818, No. 190. The Colonel's friend, Thomas Sully, was instrumental in arranging the latter; see his letter to Trumbull of 12 May 1818 at the Bland Gallery, Inc., New York.

38. This handsome pair of portraits are the property of Marshall Hill Clyde of Geneva, Switzerland. See Jean Brockway, "Portrait of an Artist's Wife: Mrs. John Trumbull," Antiques, XXXIV, November 1938, pp. 250–252.

39. The first is the property of Miss Marion Cruger Coffin of New Haven, and the second is at Yale. In all he painted his wife at least a dozen times.

40. Such as the "Gervartius" after Sir Anthony Van Dyck, now at The New-York Historical Society, and the "Duchess of Cleveland" after Sir Peter Lely, now lost.

41. "Susannah and the Elders" (now lost) painted at this time, must have appealed to him as subject matter. "Now Susanna was a very delicate woman and beauteous to behold" (Apocrypha, History of Susanna, 31), as was Sarah, his wife. It is somewhat amusing, in the light of all of the gossip which existed about Sarah's

America to the exiled couple must have looked increasingly attractive. The Colonel sounded out his old friend, Rufus King, as to the possible reception of his wife. That statesman wrote him on 25 December 1812:

> . . . I am quite sure, that both you and Mrs. Trumbull would be kindly received by all your former acquaintances, and I cannot avoid remarking, that you will ascribe greater importance to that incident than it really merits, should you be restrained by it, from revisiting your old and faithful friends in this Country.[42]

Still it was a long time before official permission to quit England was received. The Trumbulls took the first passage available. They sailed on board the "Illinois, Captain Noyes" on the 18th of August 1815, with a vast amount of luggage—21 trunks, 9 boxes, and 4 crates—leaving England forever.

Settled, once again, at New York, Sarah, poor lonely girl, respected and loved by few other than her husband, became a dipsomaniac. Such are typical records: "Mrs. Col. Trumbull was at one of the assemblies. She was irregularly dressed and looked like a washwoman. She was so drunk at Mrs. Primes party that they were obliged to carry her home." [43]

Scattered through the Rufus King–Christopher Gore correspondence there are many references to the unhappy Sarah. King, describing a ball given by the French Ambassador, wrote his friend on 19 February 1817:

> After standing and walking from room to room till I was tired, I saw a vacant chair in a corner, where I placed myself next to Monsr. Correa, the Portuguese Minister. We were engaged in conversation when of a sudden I observed Col. & Mrs. T[rumbull] coming towards me. When near she quitted her husband's arm, and sallying

---

past, that he used her for the woman in "Christ and the Woman taken in Adultery" (John 8:3–12). This large, dull canvas is now at Yale with many other religious works by the biblically trained and Bible-reading artist.

42. Ms., New-York Historical Society.

43. Letter from Edward Fenno, son of John Fenno, the proprietor and editor of the *Gazette of the United States,* to his sister, Eliza Fenno (Mrs. Gulian Crommelin Verplanck, wife of the Colonel's friend), dated New York, 14 February 1816. I am indebted to William C. Kiessel of Bergenfield, N.J., who is engaged in writing the life of John Fenno, 1751–1798, for permission to quote from this letter, and to Dr. J. Hall Pleasants of Baltimore who brought it to my attention.

towards me, almost tumbled into my arms, but by good fortune brought up on an empty chair on my right. . . .[44]

At New Haven the same story was repeated. Mrs. Benjamin Silliman wrote to her sister Faith (Mrs. Daniel Wadsworth of Hartford) on 15 August 1823: we "took a carriage and called at Uncle Trumbull's. . . . I was received with great kindness by Uncle, and treated by his wife in her best manner, tho she looked very bad and had evidently been indulging too much."[45] The same unfortunate circumstances were reported by Margaret Fuller:

> . . . before they entered the dining room they met an old friend, Colonel Trumbull, whom they naturally invited to sup with them. The Colonel hesitatingly informed them that he was married and of course they invited his wife as well. Mrs. Trumbull's appearance accounted for her husband's hesitation. Her coarse and imperious expression reflected her low habits of mind, and her exaggerated dress and gesture betrayed her lack of education. At dinner Mrs. Trumbull drank glass after glass of wine and became abusive. Colonel Trumbull asked his host to forgive him. He had married, he explained, to atone for a sin.[46]

Poor Sarah had at least two good friends, Mrs. Rufus (Mary Alsop) King, and her husband. When Mrs. King died the Colonel wrote on 5 June 1819: "To Mrs. Trumbull in particular her kindness was uniform and invaluable, and her regret for the loss of her first and best American friend will be deep and lasting."[47]

Only once, so far as this writer knows, did the Colonel complain about his wife, who, for obvious reasons, was kept quietly at home as much as possible. From London on 2 June 1810 he wrote to his intimate, Rufus King, about the "Idiocy, as well as wickedness of [certain] Federalists" and his momentary expectation of "the confiscation of all American property" by Bonaparte. "I fear no remedy but the blood-letting and Straight waistcoat of Despotism." In a fit of spleen he closed his letter with these words: "I am disgusted, my friend, sick of my Country, *Sick of my Family*, sick of Human Nature. My poor, banished, persecuted,

44. *The Life and Correspondence of Rufus King, op. cit.*, VI: 57–59.
45. Letter in the possession of Miss Maria Trumbull Dana.
46. Madeleine Bettina Stern, *The Life of Margaret Fuller* (New York: E. P. Dutton & Co., Inc., 1942), 273.
47. Rufus King Papers, New-York Historical Society.

insulted *ill tempered* Wife (curse the Scoundrel) joins in wishing health & happiness to you & yours." [48]

Marriage has been characterized as "a state of silent desperation." Perhaps it was in this case. "In any human association," wrote Professor Keller of Yale, "there is sure to be an interest-conflict more or less successfully reduced to the harmony of antagonistic cooperation." [49]

Mrs. Trumbull died at New York on 12 April 1824. Her husband painted her on her death bed! [50] The attending physician was the Colonel's old friend, Dr. David Hosack,[51] the chief backer of the American Academy of the Fine Arts, of which Trumbull was President for nineteen long years.[52] Another old friend, the Rev. Jonathan Mayhew Wainwright,[53] was the clergyman. A note [54] in the Colonel's hand gives the pallbearers as: "Peter Lanman, Mr. Charles Wilkes, Mr. Moses Rogers, Mr. Buchanan, the British Consul, Mr. I. B. Coles, and Mr. Theodore Dwight. Mr. Bronson and Benj. Huntington, if either of the above named gentlemen should not have it in his power to attend I could wish Mr. C. D. Colden and Col. Fish." [55] Ten years later her body was removed by her husband to a vault prepared under his direction beneath the Trum-

48. *Ibid.*

49. A. G. Keller, *Man's Rough Road* (New York and New Haven: Frederick A. Stokes Co., Yale University Press, 1932), 321.

50. The property of Joseph Lanman Richards of New London, Conn. See Sizer, *Works of . . . Trumbull*, plate 29. Besides the many portraits by her husband there is a miniature by the Colonel's friend, Elkanah Tisdale of Lebanon, Conn., painted at New York in the 1820's, owned by the Misses Trumbull of Norwich Town, Conn.

51. 1769–1835. His portrait by Trumbull, painted at New York in 1806, hangs in the New York Hospital, of which Dr. Hosack was Attending Physician.

52. See Sizer, "American Academy of the Fine Arts" in *American Academy of Fine Arts and American Art-Union, . . .* I: xvii–cviii.

53. 1792–1854, Episcopal minister and later bishop. Trumbull's portrait of him, painted at this time, is at the New Britain Institute, New Britain, Conn.

54. Ms., Yale Library.

55. Peter Lanman, 1771–1854, merchant of Norwich, Conn., husband of Abigail Trumbull, the daughter of David Trumbull, the artist's brother.

Charles Wilkes, *ca.* 1764–1833, President of the Bank of New York and a member and supporter of the American Academy of the Fine Arts.

Moses Rogers, 1750–1825, was a New York merchant. His portrait, painted by Trumbull in 1806, belongs to Mrs. H. Schuyler Cammann of Syosset, Long Island, N.Y.

James Buchanan, 1772–1851, British Consul at New York, instrumental (in 1821) in the removal of Major André's remains from the scene of his hanging at Tappan, N.Y., to Westminster Abbey.

John Butler Coles, 1760–1827, a New York merchant. Trumbull painted his portrait, now owned by John Knapp Hollins of Beaufort, S.C., about 1816.

bull Gallery at Yale College. It has been twice moved since and now lies—permanently, it is to be hoped—beside that of her devoted husband, "at the feet of his master," below his great portrait of Washington. May her soul rest in peace.

THE PERFECT PENDANT
Major André and Colonel Trumbull °

Every schoolboy is familiar with the hangings of two celebrated spies; of the sober-minded schoolteacher, Nathan Hale,[1] who gave his "one" life in 1776, and that of the gay and endearing Major John André, Adjutant General of His Majesty's forces in America. The latter took place at Tappan, New York, on October 2, 1780.[2] This sad tragedy is strangely linked with the life of a Connecticut Yankee.

Probably Theodore Dwight, Senior, 1764–1846, lawyer, editor, and author, brother of the Rev. Timothy Dwight, President of Yale College.

Isaac I. Bronson, *ca.* 1759–1838, office 34 Wall St., residence 12 Park Place.

Benjamin Huntington, 1777–1850, son of Gen. Jedediah Huntington of Norwich, Conn. (whom Trumbull painted *ca.* 1790) and Faith Trumbull, the artist's sister. Benjamin Huntington married Faith Trumbull Huntington; their son, Daniel Huntington, 1816–1906, was the portrait painter.

Cadwallader David Colden, 1769–1834, lawyer, former Mayor of New York, Director of the American Academy of the Fine Arts.

Col. Nicholas Fish, 1758–1833. Revolutionary officer, prominent citizen, resident of New York.

The *New-York American* for Monday Evening, 12 April 1824, carried the notice (undoubtedly written by the colonel himself) under "Deaths": "This morning, in the humble hope of a happy immortality, through the merits of the blessed redeemer, Sarah, wife of Col. John Trumbull, in the 51st year of her age. 'Blessed are the dead, who die in the Lord, for they rest from their Labours.' The friends of the family are requested to attend the funeral from No. 27 Park-Place, at 5 o'clock to-morrow afternoon." This was followed on the next day, Tuesday: "In announcing yesterday the death of Mrs. Trumbull, an error occurred, as [to] the day of interment. The funeral will take place *to-morrow*, Wednesday, at 5 o'clock, instead of to-day as announced by mistake." *The New-York Evening Post* for 12 April carried the same notice, except for "the funeral . . . on Wednesday afternoon."

The funeral costs amounted to $40.

° Reprinted from *The New-York Historical Society Quarterly*, 35 (October 1951), 400–404.

1. Of South Coventry, Connecticut. Hale graduated from Yale in 1773, Trumbull from Harvard the same year.

2. Described in gruesome detail by Winthrop Sargent, *The Life and Career of Major John André* (Boston: Ticknor and Fields, 1861), of which only seventy-five copies were printed.

In the midst of the Revolution the highly emotional John Trumbull, aged twenty-one, resigned his commission as a colonel in the Continental Army in high dudgeon. In July 1780 the "patriot-artist," to use a posthumous complimentary title,[3] was comfortably ensconced in London . . . He records . . . that [when] ". . . news arrived in London of . . . the death of Major André. . . . The deputy adjutant general of the British army, and I a deputy adjutant general in the American, and it seemed to them that I should make a perfect *pendant*." . . .[4]

André had been buried close to the scene of his execution. Forty-one years later "the Duke of York, Commander of the Forces . . . decided to remove André's corpse to England. The Rev. Mr. Demarat who now owned the ground, gave ready assent to the (British) consul's proposal," we learn from Winthrop Sargent.[5] That romantic author tells us that the work of exhumation took place on 10 August 1821, at eleven A.M. *The Annual Register*[6] describes the procedure as follows:

MAJOR ANDRÉ—The following account of the disinterment of the remains of Major André is taken from a New York paper of 14th August:—

This event took place at Tappan, on Friday the 10th inst. The British consul, with several gentlemen, accompanied by the proprietor of the ground and his labourer, commenced their operations at eleven o'clock, by removing the heap of loose stones that surrounded and partly covered the grave. Great caution was observed in taking up a small peach-tree that was growing out of the grave, as the consul stated his intention of sending it to His Majesty to be placed in one of the royal gardens. Considerable anxiety was felt, lest the coffin should not be found, as various rumours existed of its having been removed many years ago. However, when at the depth of three feet, the labourers came to it. The lid being broken, the centre had partly fallen in, and was kept up by resting on the skull. The lid being raised, the skeleton of the brave André appeared entire, with some small locks of hair. A leather thong was all that remained of his dress. As soon as the curiosity of the spectators was gratified, a large circle was formed, when the undertaker, with his assistant, uncovered the sarcophagus, into which the remains were

3. Often employed: given to him by Professor Benjamin Silliman of Yale, at the suggestion of his son, another Professor Benjamin Silliman.
4. The italics are Trumbull's.
5. *Op. cit.*, 408–409. Mr. Buchanan was the British Counsul at New York.
6. *Annual Register of the Year 1821* (London: 1822), 133.

carefully removed. This superb depository, in imitation of those used in Europe for the remains of the illustrious dead, was made of mahogany; the panels were covered with rich velvet, surrounded by a gold bordering: the rings were of deep burnished gold, and the inside was lined with black velvet: the whole was supported by four gilt balls.

The sarcophagus with the remains have been removed on board his Majesty's packet, where it is understood, as soon as some repairs on board are completed, an opportunity will be afforded of viewing it.

A week later John Pintard wrote his daughter from New York:

Sat^y [August] 18th. Yesterday at noon I rec^d an invitation from Mr Buchanan to accompany him at 1 o'clock on b^d the British packet to see the sarcophagus containing the remains of the unfortunate André, of w^h circumstance I made the following memo, on the back of the Consuls note, as soon as I returned[:]

Augt 17. Attended Ja[mes] Buchannan Esq. British Consul, on b^d the B. packet a[t] 1 o'clock, with several gentlemen . . . The Revd Mr Demarest of Tappan, to whose ca[re] the remains of Major André were intrusted, was of the party. [The sarcophagus] in the shape of a Ladies work case about 2 feet high & 1½ wide [MS. torn] designe[d by] Col. Trumbull [& executed by] Mr Eggle [so] . . .[7]

Pintard, a keen observer, must have known all about the authorship of the design for the little mahogany casket, the "superb depository, in imitation of those used in Europe for the remains of the illustrious dead." He and the "patriot-artist" had long been friends and associates. They had both been fellow officers of the American Academy of the Fine Arts. Pintard, the founder (in 1804) of The New-York Historical Society, had been painted by the colonel in 1817 for the Society.

Sargent gives the name of the British frigate as the *Phaeton* and tells of the reburial in Westminster Abbey:

In the south aisle of the Abbey wherein sleeps so much of the greatness and the glory of England stands André's monument. It is of statuary marble carved by (P. M.) Van Gelder. It presents a sarcophagus on a moulded panelled base and plinth; the panel of which is thus inscribed: "Sacred to the memory of Major John

7. *Letters from John Pintard to His Daughter, 1816–1833*, 4 vols. (New York: New-York Historical Society, 1940), II, 75.

André, who, raised of his merits, at an early period of life, to the rank of Adjutant-General of the British forces in America, and, employed in an important but hazardous enterprise, fell a sacrifice to his zeal for his King and Country, on the 2nd of October, 1780, aged twenty-nine, universally beloved and esteemed by the army in which he served, and lamented even by his foes. His gracious Sovereign, King George III, has caused this monument to be erected."

On the plinth these words are added: "The remains of Major John André were, on the 10th of August, 1821, removed from Tappan by James Buchannan, Esq., his Majesty's consul at New York, under instructions from his Royal Highness the Duke of York, and with permission of the Dean and Chapter, finally deposited in a grave contiguous to this monument, on the 28th of November, 1821." [8]

Presumably the little casket designed by Colonel Trumbull was sealed in the Abbey wall.

These two combatants in our War of Independence were alike in another respect. Both could draw prettily. On the morning of his execution André made a charming pen-and-ink self-portrait.[9] Even a posthumous parallel can be made. There was, to use 18th-century phraseology, a "translation of the relics" in both cases: André's remains were removed from Tappan to the Abbey and Trumbull's from beneath the "Trumbull Gallery" at Yale . . . What a curious set of relations existed between André and Trumbull, between these two men who never met! They were, as Trumbull said, *perfect pendants.*

TRUMBULL'S LIST OF AMERICAN HISTORICAL PAINTERS [*]

Among the Trumbull papers at the Yale Library there is a draft of a letter from the painter, Col. John Trumbull, Harvard B.A. 1773, to the statesman, Edward Everett, Harvard B.A. 1811, five times Congressman from Massachusetts, later President of Harvard, remembered today as the orator who preceded Lincoln at Gettysburg. This unpublished letter, written when the painter was seventy-one, was prompted by the criticism, in and outside of Congress, of the four large, heavy-handed paint-

8. *Op. cit.*, 411.

9. See *Yale University Portrait Index, 1701–1951* (New Haven: Yale University Press, 1951), 4; also referred to in the *Dictionary of National Biography* (London and New York: 1885), I, 398.

* Reprinted from the *Yale University Library Gazette*, Vol. 26 (April 1952).

ings, which the aged artist had finished in 1824 and which had been installed in the Rotunda of the rebuilt Capitol shortly after. Trumbull always insisted, like the sensible man he was, in being judged by his peers and not by ignorant politicians, laymen—and even portrait painters. The letter, a just and generous estimate of his contemporaries, is dated Washington, 12 January 1827.

From questions which have been put to me by the Speaker & other gentlemen of Congress, I am led to judge that there prevails a very general want of information on the subject of the Arts, especially of Painters—it seems to be supposed that historical painters abound in this Country. Talent does indeed abound but without study & cultivation talent avails as little in the Arts as in Literature. A man may possess admirable powers of acquiring knowledge but yet may not have acquired [ability to compose and paint historical subjects]. Portrait painters are many, but the difference between portrait & historical painting is almost the Same as that between a Cabinet-maker and an Architect—a man may produce exquisite cabinet work, who would be utterly incapable of combining the vast and varied Magnificence of the Capitol.

It is very probable that some members of the Committee on public buildings may entertain these erroneous notions, & it has seemed to me Not improper then for me (as President of one of the principal Academies of the Fine Arts in the Country, & at the Same time one of the Oldest Artists having commenced the regular course of Study nearly fifty years ago) to lay before you, a List of the most distinguished painters now living in this Country. I have endeavored to do it with correctness and impartiality.

List of painters who have attended to the historical branch of the profession—now living in the U.S.

Charles Wilson [i.e. Willson] Peale, Pha., aged 84 or 5 [actually 86] studied with Mr. West before the War. Painted many portraits of eminent men during the Revolution, which are to be seen in the Museum Phila., made some few attempts at history, one of which may be seen in Princeton College.*

* Trumbull refers to the celebrated "Washington at the Battle of Princeton," which Peale finished in 1784 and which has been at Princeton ever since. Though the composition includes a landscape with Nassau Hall, an actual battle scene with the dying General Mercer and two other figures, it is now regarded as a portrait—one of the most important of the Revolutionary Commander-in-Chief.

John Vanderlyn, New York. Studied with great reputation in Paris & Italy. Painted [in 1807] Caius Marius sitting among the ruins of Carthage, [then belonging to the Kip family and now at M. H. DeYoung Memorial Museum at San Francisco], which received the applause of Napoleon, Ariadne ["Ariadne on the Island of Naxos," probably painted in 1814, at the Pennsylvania Academy of the Fine Arts, Philadelphia], Venus [the old Colonel was mistaken; Vanderlyn did not paint a "Venus"], made one well known attempt in modern history, "The Murder of Miss McCrea by the Indians in 1777," [painted in 1804] which is now in the Academy of Fine Arts at New York. [Now at the Wadsworth Atheneum, Hartford].

G. W. Allston, [i.e. Washington Allston] Boston. Studied with great reputation in England & Italy, painted "the restoration of Life, to a dead man, on touching the bones of the Prophet Elijah," to be seen in the Academy at Phila. [still there]. Has been employed for some years on a painting "of Belshazzar's Feast" [deposited by the Boston Atheneum at the Museum of Fine Arts, Boston], is mostly conversant in Subjects of Classical Antiquity & Poetry, and has made no attempt in modern History, so far as I am informed.

William Dunlap, N.Y. Studied a short time under Mr. West, in early life, left the pursuit of the Arts for many years, & engaged in Commerce, Literature, the Theatre, &c; a few years ago resumed the pencil, & has painted several historical pictures, generally Ancient & Sacred Subjects, which have been generally seen, but has made no attempt at modern history so far as I know.

Daniel Sargeant, [i.e. Col. Henry Sargent, Daniel's son, whom Trumbull had known at London in his student days] Boston. Studied some time under Mr. West in London, but left the Arts on his return to America for Commerce; afterwards resumed the pencil, & has painted several subjects of Scripture history, and the "Landing of the Pilgrims at Plimouth," which have been generally seen, except the last [this, the artist's first important picture, was ruined by pitch, having been rolled on a green pine log. A replica hangs in Pilgrim Hall, Plymouth, Mass.]. Has made no attempt at Modern History, that I know of.

Rembrandt Peale, Pa., has studied in Europe—painted some years ago a fine "picture of the Court of Death" [now belonging to the Detroit Institute of Arts, deposited at the Baltimore Municipal Museum, known as the "Peale Museum"] from a poem of Dr. Porteous, late Bishop of London, [Beilby Porteus died in 1808] and more recently a "portrait of Genl. Washington on horseback" [painted in 1823 and now at the Corcoran Gallery of Art, Washington], which was shown in the Rotunda of the Capitol, & offered to Congress in 1824.

[Thomas] Sully, Phila., has studied in England, painted some years ago, "the Passage of the Delaware in 1776 by Genl. Washington," [Museum of Fine Arts, Boston] well known by a very good engraving.

S. F. B. Morse, New York, has studied in England, painted some years since "the Hall of the Representatives in the Capitol," [Corcoran Gallery of Art] which has been very generally seen.

These are the principal Artists living in this Country, who have made Attempts at historical painting, ancient or modern, so far as my information goes. They all paint portraits, and in that branch of the profession, the Name of [Gilbert] Stuart, stands almost without a Rival, in this or any country, or in any Age.

Several young men in New York, and probably elsewhere, display Talent, for the higher branches of the Arts, which only need a few Years cultivation to mature, in particular Mr [Henry] Inman & Mr [Charles Cromwell] Ingham.

[Charles Robert] Leslie & [Gilbert Stuart] Newton, fr. among all these you find not one instance of any attempt to record the Glory of our Country, and but one to record any portion of our history, that, merely disgraceful to our then Enemy. . . .

JOHN TRUMBULL
Museum Architect *

The art museum was born in an abandoned palace, the event taking place at the turn of the nineteenth century. It was the product of revolutionary bourgeois aggressiveness and tender romanticism, a union of opportunistic practicality of the present with spiritual understanding of the past. The museum's unpredetermined birthplace, the classical Renaissance palace (and its prototype, the Graeco-Roman temple), was to fix the character of its abode for a century and a half. The early museums of Germany and Britain were ponderously classical and correspondingly unfunctional. One of the earliest examples to be built in these United States was the little temple-like Trumbull Gallery at Yale.

Designed by a romantically-inclined, bellicose ex-army officer, whose

* Reprinted from the Walpole Society *Note Book*, 1940.

dramatic ideas were tempered by a serene-minded professor, the Gallery was chastely classical but eminently practical. Patriotism, opportunism, didacticism, and a newly-awakened social consciousness were all ingredients that went into its making. The justly-proportioned, prim little building only served its original purpose of an art museum for thirty-five years. It was an administrative officer for thirty-four more, and was then obliterated, leaving only a memory.

Trumbull's devoted nephew-in-law, the celebrated scientist, Professor Benjamin Silliman, amply documents this early American venture into the field of the fine arts. In a notebook, now in the Garvan Collection, prepared in 1853, the seventy-nine year old scientist records, under the heading of "History of the overtures which brought the Gallery to Yale College" the following: "In the summer of 1830, when returning from a journey, I called upon Col Trumbull at his lodgings at Miss Lentners, corner of Walker Street and Broadway New York," (then a city of less than 250,000 persons) "it being my habit to pay my respects to him whenever I was in the city. The house was large—the apartments spacious and two contiguous parlors, of uncommon dimensions, were adorned by the paintings of Col Trumbull, which were advantageously suspended all around upon the walls. I had seen many of them singly before, but had never seen them all together & some of them never before I was therefore strongly impressed and delighted by this unexpected vision, and had the good fortune to find the venerable artist in the midst of his treasures. Friendly salutations were followed by fuller explanations of some of the subjects than I had before received, but I was sorry to find that the great artist at seventy four years of age was in a position far from eligible, and although surrounded by the splendid productions of his own skill talent, and taste he was without a sure foundation upon which he might repose in the evening life."

The aged "patriot-artist" was in financial straits. He had lived handsomely in London and in New York and, as Silliman states, ". . . the practice of his profession" . . . did "not equal . . . his expences." He was deeply in debt to the American banker, Samuel Williams of London, his prints had not sold, his wife had been dead a half-dozen years, his talents were fast waning and the competition of the younger painters, such as Morse, Sully, Jarvis, and Vanderlyn was proving disastrous. Deprived of his means, "the evening twilight of a long life was now falling upon his eyes with shadows deepening still. Had he not explained his misfortunes in his autobiography, it might be indelicate in me, to report his painful remarks made in the confidential interview of which I am

now writing. He then lamented his poverty in manly but energetic and
eloquent language, which painfully touched my feelings. The very expressions which he used and his energetic action are still with me vivid
as at that moment. It was a painful one and was ended, for the time, by
a question from me and an answer from him. Referring to the paintings
around us, which he stated were his chief resource—I said—

'And what Sir do you intend to do with them?' He instantly replied—

'I will give them to Yale College to be exhibited forever for the benefit
of poor students provided the College will pay me a competent annuity
for the remainder of my life.'

'Are you in earnest Sir? Certainly I am' Am I then at liberty to go
home and act upon this suggestion? 'You are at liberty and I authorize
you to say so from me.'

'The proposition, Sir, is as grateful to me as it is surprising. 'I will return then Sir forthwith to New Haven' resolving, like Col Miller at
Lundy's Lane that I would try."

The professor of Chemistry, Mineralogy, Pharmacy, and Geology took
up the task with zeal and enthusiasm. He "found no difficulty in exciting
. . . a lively interest and a strong desire to obtain the prize that was
thus unexpectedly offered . . ." The president, Rev. Jeremiah Day, his
"immediate colleagues among the older members of the College Faculty
as well as the officers of the fiscal department were men of liberal
minds." The duty of correspondence "fell to" Silliman's "lot." The
deliberations and discussions of 1831 naturally included Daniel Wadsworth of Hartford, who, too, was related to the aged painter by marriage. Wadsworth had married Faith Trumbull, 1794, the eldest daughter of the artist's brother, Jonathan, and Professor Silliman had married
Harriet, her youngest sister, in 1809, fifteen years later. Family complications set in.

A little group of Hartford gentlemen led by Wadsworth suggested
that the Trumbull paintings be divided, and "two galleries—one in
New Haven and the other in Hartford—" be established. A long memorandum to this effect was prepared by Trumbull in September 1831
under which a fireproof building should be constructed in Hartford
and an annuity of five hundred dollars should be paid to the artist for
life. Provision was made that after his death it should be used "towards
defraying the expence of the Education of poor Scholars" at Yale. Hartford was to get thirty, or half of the miniatures, an assortment of religious
paintings, and five enlarged replicas of the Revolutionary Scenes. Difficulties arose. Silliman observed: "Mr. Wadsworth . . . being himself

an amateur artist, evidently felt that the original studies of the Revolutionary Paintings the fresh productions of the early skill of the artist were superior to the enlarged copies painted in the evening of life." As the situation grew more delicate, Mr. Wadsworth suggested that the good pictures be occasionally exchanged between the two cities, but to this the crusty colonel objected. "I felt," the scientist recorded, "my own position to be a difficult one as" . . . the "gentlemen in Hartford had . . . made liberal contributions to Yale." At length Trumbull proposed that the pictures should not be divided. "Mr. Wadsworth had the magnanimity to acquiesce." The day after the conclusion of these arrangements, Trumbull, who had graduated from Harvard in 1773, felt perhaps a bit uneasy over the transaction and wrote President Josiah Quincy of Harvard, informing him of the conveyance of the pictures to the President and Fellows of Yale College. . . .

"This first difficulty being removed" the next hurdle to be cleared was the provision for a New Haven annuity of a thousand dollars. Daniel Wadsworth headed the list with two hundred and fifty dollars, which sum was matched by Professor Silliman. The balance of the thousand was pledged by the President of the College, Jeremiah Day, and by the Secretary and Treasurer, Professor Elizur Goodrich and Stephen Twining respectively, certainly liberal contributions from administrative officers and college professors. This was to be for six years, a reasonable life expectancy for the aging artist—but he lived six more, causing thereby considerable embarrassment to the guarantors and to posterity! Trumbull made up the difference by painting copies of his earlier works and copies after copies of Old Masters brought back by visitors to Europe. Or did he use the copies in Ithiel Town's collection of 170 "oils," bought by the architect sometime between 1830 and 40 "from the Executors of Mr. Paff in N.Y."? (And where are Town's pictures to-day?) Subject material may have been furnished by the countless engravings in Town's magnificent library of eleven thousand volumes. It is only fair to point out that copies of Old Masters formed the backbone of most collections in those days . . .

Having solved the problems of locating the collection and supplying the annuity, that of securing funds for the building still remained. In May 1831, the undaunted scientist was in Hartford applying to the Legislature "for aid to Yale College." He records a "Fortunate Coincidence" as follows: "Probably my application would have been unsuccessful, had not the Episcopal Church been at the same time in the arena, in behalf of some of their peculiar objects . . ." There ensued a bit of political log rolling. The Episcopal Church "and myself pulled indeed on different ropes attached to the same machine, but pulled in the same direction, so effectively, that with the aid of our friends both within and without the Legislative Halls, we succeeded in moving the carriage of State." The energetic professor spent his whole vacation in lobbying, and finally obtained $7,000 for the building which had been paid in for a charter for a bank in Bridgeport.

"At the meeting of the corporation in September 1831—the proposals for the Gallery were received with unanimous approbation, and money was voted for the erection of the Building." The records of the corporation for 13 September 1831, read in part: "Voted that a suitable building be erected on the ground west of the College Chapel for the exhibition of Colonel Trumbull's paintings . . . provided the total expense of the building does not exceed $3000." A note in Silliman's journal is characteristic of a college building. "Our worthy and vigilant friend, Mr. Twining," Treasurer of the College, he wrote, "always laudably anxious for the most economical application of the funds of the College, was much annoyed that the charges ran up to $5000 Five Thousand Dollars, but I felt differently. My only regret on that subject is that the entire sum of $7000 Seven Thousand Dollars which I earned by my own efforts aided by my friends in the Legislature, had not been expended upon the Building."

As to the designing of the building by the artist, Silliman gives this essential background: "While Col Trumbull was a prisoner in London on a charge of high treason Mr. Burke who, with other eminent men, took a warm interest in his welfare, visited him, and advised him strongly to make himself well acquainted with architecture, as there would evidently be a great demand in America for that kind of knowledge. The advice was not neglected and great attention was paid by him to that very important & beautiful art. From drawings left by Col Trumbull, it appears that he had knowledge, judgment & taste in architecture, as well as consummate skill in delineation. He was much in consultation with Mr. Bulfinch the architect of the Capitol at Washington. A model has been preserved in the Trumbull Gallery of stair cases for the building and of the position, form and structure of the apparatus for heating and ventilation. The plan and elevation of the building for the Trumbull Gallery were furnished by him and there can be no doubt that had he devoted himself to architecture he would have taken the first rank in that department of the arts. He had a very accurate eye for form and proportions and a quick & delicate perception of beauty. His judgment was much valued in questions relating to architecture and architects were fond of his society. The late Mr. Ithiel Town the eminent and self taught architect of New Haven was often in his chamber & they passed many joyous hours in devising splendid public buildings and adorning them with grand & beautiful pictures." . . .

The reference to Ithiel Town above raises the interesting problem as to how far that New Havener, then (1830–31) living in New York, participated in the design of the little Greek Revival Gallery. Amongst the Tilney papers, deposited with the New-York Historical Society, there is a meticulous and beautifully executed watercolor drawing obviously by Alexander Jackson Davis,* Town's junior partner, and the "pupil and friend of Trumbull," entitled: "Design: Pinacotheca for Col. Trumbull's Paintings/Town & Davis, Archts." It represents a simple Greek Doric temple, diastyle in antis, with four pilasters, similar to the antae, on long side. My friend, Roger Newton, who has made a careful study of the work of the famous architectural firm of Town & Davis, formed in 1829, believes that the undated watercolor was executed about 1830 or before the Trumbull plans. It is not too much to assume that the colonel was thoroughly familiar with this ambitious project, if he himself did not unofficially suggest it, as he obviously had it in mind in designing the simplified two storied Gallery. In this, a slightly rusticated basement with shuttered windows replaced the Greek stylobate of the projected "Pinacotheca," the gable temple roof was flattened, and the columniated and predimented façade reduced to a pilastered wall. The twin Doric columns of the Town & Davis façade were used as an entrance motive but shifted to the center of the longitudinal side of the basement, in which the diminutive sunken porch seems to be rather absurd in scale. The ambitious frieze of regulation triglyphs and metopes was simplified by Trumbull. However, in both the project and in the actual building, the four corners are accentuated by identical antae and the unbroken walls relieved by the same number of Doric pilasters. Double sky-lights, indicating two rooms, were indicated on the architect's drawing and executed in the painter's building. Not only had a thoroughly functional gallery been planned by the artist but one that was in the mode of the moment. A. J. Davis records in his Diary in 1831 (in the Metropolitan Museum) that the entrance of a certain Mr. Curtis' on Bleeker Street "was the first Greek Doric Door introduced in N. York city." Trumbull was fashionable.

* Now at Yale (Franklin Collection); contained in the 3 extra-illustrated volumes of the *Autobiography, 3,* opp. p. 405.

The details of the construction of this historic example of early Republican eclecticism are worthy of record. Red East Haven sandstone conglomerate was used beneath cemented walls, coursed to resemble ashlar. The artist wrote Silliman, 26 September 1831: "I had begun with a view to external measure of the walls—30 by 60—but after seeing Mr. Town, & learning that a Room which should measure 30 by 30 inside would be most acceptable, I made my Portico & Section 34 feet exterior —I thought of imitating the Stair case of the Room in Philadelphia where Mr. West's picture is placed, which is double—but on reflection I have concluded that a Single stair as in the Drawings is amply sufficient—" The two rooms for the paintings were actually "30 feet 3 inches square inside in the clear and 15 feet high, to the base of the sky light"— simple and effective proportions. These rooms "were lined first with Pine Plank throughout that there might be both the greatest facility and security in hanging the paintings"—and we have done nothing better since. "Then, according to the taste and wishes of Col Trumbull the plank lining was covered entirely with red moreen which was regarded as a proper basis of color and a durable material as 25 years have proved, but the brilliant color," Silliman wrote, "has faded." The carpet—green —was selected by Trumbull, settees, chairs, and stools were of curly maple with cane seats. The staircase had long been a debatable matter. Stone was originally preferred by the painter-architect, who recommended that the risers measure between six and seven inches, and the treads at least eleven. The stairs were eventually made of wood. "They were not carpeted until the visit of General Andrew Jackson to New Haven in 1837 . . . I took care," Silliman wrote, "to have the stairs carpeted that very morning, and the Hero of New Orleans was the first public Dignitary who ascended them in their improved condition." But wooden stairs bothered the practical-minded Silliman, "the building being therefore not fully fire proof I added as a security a slit in the floor of each room for the quick removal of the paintings, frames and all—for the large paintings unless rolled could not descend the stairs or only with difficulty. Two slits or oblong apertures are each twelve feet long and fifteen inches wide. Through them the largest pictures when in their frames can be dropped down instantly, and if the lower room is not on fire all could be speedily extricated . . . The slits are concealed by a moveable board which is covered by the carpet." . . .

"Desiring to provide an inscription," again quoting Silliman, "which should be both permanent and beautiful, I caused an Iron plate to be cast with raised letters, and the silver platers succeeded in covering these letters with a substantial coating of silver . . . thus the Inscription

TRUMBULL GALLERY

will remain as long as stone iron & silver shall last, a splendid memorial to the honor of the great artist—and as a moral lesson to a distant posterity."

The red moreen covering was in place the first week in October 1832, and the "numerous boxes containing the Paintings arrived, under the safe conduct of the artist himself, who came to New Haven in the same Steamer which brought his treasures." The steamboat line between New York and New Haven "generously tendered a free passage to Col Trumbull & all his effects, and this was only in accordance with that gentleman's considerate & habitual benevolence as exhibited on many occasions"—those were gentler days! The colonel brought an experienced man for the hanging of the pictures and all was ready for the opening of the earliest art museum connected with an educational institution in America . . . [on Thursday, 25 October 1831] . . . ten months after the signing of the Indenture, in which it was specified "that the building shall be finished on or before the first day of October, in the year of our Lord one thousand eight hundred and thirty-two." The "Connecticut Herald" noted on 30 October that "this institution is now open for the reception of visitors." New Haven was then a city of some ten thousand souls . . .

What follows may be briefly told. Through the munificence of Augustus Russell Street, a new art building, now called Street Hall, was erected in 1864 and finished in 1866. The Corporation voted at their July meeting that year "that the remains of Colonel Trumbull and his wife be also removed." From 1867 the old Trumbull Gallery served as an office for the President and Treasurer of the University. Tall windows were cut through the walls of the two upstairs galleries. In 1901 a new administrative building, Woodbridge Hall, was opened, and the old Gallery was demolished, and the last but one of Trumbull's architectural achievements passed into oblivion. . . .

Professor Silliman, in whose honor the last of the Yale residential colleges has been named, felt that Trumbull's "posthumous fame was, in some degree, entrusted to [his] keeping . . ." and the closing thought in the Notebook: "Long may his works remain and longer still his fame."

THE REINTERMENTS OF COLONEL TRUMBULL *

John Trumbull, sometime aide to General Washington, dramatizing himself in death as in life, caused his body to be forever laid "at the feet of his master," beneath his great military portrait of "Washington at Trenton." The story which, in its final phase concerned several members of this honorable society, is, I believe, worthy of your attention; at least, in its telling we may set the record straight.

It will be recalled that Trumbull, the "patriot-artist," turned over his pictures to Yale in 1831 in exchange for an annuity, provided that a suitable building be erected from his own designs for their reception. In due course the Trumbull Gallery was built on the Old Campus and opened to the public in October 1832, one of the earliest picture galleries in the English-speaking world—a veritable museologic milepost.

The chief chronological rival to the Trumbull Gallery is, of course, the National Gallery in London, founded in 1824 or eight years earlier. Its official inception gives but an imperfect impression. The nest egg of the National Gallery, thirty-eight paintings from the Angerstein Collection, was purchased for £57,000 in December of 1823. It was not until the following May that the pictures were exhibited to the public at Mr. Angerstein's former town residence, 100 Pall Mall, and there little noticed by press or public. In 1834 the national pictures were removed to 105 Pall Mall, as no. 100 partially collapsed due to excavations for the foundations of an adjoining building. They remained in this second make-shift for four years until transferred to what became known as Trafalgar Square. On 7 April 1838, the young Queen Victoria was conducted to the newly built gallery, erected on the site of the royal stables, the King's Mews. Two days later the partially completed building was thrown open to the public—five and one-half years after the inauguration of the Trumbull Gallery. Or, to put it another way, the New Haven art museum, designed by an amateur architect, born a British subject, dates from the second year of the reign of William IV and the National Gallery, designed by William Wilkins, R. A., from the first year of the Victorian era. . . .

"Soon after the arrangement of his pictures was completed in 1832," the scientist, Benjamin Silliman, Trumbull's devoted nephew-in-law, wrote in his *Note Book*, "he [Trumbull] said to me one day when we were in the Gallery, 'It is my wish to be interred beneath this Gallery.' Looking around on the pictures he added, 'these are my children—those

* Reprinted from the Walpole Society *Note Book,* 1948.

whom they represent have all gone before me, let me be buried with my family. . . . Please, therefore, apply to your authorities of the College for leave to construct a tomb beneath this building—at my expense. I wish to have it large enough for two. I will remove the remains of my wife from New York and place them in it and when I die, I wish to be placed by her side. Let the tomb then be finally closed not to be opened again until earth and sea shall give up their dead.' " The tomb was built accordingly. The colonel's wife, the beautiful and mysterious Sarah, had died at the age of fifty-one in 1824—she who was alone loved by her socially conscious husband in spite of ill-concealed hostility of family and friends. "Mrs. Trumbull's Remains were originally deposited in one of the Church Yards of New York," Silliman noted, "and to prevent a possible disturbance by city improvements her grave was sunk to the depth of twelve feet where they remained until the pious affection of her husband gave her a new tomb in New Haven to which her remains were removed in 1834." Nine years later the colonel died at the ripe age of eighty-seven years and five months on 10 November 1843 at Mrs. Lentner's in New York. The following day his body was brought to New Haven by steamer and thence to Professor Silliman's home at the corner of Hillhouse Avenue and Trumbull Street. Services were held in the College Chapel on the twelfth, Professor Eleazur Thompson Fitch "sketched the principal events from the cradle to the grave in the life of Col. Trumbull . . . the text was appropriate (Genesis XXV, verses 8–9–10)." "There was a large attendance of citizens at the funeral," the scientist wrote, and "an earnest desire was manifest to look into the tomb . . . multitudes availed themselves of the opportunity to gaze upon the last earthly abode of the man and woman. She once beautiful and animated, he heroic and renowned. . . ." The conscientious professor superintended every detail. Beneath the full-length Washington the portraits of Col. Trumbull and his wife were hung, between which "a trophy sword taken by Trumbull in the battle of Rhode Island" and the artist's palette and brushes (his "pencils") were displayed. On the dado immediately under these patriotic and professional symbols he caused a black marble tablet to be erected with the inscription: "Colonel John Trumbull, Patriot and Artist, Friend and aid of Washington. . . . To his country he gave his SWORD and his PENCIL." What more could a proud man desire!

"Some centuries hence," Silliman wrote, "when the firm stones of the Trumbull Gallery have fallen those who dig among the ruins will discover the tomb in this obscure crypt and will be warned not to violate it when they read the . . . inscription. . . ." But man is ever the de-spoiler—usually in the name of progress. Yale had achieved a new and larger art museum—one in fashionable Venetian Gothic, bepraised by Mr. Ruskin, and abandoned the prim, well-proportioned, neo-classical edifice designed by the "patriot-artist." We therefore find that in less than twenty-three years "the Reverend Honorable Corporation of Yale College" voted (24 July 1866) "to permit the paintings of Colonel Trum-bull to be removed from the Trumbull Gallery to the Art Building . . . provided there is no legal impediment; and, if the paintings are removed, voted, that the remains of Colonel Trumbull and his wife be also re-moved." This must have been quietly performed for I can find no men-tion of the act in the New Haven papers of the time.

Sixty-one years later a future Walpolean happened to be in charge of a newly constructed art museum, Yale's third, and found himself under the necessity of supervising the transfer of the bodies, along with the pictures, in fulfillment of the University's legal and moral obliga-tion . . . The time for the "translation of the relics," to use the ecclesi-astical term, was set by the University administration for the spring recess (1928), fearing that if it took place during term time it might offer an irresistible excuse for a student demonstration. There was a tablet (since destroyed) on the south side of the Art Building (now known as "Street Hall"), marking, apparently, the tomb site. Workmen with pick and shovel made an enormous excavation between Street and Vanderbilt Halls as a little company of Trumbull and Silliman descend-ants, and faculty . . . stood as silent witnesses.

As the pit grew hopes fell. At last someone suggested shifting the attack indoors. Equally interested excavators and spectators marched to the basement of the Art Building. The floor was ripped up inside the wall bearing the tablet. A well-constructed brick crypt was speedily re-vealed to an awed group. The coffin containing the thrice buried Sarah was not in good condition. At the time of this lady's second burial Pro-fessor Silliman had noted that "Mrs. Trumbull had been interred 19 years but the coffin had not failed—its form was preserved although the lid was distorted and was in part separated from the sides, but the re-mains were not exposed to view." When it was gently lifted the bottom gave way. Her body was reverently placed in a new casket by awaiting undertakers. The colonel's mahogany coffin, however, was in a perfect state of preservation. Press and photographers being barred from these solemn proceedings, the writer made a rapid pencil sketch of the beauti-ful nail-head coffin, and falling on his knees, noted its several dimensions. As silent workmen stood with bared heads the flag-draped coffins were carried across High Street, followed by a small procession, to the new impressive tomb in the still incomplete Gallery. . . . A full account of what happened that day, the signatures of those who witnessed the proceedings, and an extract of Professor Silliman's notes on the Trumbull Gallery burial of eighty-five years before were bricked up in the new and spacious vault. This took place on 11 April 1928, and was noticed in the press on the following days. . . .

Here is a typical example of a latter-day legend, this from the *Saturday Review of Literature* of 18 March 1939: "The distinguished English artist, A. Hugh Fisher, tells a good tale of some embarrassment at New Haven ten or twelve years ago . . . the trouble was to find exactly *where* he had been buried. They were plowing up the campus all around the building for days and finally found the coffin somewhere under one corner of the walls. As they were carrying the very decrepit coffin from one building to the other and had got halfway across, the bottom fell out and out came John Trumbull! Of course there was great consternation but the janitor of the school, a crabby old fellow named Enos, had a bright idea. He rushed out with a dustpan and broom and swept John Trumbull back into the coffin, which was turned upside down for the purpose, and the removal proceeded satisfactorily." Distortion is often more arresting than the factual.

The true story does not end here. When the new Gallery was finally completed, some months after the reinterment, the writer ceremoniously placed Col. Trumbull's maulstick in the empty building, first object to be brought within its portals. The old colonel, who appreciated protocol, would have liked that! Then on 6 June 1928, the one hundred and seventy-second anniversary of the birth of the celebrated "patriot-artist," a special memorial service was held directly above the new vault. President Angell, in his robes of office, presided over a distinguished company composed of Trumbull and Silliman descendants, friends, faculty, and students. The . . . University Chaplain, reenacted the original burial service of 1843 [and] . . . John Hill Morgan, concluded the ceremony by paying eloquent tribute to him who gave his SWORD and PENCIL to his country.

A Supplement to the "Check List"

APPEARING IN *The Works of Colonel John Trumbull,
Artist of the American Revolution,*
NEW HAVEN, YALE UNIVERSITY PRESS, 1950.

The editor of this book is astonished—and saddened—by the large number of "Trumbulls" which have come to his attention since the publication of his check list in 1950. Most of these are portraits of Revolutionary worthies (in sepia wash, watercolor, and oil; miniatures, small drawings, and bust portraits of unusual sizes). Some erroneous attributions, of course, have been made in all good faith, due to faulty family tradition, misinformation, ignorance, and perhaps wishful thinking. Some of the fraudulent productions, however, the editor cannot help but believe, are knowingly misrepresented. There must be as many "Trumbulls" as there are genuine Trumbulls. *Caveat emptor!*

Some of the following have been previously noted in the *Works.* They are here repeated, in a more perfect order, for purposes of clarity; additional information has been supplied as an aid in the identification of lost pictures.

Names in full capitals indicate individual portraits, as distinguished from representations in historical pieces, which are in small capitals.

PORTRAITS

SAMUEL BLODGET, JUNIOR (1757–1814), Revolutionary officer from New Hampshire, merchant, architect, first superintendent of Public Buildings in the District of Columbia; "Small whole length of Mr. Sam Blodget, sitting, in a purple morning gown . . . done in London 1784 . . . 10 Gns."; Mrs. I. Harding Hughes, Raleigh, N.C.

——— an identical picture, in a harder manner, probably painted shortly before the above (in 1784, a year of abrupt stylistic change, from the "early Copley manner" to that of the current British school), unrecorded by the artist; Insurance Company of North America (of which the subject was a director in 1792), Philadelphia.

——— (?) pencil drawing, head only, labeled by the artist on reverse "Capt. L. Blodget, Princeton," most probably Capt. Samuel Blodget,

Junior, of the 8th Continental Foot (formerly the 2d New Hampshire), which unit was present at Princeton; possibly intended for inclusion in the "Battle of Princeton"; probably 1786 at London; Yale, No. 1931.66.

—————— "Portrait, Mr. Blodget in a Rifle dress—Recd 15 Gns . . . a beautiful little picture . . . finished in 1786" at London, probably after the above study; destroyed by fire about 1925. [*Substitute for* entries under Capt. L.(?) Blodget & Samuel Blodget, p. 17.]

(ESTHER MARGARET BULL, see Mrs. Thomas Chester.) [*Add*, p. 18.]

JOSEPH BULL (1736/7–1797), of Hartford, Conn., half-length, posthumous, after "a miserable old crayon portrait and 2 small miniatures" (Mrs. Benjamin Silliman to her sister Mrs. Daniel Wadsworth, 12 January 1838); 1838 at New Haven; James Chetwood Leatty, Rye, N.Y. [*Add*, p. 18.]

COL. DONALD CAMPBELL, Deputy Quartermaster General, New Yor'· ⌐ nt.; pencil sketch, idealized, 1785 at London, for No. 4 in *Queu* ᵢale, No. 52.3.2a.

COL. DONALD CAMPBELL, from the above, No. 4 in *Quebec*. [*Substitute for* entry under Col. Donald Campbell, p. 19.]

CHILDREN OF CHARLES I, "HEADS OF TWO BOYS" (CHARLES, 1630–1685, later Charles II, and JAMES, 1633–1701, later James II); British, after John Smibert's copy (now lost) of one of the many Van Dyck portraits, 1778 at Boston, Mass., *Autobiography* No. 38; unlocated. [*Substitute for* entry under Children of Charles I, *in first printing only*, p. 19.]

CAPT. JACOB CHEESEMAN, Aide-de-Camp to Gen. Montgomery (killed in action at Quebec 1775); pencil sketch, posthumous, 1785 at London, for No. 2 in *Quebec;* Yale, No. 52.3.2b.

CAPT. JACOB CHEESEMAN, from the above, No. 2 in *Quebec*. [*Substitute for* entry under Capt. Jacob Cheeseman, p. 19.]

MRS. THOMAS (ESTHER MARGARET BULL) CHESTER (1777–1844), of Wethersfield and Hartford, Conn., daughter of Col. Joseph Bull, wife of Thomas Chester (1764–1831, Yale 1780, Clerk of the Court of Common Pleas in 1796, and of the Superior Court in 1806); 1838 at New Haven; unlocated. [*Add*, p. 19.]

DUCHESS OF CLEVELAND, Barbara Villiers, Countess of Castlemaine and Duchess of Cleveland (1641–1709), after (a copy of?) a portrait by Sir Peter Lely (ex coll. Sir Joshua Reynolds and Charles Wilkes of New York, exhibited at the American Academy

1820, No. 36; 1824, No. 57: and 1825, No. 74; unlocated); half-length (Trumbull's copy American Academy Cat., 1824, No. 106 or 108. "Portrait of a Lady"); probably painted between 1820 and 1824; unlocated. [*Substitute for* entry under "Duchess of Cleaveland," p. 20.]

T. FARMER (?), possibly Thomas Farmer, New York merchant, "Portrait of a Gentleman, Lent by T. Farmer" (American Academy Cat., 1818, No. 167); bust (?); lost (?). [*Add,* p. 25.]

(———?) GAHN, probably HENRY GAHN (d. 1834), Consul General for Sweden at New York (portrait of "Gahn" mentioned in packing list of 23 June 1808, included item 46, New-York Historical Society), before 1808 at New York; unlocated. [*Add,* p. 26.]

CHILDREN OF ARCHIBALD GRACIE (?), (Archibald Gracie, 1755–1829, m. Esther Rogers by whom he had eight children) possibly the "Portrait of Children. Lent by A. Gracie, Esq." (American Academy Cat., 1817, No. 96); lost (?). [*Add,* p. 27.]

CHRISTOPHER GORE, miniature, 1790 or 1793 at Boston; John Morse Elliot, Boston, Mass. [*Add,* p. 27.]

ALEXANDER HAMILTON, full-length, life-size (American Academy Cats., 1817, No. 94; 1819, No. 25; 1820, No. 29; 1821, No. 31; 1822, No. 12; and 1823, No. 13); possibly one of the above; lost (?).

——— "Feby, 19th. Recd. of Mr. Vaughan for Hamilton's portrait—£31"; possibly one of the above; lost (?).

——— "Mr. Hamilton," probably one of the above (Royal Academy, London, 1811, No. 427); lost (?). [*Substitute for* entry under Hamilton, "(type unknown)," p. 30.]

JAMES HEWLETT (1789–1836), British, "the eminent flower painter of Bath," probably 1813 at Bath (American Academy Cat., 1817, No. 130); unlocated. [*Add,* p. 31.]

THOMAS HEYWARD, JUNIOR (1746–1809), Signer, Revolutionary officer, jurist; sketch or miniature (?), 1791 at Charleston, S.C.; unlocated.

THOMAS HEYWARD, JUNIOR, from the above, No. 15 in the *Declaration.* [*Substitute for* entry under Thomas Heyward, p. 31.]

DR. DAVID HOSACK (1769–1835), attending physician at the New York Hospital, botanist, professor at Columbia College, philanthropist, art patron, incorporator and chief backer of the American Academy of the Fine Arts; ("cash recd. From Dr. Hosack for a portrait 140 [dollars]," accounts for 15 November 1806; possibly the same as "Portrait of a Gentleman. Lent by Dr. Hosack," American Academy Cat. 1817, No. 128); or possibly the following; lost (?).

—— "Portrait of the late David Hosack, M.D., F.R.S. Painted by Col. John Trumbull for Richard Pennell, M.D." (Royal Academy, London, 1818, No. 275; Apollo Association, New York, 1839, October Exhibition, No. 38), presented in 1866 by Mary C. and Geo. C. Pennell to the New York Hospital, half-length, on wood, 1806 at New York; New York Hospital. [*Substitute for* entry under Dr. David Hosack, p. 32.]

THOMAS JEFFERSON, miniature, a replica, 1788 at London, for Maria (Hadfield) Cosway, 1759–1838, wife of the English miniature painter, Richard Cosway; Collegio Maria S. S. Bambina (founded by Maria Cosway), Lodi, Italy. [*Substitute for* entry for the third miniature under Thomas Jefferson, p. 35.]

MAJ. GEN. CHARLES LEE (1731–1782), pencil sketch, posthumous, 1785 at London; probably for the projected *Attack on Charleston, S.C.*; Yale, No. 52.3.5. [*Add*, p. 37.]

"COL. JOSEPH LEWIS" (or LOUIS), chief of the Oneida Indians, pencil sketch, idealized, 1785 at London, for No. 6 in *Quebec*; Yale, No. 52.3.4.

"COL. JOSEPH LEWIS," from the above, No. 6 in *Quebec*. [*Substitute for* entry under "Col. Joseph Lewis," p. 38.]

CAPT. JOHN MACPHERSON (1754–1775; killed in action at Quebec), pencil sketch, posthumous, 1785 at London, for No. 3 in *Quebec*; Yale, No. 52.3.3. [*Add*, p. 40.]

JAMES MADISON (1751–1836), fourth President of the United States; probably after Gilbert Stuart's 1804 portrait or one of the replicas, No. 17 in the *Resignation*. [*Substitute for* entries under James Madison, p. 40.]

MAJ. GEN. RICHARD MONTGOMERY (1738–1775; killed in the assault on Quebec), Continental Army; pencil sketch, posthumous, 1785 at London, for No. 1 in *Quebec*; Yale, No. 52.3.1b.

MAJ. GEN. RICHARD MONTGOMERY, from the above, No. 1 in *Quebec*. [*Substitute for* entry under Maj. Gen. Richard Montgomery, p. 41.]

THOMAS PALMER, possibly T. Palmer, Junior, London architect, who exhibited at the Royal Academy in 1798 and 1799 and a painting (?) in 1804; or Thomas Palmer (1754?–1833), engraver from Hounslow, near London (note to Dr. David Hosack, 9 May 1828); probably the same picture as that of "Mr. Palmer, an Artist of London"

(1844 auction sale No. 40, purchased by a Mr. Lanman), *ca.* 1810 at London; unlocated. [*Substitute for* entry under "Mr. Palmer," p. 44.]

JOHN HOWARD PAYNE (1791–1852), dramatist, editor, and actor (played in England); bust (?), exhibited at the Liverpool Academy of Arts (No. 68), Liverpool, England, in August 1813 and painted at London earlier that year; unlocated. [*Add,* p. 44.]

MISS POGGI (probably a daughter of Antonio C. de Poggi of London, publisher of Trumbull's engravings, note to Dr. David Hosack, 9 May 1828); *ca.* 1786 (?) at London; unlocated. [*Add,* p. 45.]

MOSES ROGERS (1750–1825), New York merchant; bust, 1806 at New York; possibly the same as a "Portrait of a Gentleman, Lent by M. Rogers, Esq." (American Academy Cat., 1817, No. 133); Mrs. H. Schuyler Cammann, Syosset, Long Island, N.Y. [*Substitute for* entry under Moses Rogers, p. 47.]

MRS. MOSES (SARAH WOOLSEY) ROGERS (?) (1750–1816), possibly the "Portrait of a Lady, Lent by M. Rogers, Esq." (American Academy Cat., 1817, No. 135); lost (?). [*Add,* p. 47.]

MRS. SEWALL AND HER TWO SONS, bequeathed by the artist to Catherine Lentner, sister of Mrs. Sewall; unlocated. [*Substitute for* entries under Mrs. Sewall, p. 49.]

"L. SIMOND, a portrait of himself with hands," probably LEWIS (LOUIS) SIMOND, (b.?–d. before 1821), New York West Indian merchant, incorporator of the American Academy of the Fine Arts in 1808, member of the New-York Historical Society in 1812, married Frances Wilkes at New York in 1791; 1806 at New York; unlocated. [*Substitute for* entry under L. Simond, p. 50.]

MRS. JOHN (SARAH HOPE HARVEY) TRUMBULL (1774–1824), half-length (formerly attributed to Samuel Lovett Waldo), 1804–1808 (?) at New York (?); Yale, No. 1929.1.

——— half-length, identical to the above, probably the original (and the above a later replica), painted between 1800–1804 at London; Mrs. John W. (Mary Brinley) Muir, Chestnut Hill, Philadelphia. [*Substitute for* fifth entry under Mrs. John Trumbull, p. 56.]

JONATHAN TRUMBULL, SENIOR (1710–1785), "Portrait of Jonathan Trumbull, Governor of Connecticut, during the Revolution," (American Academy Cat., 1820, No. 51), probably one of the above; lost (?). [*Add* after entries for Jonathan Trumbull, Senior, p. 57.]

JOHN TYRRELL (also spelled TERRILL and TERRELL), (1776–

1857), son of the American Loyalist, William Terrill, secretary to his uncle, Sir George Nugent, Governor of Jamaica, in 1804; bust with hands, 1806 at New York; Rear Admiral Sherbrooks Popham, U.S.N. (ret.), Charleston, S.C. [*Substitute for* entry on p. 59.]

RICHARD VARICK, "Portrait of a Gentleman, Lent by Richard Varrick, Esq." (American Academy Cat., 1817, No. 129), probably one of the above; lost (?). [*Add,* p. 60.]

JEREMIAH WADSWORTH, enlarged replica (of the bust only, figure of young Daniel Wadsworth omitted), from the above, 1838–39 at New Haven, Conn.; Estate of James Wadsworth, Geneseo, N.Y., [*Add,* p. 61.]

MRS. JONATHAN MAYHEW (AMELIA MARIA PHELPS) WAINWRIGHT (married 1818), half-length, seated, 1822 at New York; Mrs. Ruth Wainwright Wallace, Farmington, Conn. [*Add,* p. 61.]

LIEUT. COL. BENJAMIN WALKER (1753–1818), Revolutionary officer, Naval Officer of the Port of New York (note to Dr. David Hosack, 9 May 1828); bust (?), used for the following; unlocated. [*Add,* p. 61.]

LIEUT. COL. BENJAMIN WALKER, from the above, No. 23 in the *Resignation.* [*Substitute for* entry under Lieut. Col. Benjamin Walker, p. 61.]

MAJ. GEN. JOSEPH WARREN (b. 1741–killed at Bunker's Hill 1775), pencil sketch, posthumous, 1785 at London, for No. 1 in *Bunker's Hill;* Yale, No. 52.3.1a. [*Add,* p. 61.]

GEN. GEORGE WASHINGTON (1732–1799), "Full-length Portrait of General Washington" (American Academy Cat., 1816, No. 43); probably one of the "Yale Type" replicas; lost (?). [*Add,* under "*Type Unknown,*" p. 64.]

ARTHUR WELLESLEY, DUKE OF WELLINGTON (1769–1852), "Portrait of the Duke of Wellington" (American Academy Cat., 1816, No. 42), probably one of the above; lost (?). [*Add* at end of entries under Duke of Wellington, p. 66.]

"MR. WOODFORDE" (unidentifiable; note to Dr. David Hosack, 9 May 1828), bust (?); unlocated. [*Add,* p. 68.]

REV. RALPH WORSLEY (or WORSELEY) (1766–1848), British, of Finchley, Middlesex, officiating minister at the Church of St. Mary's, Parish of Hendon, Middlesex (seven miles northwest of London) at the marriage of the artist and Sarah Hope Harvey on 1 October 1800; probably painted at that time (listed erroneously as "Ralph Worley" in note to Dr. David Hosack, New York, 9 May 1828); bust (?); unlocated. [*Add,* p. 68.]

Unidentified Men

"Soldier of the King's Horse Guards," sketch, 1785 at London; unlocated.
"Portrait of a soldier in the horse grenadiers," probably after the above
(Royal Academy, London, 1785, No. 432); unlocated. [*Substitute*
for entry under "Soldier of the King's Horse Guards," p. 68.]
"Portrait of a Gentleman" (Royal Academy, London, 1785, No. 72),
probably a duplicate of a portrait listed; lost (?).
"Portrait of a Gentleman" (Royal Academy, 1785, No. 94), probably a
duplication; lost (?).
"Portrait of a Gentleman" (Royal Academy, 1809, No. 356), probably a
duplication; lost (?). [*Add*, p. 68.]

Unidentified Women

"Portrait of a Lady" (Royal Academy, 1811, No. 457), possibly the "Portrait of a Lady," 1800 at London; lost (?). [*Add* after "Portrait of a
Lady," 1800 at London, p. 69.]
"THE PEARL NECKLACE, from Paris Bordone," exhibited at the
Boston Athenaeum, 1829 (No. 62 under works by "Living Artists"),
a copy from the Venetian, Paris Bordone, 1495–1570, probably
painted at London during the War of 1812, possibly after the Earl
of Dudley's picture, now called "The Mirror"; unlocated. [*Add*,
p. 69.]

HISTORICAL SUBJECTS

(Listed in chronological order of events represented)

THE RAPE OF LUCRECE (LUCRETIA) (?), possibly the "Brutus
and his Friends at the Death of Lucretia"; once belonging to the
David Trumbull Lanman family; lost (?). [*Add* after "Brutus and
his Friends," p. 70.]
THE DEPUTATION FROM THE SENATE PRESENTING TO
CINCINNATUS THE COMMAND OF THE ROMAN AR-
MIES, "four small figures on a half-length cloth," 1784 at London
(Royal Academy, 1784, No. 153); unlocated. [*Substitute for* entry
"four small figures" under Cincinnatus, p. 70.]
"A Variation from a Picture of CLEOPATRA, by Titian . . . the origi-
nal was beautifully colored, and represented a beautiful woman,
but with arms that might have belonged to a blacksmith" (no such
composition known; possibly after Titian's "Lucretia" at Hampton
Court), *ca.* 1812 at London or a copy made at New Haven; or at

New York in the late 1830's (Apollo Assn. Cats., Oct. 1838, No. 16; Jan. 1839, No. 14; and May 1839, No. 170); unlocated. [*Add* after "The Dead Body of Brutus," p. 71.]

PETER THE GREAT (of Russia) AT THE CAPTURE OF NARVA, 1704; large oil, 1812 at London (British Institute, London, 1813, No. 34, and repeatedly exhibited at the American Academy 1817 to 1831); Yale, No. 1832.88. [*Substitute for* third entry under Peter the Great, p. 71.]

THE SORTIE MADE BY THE GARRISON OF GIBRALTAR, 27 November 1781. Replica, 117 by 126 inches, probably between 1808 and 1812 (British Institution, London, 1812, No. 26); unlocated. [*Add,* at the bottom of p. 76.]

LITERARY SUBJECTS

LADY OF THE LAKE, from Scott's *Lady of the Lake* (published in 1810), large oil, 1811 at London (this or the following exhibited at the Royal Academy, London, 1811, No. 237); owned by the artist in 1837 and now by Mrs. Cyrus L. (Harriet Sharp Lanman) Fulton, Lancaster, Ohio.

———— a smaller version, probably 1811 at London (American Academy Cat., 1816, No. 10; 1824, No. 95; and 1831, No. 28; Pennsylvania Academy Cat., 1818, No. 50; and Cat. of Paintings in the Wadsworth Gallery, Hartford, 1863, No. 124); owned by Daniel Wadsworth before 1837, then by the Wadsworth Atheneum; now unlocated. [*Substitute for* entries under "Lady of the Lake," p. 79.]

RELIGIOUS SUBJECTS

Scenes from the Apocrypha

SUSANNAH AND THE ELDERS or THE CHASTITY OF SUSANNAH, oil, 1811 at London (American Academy Cats., 1831, No. 27 and 1833, No. 41; Apollo Assn. Cats., 1838, No. 20 and 1839, No. 18; 1844 auction sale, No. 3); unlocated. [Substitute for entry under "Susannah and the Elders," p. 80.]

Scenes from the Life of Christ

MADONNA AND CHILD, HOLY FAMILY, or "COPY OF VANDYK," after the "Madonna and Infant Saviour" by Sir Anthony Van Dyck, once owned by Trumbull and sold by him in 1797 (now in the Dulwich College Gallery, London); copy made before 1815 at London (American Academy Cat., 1819, No. 53, and 1844 auction sale, No. 1); unlocated. [*Substitute for* entry under Holy Family and "Copy of Vandyk," p. 81.]

HOLY FAMILY, six small individual pictures, probably near replicas (American Academy Cats., 1826, Nos. 49, 50, and 105; 1827, Nos. 51, 98, 100, 101, and 128; 1828, No. 66, and 1831, No. 48), probably all painted between 1826 and 1827 at New York; one of the above, private collection, New Haven, Conn., destroyed; the other five unlocated.

HOLY FAMILY "with a group of Angels in the Sky," "small picture," given to the American Academy by the artist in 1826 "as a Specimen of his Talents," probably one of the above; lost (?).

HOLY FAMILY WITH ST. JOHN AND HIS PARENTS (Madonna and Child with Saints Zacharias, Elizabeth, and John the Baptist), 1809 at London (Royal Academy, 1809, No. 9), probably the same as "Holy Family, Eleazer, St. Elizabeth, and St. John" (American Academy Cat., 1817, No. 36); Connecticut Historical Society, No. 102. [*Substitute for* first five entries under Holy Family, top of page 82.]

Scenes from the New Testament

DOUBTING THOMAS or THE UNBELIEF OF THOMAS (John 20:19–30), projected in 1834 at New York (possibly never executed); lost (?) [*Add*, p. 83.]

Post-Biblical Scenes

ST. JEROME, referred to by the artist as "THE SPAGNIOLET," a copy after "Lo Spagnoletto" (José Ribera, *ca.* 1590–*ca.* 1652); given by the artist to the American Academy in 1826 "as a Specimen of his Talents"; Wadsworth Atheneum, No. 1855.99. [*Add*, p. 83.]

LANDSCAPES

Connecticut

VIEW OF THE WEST MOUNTAIN NEAR HARTFORD, sepia wash, 1791 (2d Silliman Sale No. 840); Yale, No. 1938.290.

—————— oil (?) (American Academy Cat., 1817, No. 168), probably the following; lost (?).

"LANDSCAPE VIEW NEAR HARTFORD" (American Academy Cat., 1824, No. 45), probably the following; lost (?).

"MONTE VIDEO" (Daniel Wadsworth's country seat), Talcot Mountain, Avon, Conn., oil, 1806 or 1816; Miss Marion Coffin, New Haven, Conn.

THE GREAT FALLS OF THE CONNECTICUT RIVER AT WAL-POLE, "a view of the first timber cantilever bridge erected in this country," India ink, 1791 (1st Silliman Sale No. 60); Fordham.

NORWICH NEAR THE PAPER MILLS, pencil, 1806; Yale, No. 1935.3.3.

——— pencil, 1806; Yale, No. 1935.3.5.

NORWICH FALLS or THE FALLS OF THE YANTIC AT NOR-WICH, pencil, 1804; Yale, No. 1935.3.2.

——— pencil, 1804; Yale, No. 1935.3.8.

——— pencil, 1804; Yale, No. 1935.3.10.

——— pencil, 1804; Yale, No. 1935.3.11.

——— from the grounds of Mr. Vernet, pencil, 1806 (portraits of John Vernet and his family painted that year); Yale, No. 1935.3.7.

——— oil, 1806; Slater Memorial Museum, Norwich, Conn.

——— oil, 1806; Garvan Collection, Yale, No. 1947.186. (The above two oils, Pennsylvania Academy Cat., 1818, Nos. 35 and 41; American Academy Cats., 1817, Nos. 64 and 67; 1824, Nos. 7 and 11; and 1831, Nos. 21 and 22).

——— oil, probably 1806 (the artist referred to "my three pictures of Norwich Falls"); unlocated. (Note: two of the above, both entitled "View of the Falls of the Yantick, a branch of the river Thames near Norwich in North America," exhibited at the Royal Academy, London, 1809, Nos. 85 and 198). [*Substitute for* all entries under Connecticut, pp. 87–88.]

Unidentified

LANDSCAPE, oil (?) (American Academy Cat., 1817, No. 65), probably one of the above; lost (?). [*Add,* p. 89.]

Romantic

ROMANTIC LANDSCAPE WITH TREES AND WATERFALL, and ROMANTIC LANDSCAPE WITH FIGURES AND SHEEP, both small pen-and-wash sketches probably after prints after Italian (or French?) paintings, 1783, probably at Boston; given to Theodore Dwight (Senior or Junior?) in the late 1820's; Stephen B. Luce, Boston, Mass.

"COMPOSITION, suggested from No. 120," by "an Unknown Artist, lent by Mrs. Rogers" (American Academy Cat., 1825, No. 99), a landscape (?); unidentified; lost (?). [*Add,* p. 90.]

MISCELLANEOUS DESIGNS

Design for a mahogany SARCOPHAGUS "containing the remains of the unfortunate André . . . in the shape of a Ladies work case about 2 feet high and 1½ wide . . . designed by Col. Trumbull . . ." *Letters from John Pintard to his daughter, 1816–1833* (New-York Historical Society, 1940), 4 vols., 2, 75, letter of 18 August 1821; presumably enclosed in Major André's tomb designed by P. M. Van Gelder, in Westminster Abbey, London. [*Add*, p. 92.]

ERRATA

to the "Check List"

p. 19, Under HARRIET CHEW, *insert the word* miniature.

p. 20, Under MRS. JOHN BARKER (ANGELICA SCHUYLER) CHURCH, CHILD (PHILIP CHURCH), and SERVANT, *for* unlocated *read* Peter Butler Olney, Old Saybrook, Conn.

p. 24, Under LIEUT. GEN. GEORGE AUGUSTUS ELIOTT, *for* unlocated *read* (Trumbull-Silliman letters, scrapbook 1, p. 5) Connecticut Historical Society, Hartford.

p. 26, Under GEORGE GALLAGHER, *for* Dr. Joseph Gardner Hopkins, New York *read* Mrs. Robert A. (Alice Gardner Hopkins) Eyerman, Wilkes-Barre, Penna.

p. 31, Under DR. LEMUEL HOPKINS, *for* Dr. Joseph Gardner Hopkins, New York *read* Mrs. Robert A. (Alice Gardner Hopkins) Eyerman, Wilkes-Barre, Penna.

Under SAMUEL MILES HOPKINS and MRS. SAMUEL MILES (SARAH ELIZABETH ROGERS) HOPKINS, *for* Dr. Joseph Gardner Hopkins, New York *read* Mrs. George (Virginia Hopkins) Mayakis, Burbank, Calif.

p. 33, Under ROBERT BALL HUGHES, *for* Frederick R. Brown, "Kings Prevention," Chestertown, Md. *read* Frederick R. Brown, Junior, Ridgefield, Conn.

p. 33, Under GEN. DAVID HUMPHREYS, *for* probably late 1830's at New York *read* before 1824 at New York.

p. 36, Under MARY HUNTINGTON LANMAN, *for ca.* 1879 *read* 1880; and ABIGAIL TRUMBULL LANMAN, *for ca.* 1870 *read* 1891.

p. 38, Under ROBERT LENOX, *for* Estate of Waldron Phoenix Belknap, Junior, Boston, Mass. *read* the New-York Historical Society, No. 1950.225.

Under MRS. ROBERT (RACHEL CARMER) LENOX, *for* Estate of Waldron Phoenix Belknap, Junior, Boston, Mass. *read* the New-York Historical Society, No. 1950.226.

p. 38, *Delete entirely* entry under MRS. LAWRENCE (ELEANOR PARKE CUSTIS) LEWIS.

p. 40, JAMES MADISON, *delete* entry.

p. 41, Under THOMAS MIFFLIN, *delete* entry, "—(?), miniature; lost (?)."

p. 47, Under MAJ. GEN. CHARLES ROSS, *for* (d.1814) *read* (d.1797).

p. 48, Under EDWARD RUTLEDGE, ELIZA (ELIZABETH) RUTLEDGE, MRS. JOHN (ELIZABETH GRIMKÉ) RUTLEDGE, and STATES RUTLEDGE, *for* 1790 *read* 1791.

p. 49, Under MR. SANDERSON, *for* before 1815, probably at London, *read* 1811 at London.

Under MRS. SANDERSON, *add* (Royal Academy, London, 1811, No. 87); unlocated.

p. 50, Under MRS. CHARLES (LYDIA HUNTLY) SIGOURNEY, *for* 1834 at Hartford *read* 1838 at New Haven.

p. 51, Under DAVID SPROAT, *for* Estate of Waldron Phoenix Belknap, Junior, Boston, Mass. *read* New-York Historical Society, No. 1950.224.

p. 61, Under REV. JONATHAN MAYHEW WAINWRIGHT, *insert before New Britain Institute* probably the same as a "Portrait of a Clergyman" (American Academy Cat., 1822, No. 33), and *for ca.* 1820 read 1822.

p. 67, Under THOMAS WILLING, after *"ca.* 1790 at Philadelphia" *insert* or later, and not from life, but from description furnished by Thomas Jefferson.

p. 68, MRS. OLIVER (ELIZABETH STOUGHTON) WOLCOTT, JUNIOR, *add* Estate of (Oliver Wolcott Roosevelt, New York).

p. 69, Under Charlestonians . . . about 20 heads . . . , *for* 1790 *read* 1791.

p. 73, Under THE DECLARATION OF INDEPENDENCE, U.S. postage stamp No. 120, in first printing only, *for* 1896 *read* 1869.

Under CAPTURE OF THE HESSIANS AT TRENTON, replica, large oil, in the first printing only, *for* 1832 *read* 1830.

p. 78, Under PRIAM RETURNING WITH THE BODY OF HECTOR, study, ink(?), *for* unlocated *read* Mrs. Percy Chubb, Chester, N.J.

p. 95, Under Addenda & Corrigenda, *delete* all entries.

INDEX

Abercromby, Gen. James, 32
Accademia Reale di Belle Arti, 169 n
Accademia Romana di San Luca, 169 n
Adams, Charles, 78
Adams, John, 60, 74, 92, 147, 311–312, 326
Adams, John Quincy, 60, 235, 269, 275, 313–314, 322
Adams, Mrs. John Quincy, 270
Addington, William, 66
Alden, Judah, 16
Alden, Roger, 16
Alexander, Emperor of Russia, 121
Allston, Washington, 293, 294, 306, 316, 319, 321, 370
American Academy of the Fine Arts, xii, xvii, 169 n, 261, 268, 268 n, 269 n, 297, 300, 317, 318, 321, 322, 324, 364
American Philosophical Society, 169 n
Amherst, Lord Jeffrey, 18
Anderson, Joseph, 272
André, Major John, xvi, 63, 365–368
Angiviller, comte de, 114
Anstey, John, 193
Apollo Association, 300
Arnold, Gen. Benedict, 29, 30, 32, 35, 38, 63
Arnout, see Arnoux
Arnoux, Abbé, 118
Art collections:
    Bath, Daniel Webb, 62
    Brussels: cathedral, 142–143; M. Lavocat (?), 145; Royal, 143–144
    Dusseldorf, Gallery, 136–139
    Frankfort, Johann Friedrich Städel, 128
    London, Marquis of Stafford, 62
    New York, Charles Wilkes, 256

    Paris: Bibliothèque du Roi, 100; Church of the Carmelites, 104; Louis Stanislas Fréron (?), 104; Sir John Lambert, 119–120; Louvre, 101–103, 108–109, 116–118; Luxembourg, 107–108; Jean Massard, 119; Comte d'Orsay, 105; Sir Gregory Page, 117; Palais Royal, 103, 119; Duc de Praslin, 119; Church of the Sorbonne, 109; St. Sulpice, 107; Comte de Vaudreuil, 97
    "Strawberry Hill," Horace Walpole, 151 n
    Versailles, 111–116
Arthois, Jacques, 143

Bailey, John, 339
Balbastre, Claude Louis, 118
Barbé-Marbois, François, marquis de, 217
Barber, John Warner, 324
Barbour, James, 310
Baring, Sir Thomas, 149, 338
Barney, Commodore Joshua, 76, 78
Barocci, Federico, 137
Barthélemy, François, marquis de, 217
Bates, Mr., 39, 43, 44
Baylor, George, 23
Beauharnais, Marie Françoise (?), 121
Beckford, William, xv, 306, 307
Beckford's landholdings in western New York, see Genesee
Belesaire, see Bélisart
Bélisart, Claude Billard de, 107, 111
Berchem, Nicolaes, 115, 117
Blackman, Alfred, 305
Blanchard, Jean Pierre, 140
Boileau, Jacques, 111, 118, 119